University Keywords

Critical University Studies
Jeffrey Williams and Christopher Newfield, Series Editors

University Keywords

edited by
Andy Hines

 JOHNS HOPKINS UNIVERSITY PRESS BALTIMORE

Printed in the United States of America on acid-free paper
9 8 7 6 5 4 3 2 1

Johns Hopkins University Press
2715 North Charles Street
Baltimore, Maryland 21218
www.press.jhu.edu

Library of Congress Cataloging-in-Publication Data is available.

A catalog record for this book is available from the British Library.

ISBN 978-1-4214-5235-7 (hardcover)
ISBN 978-1-4214-5236-4 (ebook)

EU GPSR Authorized Representative
LOGOS EUROPE, 9 rue Nicolas Poussin, 17000, La Rochelle, France
E-mail: Contact@logoseurope.eu

Contents

University Keywords

University

An Introduction

Andy Hines

The essays in *University Keywords* bridge, expand, and define 27 terms that drive recent public and scholarly conversations about the history, structure, and function of the American university. This work is necessary because it has become common to think of the university as a mere appendage of the larger bundle of functions of which education is a vanishingly small part: a hedge fund (A. Taylor 2016), a real estate developer (Russell 2015), a debt engine (Shermer 2021), a hospital system (Richman 2023), and a corporate-cum-military R&D department (Giroux 2007) with a university attached. Readers of this book will learn about these political economic functions of American higher education, as well as how many of these supposedly auxiliary functions have long been central to the structure and success of colleges and universities. The book, thus, offers an answer to the broad questions of "what is the American university?" and "what does it do?"

To approach these questions, this book adopts a cultural studies method to glimpse the intersection of the political economic field and function of higher education in the United States, with its animating but never singular educational purpose. Raymond Williams suggested a *Keywords* project to grasp the shifting terrain animating political and cultural activity within a shared language: "[These] are significant, binding words in certain activities and their interpretation; they are significant, indicative words in certain forms of thoughts. Certain uses bound together certain ways of seeing culture and society, not least in these two most general words. Certain other uses seemed to me to open up issues and problems, in the same general area, of which we all needed to be very much more conscious" (1985, 15). Williams's idea in outlining keywords is to establish a common language for study, analysis, and, ultimately, connection. These connections need to be made because the common language spoken between others has lost a shared sense of meaning as a result of significant social, cultural, and political upheaval. Establishing a language-in-common requires an excavation of past and present denotations, as well as a materialist study of language's connotations. In this respect, *Keywords* may appear as an investigation of terms, but this is more fundamentally a project that plumbs the structure of "culture and society" and the manifold epistemologies colliding within.

There is no shortage of keywords projects in the academic present (see Edwards, Ferguson, and Ogbar 2018; Tompkins et al. 2021; and Leary 2018). While those projects hold to Williams's guiding idea, the broader circulation and adoption of keywords has taken his remit of understanding the common language of *culture* and *society* to be limited to disciplinary formations. Arguably, this movement from an analytical and political project rooted in a bloc for analyzing culture and society to the limits of an academic discipline has been the story of cultural studies since its arrival in the United States; it is also, in certain ways, the story of the university that I describe in this introduction. This may explain the appeal of keywords projects to interdisciplines: Part of these projects' design has always been assembling an interpretive community beyond the limits of existing formations. They are, as Williams outlines, about binding uses and ways of seeing to make "all . . . much more conscious."

The gambit of this book is that the US university is a site that both requires and benefits from the clarifying challenge of generating new forms of shared understanding and establishing purposes for that understanding across distinctive domains. Embracing Williams's aim for keywords means that this book brings together different audiences. *University Keywords* might be encountered by undergraduate students assigned to read it in a course, graduate students power mapping in a union meeting, faculty sitting on a hastily assembled committee, nurses trying to grasp the public purpose of their new employer, janitors questioning why they have more to clean in fewer hours, and community members organizing against a new building, police force, or bond issue.

These audiences are not always so distinct. They can sometimes all be found in the same classroom or even embodied in the same person. The university in its complexity seeks to disaggregate these groups and to provide them with competing purposes and modes of reason. The university catalyzes a social process that puts these groups in relation. This book invites us to grasp how the university produces these particular social groupings while maintaining their isolation.

The perpetual but intensifying crisis framing of US higher education occasions understanding the university as a social process, which I see to be a central insight of this book. In humanities discourse, *crisis* has become less a description of a turning point, and more a long-standing structuring trope (Boggs and Mitchell 2018; Reitter and Wellmon 2021). But that's not what I invoke here. Researchers in political economy have a different definition of the term. They define *crisis* "as produced through the accumulation of contradictions in the social formation so that it can no longer reproduce itself" (Pelot-Hobbs 2023, 6; Gilmore 2007, 26). In this tradition, crisis describes a social and political struggle and thus rests at an intersection of state, capital, and civil society (Hall et al. 1978). The university can be viewed not only as a significant institution with which to manage crisis (Boggs et al. 2019; Caffentzis 1975; Wallerstein 1969) but also as crucial to the very production of crisis. The university produces the distinctive categories—faculty, staff, student, community, and so on—and related ways of knowing that this project invites its readers to bridge. In other words, I offer a definition by which we can analyze higher education: the university is a social process that brings distinctive groups in relation but in doing so produces the appearance of asymmetrical distinction and isolation between these groups for the purpose of capital accumulation.

If *university* describes a social process for bringing distinctive groups into relation mediated by administration, then a study of its political economic function requires an attention to the divisions it produces at various scales. *University* does not exclusively describe elite and wealthy private institutions, like Harvard and Stanford, nor does it solely denote public flagship schools, like the University of California or the University of Michigan. Studying the university requires thinking beyond these commonly metonymic institutions (Casselman 2016) and reaching toward those that frequently evade representation: regional comprehensive public universities, for-profit colleges, historically Black colleges and universities, tribal colleges, small liberal arts colleges, and any number of other institutional types (Hamilton and Nielsen 2021). What becomes clear when thinking across the full range of these institutions is that the university, or higher education in the United States, operates as a system, with each part performing distinct functions on and on behalf of different people.

Universities are frequently looked to as a Swiss Army knife–style tool to solve the problems of postindustrial capitalism. These myriad functions—

large employer, land developer, health system, site of job re/training, cultural hub, and others—mean that the political economic functions of particular institutions differ significantly within the hierarchized higher education system. For example, Tressie McMillan Cottom (2017) shows how the "education gospel" of the moral and economic value of postsecondary education connects these institutions. The activities of the most elite universities make possible the exploitation of the most vulnerable student populations and arguably of the most vulnerable institutions as well. These connections are also borne out by flows of capital. As Charlie Eaton (2022) describes, some of the wealthiest universities in the country have invested their endowments in for-profit colleges, which nominally make clear the pursuit of capital accumulation on the backs of a disproportionate number of students of color, women, and working-class students.

The logics of profit-driven education, often bolstered by private equity principles, have boomeranged back to the elite, suggesting a multidirectional exchange. At many campuses, the pursuit of ed tech solutionism through asynchronous and massively scaled education to reduce labor and facilities costs is yet another way to splinter and isolate student populations, as well as a vanishing cadre of faculty (Hamilton et al. 2022; Seybold 2023). Revenue-generating graduate degree programs at highly selective schools rely on the same federally expanded student debt opportunities for graduate students that for-profit colleges also depend on (Korn and Fuller 2021). Indeed, for-profit education has come to be embedded within the structure of public education: the private equity owner of the University of Phoenix, Apollo Global Management, has worked to sell the beleaguered institution to the University of Idaho, following the sale of for-profit Kaplan University to Purdue University in 2018. Even the country's most elite institutions are subject to these schemes: Marc Rowan, Apollo Global Management's CEO, has sought to radically reconfigure the priorities and principles of the University of Pennsylvania via a donor revolt, which gained strength in the wake of the Israel-Gaza War, though his campaign started prior to October 7, 2023 (Snyder 2023; Tkacik 2023).[1] These developments replicate within in-

1. Apollo connects private equity investments in higher education to hospitals. It owns more hospitals in the United States than any other private equity firm and was one of the final investor groups in Philadelphia's Hahnemann Hospital, which had been the teaching hospital for Drexel University before its closure; see "PESP Private Equity Hospital Tracker" (2024); and Pomorski (2021).

stitutions a dynamic that has played out across the system at least since the 1980s: Higher education becomes a hierarchized multitiered system, with the vast array of resources distributed to the wealthiest institutions with the highest barriers to access (B. J. Taylor and Cantwell 2019). Yet these differentiated institutions remain connected. A predatory scheme or the destruction of governance norms in one part of the system inevitably spreads throughout it.

There is much more to understand about the interactions between and within higher education institutions and how these relations work across several domains to enforce and reproduce the myriad asymmetries essential to capital accumulation in a financialized system. We might consider the relationships between the populations that colleges and universities bring together. We might also recognize the multifaceted dimensions of these institutions, particularly the largest among them. Parts of the university, for instance, may engage in meaningful community activities at the same time as, say, the real estate office, or the division of public safety, actively undo that work (Baldwin 2021, 36–41). There is a range of complexity within given institutions, between institutions, and between state-anchored higher education systems, not to mention in the manifold global relationships maintained through universities.

This book focuses primarily on institutions within the United States. This is an unfortunate limit that reflects my editorial choices, as well as a tendency in critical scholarship on the university. Several exceptions highlight the importance of contextualizing the links between the US higher education system and that of the rest of the world. Maya Wind (2024), for instance, shows how the development of higher education in Israel draws on the geographic strategies of the US system—for the purpose of expanding territorial sovereignty, for instance—as well as spearheading practices of student, faculty, and community surveillance and policies of repression that return to North America. At the same time, Wind illustrates that the power of donors such as Sheldon Adelson and the broader Koch Donor Network solidifies connections between universities in Israel and those in the United States (Wilson and Kamola 2021; Wind 2024). These comparisons highlight the integration of US higher education with international systems and suggest the many insights possible with future scholarship of this kind (see Kamola 2019; Vora 2018; and Watkins 2021). There also is room for further study of the interactions between postsecondary education and K–12 education, which are often stymied by the norms of scholarly disciplines.[2]

A book alone cannot resolve a destabilization of the hegemonic grasp of the university's function: That requires a broad social struggle. A book can, however, offer some insight into what has been stirred up in the process. In the next section, I draw attention to the apparent limits of mainstream historical accounts of the development of the US system of higher education to bring attention to the contours and purposes of the social processes that higher education has engaged to reproduce the US political economy.

Whose University?

How do you narrate the history of "the university"? This is particularly challenging if the university describes a system, a political realm, and a mode of accumulation, not to mention specific institutions and the groups that exist within and in relation to these processes and entities. There are students, workers of various categories, presidents, provosts, vice provosts, as well as an explosion of disciplines, interdisciplines, and antidisciplines. The university, in effect, can describe the history of the state itself, the development of capitalism, or even the development of colonialism and racism. In other words, even if a historical subject is ascertained, the myriad functions of universities complicate things even further.

As Olúfẹ́mi O. Táíwò (2024) has recently proposed, we can think about five different frames for understanding the university: a workplace; a site for ideological struggle; a site for financial struggle; a site for resource generation; or a site for intellectual generation. We can easily add to this list: a site for social reproduction; an animating force in the care and service economies; and a producer of capitalist society via credentials and cultural comportment. As Táíwò suggests, these framings can be particularly useful for clarifying what we mean when we talk about universities. One person may be thinking of one of these framings, while another may be thinking of multiple ones, or none of them. To push this further, we must consider how these different domains develop in relationship to one another, a complicating factor in trying to attend to a historical account useful to framing present questions about higher education.

---

2. For exemplary studies examining the connection of higher education to K–12 education, see Abrams (2023); Anderson (1995); and Groeger (2021).

The questions of education, campus maintenance, colonization, economic development, racial science, national sovereignty, and many others have almost always been tightly bound within the scores of documents that attempt to define the university and its purpose. The Harvard College Charter of 1650, one of the first in colonial North America, foregrounds "the advancement of all good literature arts and sciences" and assures the maintenance of "all accommodations of buildings and all other necessary provisions that may conduce to the education of the English and Indian youth of this country in knowledge and godliness" ("Harvard Charter of 1650" [1650] 2020). From the beginning, what would become the US university would be poised among the liberal arts, the maintenance and construction of facilities to support such an educational commitment, and the competing aims of colonial, racial capitalism: assimilation, elimination, and differential exclusion. Indigenous dispossession, not to mention the proceeds of the slave trade, would provide essential funding for the expansion of the university system (la paperson 2017; Stein 2017; Wilder 2013).

Further developments in the state and in its entanglement with capital would refine and expand this definition of the university. The federal Morrill Land Grant Act of 1862 provided stolen Indigenous land for the endowment in the states of "at least one college where the leading object shall be, without excluding other scientific and classical studies, and including military tactics, to teach such branches of learning as are related to agriculture and the mechanic arts . . . in order to promote the liberal and practical education of the industrial classes in the several pursuits and professions in life" (US Congress 1862; Lee and Ahtone 2020). To meet the needs of an industrializing nation amid civil war, the Morill Act codified the university's entanglement with capital's conquest to reach the ends of the earth and to grow through its soils; it also entrenched the structuring opposition of practical and liberal pursuits.

With this framework, the American university grew as a blunt instrument of economic development in both its technological innovations and its capacities to produce, reproduce, and mediate the cultural and practical trappings of class. In the early twentieth century, Morris Llewelyn Cooke (1910, 8), one of Frederick Winslow Taylor's chosen disciples of scientific management, completed a report for the Carnegie Foundation for the Advancement of Teaching in which he drew on terms of industrial management to insist that "highest efficiency" within universities would be most appealing to "public benefactors." The growing influence of capital on the governing boards and subsequently the administration of colleges and universities would lead Thorstein Veblen ([1918] 2015, 68) to suggest that "the graver issues of academic policy which now tax the discretion of the directive powers, reduce themselves in the main to a question between the claims of science and scholarship on the one hand and those of business principles and pecuniary gain on the other hand." Veblen posits the opposition between liberal arts and applied education as an opposition between an academic ideal and capitalist reality. This was a university that ran at the pleasure of the titans of industry. Faculty and students whose teaching, research, and learning challenged the smooth function of capitalism—including its racial science and imperial aims—faced material threats from industrial leaders on university boards (Barrow 1990; Harris 2023; Newfield 2003; Sinclair 1923; Tiede 2015). As universities embraced the terms of professionalization and industrial management rather than workerism (Cain 2010), this period saw the rise of academic disciplines as professional organizations, as well as the founding of the American Association of University Professors (AAUP).

Meanwhile, agitation by Black people and women (A. Cooper [1892] 2017, 48–80) opened the question of differential and limited access to this system, which had been significantly segregated and unevenly funded. Indeed, the growing power of southern interests within the state codified segregated forms of postsecondary education with the Second Morrill Act (1890). W. E. B. Du Bois ([1933] 2001, 115), who reflected frequently on the concerns of higher learning for Black people specifically and for the United States more broadly, recognized that the social base for a democratic university was "the mass of men." Should an institution be separated from this, he argued, it would "become a university of the air." In other words, Du Bois argues that if a university loses touch with a clearly and democratically defined social base, then it would be a disconnected idealist exercise, more subject to being wielded for purposes countervailing to democracy.

Much of the contestation of the American university system relied on who constituted this "mass of men," and arguments proliferated about what purpose that mass ought to be devoted to. Conservative foreman William F. Buckley Jr. (1951, xiv) argued that Yale's base was its alumni, and like those alumni, its trustees "are committed to the desirability of fostering both a belief in God, and a recognition of the merits of our economic system." This idea was, of course, widely challenged. Writing about Yale in 1970, during a student strike in support of the imprisoned New Haven Nine, the Africa Research Group (1970, 2) suggests that "the Yale University-Corporation is in the vanguard of liberal repression."

Amid the tumult of widespread student and social unrest in the sixties and seventies, the university system in the United States only grew larger. The administered activities of its students and faculty further shifted away from ideals about education and toward those of knowledge production. This was Clark Kerr's (2001, 15) multiversity, "a series of individual faculty entrepreneurs held together by a common grievance over parking." Kerr's quip signals the changing figuration of faculty work (resentful and petty "entrepreneurs") as well as the solidification of the idea that administrators, rather than faculty or students, must maintain the university's operation. The state response to the Great Depression brought significant forms of redistributive resource allocation, which greatly expanded the university system, with perhaps the most important of those forms being the intensification of American military power. Greater capacity for research, the pressure to avoid unemployment for returning soldiers, and the early and uneven signals of deindustrialization made universities an appealing lever for economic expansion (Loss 2012). All of this required the kinds of managerial structures necessary to "administer the present," as Kerr put it in 1957 (Schrum 2012). In effect, the postwar university came to be defined by the struggle between the promise of the kind of democratic institution intimated by Du Bois's invocation of a university connected to a "mass of men" and the logic ensuring that power flowed through university buildings, allowing for the management of capital's unwieldy surpluses.

The neoliberal phase that followed placed the primary onus for funding the system on students via state-backed debt and market-inspired revenue opportunities supported by laws like the Bayh-Dole Act of 1980, which allowed universities to own the patents of federally funded campus-based research (Slaughter and Rhoades 2009). These policies and rising costs justified withdrawal of state support, which would only intensify with the 2008 financial crisis, further instilling austerity for institutions, casualization for faculty, and "predatory inclusion" via student debt (Seamster and Charron-Chénier 2017) for the many students pursuing a credential for a vanishing horizon of secure employment. The demand for job readiness, the competition for students, and internal competition for increasingly small pots of funding would dramatically reshape the built landscape of the college, the characteristics of academic work and university management, and the reordering of subjects thought to be essential to a liberal education.

Writing on the development of a Black university, Toni Cade Bambara (2017, 14) encapsulates the challenge of the existing US university system: "Let's just agree from the jump that whatever its motives, ideals, dreams, purposes, what the college does at best is to critically re-appraise and renew the cultural heritage, and what the college does at its worst is to merely study and perpetuate the idea of our cultural heritage—the idea, not what it is necessarily, but what we have traditionally believed it to be." Bambara speaks to the countervailing challenges about authorizing Black culture within academia specifically, but there is another insight within her observation. The university's emphasis on its cultural heritage—the "advancement of all good literature arts and sciences," as the Harvard charter put it—operates as the university's grand potential, while, in fact, justifying its manufacture of material and intellectual strategies that insist on reproducing the regimes of colonial, racial capitalism.

Today the question of reappraising and renewing a cultural heritage draws the university into the center of a white-hot political struggle. Part of this has to do with the material realities of the scarcity of seats at well-resourced elite institutions like Harvard and Yale. As Ashon Crawley (2018, 213) has written, "The university, with the power to produce and grant degrees, is a site of struggle and contestation precisely because it is a site of power to confer or to withhold." The degree-granting power animates a cultural debate about the content of that degree and who has access to it, igniting a culture war. Wokeism and DEI have replaced political correctness as the glyphs by which to discuss the shape of the US political economy and the hierarchies of race, ethnicity, gender, sexuality, and ability that produce the social organization possible to achieve that economic order. These tendencies grow from a well-organized and well-funded strategy fueled largely by the joint forces of the neoliberal and socially conservative Right (M. Cooper 2017; Nations 2021; Shepherd 2023; Wilson and Kamola 2021).

Here I would be remiss to forget the importance of "buildings and provisions" to the maintenance not just of the university, but of the broader US economy. Public universities are the largest employers in many states, as are university-affiliated health systems. US cities have come to be dominated by large universities and hospitals, a state-sponsored solution for deindustrialization since the mid-twentieth century. US universities hold approximately $839 billion in endowments, annually generate $745 billion in revenue, and pay out $719 billion (NACUBO 2024; NCES 2023a, 2023b). This significant economic footprint has changed public perception and granted more power to financiers and debt-rating agencies, like Moody's, to dictate university administrative policies. This situation is facilitated by the fact that many more institutions of significant size have debt bills as long as their deferred maintenance list, jeopardizing educational quality for their students, security of employment for their workers, and, in some cases, the economic viability of entire regions (CACD 2024). Indeed, like the industrial magnates they replaced—though many of those names remain emblazoned on university buildings—universities are at the forefront of a growing struggle over labor and the uneven distribution of wages, wealth, and opportunity across the country.

Arguably, we are in the midst of a crisis shaping this periodization, the kind of crisis of hegemony that makes possible a new narrative of the history of higher education. Israel's unceasing genocidal military assault on Gaza after the horrific October 7, 2023, Hamas attack has solidified a new set of alignments within the sphere of US higher education (Toscano 2024), alignments that have only hardened in the opening weeks of the second Trump presidency. Donor power has allied with a Republican-Democratic coalition via the politicization of antisemitism. The result has been lockdowns on campus speech, new justifications for academic austerity, and the end of job security for the few remaining tenured faculty. But October 7 didn't itself generate this reconfigured arrangement of liberalism and capitalism. This form had been emergent already. It was present in, among many other examples, the litany of antiwoke legislation directed by Ron DeSantis in Florida (Jafar et al. 2023), the unprecedented but aggressive stance against a graduate student union strike at Temple University (Fuelling 2023), and the consultant-led assault that has enacted "academic transformation" at a growing list of public universities, including West Virginia University, University of North Carolina–Greensboro, and Miami University in Ohio (Casey, Wilkerson, and Winant 2023; Hogan 2023). In other words, what may have appeared as distinctive tendencies of MAGA culture warriors and neoliberal austerity hawks have been in a strategic but tenuous alignment to transform and extract capital from the higher education system.

A focus on the university's embeddedness in broader political and economic dynamics supplies an important insight for scholarship and potentially for organizing and political action. Neither faculty nor their teaching and research have been the exclusive or even central domain of the American university across its lengthy history. Certainly, over four centuries, faculty have played a dominant role in shaping the narrative of the institution's political, social, and economic value, but the long twentieth century (from the founding of the AAUP in 1915 to the early 2000s) constitutes the peak of faculty's ideological and cultural relevance.

We can glimpse this in the diminishing ranks of the faculty over the last several decades. As of 2023, 68 percent of faculty were in positions not eligible for tenure. Forty years ago, about 70 percent of faculty had tenure or were on the tenure track. Now, 48 percent of all faculty have part-time appointments (AFT 2023, 1). We can also witness the diminishing power of faculty among the struggles waged by those who have managed to hold on to tenure. What has been so striking about the developments in higher ed in the wake of consultant-driven restructuring, the consistent withdrawal of state funding, and the donor revolt is how the country's most elite institutions have intensified their role in significant repression in terms of reduced governance power and disregard of academic freedom for faculty, staff, and students.

Public discourse about the place of education in the university has admittedly shifted as well. There is no shortage of writing on the organization of college curriculum, its connection to job readiness, and, most expansively, the degree to which it ought to involve (or not) the study of the history of racism, gender, sexuality, colonialism, capitalism, and even sociology itself. Even so, increasing focus has been directed toward the wealth of a subset of institutions, the overwhelming amount of student debt held even after several waves of federal cancellations, and the noneducational activities on which universities expend their precious cash. This means special attention to the construction of university campuses, police departments that patrol those campuses, the growth of its hospitals and medical centers, and the vexed relationships universities have with their surrounding communities (Baldwin 2021; Krupar 2023; McKee 2023; Suriel et al. 2023; Winling 2018). These activities of university wealth management are not the domain of faculty, nor have they ever been at scale. Indeed, the increased scholarly attention to higher education's political economy might be but a symptom of the growing contingency of faculty (or those who wish to be faculty) *and* of the structural minimization of faculty activities that determine the shape of universities.

Political economic accounts of higher education, like the important and far-reaching *In the Shadow of the Ivory Tower*, by Davarian Baldwin, did not come out of nowhere. The insurgent 1960s movements for Black studies, ethnic studies, feminist studies, and Indigenous studies identified the extra-educational dimensions of higher education. Some of the most prominent groups within these movements, like the Black Panther Party, grew out of study groups in and frustrations with the higher education system (Murch 2010). Student and political groups in the 1970s continued this argument, such as the Africa Research Group and the New Left radical paper the *Old Mole*, who argue in the pamphlet *How Harvard Rules* (1969) that "the proverbial absent-minded professors, the archive rats, the bohemians, and the assorted academic odd-balls . . . are only the sad but noble remnants of an utterly shattered classical bourgeois ideal of Universitas. Today . . . American universities are absolutely central components of the social system of technological warfare-welfare capitalism." In other words, the ample analytical tradition of grasping the political economic function of universities beyond their educational capacity can be traced through sixties and seventies social movements; the Black Left in the 1940s, through figures like W. E. B. Du Bois and Doxey A. Wilkerson; and the professor's literature of protest of the early twentieth century, helmed by Thorstein Veblen. This critical analytical tradition also includes forming autonomous institutions subject to "vernacular authorizing authorities," such as the Jefferson School of Social Science, the Institute of the Black World, and Highlander Folk School among others (Hines 2022; Loggins and Douglas 2021; Melamed and Reddy, forthcoming; Meyerhoff 2019; Slate 2022; White 2012). In other words, there has long been work that has sought to counterbalance the "negotiated class compromise" among faculty and trustees, administrators, and state elites (Barrow 1990) and thus to describe the broader machinations of universities beyond their academic promises. This is not to erase fully the relevance of education to colleges and universities and to our study of them. In fact, education enables and unleashes an array of accumulative activities that these institutions have the power to undertake only because of its invocation.

Practically, this observation may be a difficult pill to swallow, especially for faculty. To focus on the actions of a subset of workers within higher education as deterministic of the entire sector reinforces existing myths about colleges and universities, as well as distracts us from understanding how these institutions are embedded within wider political, economic, and social dynamics in a series of overlapping contexts. Faculty are one group on campus among many, and recent efforts to build coalitions of unions—shorthand for building alliances, or labor tables, across groups on campuses—or to leverage existing "industrial" unions have been incredibly successful in building power on university campuses (Denvir 2023). Faculty and students may have unique claims on the educational activity of the institution, but that unique claim carries purchase only when it connects to other dimensions of the university's operations, such as construction of buildings, its endowment, or, increasingly, the revenue large institutions generate from patient care. Making these types of analytical, social, and political connections expands beyond the traditional domain of arguments about the value of a university education, the humanities, or particular disciplines. It expands the project of studying the university, as this book does, echoing Raymond Williams, by opening issues and problems to a general understanding.

The Keywords

Choosing the terms that anchor this book has been a challenge. It is easy to imagine terms left out that are of paramount importance to some, as well as to say that the approaches taken by some contributors to a certain phenomenon are controversial. My goal in curating these terms was to choose those that allowed for the most exploration of the cross-cutting but otherwise separated spheres within, between, and beyond colleges and universities. Why? It is increasingly clear that the critical study of the university is a necessarily interdisciplinary endeavor that cannot be limited solely to the domain of higher education for fear of missing the predominance of universities in wider US and global political economies. Part of this means that any given entry in this book on a particular term is not meant to be the authoritative answer on that subject; it instead offers an argument, a carefully considered set of points of departure for further conversation, study, and analysis.

With this in mind, I sought authors for this book who had varying relationships to the university and worked at many different types of institutions. I include faculty at research-intensive institutions, at teaching-driven ones, at large universities, and at small liberal arts colleges. There are graduate student contributors, several contingent faculty, and others, like me, who are not faculty at all. There are scholars writing with expertise expanded by various forms of struggle. I had always imagined that this would be a collaborative project—the vast and complex nature of the university requires working together to grasp its broader functions—but even I was surprised at the number of contributors who asked if they could submit something they had been working on with others. While multiauthored works are familiar in some disciplines, critical work in the humanities and social sciences has been slower to embrace collaboration. The fruits of the collaborations in this volume speak to what is possible when researchers within colleges and universities challenge the regimes that otherwise individuate them and set them in competition.

In that spirit, I include in a short appendix the questions that I shared with contributors to guide their approach to writing for this book. My hope in sharing these questions is to offer readers a chance to continue the work of writing this book beyond its publication. These may make for a good classroom assignment, as they would for a writer (or a group of writers) to develop analyses of terms that have gained relevance that I simply could not have foreseen. That is the thing about keywords: If we are to accept that they bind together certain ways of seeing culture and society, then the relevant terms inevitably shift with the terrain. We share a mutual responsibility in finding mechanisms for understanding those shifts, which, perhaps to some, require the development of new strategies to achieve a political horizon for higher education that does not rely on social separation for the purpose of accumulation.

This book, I hope, will be a repository of knowledge for those struggling against repressive regimes acting within and through the university. Collecting knowledge can be important for struggle, and this book offers a first step. In that sense, *University Keywords* speaks to the desire of many academic workers to understand deeply before finding the means for organizing and action, a desire that, at times, can lead to the splintering of solidarity and at worst the dissolution of movements. Each entry is meant to be as much an introduction to a particular topic as an argument, and the references in each essay give readers many opportunities for further research. While I don't claim that this introduction is definitive, the difficult work of analyzing a certain set of emergent dynamics on a campus or across campuses has at least begun in these pages.

Entries can stand alone, but they also speak across one another, and the book could be read from start to finish. Reading across the book encourages the kind of cross-domain connection essential to the critical work of study. Indeed, one thing to learn from the kinds of political movements that have long analyzed the university's political economy is their tendency to interrupt assumed categories. What does free breakfast have to do with the struggle for racial justice? How can there be unions of debtors and tenants? Ought housework or schoolwork be waged? Can property be made free?

Whether this book finds you looking at a stack of discarded books marked free in an academic corridor, in a classroom, in a library, in a union hall, in a study group, in a provost's office, or on a picket line, know that you have picked up not an encyclopedia or even a dictionary, but instead an invitation to join in study. As these pages suggest, making time and space for learning within the university, despite that being its nominal purpose, has been made increasingly difficult. Studying and learning together—among the most essential social activities of modern life—have been thrown into a complex terrain of struggle.

References

Abrams, Annie. 2023. *Shortchanged: How Advanced Placement Cheats Students.* Baltimore: Johns Hopkins University Press.

Africa Research Group. 1969. *How Harvard Rules: Being a Total Critique of Harvard University, Including New Liberated Documents, Government Research, the Educational Process Exposed, Strike Posters and a Free Power Chart.* Cambridge, MA: A. R. G. and the Old Mole.

Africa Research Group. 1970. *Go to School, Learn to Rule: The Yale Method.* New Haven, CT: A. J. M and A. R. G.

AFT (American Federation of Teachers). 2023. *An Army of Temps: AFT 2022 Contingent Faculty Quality of Work/Life Report.* Washington, DC: AFT, AFL-CIO. https://www.aft.org/sites/default/files/media/documents/2023/Contingent_Faculty_Survey_2022_interactive.pdf.

Anderson, James D. 1995. *The Education of Blacks in the South, 1860–1935.* Chapel Hill: University of North Carolina Press.

Baldwin, Davarian L. 2021. *In the Shadow of the Ivory Tower: How Universities Are Plundering Our Cities.* New York: Bold Type.

Bambara, Toni Cade. 2017. "Realizing the Dream of a Black University." In *"Realizing the Dream of a Black University" and Other Writings, Part I,* edited by Makeba Lavan and Conor Tomás Reed, 2:13–26. Lost and Found: The CUNY Poetics Document Initiative 7. New York: CUNY.

Barrow, Clyde W. 1990. *Universities and the Capitalist State: Corporate Liberalism and the Reconstruction of American Higher Education, 1894–1928.* History of American Thought and Culture. Madison: University of Wisconsin Press.

Boggs, Abigail, Eli Meyerhoff, Nick Mitchell, and Zach Schwartz-Weinstein. 2019. "Abolitionist University Studies: An Invitation." *Abolition Journal,* August 28. https://abolitionjournal.org/abolitionist-university-studies-an-invitation/.

Boggs, Abigail, and Nick Mitchell. 2018. "Critical University Studies and the Crisis Consensus." *Feminist Studies* 44 (2): 432–63.

Buckley, William F. 1951. *God and Man at Yale: The Superstitions of Academic Freedom*. Chicago: Regnery.

CACD (Coalition Against Campus Debt). 2024. *Lend and Rule: Fighting the Shadow Financialization of Public Universities*. Philadelphia: Common Notions.

Caffentzis, George. 1975. "Throwing Away the Ladder: The Universities in the Crisis." *Zerowork* 1 (December): 128–42.

Cain, Timothy Reese. 2010. "The First Attempts to Unionize the Faculty." *Teachers College Record* 112 (3): 876–913.

Casey, Rose, Jessica Wilkerson, and Johanna Winant. 2023. "An Open Letter from Faculty at West Virginia University." *Boston Review*, September 7. https://www.bostonreview.net/articles/an-open-letter-from-faculty-at-west-virginia-university/.

Casselman, Ben. 2016. "Shut Up about Harvard." *FiveThirtyEight* (blog), March 30. https://fivethirtyeight.com/features/shut-up-about-harvard/.

Cooke, Morris Llewellyn. 1910. *Academic and Industrial Efficiency: A Report to the Carnegie Foundation for the Advancement of Teaching*. New York: Carnegie Foundation.

Cooper, Anna J. (1892) 2017. *A Voice from the South: By a Black Woman of the South*. Chapel Hill: Chapel Hill Library, University of North Carolina.

Cooper, Melinda. 2017. *Family Values: Between Neoliberalism and the New Social Conservatism*. New York: Zone Books.

Cottom, Tressie McMillan. 2017. *Lower Ed: The Troubling Rise of For-Profit Colleges in the New Economy*. New York: New Press.

Crawley, Ashon. 2018. "University." In *Keywords for African American Studies*, edited by Erica R. Edwards, Roderick A. Ferguson, and Jeffrey O. G. Ogbar, 213–16. New York: New York University Press.

Denvir, Daniel. 2023. "Higher Ed Industrial Unionism w/ Donna Murch and Todd Wolfson." *Dig*, podcast, February 17. https://thedigradio.com/podcast/higher-ed-industrial-unionism-w-donna-murch-and-todd-wolfson/.

Du Bois, W. E. B. (1933) 2001. "The Field and Function of the Negro College." In *The Education of Black People: Ten Critiques, 1906–1960*, edited by Herbert Aptheker, 111–33. New York: Monthly Review Press.

Eaton, Charlie. 2022. *Bankers in the Ivory Tower: The Troubling Rise of Financiers in US Higher Education*. Chicago: University of Chicago Press.

Edwards, Erica R., Roderick A. Ferguson, and Jeffrey Ogbonna Green Ogbar, eds. 2018. *Keywords for African American Studies*. New York: New York University Press.

Fuelling, Mathias. 2023. "Blow It Up." *Verso Blog*, February 16. https://www.versobooks.com/blogs/news/5563-blow-it-up.

Gilmore, Ruth Wilson. 2007. *Golden Gulag: Prisons, Surplus, Crisis, and Opposition in Globalizing California*. Berkeley: University of California Press.

Giroux, Henry A. 2007. *The University in Chains: Confronting the Military-Industrial-Academic Complex*. Boulder, CO: Paradigm.

Groeger, Cristina V. 2021. *The Education Trap: Schools and the Remaking of Inequality in Boston*. Cambridge, MA: Harvard University Press.

Hall, Stuart, Chas Critcher, Tony Jefferson, John Clarke, and Brian Roberts. 1978. *Policing the Crisis: Mugging, the State and Law and Order*. London: Macmillan.

Hamilton, Laura T., Heather Daniels, Christian Michael Smith, and Charlie Eaton. 2022. *The Private Side of Public Universities: Third-Party Providers and Platform Capitalism.* UC Berkeley Research and Occasional Papers Series no. 3.

Hamilton, Laura T., and Kelly Nielsen. 2021. *Broke: The Racial Consequences of Underfunding Public Universities.* Chicago: University of Chicago Press.

Harris, Malcolm. 2023. *Palo Alto: A History of California, Capitalism, and the World.* New York: Little, Brown.

"Harvard Charter of 1650." (1650) 2020. Transcription, Harvard University Archives Research Guides. Harvard Library. Last updated December 1, 2020. https://guides.library.harvard.edu/c.php?g=880222&p=6323072.

Hines, Andy. 2022. *Outside Literary Studies: Black Criticism and the University.* Chicago: University of Chicago Press.

Hogan, Dennis M. 2023. "Capture the Flagship." *Baffler*, August 30. https://thebaffler.com/latest/capture-the-flagship-hogan.

Jafar, Afshan, Henry Reichman, Davarian Baldwin, Emily M. S. Houh, Anil Kalhan, Charles Toombs, and Brian Turner. 2023. *Report of a Special Committee: Political Interference and Academic Freedom in Florida's Public Higher Education System.* American Washington, DC: Association of University Professors. https://www.aaup.org/file/AAUP_Florida_final.pdf.

Kamola, Isaac A. 2019. *Making the World Global: US Universities and the Production of the Global Imaginary.* Durham, NC: Duke University Press.

Kerr, Clark. 2001. *The Uses of the University.* 5th ed. Cambridge, MA: Harvard University Press.

Korn, Melissa, and Andrea Fuller. 2021. "'Financially Hobbled for Life': The Elite Master's Degrees that Don't Pay Off." *Wall Street Journal*, July 8, sec. US. https://www.wsj.com/articles/financially-hobbled-for-life-the-elite-masters-degrees-that-dont-pay-off-11625752773.

Krupar, Shiloh R. 2023. *Health Colonialism: Urban Wastelands and Hospital Frontiers.* Minneapolis: University of Minnesota Press.

la paperson. 2017. *A Third University Is Possible.* Minneapolis: University of Minnesota Press.

Leary, John Patrick. 2018. *Keywords: The New Language of Capitalism.* Chicago: Haymarket.

Lee, Robert, and Tristan Ahtone. 2020. "Land-Grab Universities." *High Country News*, March 30. https://www.hcn.org/issues/52-4/indigenous-affairs-education-land-grab-universities/.

Loggins, Jared A., and Andrew J. Douglas. 2021. *Prophet of Discontent: Martin Luther King Jr. and the Critique of Racial Capitalism.* Athens: University of Georgia Press.

Loss, Christopher P. 2012. *Between Citizens and the State: The Politics of American Higher Education in the 20th Century.* Princeton, NJ: Princeton University Press.

McKee, Guian A. 2023. *Hospital City, Health Care Nation: Race, Capital, and the Costs of American Health Care.* Philadelphia: University of Pennsylvania Press.

Melamed, Jodi, and Chandan Reddy. Forthcoming. *Operationalizing Racial Capitalism: On Liberalism's Command Powers.* New York: Verso.

Meyerhoff, Eli. 2019. *Beyond Education: Radical Studying for Another World.* Minneapolis: University of Minnesota Press.

Murch, Donna Jean. 2010. *Living for the City: Migration, Education, and the Rise of the Black Panther Party in Oakland, California.* Chapel Hill: University of North Carolina Press.

NACUBO (National Association of College and University Business Officers–Commonfund Institute). 2024. "Presentation of Key Insights from the 2023 NCSE." *2023 NACUBO-Commonfund Study of Endowments.* NACUBO, February 15.

Nations, Jennifer M. 2021. "How Austerity Politics Led to Tuition Charges at the University of California and City University of New York." *History of Education Quarterly* 61 (3): 273–96.

NCES (National Center for Education Statistics). 2023a. "Postsecondary Institution Expenses." *Condition of Education*. US Department of Education, Institute of Education Sciences. https://nces.ed.gov/programs/coe/indicator/cue.

NCES (National Center for Education Statistics). 2023b. "Postsecondary Institution Revenues." *Condition of Education*. US Department of Education, Institute of Education Sciences." https://nces.ed.gov/programs/coe/indicator/cud/postsecondary-institution-revenue.

Newfield, Christopher. 2003. *Ivy and Industry: Business and the Making of the American University, 1880–1980*. Durham, NC: Duke University Press.

Pelot-Hobbs, Lydia. 2023. *Prison Capital: Mass Incarceration and Struggles for Abolition Democracy in Louisiana*. Chapel Hill: University of North Carolina Press.

"PESP Private Equity Hospital Tracker." 2024. Private Equity Stakeholder Project. https://pestakeholder.org/private-equity-hospital-tracker/.

Pomorski, Chris. 2021. "The Death of Hahnemann Hospital." *New Yorker*, March 31. https://www.newyorker.com/magazine/2021/06/07/the-death-of-hahnemann-hospital.

Reitter, Paul, and Chad Wellmon. 2021. *Permanent Crisis: The Humanities in a Disenchanted Age*. Chicago: University of Chicago Press.

Richman, Barak. 2023. "Universities Are Prioritizing Their Health Systems over Teaching. That's Killing Academic Freedom." *Politico*, December 31. https://www.politico.com/news/magazine/2023/12/31/universities-no-longer-fight-for-academic-freedom-blame-the-hospitals-00133272.

Russell, Jim. 2015. "University as Real Estate Developer." *Pacific Standard*, February 27. https://psmag.com/education/university-as-real-estate-developer.

Schrum, Ethan. 2012. "To 'Administer the Present': Clark Kerr and the Purpose of the Postwar American Research University." *Social Science History* 36 (4): 499–523.

Seamster, Louise, and Raphaël Charron-Chénier. 2017. "Predatory Inclusion and Education Debt: Rethinking the Racial Wealth Gap." *Social Currents* 4 (3): 199–207.

Seybold, Matt. 2023. "Jason Wingard's EdTech Griftopia." *Los Angeles Review of Books*, February 23. https://lareviewofbooks.org/article/jason-wingards-edtech-griftopia.

Shepherd, Lauren Lassabe. 2023. *Resistance from the Right: Conservatives and the Campus Wars in Modern America*. Chapel Hill: University of North Carolina Press.

Shermer, Elizabeth Tandy. 2021. *Indentured Students: How Government-Guaranteed Loans Left Generations Drowning in College Debt*. Cambridge, MA: Harvard University Press.

Sinclair, Upton. 1923. *The Goose-Step : A Study of American Education*. Girard, KS: Haldeman-Julius.

Slate, Nico. 2022. "'The Answers Come from the People': The Highlander Folk School and the Pedagogies of the Civil Rights Movement." *History of Education Quarterly* 62 (2): 191–210.

Slaughter, Sheila, and Gary Rhoades. 2009. *Academic Capitalism and the New Economy: Markets, State, and Higher Education*. Baltimore: Johns Hopkins University Press.

Snyder, Susan. 2023. "Penn Faculty Fear the Donor Who Started the Effort to Oust Liz Magill Is Attempting to Set the Agenda for Trustees." *Philadelphia Inquirer*, December 12. https://www.inquirer.com/education/marc-rowan-university-pennsylvania-agenda-20231212.html.

Stein, Sharon. 2017. "A Colonial History of the Higher Education Present: Rethinking Land-Grant Institutions through Processes of Accumulation and Relations of Conquest." *Critical*

Studies in Education, ahead of print, December 2, 1–17. https://doi.org/10.1080/17508487.2017.1409646.

Suriel, Yalile, Grace Watkins, Jude Paul Matias Dizon, and John Joseph Sloan III, eds. 2023. *Cops on Campus: Rethinking Safety and Confronting Police Violence*. Seattle: University of Washington Press.

Táíwò, Olúfẹ́mi O. 2024. Presentation at the Universities and Democracy: The Politics of US Higher Education Today, Haverford College, February 23.

Taylor, Astra. 2016. "Universities Are Becoming Billion-Dollar Hedge Funds with Schools Attached." *Nation*, March 8. https://www.thenation.com/article/archive/universities-are-becoming-billion-dollar-hedge-funds-with-schools-attached/.

Taylor, Barrett J., and Brendan Cantwell. 2019. *Unequal Higher Education: Wealth, Status, and Student Opportunity*. New Brunswick, NJ: Rutgers University Press.

Tiede, Hans-Joerg. 2015. *University Reform: The Founding of the American Association of University Professors*. Baltimore: Johns Hopkins University Press.

Tkacik, Maureen. 2023. "The University of Phoenixification of Elite Education." *American Prospect*, December 22. https://prospect.org/api/content/9ae2353e-a0ec-11ee-b216-12163087a831/.

Tompkins, Kyla Wazana, Aren Z. Aizura, Aimee Bahng, Karma R. Chávez, Mishuana Goeman, and Amber Jamilla Musser, eds. 2021. *Keywords for Gender and Sexuality Studies*. New York: New York University Press.

Toscano, Alberto. 2024. "The War on Education—in Gaza and at Home." *In These Times*, February 15. https://inthesetimes.com/article/campus-wars-gaza-higher-ed-christopher-rufo.

US Congress. 1862. Act of July 2, 1862 (First Morrill Act). Washington, DC: US Government Printing Office.

Veblen, Thorstein. (1918) 2015. *The Higher Learning in America: A Memorandum on the Conduct of Universities by Business Men*. Edited by Richard F. Teichgraeber. Baltimore: Johns Hopkins University Press.

Vora, Neha. 2018. *Teach for Arabia: American Universities, Liberalism, and Transnational Qatar*. Stanford, CA: Stanford University Press.

Wallerstein, Immanuel. 1969. *University in Turmoil: The Politics of Change*. New York: Atheneum.

Watkins, Grace. 2021. "'Cops Are Cops': American Campus Police and the Global Carceral Apparatus." *Comparative American Studies*, online, March 30, 1–15.

White, Derrick E. 2012. *The Challenge of Blackness: The Institute of the Black World and Political Activism in the 1970s*. Gainesville: University Press of Florida.

Wilder, Craig Steven. 2013. *Ebony and Ivy: Race, Slavery, and the Troubled History of America's Universities*. New York: Bloomsbury.

Williams, Raymond. 1985. *Keywords: A Vocabulary of Culture and Society*. Oxford: Oxford University Press.

Wilson, Ralph, and Isaac A. Kamola. 2021. *Free Speech and Koch Money: Manufacturing a Campus Culture War*. London: Pluto.

Wind, Maya. 2024. *Towers of Ivory and Steel: How Israeli Universities Deny Palestinian Freedom*. London: Verso.

Winling, LaDale C. 2018. *Building the Ivory Tower: Universities and Metropolitan Development in the Twentieth Century*. Philadelphia: University of Pennsylvania Press.

A

Academic Freedom

Jennifer Ruth and Ellen Schrecker

Academic freedom is one of those variable concepts that, as Supreme Court Justice Potter Stewart so famously noted when discussing pornography, "I know it when I see it." Although academic freedom is usually assumed to protect controversial faculty members from outside interference with their teaching, research, and what the American Association of University Professors (AAUP) calls "extramural utterances," who exactly can benefit from this protection and under what circumstances has long been unclear. Just individual faculty members? Or the institutions as a whole? What about K–12 teachers? What about students?

The concept is barely a century old. Borrowed from a German precedent, it was developed at the end of the nineteenth and beginning of the twentieth centuries as the modern American research university came into being. The new cohort of highly trained and ambitious scholars and scientists who taught at these institutions were eager to raise the status of their profession. The colleges and universities employing these people were funded by industrial barons, whose interests conflicted at times with the positions taken by faculty members in their research and teaching. A few nationally publicized dismissals at schools like Chicago, Brown, and Stanford prompted a handful of eminent professors to create a new organization to protect and empower the professoriate. Initially an elitist group, whose members had to be nominated by their colleagues and teachers, the AAUP soon became the main organization representing the American professoriate—its statements and reports defining the parameters of academic freedom (Tiede 2015). As a result of the AAUP's efforts, the concept of academic freedom entered the public lexicon as a right of faculty working in higher education—both tenured individuals and the collective faculty through shared governance. While students and K–12 teachers have at times attempted to claim academic freedom, and academic administrators have tried with more recent success to appropriate the concept for the institutions they run, the term developed primarily with reference to the faculty members of colleges and universities (Rabban 1990, 231).

From the start, the organization's founders tackled the conundrum of their profession: To do their work with integrity, they required the autonomy and status of their fellow professionals in fields like law and medicine, yet they were employees of the institutions at which they worked, hired and fired by administrators beholden to political and moneyed interests. Rejecting unionization and its associations with the working class, they developed the concept of academic freedom to gain control over their work and insulate themselves from the interference of nonexperts outside their fields. For the knowledge faculty produced to honestly serve the common good, faculty must be able to "bite the hand that feeds them" when necessary, according to the AAUP *1915 Declaration of Principles on Academic Freedom and Academic Tenure.* This founding document established both the general assumptions that defined academic freedom as a public good and the specific conditions required for that protection, primarily through faculty governance and, especially, tenure.

Although the *1915 Declaration,* with its emphasis on "enhanc[ing] the dignity of the scholar's profession" to attract "men of the highest ability, of sound learning, and of strong and independent character," contained a whiff of snobbish self-interest, it articulated a fundamental tenet that has withstood the test of a century's worth of time yet now finds itself under concerted partisan attack: knowledge is trustworthy only when neither the market nor the state can dictate its content (AAUP 1915, 294). The document insists on the faculty's control of its own business, specifically demanding that decisions involving the termination of a professor's appointment "be taken only with the advice and consent of some board or committee representative of the faculty" (300). Outsiders, like politicians, donors, and trustees who lacked the rigorous training of academic professionals, the *1915 Declaration* explained, "have neither competency nor moral right to intervene" in cases of professors who transgress their professional obligations (295).

During the 25 years after its founding, the AAUP reached out to gain broader acceptance for this vision of academic freedom and the professional identity it implied. In 1940, it revamped its founding document in a revised *Statement of Principles on Academic Freedom and Tenure* (AAUP 1940), produced in collaboration with the Association of American Colleges. As with the *1915 Declaration*, the *1940 Statement* emphasized tenure, the economic job security that, its authors claimed, was "indispensable to the success of an institution in fulfilling its obligations to its students and to society" (14). The new document described the procedures and timetable for awarding tenure, as well as detailing the quasi-judicial machinery required for dismissing a tenured professor. It paid more attention to the off-campus political activities of individual faculty members than the 1915 document had. "When they speak or write as citizens," the *1940 Statement* declared, professors "should be free from institutional censorship or discipline" (14). But they should also fulfill their "special obligations" to the institutions that employed them: "They should at all times be accurate, should exercise appropriate restraint, should show respect for the opinions of others, and should make every effort to indicate that they are not speaking for the institution" (14).

The *1940 Statement* was a great success, reshaping higher education to a remarkable—if incomplete—degree around its vision of the primacy of an independent faculty. As of 2014, that document—updated by seven "Comments" added in 1970—has been officially endorsed by 275 scholarly organizations and, according to a 2020 AAUP report, incorporated directly into or cited by the faculty handbooks and union contracts of some 600 four-year institutions with a tenure system (Tiede 2020).

The AAUP's leaders saw themselves as judges—disinterested but well-informed arbitrators who provided unbiased assessments. Their investigations of violations of academic freedom and their policy reports created a record that they hoped would become the basis for a kind of academic common law to which the nation's colleges and universities might be expected to adhere. Accordingly, they were reluctant to risk the organization's reputation by seeming to take sides on political issues or by embracing professors whose teaching, research, and outside activities strayed too far from that of their peers. Whenever possible, the organization's officers and staff members hoped to mediate between the parties (usually, an overreaching administration and an aggrieved faculty member) to reach a settlement without having to mount a full-scale investigation, which would lead to a published report and censure of the errant institution. They also refrained from seeking reinstatement for the academic dissidents who lost their jobs. Not only was such an objective unlikely to be achieved, but it might also align the new organization too closely with the controversial individuals it defended instead of the broader principles their cases involved. In the process, the AAUP's early activities created an institutional culture of quasi-legal investigations and judicious behavior that would mark its work for the decades to come. Or, as one recent scholar put it, because of the AAUP's organizational limitations, "the discourse of academic freedom acquired a bureaucratic tone" (Gordon 2015, 69). And, perhaps because of its elitist past, until the 1980s it paid little attention to the academic freedom of the growing ranks of instructors off the tenure track.[1]

The outcome of the AAUP's early cases was mixed. Some investigations by the AAUP's newly formed Committee A on Academic Freedom and Tenure seem to have induced the institutions they censured to change their ways. The University of Pennsylvania, for example, revised its personnel procedures in response to an early report condemning its trustees' abrupt dismissal of a leftwing economist despite the unanimous support of his department and dean. But in other cases, the AAUP's findings were ignored, and the organization did not have the capacity to investigate every apparent violation of academic freedom brought to its attention.

World War I was toxic for academic freedom. Although we have no official casualty figures, likely dozens of professors lost their jobs for opposing US participation in the war (Gruber 1975; Tiede 2015, 147–71). If the founders of the AAUP had qualms about the conflict, they did not act on them. Most, no doubt, agreed with the chair of Committee A that "we have to recognize that some things are just at present vastly more important than is academic freedom" (Tiede 2015, 151). Instead of investigating the 20 or so violations of academic freedom brought to its attention, the AAUP released a statement entitled "Academic Freedom in Wartime," advising faculty members against engaging in any type of antiwar activity and, worse yet, warning professors of German or Austrian descent to avoid talking about the war in public with their friends and neighbors (Schrecker 1986, 19–23; Tiede 2015, 131–69). Once the war ended, some of those involved regretted this unfortunate statement, and the organization never again wavered rhetorically in its adherence to the primacy of academic freedom. Unfortunately, however, words were not enough to preserve the professoriate's autonomy when an unprecedented wave of political repression inundated the nation's campuses in the early years of the Cold War.

1. There is a useful addendum about contingent faculty in Gilmore (2021).

During the late 1940s, when it was not yet clear how devastating McCarthyism would become, the AAUP's leadership took up the question of whether membership in the Communist Party disqualified someone from an academic position. Committee A's initial answer in fall 1947—and reaffirmed by its ruling council repeatedly throughout the Cold War Red Scare—was "no." As long as the party was legal, belonging to it was not "sufficient grounds for dismissal," Committee A explained. Rather, there had to be some kind of concrete misbehavior, like advocating the overthrow of the government, proselytizing in class, or showing a "more than normal bias so uncritical as to evidence professional unfitness," to justify a dismissal. To do otherwise, to punish professors for their political views, Committee A declared (Shannon 1948, 1949), "would readily lead to discrimination against teachers with other unorthodox views." Campuses "would become havens of cautious mediocrity," and higher education "would be ready to become an instrument of indoctrination for an authoritarian society."

The organization's leaders hoped that their opposition to firing faculty members who belonged to the Communist Party or, later, had invoked the Fifth Amendment in an anti-Communist investigation would encourage administrators to do the right thing. But the AAUP's inactions spoke more loudly than its statements. Beginning with the University of Washington's dismissal of three tenured professors for political reasons in early 1948 and the University of California's imposition of an anti-Communist loyalty oath on its faculty the following year, the AAUP did not act. It was not until 1956, when the worst of the inquisition had passed, and about 100 faculty members had lost their jobs for political reasons, that the organization released a special report on some specific violations of academic freedom that had occurred during the previous eight years. That delay was devastating. Until the current wave of state legislation banning education on racial, gender, and social justice issues and the attacks on universities after the outbreak of the Middle East conflict in fall 2023, that period in the 1950s had been widely viewed as the most dangerous moment for academic freedom since its conceptualization in the early twentieth century.

Significantly, the faculty members targeted by McCarthyism were never charged with subverting the government or indoctrinating students. Their universities felt obliged to act simply because these people refused to cooperate with an official investigation into their political beliefs. Because the

Supreme Court did not protect their refusal to name names, the only way they could avoid an indictment for contempt of Congress was to rely on the Fifth Amendment's provisions against becoming a witness against themselves by refusing to answer the committees' questions about their politics. Administrators at institutions of higher education that housed so-called Fifth Amendment Communists sometimes fired these people outright without employing any of the procedural machinery the AAUP specified; others went through the motions but ended up with the same result. There was little effective opposition from their faculties. Only a tiny handful of institutions kept unfriendly witnesses with tenure on their payrolls. How did universities reconcile their ostensible commitment to academic freedom with the dismissal of or refusal to hire professors whose only offense was to invoke a constitutional protection? Proving "unfitness" in teaching and research would have been the only way the institutions could have fired the supposed Communists and unfriendly witnesses on their faculties without violating academic freedom principles. But at no point was any evidence produced that these people's political activities impaired their teaching or scholarship.

Until McCarthyism petered out in the late 1950s, self-censorship was rampant. Leftwing politics disappeared from almost all the nation's campuses. Professors pruned their reading lists and avoided researching controversial topics. The eminent cultural critic Leo Marx recalled that he stopped using the word *capitalism* in his lectures, substituting *industrialism* instead. It took a decade for the chill to dissipate—pushed off the nation's campuses by the civil rights movement, the Vietnam War, and student unrest that forced the academic community to confront serious real-world issues instead of McCarthyism's hyped-up controversies.

At around the same time, the Supreme Court began to protect the rights of college teachers. By the end of the 1950s, the justices were nibbling away at the purges in universities and elsewhere, mainly by questioning such technicalities as the vagueness of the statutes that denied supposed Communists their jobs. Within a decade, the Warren Court's new liberal majority had also jettisoned its reliance on Cold War tropes of national security and the evils of communism and began to pay more substantive attention to the Bill of Rights. Justice William Brennan's 1967 majority opinion in *Keyishian v. Board of Regents* (385 US 589 (1967)), the case of five SUNY-Buffalo professors who refused to submit to New York State's anti-Communist loyalty program, epitomized that transformation by extending the First Amendment's protection to faculty members in public universities. As Brennan put it: "Our Nation is deeply committed to safeguarding academic freedom, which is of transcendent value to all of us, and not merely to the teachers concerned. That freedom is therefore a special concern of the First Amendment, which does not tolerate laws that cast a pall of orthodoxy over the classroom." To this day, that opinion stands as the most powerful defense of academic freedom in the United States offered by the Supreme Court.

Brennan's stirring language about the "transcendent value" of academic freedom to the American polity did not, however, create a new consensus about what that freedom actually protected, and this ambiguity would continue to deepen as racial and gender justice and antiwar movements hit the nation's campuses during the sixties and early seventies. African Americans, women, and LGBTQ and other marginalized groups demanded access to the ivory tower (Ferguson 2017). These constituencies raised questions about the degree to which higher education could claim to serve the common good when it excluded entire groups of citizens from sharing in the production, dissemination, and consumption of knowledge. The pretense to universality and neutrality, so central to the justifications of academic freedom and higher education that had earlier gained a high degree of acceptance, could not be sustained in the face of people whose exclusion had demonstrably warped the very disciplines around which universities were organized. The largely procedural and discipline-based approach to academic freedom—accountability to disciplinary peers, but independence from outside influence—had rested on a philosophical presumption that politics could be bracketed from knowledge production. Now, arguments emerging from within the academy and outside it from historically excluded groups have made clear that politics shapes knowledge as much as it sometimes distorts it, complicating any consensus on academic freedom and whose interests the concept serves.

Political neutrality, it had long been assumed, was the institutional equivalent of the professoriate's obligations of impartial scholarship and civility. Forced by student protests to address the issue directly, the academic community unofficially adopted the formulation offered in the "Report on the University's Role in Political and Social Action" (Kalven 1967), by a University of Chicago committee chaired by law school professor Harry Kalven Jr. The so-called Kalven Report, which received widespread attention, asserted that taking positions on controversial political issues would undermine the university's primary mission—that is, "the discovery, improvement, and dissemination of knowledge." To do otherwise would create dissension within the faculty and, thus, conflict with the academy's "respect for free inquiry and the obligation to cherish a diversity of viewpoints." The report argued that institutions can protect the academic freedom of the individuals housed within them only by maintaining neutrality on the broad issues facing society.

The Kalven Report did little to assuage deep-seated concerns that the concept of academic freedom did more to maintain the status quo than to enable social progress. Criticisms in this vein began to appear with increasing exigency and continue in the present. In addition to the growing awareness that knowledge is shaped by gender, class, race, and sexuality, another major factor exposing the inadequacy of academic freedom as procedurally practiced and conceptually understood is the structural erosion of tenure, which, beginning with the decline of state funding in the seventies, continues to disempower faculty members and marginalize them in the governance of their institutions. Most of the time, over the last half century, the erosion occurred so gradually that many senior professors, who might have countered it, were unaware of just how much power and autonomy the faculty as a whole was losing. But today, contingent instructors without access to basic due-process procedures or inclusion in governance activities outnumber tenured and tenure-track ones by a ratio of three to one (Kezar, DePaolo, and Scott 2019). While the AAUP and other higher education organizations continue to claim the right to academic freedom for all faculty, in practice only a small minority can reliably count on its protections or contribute to the shared governance on which academic freedom also depends. As such, academic freedom is in danger of becoming a phrase that more often proffers the appearance of protection without the reality of ensuring the integrity of faculty work.

The knowledge gains and social progress made in the sixties and seventies with the incorporation of ethnic and women's studies programs and other interdisciplinary efforts met with swift backlash from conservative politicians, business leaders, and pundits. A coterie of reactionary billionaires and intellectuals mounted a long-term lavishly funded campaign to move American political culture to the right. Theirs was—and is—a campaign specifically designed to undermine support for public education, and it paid off handsomely in the eighties and nineties, as states began dramatically shrinking their education budgets. The resulting combination of straitened finances and the growing influence of a neoliberal ideology hostile to the public sector and the common good transformed higher education (MacLean 2018). The academy's administrative leaders normalized austerity, raised tuitions, and adopted a corporate mindset that favored an institution's financial well-being over its educational activities.

In addition, the administrative class has grown exponentially, posing another challenge to the centrality of faculty and the integrity of the educational mission that academic freedom is intended to foster. As institutions of higher education took on ever more complex functions over the last decades, not only do they employ more administrators than instructors, but those administrators also intervene in areas like curriculum, faculty status, and student affairs where faculty members traditionally had primary responsibility. Coupled with the dramatic loss of faculty job security in what is essentially academia's gig economy, this growth in administrative power has meant the further diminution of the influence of academic freedom in concept and practice. The fact that this structural disempowerment of faculty occurred at the same time the demographics of faculty began to become more diverse is also important to note.

Academic freedom, articulated as independence from external coercion in 1915 and buttressed by the infrastructure recommended in the *1940 Statement* (peer review, tenure, shared governance), made the US higher education system the envy of the world. And yet it has repeatedly been observed in the breach, its putative defenders lacking the collective will to buttress the infrastructure essential to its survival. As a result, academic freedom now faces an existential threat in the form of a rightwing culture war determined to abolish tenure and silence faculty. The university's official leaders seem unable—or unwilling—to protect it. As all but a few respond with repression to the recent student protests against the Israeli government's violent attacks on the people of Gaza, they slough off their supposed political neutrality and disregard their internal regulations. The Kalven Report, already questionable in its endorsement of neutrality at the time, is exceedingly unhelpful today, though many administrators (Diermeier 2023) seek to resuscitate it. With higher education the target of a massive rightwing campaign, which has now added a misguided version of antisemitism to its charges against the university's supposedly "woke" culture, relying on "neutrality" is a farcical exercise in denial.

Academic freedom, at heart, is the faculty's collective right to control the content and method of higher education research and instruction. Without this ability, in a scenario in which politicians, trustees, and wealthy donors dictate what can and cannot be taught, and what research will or will not be funded, and precarious faculty members without job security must comply or suffer unemployment, academic freedom no longer exists.

References

AAUP (American Association of University Professors). 1915. *1915 Declaration of Principles on Academic Freedom and Academic Tenure.* Washington, DC: American Association of University Professors. https://www.aaup.org/NR/rdonlyres/A6520A9D-0A9A-47B3-B550-C006B5B224E7/0/1915Declaration.pdf.

AAUP (American Association of University Professors). 1940. *1940 Statement of Principles on Academic Freedom and Tenure.* Washington, DC: American Association of University Professors. https://www.aaup.org/report/1940-statement-principles-academic-freedom-and-tenure.

Diermeier, Daniel. 2023. "The Need for Institutional Neutrality at Universities." *Forbes*, December 20.

Ferguson, Roderick A. 2017. *We Demand: The University and Student Protests.* Oakland: University of California Press.

Gilmore, Shawn. 2021. "Are We Really Supporting the Inclusion of Contingent Faculty in Governance?" *Academe* 107 (4). https://www.aaup.org/article/are-we-really-supporting-inclusion-contingent-faculty-governance.

Gordon, Daniel. 2015. *What Is Academic Freedom? A Century of Debate, 1915–Present.* London: Routledge.

Gruber, Carol S. 1975. *Mars and Minerva: World War I and the Uses of Higher Learning in America.* Baton Rouge: Louisiana State University Press.

Kalven, Harry, Jr. 1967. "Kalven Committee: Report on the University's Role in Political and Social Action." *Record*, November 11. https://provost.uchicago.edu/sites/default/files/documents/reports/KalvenRprt_0.pdf.

Kezar, Adrianna J., Tom DePaola, and Daniel T. Scott. 2019. *The Gig Academy: Mapping Labor in the Neoliberal University.* Baltimore: Johns Hopkins University Press.

MacLean, Nancy. 2018. *Democracy in Chains: The Deep History of the Radical Right's Stealth Plan for America.* New York: Penguin.

Rabban, David M. 1990. "A Functional Analysis of 'Individual' and 'Institutional' Academic Freedom under the First Amendment." *Law and Contemporary Problems* 53 (3): 227–301.

Schrecker, Ellen. 1986. *No Ivory Tower: McCarthyism and the Universities.* New York: Oxford University Press.

Shannon, George Pope. 1948. "Academic Freedom and Tenure: Report of Committee A for 1947." *Bulletin of the American Association of University Professors* 34 (1): 119–32.

Shannon, George Pope. 1949. "Academic Freedom and Tenure: Report of Committee A for 1948." *Bulletin of the American Association of University Professors* 35 (1): 49–65.

Tiede, Hans-Joerg. 2015. *University Reform: The Founding of the American Association of University Professors*. Baltimore: Johns Hopkins University Press.

Tiede, Hans-Joerg. 2020. *Policies on Academic Freedom, Dismissal for Cause, Financial Exigency, and Program Discontinuance*. Washington, DC: American Association of University Professors. https://www.aaup.org/file/PoliciesonAcademicFreedom.pdfhttps://www.aaup.org/report/policies-academic-freedom-dismissal-cause-financial-exigency-and-program-discontinuance.

A

Adjunct

Heather Steffen

An adjunct faculty member is a part-time contingent teacher-scholar in US higher education. To be contingent means to be employed without job security, usually on limited short-term contracts with no guarantee of future employment beyond the contract term and no expectation of contract renewal. Adjuncts may be referred to by various different titles, including lecturer, teaching professor, or professor of the practice. Adjunct teaching contracts usually last between one semester or quarter and one academic year, and they offer pay per course but neither health benefits nor retirement contributions. The average pay per course for adjuncts in the United States is about $3,000, meaning an adjunct faculty member teaching four courses a year at each of two institutions (i.e., eight courses in the academic year and very much full time) will bring home $24,000, and indeed most adjuncts make around $20,000 per year from the work (Fure-Slocum 2024, 4). Assistant professors, the bottom tenure-track faculty rank, average salaries around $90,000, usually while teaching between four and eight courses per year, conducting research, and providing institutional service (AAUP 2023, table 1). The current goal of the adjunct labor movement's fight for better pay is a minimum of $5,000 per course.

The work for which an adjunct teacher-scholar is responsible, in most cases, is the design, delivery, and assessment of student coursework. Adjuncts are not compensated for research or service they may perform alongside or in support of their teaching duties. Neither are adjuncts typically involved in shared governance (e.g., faculty senates or departmental decision-making processes), meaning the contingent majority has little to no say in developing the curricular policies and procedures that determine their working conditions and their students' learning conditions. Academic freedom is another scholarly value and right that adjuncts do not enjoy alongside their tenured colleagues. Instead, an adjunct's abject lack of job security beyond the current contract constrains their freedom to teach, to research and publish, and to speak as members of the public without fear of retaliatory employment consequences if they anger a manager, administrator, or donor.

Adjunct teacher-scholars are unlikely to have access to university resources and amenities available to other (full-time or tenure-stream) teachers. Adjuncts are not issued laptops or dedicated desktop computers; nor are they provided with private workspace on campus. Contingent faculty are often not listed in course catalogs nor included in the faculty list on departmental websites, making it difficult for students to locate them and for adjuncts to build public profiles as scholars, artists, writers, or community organizers. Not long ago in the fight for adjunct labor rights, contingent instructors struggled simply to have institutional email addresses. Further, adjuncts are typically ineligible to apply for internal and external funding opportunities, like those that support research and conference attendance and presentations, as well as those that provide time off from teaching to pursue research or community engagement projects. One benefit many adjunct unions seek in collective bargaining is a "professional development fund," usually a small fund (several hundred dollars a year per adjunct) provided by the university to support adjunct attendance at conferences or other professional development events.

Many adjuncts work multiple jobs, either as "freeway flyers" jetting between courses at different institutions or as part of the vast US part-time gig economy. Adjunct college instructors I have known have also worked as entrepreneurs and business owners, consultants, editors, curators, tutors and test prep specialists, nannies and caregivers, restaurant servers, events managers, Uber drivers, university staff members, and sex workers, both part and full time, while teaching. The anonymous author of *In the Basement of the Ivory Tower* (Professor X 2012) works a full-time day job "in a rather dreary corner of the government" in addition to adjunct teaching in the evenings. Many adjuncts work for their institutions for a very long term of service (20+ years), always on a series of short-term contracts and with no hope of promotion.

The creation of adjunct positions was driven by colleges and universities' desire to access the expertise of working professionals as a resource for students. By hiring nonacademic professionals on a per-course basis, colleges and universities take advantage of community knowledge for a reasonable price, and these teachers already have full-time jobs outside higher education that supply them with living wages and benefits. Adjuncts of this sort—the professional moonlighting at the local college—were never meant to become a meaningful percentage of higher education faculty. Adjuncts now make up the clear majority, almost three-quarters, of the teaching workforce in US colleges and universities. As of 2017, adjunct faculty composed "about 61.4 percent of the instructional positions at 4-year institutions, 83.5 percent at 2-year institutions, and 99.7 percent at for-profit institutions," according to the Government Accountability Office (quoted in Fure-Slocum 2024, 4). Most college students in the United States are found in the types of institutions with the highest percentages of contingent instructors.

Not all contingent workers experience precarity in the same way or to the same degree. To be sure, some adjunct faculty choose and are satisfied with part-time work for multiple reasons. But more common is an experience of compounded contingency, one might say hypercontingency. Women and teacher-scholars of color are disproportionately likely to be found in the adjunct and other contingent ranks. When women of color work as part-time adjunct faculty, they experience a version of hypercontingency due to the overlapping and reinforcing effects of institutional racism and sexism intersecting with precarious employment. Sekile M. Nzinga (2020, 60) argues that faculty of color, particularly women of color, are both "contractually contingent" in the senses discussed above and "structurally contingent . . . because regardless of their contracted appointment status, they remain particularly disposable given enduring inequities that are maintained and reproduced through institutionalized forms of racism and sexism within the university's academic workforce." Far from new phenomena, then, contingency and precarity have marked the academic lives of scholars of color throughout their history in US higher education: "The contractual contingency that comes for growing masses of part-time faculty members in the morning has already been coming for vulnerable women and people of color faculty at night for some time now, regardless of their contract" (Nzinga 2020, 52).

For Herb Childress (2019), the massive growth in the use of adjuncts in place of full-time teaching faculty over recent decades signals the steep inequality within US higher education. "Our reliance on adjunct faculty isn't an accident," he writes. "It's a standard operating feature of a system of higher education designed to offer vastly different tiers of service to vastly different populations of privilege" (15). In Childress's formulation, the casualization of college teaching is a symptom of the tiered nature of the US higher education system, in which very few students actually enjoy the well-resourced, wealthy, prestigious institutions that come to mind most readily when we think of college. The reality is that most of today's college students attend two-year institutions or community colleges, for-profit institutions, and lower-tier public universities. These institutions are also the most likely to employ large percentages of contingent instructors. That is to say, "the least privileged students are likely to have the least privileged teachers" (Childress 2019, 15).

Childress's conclusion raises a question: Does the fact that a student has an adjunct for a teacher rather than a full-time permanent lecturer or tenure-stream professor affect the quality of education the student receives? As Eric Fure-Slocum summarizes, studies of adjunct teaching quality have concluded that "the quality of teaching offered by contingent faculty members is often equal to, if not better, than that of their tenure-stream peers" (2024, 5). Although adjunct teaching quality is high, however, Fure-Slocum reminds us that contingent instructors are constrained by their working conditions when it comes to their ability to serve students and to grow and develop as teacher-scholars: "Faculty instability discourages pedagogical innovation, undermines continuity in learning, hampers student-teacher relationships, and subverts the possibility of longer-term mentoring" (5). Students are denied the multiyear contact with faculty members that can lead to in-depth learning and to research assistantships, mentored independent projects, service-learning opportunities, and independent studies, all among the high-impact learning practices recommended by scholars of teaching and learning.

In light of these working conditions and their effects on students, teachers, and researchers, adjunct and contingent faculty in the United States have engaged in a constantly growing wave of organizing for collective bargaining, for research and activism, and for solidarity. The contingent academic labor movement is responsible for or involved in some of the most forward-looking organizing on campuses and in workplaces today. For instance, SEIU Local 500 pioneered the "metropolitan organizing strategy" in the Washington, DC, region, organizing adjunct faculty at many institutions around the city at roughly the same time and bargaining higher wages into all contracts, effectively raising the floor for adjunct pay throughout the region. One of the oldest academic unions in the nation, Rutgers AAUP-

AFT is a model of "wall-to-wall" campus organizing, in which as many types of campus worker as possible are included within the same union so that bargaining and activism can be coordinated across job categories. The New Faculty Majority and the Coalition of Contingent Academic Labor are two nonunion adjunct organizations that have produced studies and collate examples of adjunct working conditions, collective bargaining wins, and resources for adjunct workers.

Although adjuncts have drawn the most public attention because of their bare-bones working conditions and strong labor activism, adjunct work is but one variety of contingent labor in today's colleges and universities. Other types of contingent labor currently used on US campuses include the following groups:

- Graduate student employees are usually full-time doctoral students who work for the institution at which they study, although master's students also sometimes work on campus during their studies. Graduate students on US campuses design and teach classes, conduct research, and serve as research and teaching assistants to faculty, as well as filling numerous other staff and service roles.
- Postdoctoral workers ("postdocs") have recently earned doctorates and are employed on short-term (usually 1- to 3-year) contracts to conduct further research. The purpose of postdoctoral positions can vary, but they are often meant as a period of mentored research training, during which the postdoc deepens exploration into their own project, usually by authoring articles or a book manuscript, or expands their training by taking on a new subspecialty within their field. Postdoctoral researchers work either for a supervisor on their research projects or as *fellows* pursuing their own investigations. Postdoctoral *fellowships* are most common in the humanities and social sciences, while postdoctoral employment on a supervisor's project is most common in science, technology, engineering, and mathematics (STEM) fields. Almost all STEM scholars who go on to work in universities or national laboratories will do at least one postdoc after graduate school, with some completing over a decade of research in various postdoctoral positions while seeking permanent employment; only a minority of humanities and social sciences PhDs do the same.

- Research scientists are scholars conducting scientific research on a contract basis rather than as professors with an expectation of continuing employment. Funding to pay research scientists is typically dependent on grant funding, making their employment contingent on the continued availability of that funding to the scientist or their professor-employer.
- The phrase "college and university staff" encompasses an incredibly wide array of job categories, from department administrative assistants, student advisers, and accountants to IT professionals, custodians, and microscope technicians. We can understand *staff* here as naming those workers on college campuses whose primary responsibility is neither teaching nor research but support, in whatever capacity, of those institutional priorities. Staff are workers rather than managers or administrators, because they do not have a direct role in institutional decision making, though midlevel managers are increasingly common in higher education and make classification difficult. Included within the staff category are most undergraduate campus workers, because most are engaged in support of teaching, research, student affairs, or another aspect of campus life.

Contingent labor is now the foundation of the contemporary US higher education system, and today's contingent campus workers are the fundamental force that enables colleges and universities to fulfill their teaching and research missions. How did we get here? And how does the existence of a majority-contingent workforce affect life in colleges and universities, especially for contingent workers themselves?

The question of how we got here begins with cuts to state funding for US higher education that began in the 1980s and have continued into the present. As colleges and universities lost funding from their states, they undertook several strategies to cut costs and raise additional funds. On the one hand, institutions shifted costs onto students. Tuition increases drastically outpaced inflation throughout this period, and student debt has ballooned as a result. On the other hand, colleges and universities began to adopt various cost-saving and management strategies borrowed from the world of business and management theory. The use of contingent workers is one strategy in this neoliberalization of US higher education.

Neoliberalism is a concept that recurs throughout this book because many observers name the current era in US higher education the moment of the "neoliberal university." In one basic definition, neoliberalism names the set of economic, political, social, and cultural processes through which free markets have come to serve as our dominant model for social relations and institutional organization:

- Social relationships become defined primarily through their economic facets. Students are regarded by their educational institutions as customers rather than learners, and, as Childress writes, "College has become a form of indispensable employment insurance, available for purchase on the open market at protection levels from community college bronze to Ivy League platinum" (2019, 48).
- Public goods and services become privatized. Formerly public enterprises are now run by for-profit entities (e.g., for-profit charter schools; private prisons; privately held patents on the results of publicly funded research).
- Individuals behave like entrepreneurs, and organizations behave like businesses: we imagine ourselves as mini-enterprises trying to grow our capital in the world's marketplace (e.g., the concept of human capital, resume building for high schoolers). Organizations and institutions like nonprofits, universities, government agencies, and NGOs function on the model of for-profit businesses, despite their not-for-profit tax designation. Public institutions that have not formally been privatized become neoliberalized in that they behave like businesses.
- Responsibility and risk are individualized. Rather than viewing the responsibility to employ, feed, clothe, and house everyone as society's responsibility, our society views it as each person's responsibility to fend for themselves (e.g., the transition from welfare to workfare, drastic wealth/income inequalities). Similarly, we expect risks to be borne by individuals rather than employers or social welfare services (e.g., an adjunct's laptop, an Uber driver's car, student debt).
- Labor under neoliberalism is casualized. In other words, the dominant model for employment is that of the contingent or precarious worker. In neoliberalism, workers expect to labor for many employers over their

> working lives, often shifting careers several times. Employers extract cost savings through tactics like automated scheduling, keeping workers just under the number of hours needed to gain benefits, falsely defining workers as "contractors" or "consultants," outsourcing, and speed-up (being tasked with more work but not more time to do it in).

Adrianna Kezar, Tom DePaola, and Daniel T. Scott (2019) map this last process—the casualization of campus labor—and how it affects campus culture, student learning, and workers' ability to organize and improve their working conditions. Kezar, DePaola, and Scott ask, what does it mean for the foundational values and practices of academic life that "the majority of all nonmanagement university workers, both academic and nonacademic, are employed on a part-time, temporary, or contingent basis" (Kezar, DePaola, and Scott 2019, 16)? Their answer is essentially that the casualization of campus labor shreds the social fabric of the higher education workforce, breaking up communities, isolating workers from one another, and making collective action extremely challenging. The neoliberal university (or what the authors call the "gig academy") breaks campus communities apart by outsourcing, misclassifying long-term workers as short-term contractors, unbundling workers' roles (like splitting teaching away from research and service in adjunct positions), and encouraging individualism and entrepreneurialism in workers viewed as repositories of human capital. For workers, the experience of employment in the neoliberal university is one of "devaluation and vulnerability," marked by anxiety and isolation.

In contrast, Kezar, DePaola, and Scott offer a vision of "workplace democracy" and a campus where every worker has some control over their working conditions and the decisions that affect teaching, learning, research, and community engagement. In this fight, the contingent majority have history on their side, despite all that is arrayed against them, because "higher education is one of the few sectors where the belief that some degree of democratic control over the workplace may be structurally necessary was not a radical or unusual position either for the people employed there or the general public to hold" (Kezar, DePaola, and Scott 2019, 150–51).

References

AAUP (American Association of University Professors). 2023. *The Annual Report on the Economic Status of the Profession, 2022–23*. Washington, DC: AAUP. https://www.aaup.org/file/ARES-2022-23.pdf.

Childress, Herb. 2019. *The Adjunct Underclass: How America's Colleges Betrayed Their Faculty, Their Students, and Their Mission*. Chicago: University of Chicago Press.
Fure-Slocum, Eric. 2024. "Introduction: A Labor History of Contingent Faculty." In *Contingent Faculty and the Remaking of Higher Education: A Labor History*, edited by Eric Fure-Slocum and Claire Goldstene, 3–16. Urbana: University of Illinois Press.
Kezar, Adrianna J., Tom DePaola, and Daniel T. Scott. 2019. *The Gig Academy: Mapping Labor in the Neoliberal University*. Baltimore: Johns Hopkins University Press.
Nzinga, Sekile M. 2020. *Lean Semesters: How Higher Education Reproduces Inequity*. Baltimore: Johns Hopkins University Press.
Professor X. 2012. *In the Basement of the Ivory Tower: The Truth about College*. New York: Penguin.

A

Admissions

Scott Gelber

Admissions, when defined as the process in which colleges select students from a substantial pool of qualified applicants, has mattered to a relatively small number of people during a fairly recent era. Most students have not experienced a significant distinction between admissions and *access*—the feasibility of attending college as determined by family wealth, academic preparation, gender, race, and geography. For much of American history, enrollment tended to be virtually automatic for the small number of white men who were interested in higher learning, had received a bare minimum of scholastic training, and could afford to spend four years without full-time work. Meanwhile the enrollment of white women and students of color depended largely on their geographic location and the legal or de facto extent of their freedom.

Gender and Race

Having been excluded from the first wave of East Coast private higher education during the seventeenth and eighteenth centuries, scholarly women established academies whose rigorous curricula lay the foundation for the growth of single-sex colleges during the nineteenth century. These institutions were predominantly white, though they also enrolled small yet significant numbers of Black women. Motivated by a combination of democratic principles, a desire for higher enrollments, and pressure from aspiring students, most public universities (with varying degrees of enthusiasm) started to accept women during the Gilded Age. Economic factors also prompted a substantial number of private colleges to become coeducational in this era. Southern state legislatures were slower to embrace coeducation and often opted to found separate women's colleges. Public and private colleges in all regions tended to treat women as second-class students. The pace of women's enrollment stalled after the Second World War but regained momentum during the 1960s. Beginning in that decade, a second wave of private college conversions to coeducation was driven by a desire to increase revenue and selectivity. Passed in 1972, the Title IX amendment to the Civil Rights Act of 1964 promoted more equitable treatment at most institutions by banning gender discrimination in schools that received federal funding. While underrepresented in some majors and professional schools, women college students outnumbered men by the end of the 1980s (Gordon 1990; Perkins 1997; Solomon 1985).

In contrast, racial barriers to college access were more durable. During the antebellum era, a small number of Black students attended northern and midwestern colleges. Although few of these schools explicitly promoted segregation, limited access to secondary schooling, financial constraints, and informal hostility restricted the number of Black applicants. It was also common for these institutions to permit enrollment but exclude Black students from dormitories and extracurricular activities (Diner 2017, 3–18). Most southern states prohibited formal education for free and enslaved Black people alike. Between the end of the Civil War and the civil rights movement, historically Black colleges and universities (HBCUs) provided the primary route to higher education for Black students (J. D. Anderson 1995, 198). In all regions of the nation, college attendance was impeded by segregated school systems, underfunded Black high schools, and students' financial responsibilities to their families. By the 1930s, less than 20 percent of Black teenagers attended school, compared to 55 percent of white teens (Wilkerson 1939, 36). This lack of preparation required HBCUs to maintain relatively permissive admissions standards well into the twentieth century (Drewry, Doermann, and Anderson 2001, 46, 51, 75; Thompson 1933, 260–64).

Less is known about the early higher education of other students of color. Following brief initiatives at Harvard College and Henrico College in the seventeenth century, a small number of Native Americans gained access to higher education during the eighteenth and nineteenth centuries. Some Indigenous students attended HBCUs, while others matriculated at predominantly white institutions. Most white reformers and policymakers in the nineteenth century opposed the formation of separate tribal colleges because they believed that Native American students should assimilate into European culture. As late as the 1930s, fewer than five hundred Indigenous students attended institutions of higher education (Szasz 1999). Legally, Latinx students tended to be categorized as white, though unequal provision of secondary education impeded college access. In 1930, for example, Mexican Americans composed 15 percent of Texas's population but less than 1 percent of the state's college enrollment. Missionaries recruited some Asian students to American colleges in the late nineteenth century, and the Chinese government encouraged small numbers of young people to pursue higher education overseas. By the 1920s, several thousand second-generation Japanese and Chinese Americans enrolled in institutions of higher education, especially on the West Coast. Between the Spanish-American War and the 1930s, the US government also facilitated the enrollment of hundreds of Filipino college students (Wechsler and Diner 2022, 51–63).

Academic Standards

For white male students with sufficient means, the modern admissions process did not exist at most institutions of higher education until the second half of the twentieth century. Until then, custom, law, and a lack of eligible students prevented all but a handful of colleges from enacting substantial academic entrance standards. Some schools rejected applicants who did not satisfy baseline requirements, but almost none was "selective" in the sense of admitting a group of students out of a larger pool of qualified candidates. At the start of the nineteenth century, entrance requirements at a typical college consisted of semiformal examinations in classics, basic mathematics, some philosophy, and perhaps elementary science. After the Civil War, secondary school principals successfully lobbied colleges to allow applicants to replace Greek or Latin with examinations in scientific subjects, history, English, or modern languages (Broome 1963, 82; VanOverbeke 2008, 102–3, 120–23). Western and southern public universities (especially institutions funded by the Morrill Land Grant Act of 1862) often maintained less exacting requirements, in part because of political pressure and in part because of a lack of rural secondary schooling (Dennis 2001, 4, 92–93; Douglass 2007b; Eddy 1973, 66–67). These universities tended to regard the first two years of enrollment (rather than the moment of initial registration) as the time for identifying unqualified students (Duffus 1936, 178). These flexible entrance policies served the interests of most college presidents, who hoped to expand access either for the sake of institutional survival or because they regarded large enrollment as a sign of prestige.

As a result, the distinction between secondary and higher education was blurry. To increase their enrollment, colleges created remedial departments, which sometimes educated greater numbers of students than their regular courses of study. All colleges offered conditional enrollment to unqualified applicants and invited them to address their deficiencies after they set foot on campus. Even at institutions such as Harvard, Yale, Princeton, and Columbia, half of first-year students were admitted conditionally as late as 1907 (Henderson 1912, 24; McKown 1925, 127–28; Wechsler 1977, 24, 121–22). State universities also adopted a system of "admission by certificate." Originating at the University of Michigan during the 1870s, this system guaranteed admission to students who completed the college-preparatory track of any high school that had been accredited by university faculty. By the turn of the century, most students who entered college did so through this type of automatic process. Although the system empowered state universities to shape high school curricula, faculty eventually tired of inspecting high schools and ceded control of accreditation to state officials or regional associations (Henderson 1912, 76; MacLean 1913, 40–41; Wechsler 1977, 17, 24, 40).

"Meritocratic" Admissions and Institutional Stratification

During the first decades of the twentieth century, institutions began to rethink this relatively permissive approach to admissions. The increasing availability of public secondary education encouraged colleges to shrink or discontinue remedial programs. Meanwhile, the capacity of public universities to welcome nearly all applicants came under pressure from enrollments that began to outpace state funding. Faculty also questioned the practice of devoting resources to semiprepared students who were likely to fail. Aided by the emerging field of educational measurement, many institutions began requiring applicants to possess a minimum grade point average or high school class rank. Starting in 1935, Harvard University asked all candidates to submit scores from the Scholastic Aptitude Test (SAT), a practice that spread throughout the nation in subsequent decades. Even land grant institutions implemented new admission standards despite their legal and historical commitment to accessibility (Geiger 1986, 129; Klein 1930, 2:25–27; Lemann 2000; Levine 1986, 162–66; Wechsler 1977, 45, 58, 238–47). Elite private institutions pioneered the practice of considering qualitative measures such as interviews, letters of recommendation, and essay questions. Many college officials worried that large numbers of high-scoring Jewish and working-class applicants would alienate the traditional constituencies of their institutions and started to rely on these subjective elements to lower their acceptance rates (Karabel 2006, 484–90; Wechsler 1984).

These qualitative components enabled prestigious institutions to embrace a rhetoric of meritocracy without worrying that they might enroll a substantially more diverse student body. Although the establishment of "merit-based" criteria expanded opportunities for some high-achieving students from marginalized communities, the concept also became an obstacle to equitable access. Even state universities, which once viewed mass higher education as the means of maximizing their service to the public interest, pivoted to an emphasis on enrolling relatively smaller numbers of high-scoring students, along with research productivity and extension programs (Douglass 2007a; Nidiffer and Bouman 2001). Whereas most colleges had previously struggled to fill their seats with qualified students, the post-WWII baby boom enabled more institutions to bolster their prestige by becoming more selective. During the 1970s, when the tidal wave of students subsided, selective institutions embraced the common application form and reduced their class sizes as a dual-prong strategy for attracting more candidates and maintaining their rejection rates (Duffy and Goldberg 2014, 30, 35–37, 57; Freeland 1992). In 1983, the inaugural rankings published by *U.S. News and World Report* reified selectivity as a key metric of institutional status (McDonough et al. 1998; Solorzano and Quick 1983). Admissions offices rebranded themselves as centers of "enrollment management" and embraced market research and sophisticated approaches to financial aid to maximize their selectivity, yield, and revenue (Duffy and Goldberg 2014, 63–64).

This shift toward more stratification between different types of institutions was facilitated by the growth of regional state colleges and community colleges that accommodated growing demand from students who were unable to attend selective institutions (Levine 1986, 21, 113–14, 133). Greater capacity at these more egalitarian institutions allowed flagship universities to reject students without diverting them from higher education altogether (Jarausch 1983). Established in the early twentieth century, community colleges substantially increased access to education but slowed the pace of enrollment gains at four-year colleges. After the Second World War, when the GI Bill, economic prosperity, and a demographic surge sparked an unprecedented period of enrollment growth, two-year institutions educated nearly half of all American college students (Brint and Karabel 1986; Dougherty 1994). By 1970, only one out of every four college students attended a private four-year institution (Duffy and Goldberg 2014, 11).

Racial Integration

Although college enrollment increased steadily during the early twentieth century, at the start of the Second World War, Black children remained one-fifth as likely to attend as white children. The GI Bill compounded this inequity by increasing access for white veterans, while thousands of Black veterans were turned away from overcrowded HBCUs (Turner and Bound 2003). This state of affairs underscored the importance of the NAACP's legal campaign against segregation, which started by targeting graduate programs before culminating with *Brown v. Board of Education*. Two years later, the Supreme Court affirmed that the *Brown* decision applied to institutions of higher education (*Brown v. Board of Education of Topeka* 347 US 483 (1954); *Florida ex Rel. Hawkins v. Board of Control*, 350 US 413 (1956)). Despite some reservations about the hostile environment for Black students within predominantly white colleges and universities, NAACP lawyers believed that integration was a prerequisite for equal educational opportunity (McNeil 1985). Yet legal victories proved to be insufficient. Many southern state university systems resisted integration, the admission of a few individuals rarely paved the way to proportional enrollment, and institutions across the nation made little effort to recruit or welcome students of color (Olivas 2013, 74).

Nevertheless, at least one Black student attended every southern state university by the midsixties. More substantial integration occurred toward the end of that decade, when the federal government intensified its enforcement of the Civil Rights Act of 1964 and the Higher Education Act of 1965. Whereas HBCUs had previously provided the lion's share of access, more than half of Black college students attended predominantly white institutions by the end of the seventies (Wallenstein 2008; Williams 1997). The sixties and seventies were also decades of substantial growth for Native American higher education. Federal funding helped to convert Bureau of Indian Affairs boarding schools into two-year colleges. In 1968, the Navajo Community College (later renamed Diné College) became the first institution of higher education founded and controlled by tribal authorities. Inspired by schools such as Diné, the Indian Education Act of 1972 authorized funding for the establishment of other Native American colleges (Szasz 1999; Wollock 1997). Latinx students also benefited from new federal policies, such as the Educational Opportunities Program. Despite persistent discrimination and underfunded primary and secondary school systems, Latinx enrollment in colleges and universities increased dramatically (Bernal 1999). In this era, Asian American college students gained greater visibility by supporting protests for civil rights, ethnic studies, and admissions reform. As a result of enrollment gains stemming from the Immigration and Nationality Act of 1965, the University of California stopped considering Asian Americans to be an underrepresented population in 1984. Advocates suspected that selective schools encouraged unofficial quotas to limit overall Asian American enrollment, even though some communities remained underenrolled compared to their population levels (Takagi 1990).

In addition to federal policies that promoted this increased level of access, many colleges started their own recruitment initiatives, summer orientation sessions, and targeted scholarships to attract students of color. Typically these efforts were responses to student activists who pressured institutions to become more inclusive, not only in terms of recruitment, but also by hiring faculty, starting ethnic studies programs, and establishing campus centers (Higginbotham 2001; Higgins 2023; Wechsler and Diner 2022, 153). Ultimately, these approaches expanded college access for a relatively small number of predominantly middle-class students with test scores and grades that approximated or exceeded the usual admission standards of these institutions. Admission to elite colleges and universities remained out of reach for most students of color, who disproportionately attended unselective poorly funded institutions with high rates of attrition. More troublingly, overall Black and Latinx enrollment declined following a retreat of political and judicial will in the late seventies and early eighties (Baker 2001; Karen 1991; Williams 1997, 15–27).

Although formal affirmative action policies had a small impact by shaping the admissions policies of a limited number of selective institutions, they attracted a great deal of attention from proponents and critics alike. Affirmative action lawsuits became the most common category of college access litigation in the late twentieth century, despite evidence indicating that these policies achieved their institutional goals while also diversifying leadership positions nationwide (Bowen and Bok 2019; Olivas 2013, 74). Affirmative action remained legally and politically vulnerable in part because of the tendency of school officials to emphasize the recruitment of talented youth rather than reconsidering their definitions of merit or rearticulating their institutions' commitment to equitable outcomes. Thus, advocates for these programs were put on the defensive when colleges and universities paid increasing attention to standardized tests, which tended to identify fewer high-achieving students of color compared to other methods of evaluation (Reuben 2001).

In *Regents of the University of California v. Bakke* (438 US 265 [1978]), the Supreme Court concluded that the goal of preparing doctors to work with heterogeneous populations justified the efforts of a medical school to enroll more students of color. This emphasis on the benefits of affirmative action for society at large (rather than as a response to historical discrimination or flawed evaluation metrics) has remained a core principle of affirmative action jurisprudence. More recently, the Court rejected a formal point system employed by the University of Michigan's undergraduate admissions office, while accepting its law school's more qualitative method for promoting racial diversity (*Grutter v. Bollinger*, 539 US 306 (2003); *Gratz v. Bollinger*, 539 US 244 (2003)). In 2023, the Supreme Court essentially overturned the legal basis for affirmative action. In the wake of this decision, selective institutions are likely to invest more heavily in recruitment from underrepresented communities, further emphasize social class and geographic origin in their decision-making processes, and reduce or eliminate their reliance on standardized test scores. Despite these efforts, the numbers of Black and Latinx students at prestigious institutions seem likely to decrease (N. Anderson and Syrluga 2023; Kahlenberg 2023).

Conclusion

Regardless of these important debates at a small number of highly selective institutions, acceptance rates remain relatively high at most colleges and universities. Community colleges and many regional state universities continue to enroll most interested students, and even some flagship institutions admit over half of their applicants. Equally significant as these low entrance standards, most public universities continue to offer some forms of remediation (Fullinwider and Lichtenberg 2004; Hoxby 2009; Romaniuk 2019; Soliday 2002). Increasing numbers of institutions are focusing on expanding the pipeline into college by tightening the alignment between secondary and tertiary school curriculum, streamlining the application process, and operating dual enrollment programs, which award college credit for classes that students take during their high school years (Vargas 2004).

Still, contemporary debates about admissions tend to focus on the policies of a few elite institutions that enroll a small fraction of that nation's college-going population. In particular, it is troubling that the mechanisms of selection dramatically favor the types of academic preparation and extracurricular portfolios available mostly to the nation's wealthiest young people. Students whose families rank in the top 1 percent of earners are more than 75 times more likely to gain admission to the most selective universities than students from families with annual incomes in the bottom quintile (Chetty et al. 2017). As a result, selective colleges are facing pressure to justify practices that advantage affluent students, such as early decision, legacy preferences, and an emphasis on athletics and other unpaid activities (Bussey et al. 2021). The rise of test-optional policies (a trend that was accelerated by the COVID-19 pandemic) has also attracted a great deal of attention, even though standardized test scores have a make-or-break impact at relatively few schools (Rodriguez and Camacho 2022). While debates about the admissions processes of the most selective institutions are inherently compelling, the more significant dynamics of college access arguably consist of the equitable provision of secondary education, the affordability of tuition, and the extent to which adequate resources are devoted to the types of public and private institutions that educate the vast majority of students.

References

Anderson, James D. 1995. *The Education of Blacks in the South, 1860–1935*. Chapel Hill: University of North Carolina Press.

Anderson, Nick, and Susan Syrluga. 2023. "Without Affirmative Action, How Will Colleges Seek Racial Diversity?" *Washington Post*, July 1.

Baker, R. Scott. 2001. "The Paradoxes of Desegregation: Race, Class, and Education, 1935–1975." *American Journal of Education* 109 (3): 320–43. https://doi.org/10.1086/444274.

Bernal, Dolores D. 1999. "Chicana/o Education from the Civil Rights Era to the Present." In *The Elusive Quest for Equality: 150 Years of Chicano/Chicana Education*, edited by José F. Moreno. Cambridge, MA: Harvard Educational Review.

Bowen, William G., and Derek Curtis Bok. 2019. *The Shape of the River: Long-Term Consequences of Considering Race in College and University Admissions*. 20th Anniversary edition. Princeton, NJ: Princeton University Press.

Brint, Steven, and Jerome Karabel. 1986. *Diverted Dream: Community Colleges and the Promise of Educational Opportunity in America, 1900–1985*. New York: Oxford University Press.

Broome, Edwin Cornelius. 1963. *A Historical and Critical Discussion of College Admission Requirements*. Columbia University Contributions to Philosophy, Psychology and Education. Princeton, NJ: College Entrance Examination Board.

Bussey, Karen, Kimberly Dancy, Alyse Gray Parker, Eleanor Eckerson Peters, and Mamie Voight. 2021. *"The Most Important Door that Will Ever Open": Realizing the Mission of Higher Education through Equitable Recruitment, Admissions, and Enrollment Policies*. Washington, DC: Institute for Higher Education Policy (IHEP). https://live-ihep-wp.pantheonsite.io/wp-content/uploads/2021/06/IHEP_JOYCE_full_rd3b-2.pdf.

Chetty, Raj, John N. Friedman, Emmanuel Saez, Nicholas Turner, and Danny Yagan. 2017. "Mobility Report Cards: The Role of Colleges in Intergenerational Mobility." NBER Working Papers, July. https://opportunityinsights.org/wp-content/uploads/2018/03/coll_mrc_paper.pdf.

Dennis, Michael. 2001. *Lessons in Progress: State Universities and Progressivism in the New South, 1880–1920*. Urbana: University of Illinois Press.

Diner, Steven J. 2017. *Universities and Their Cities: Urban Higher Education in America*. Baltimore: Johns Hopkins University Press.

Dougherty, Kevin J. 1994. *The Contradictory College: The Conflicting Origins, Impacts, and Futures of the Community College*. Albany: State University of New York Press.

Douglass, John Aubrey. 2007a. *The California Idea and American Higher Education: 1850 to the 1960 Master Plan*. Stanford, CA: Stanford University Press.

Douglass, John Aubrey. 2007b. *The Conditions for Admission: Access, Equity, and the Social Contract of Public Universities*. Stanford, CA: Stanford University Press.

Drewry, Henry N., Humphrey Doermann, and Susan H. Anderson. 2001. *Stand and Prosper: Private Black Colleges and Their Students*. Princeton, N.J.: Princeton University Press.

Duffus, R. L. 1936. *Democracy Enters College: A Study of the Rise and Decline of the Academic Lockstep*. New York: Scribner.

Duffy, Elizabeth A., and Idana Goldberg. 2014. *Crafting a Class: College Admissions and Financial Aid, 1955–1994*. Princeton, N.J.: Princeton University Press.

Eddy, Edward Danforth. 1973. *Colleges for Our Land and Time: The Land-Grant Idea in American Education*. Westport, CT: Greenwood.

Freeland, Richard M. 1992. *Academia's Golden Age: Universities in Massachusetts, 1945–1970*. New York: Oxford University Press.

Fullinwider, Robert K., and Judith Lichtenberg. 2004. *Leveling the Playing Field: Justice, Politics, and College Admissions*. Lanham, MD: Rowman and Littlefield.

Geiger, Roger L. 1986. *To Advance Knowledge: The Growth of American Research Universities, 1900–1940*. New York: Oxford University Press.

Gordon, Lynn D. 1990. *Gender and Higher Education in the Progressive Era*. New Haven, CT: Yale University Press.

Henderson, Joseph Lindsey. 1912. *Admission to College by Certificate*. Library of American Civilization. New York: Teachers College, Columbia University.

Higginbotham, Elizabeth. 2001. *Too Much to Ask: Black Women in the Era of Integration*. Gender and American Culture. Chapel Hill: University of North Carolina Press.

Higgins, Andrew Stone. 2023. *Higher Education for All: Racial Inequality, Cold War Liberalism, and the California Master Plan*. Chapel Hill: University of North Carolina Press.

Hoxby, Caroline M. 2009. "The Changing Selectivity of American Colleges." *Journal of Economic Perspectives* 23 (4): 95–118.

Jarausch, Konrad Hugo. 1983. *The Transformation of Higher Learning, 1860–1930: Expansion, Diversification, Social Opening, and Professionalization in England, Germany, Russia, and the United States*. Chicago: University of Chicago Press.

Kahlenberg, Richard D. 2023. "A New Path to Diversity." *Dissent*, March 23. https://www.dissentmagazine.org/online_articles/a-new-path-to-diversity/.

Karabel, Jerome. 2006. *The Chosen: The Hidden History of Admission and Exclusion at Harvard, Yale, and Princeton*. Boston: Houghton Mifflin.

Karen, David. 1991. "The Politics of Class, Race, and Gender: Access to Higher Education in the United States, 1960–1986." *American Journal of Education* 99 (2): 208–37. https://doi.org/10.1086/443979.

Klein, Arthur J. 1930. *Survey of Land-Grant Colleges and Universities*. United States Office of Education Bulletin no. 9. 2 vols. Washington, DC: Government Printing Office.

Lemann, Nicholas. 2000. *The Big Test: The Secret History of the American Meritocracy*. 1st rev. pb. ed. New York: Farrar, Straus and Giroux.

Levine, David O. 1986. *The American College and the Culture of Aspiration, 1915–1940*. Ithaca, NY: Cornell University Press.

MacLean, George Edwin. 1913. *Present Standards of Higher Education in the United States*. United States Bureau of Education Bulletin no. 4. Washington, DC: Government Printing Office.

McDonough, Patricia M., Anthony Lising Antonio, Marybeth Walpole, and Leonor Xóchitl Pérez. 1998. "College Rankings: Democratized College Knowledge for Whom?" *Research in Higher Education* 39 (5): 513–37.

McKown, Harry Charles. 1925. *The Trend of College Entrance Requirements, 1913–1922*. United States Bureau of Education Bulletin no. 35. Washington, DC: Government Printing Office.

McNeil, Genna Rae. 1985. *Groundwork: Charles Hamilton Houston and the Struggle for Civil Rights*. Philadelphia: University of Pennsylvania Press.

Nidiffer, Jana, and Jeffrey P. Bouman. 2001. "The Chasm between Rhetoric and Reality: The Fate of the 'Democratic Ideal' When a Public University Becomes Elite." *Educational Policy* 15 (3): 432–51. https://doi.org/10.1177/0895904801015003005.

Olivas, Michael A. 2013. *Suing Alma Mater: Higher Education and the Courts*. Baltimore: Johns Hopkins University Press.

Perkins, Linda. 1997. "The African American Female Elite: The Early History of African American Women in the Seven Sisters Colleges, 1880–1960." *Harvard Educational Review* 67:718–57.

Reuben, Julie. 2001. "Merit, Mission, and Minority Students: The History of Debate over Special Admissions Programs." In *A Faithful Mirror: Reflections on the College Board and Education in America*, edited by Michael C. Johanek. New York: College Board.

Rodriguez, Awilda, and Sayil Camacho. 2022. "Why 'Test-Optional' Admissions Are Not a Game-Changer for Equity after All." *Hechinger Report*, July 13.

Romaniuk, Bohdan R., ed. 2019. *The College Blue Book*. 46th ed. Farmington Hills, MI: Macmillan Reference.

Soliday, Mary. 2002. *The Politics of Remediation: Institutional and Student Needs in Higher Education*. Pittsburgh Series in Composition, Literacy, and Culture. Pittsburgh, PA: University of Pittsburgh Press.

Solomon, Barbara Miller. 1985. *In the Company of Educated Women: A History of Women and Higher Education in America*. New Haven, CT: Yale University Press.

Solorzano, Lucia, and Barbara E. Quick. 1983. "Rating the Colleges: Exclusive National Survey." *US News and World Report* 95 (3): 41–46, 48.

Szasz, Margaret. 1999. *Education and the American Indian: The Road to Self-Determination since 1928*. 3rd ed. Albuquerque: University of New Mexico Press.

Takagi, Dana Y. 1990. "From Discrimination to Affirmative Action: Facts in the Asian American Admissions Controversy." *Social Problems* 37 (4): 578–92.

Thompson, Charles H. 1933. "Introduction: The Problem of Negro Higher Education." *Journal of Negro Education* 2 (3): 260–64.

Turner, Sarah, and John Bound. 2003. "Closing the Gap or Widening the Divide: The Effects of the GI Bill and World War II on the Educational Outcomes of Black Americans." *Journal of Economic History* 63 (1): 145–77.

VanOverbeke, Marc A. 2008. *The Standardization of American Schooling: Linking Secondary and Higher Education, 1870–1910*. New York: Palgrave Macmillan.

Vargas, Joel. 2004. "Dual Enrollment: Lessons from Washington and Texas." In *Double the Numbers: Increasing Postsecondary Credentials for Underrepresented Youth*, edited by Richard Kazis, Joel Vargas, and Nancy Hoffman. Cambridge, MA: Harvard Education Press.

Wallenstein, Peter. 2008. "Black Southerners and Nonblack Universities, 1935–1965." In *Higher Education and the Civil Rights Movement: White Supremacy, Black Southerners, and College Campuses*, edited by Peter Wallenstein, 17–59. Gainesville: University Press of Florida.

Wechsler, Harold S. 1977. *The Qualified Student: A History of Selective College Admission in America*. New York: Wiley.

Wechsler, Harold S. 1984. "The Rationale for Restriction: Ethnicity and College Admission in America, 1910–1980." *American Quarterly* 36 (5): 643–67.

Wechsler, Harold S., and Steven J. Diner. 2022. *Unwelcome Guests: A History of Access to American Higher Education*. Baltimore: Johns Hopkins University Press.

Wilkerson, Doxey A. 1939. *Special Problems on Negro Education*. Washington, DC: Advisory Committee on Education.

Williams, John B. 1997. *Race Discrimination in Public Higher Education: Interpreting Federal Civil Rights Enforcement, 1964–1996*. Westport, CT: Praeger.

Wollock, Jeffrey. 1997. "Protagonism Emergent: Indians and Higher Education." *Native Americas* 14 (4): 12.

A

Alternative Institutions

Andy Hines and Eli Meyerhoff

In spring 2024 students formed hundreds of Gaza solidarity encampments on college and university campuses in the United States and around the world. While the demands of the protestors making generative reuse of university space were myriad, they most often cohered around the divestment of university endowments and activities from the state of Israel and entities that supported its total war on Gaza. As part of efforts to distinguish the encampments from the institutions that surrounded them, organizers formed what many called "the People's University." What constituted these alternative institutions varied widely: they created libraries, often named in honor of Palestinian martyrs like Professor Refaat Alareer, with books, printable pamphlets, and shared PDFs about the struggle of Palestinian and Jewish peoples; they featured teach-ins on the colonial-capitalist dimensions of their institutions; they produced knowledge through careful research about the entanglements of American universities with the devastation of Gaza, which led to the destruction of all universities in the region; and they built new relationships through conversations and creative practices, like painting signs and banners, that were intertwined with their studying and organizing. This crucial part of political education within the encampment marked students (and sometimes faculty, staff, and wider community members) enacting a new formation for study, aside from but in unavoidable relationship to the mainstream system of higher education. They prefigured a possible future alternative university, against which the current university can be judged as failing to live up to its own ideals. Professor Eman Abdelhadi told students at the University of Chicago encampment: "This is a dispatch from the liberated future that we're all hoping for" (Abdelhadi 2024).

Not unique to 2024, alternative institutions have been ever-present within higher education in North America and beyond. They are viewed most often as an experimental novelty, but from another perspective, they offer a repertoire for imagining alternative modes of study. They also supply different viewpoints from which to analyze the forces that coalesce to shape the dominant, capitalist-statist mode of higher education. Certain examples in the United States might immediately come to mind. There are mid-twentieth century experimental arts colleges, like Black Mountain in North Carolina, that proved pivotal to the development of modernist Cold War aesthetics (Menand 2021). Some historical alternatives have been incorporated and integrated into the dominant system, despite insisting on their radical bona fides as a brand distinction (e.g., the New School for Social Research or the Experimental College at Oberlin College). Though this chapter focuses largely on the United States, alternative institutions are not an exclusively US phenomenon. Some of these international education projects include "militant education" affiliated with the African Party for the Independence of Guinea Bissau and Cape Verde (Borges 2019), "popular education" in the Brazilian Landless Workers Movement (Pahnke 2018), and the "rebel education" of the Zapatistas in Mexico (Gallardo and Gálvez 2023).[1]

As with the Gaza solidarity movement, alternative institutions for education have been central to present and historical social movements: from the fugitive learning school founded by Black abolitionist Mary S. Peake, which would become Hampton Institute (Singh 2023), to the demand exercised for Black studies and the Black university concept (Loggins and Douglas 2021, 74–95; Rickford 2016). Yet, there are also prominent reactionary examples. These include explicitly rightwing projects like Praeger U, the University of Austin, and the Koch network–funded Mercatus Center and Institute for Humane Studies (Wilson and Kamola 2021), as well as radical evangelical Christian colleges (Liberty University) and the techno-utopian visioning of twenty-first-century neoliberals (e.g., massive open online courses, or MOOCs). It might be fair to say that the current conservative transformation of higher ed—away from liberal arts curricula and basic research and toward exclusively professional and career-driven modes—stands as an alternative vision of higher education that its promoters are trying to solidify as the mainstream (Shepherd 2023).

These genealogies are myriad, and it would be too ambitious to cover them all here. Instead, we offer a definition of alternative institutions, an

1. For a wide range of examples of schools and writing about them, see Shannon Mattern's "Para-/Extra-Institutional Schools," Are.na, last modified December 20, 2024, https://www.are.na/shannon-mattern/para-extra-institutional-schools; and Carson Salter's "tTF Programs," Are.na, last modified November 30, 2021, https://www.are.na/carson-salter/ttf-programs.

argument about how and why these institutions are distinctive and valuable to historical inquiries and political imaginings, as well as making a case for why focusing on these institutions necessitates a new analytical framework with which to grasp modes of study. We begin by explaining what we mean when we invoke *alternative institutions* and then turn to describing a schematic for analyzing the activities of these institutions, which can, in turn, be useful for defamiliarizing dominant forms of higher education. We draw on Marxist social theory and decolonial theory for this schematic to foreground how the infrastructure for study grows from our lives and relations to each other, to the land, and to the more-than-human, as well as from a struggle with the terms of colonial-capitalist modernity. We close by putting our schematic to work on two case studies, one on Communist labor schools of the mid-twentieth century and an early twenty-first-century ongoing project, the Dechinta Centre for Research and Learning, an Indigenous land-based education initiative.

What Are Alternative Institutions?

When we talk about alternative institutions, we mean an interconnected set of practices for study that are set against, or are distinct from, those institutions that make up the dominant system of education. In our account, the social relations that constitute these studying practices are relatively stabilized and endow "individuals with power, status and resources of various kinds"—that is what makes them an institution (J. B. Thompson 1991, 8). In addition, more spontaneous, ephemeral forms of collective study that do not achieve this durable stabilization still demand analysis. *Institution* may not be the perfect term to describe all these alternative formations, and in fact, many of the schools, research centers, and fugitive modes of study found within it may take an explicitly anti-institutional stance. We do not seek to turn those self-descriptions, which often emphasize process, into a reified fact.

As a term *alternative institutions* sets the activities it describes in relation to institutions shaped by liberal-capitalist modernity and coloniality (Melamed 2011), even though these alternatives seek to differentiate themselves from those dominant institutions. The present education system is based on an organizational structure with a *verticalist* form, emphasizing the ascent of a ladder—with individuals rising up the grade levels toward higher education—and developing an interlocking set of hierarchies for demarcating and enforcing which types of individuals have the capacity to be educated (Meyerhoff 2019). These hierarchies include seemingly objective, meritocratic measures that otherwise enforce distinctions reproduced by prevailing ideas about race, class, gender, sexuality, age, and ability: grade levels, grades, credentials, and institutional rankings. These measures bolster modernist colonial definitions of capitalist development, which gain differential force by positioning ways of knowing that are out of step with capitalist reason as "backwards," "stuck in the past," or "of another time." This web of forces coheres in the imaginative scenes of the school and the classroom, where the teacher as knowledge giver and student as knowledge receiver meet. The classroom assumes a disciplinary relation between the knowledgeable and the ignorant, but historical practice suggests that this assumption can be upended by recognizing that knowledge can be made together when people with different ways of knowing share these ways, or by the alignment of student and teacher against the forces that discipline them (Givens 2021; Slate 2022).

Positioning the dominant beside its alternative encourages us to consider a dialectical approach for understanding study practices.[2] Nicos Poulantzas (1975, 229–52) has suggested that the state organizes the ruling class, while disorganizing the working classes, and the education system is part of this process. Yet Stuart Hall's ([1983] 2016) critique and elaboration of Poulantzas registers how modes of study can catalyze forms of organization themselves, influencing the shape of political development. Alternative institutions can create forms of organization for working, dispossessed, and marginalized peoples in association with the land and other-than-human actors. These forms of organization thus supply mechanisms to disorganize the state, capital, and coloniality. Organizers shape alternative institutions in ways that are responsive to their particular historical conjunctures, designing and adapting them in light of the shifting contextual features of both the dominant political-economic regime and the movements of resistance and subversion to that regime.

If the use of *alternative* alerts us to the dialectical activities shaping the dominant hierarchized and individuating structure of the school, then *insti-*

---

2. George Ciccariello-Maher (2017, 2) defines dialectics as "the dynamic movement of conflictive opposition." The history of dialectics is long and, like alternative institutions, does not necessarily carry a particular political character. Maher's account of decolonial dialectics reminds us to focus not on the moments of ideal synthesis between these oppositions, but instead on rupture and practice.

tution overrepresents permanence. Institutions tend to be valued for both their stability and their scale. Colleges and universities organize their accumulated assets toward an imagined future in which they will forever exist (i.e., the endowment). While projections of permanence enable various schemes for dominant higher education institutions, many of these cohere around the capacity for the institution to own and hold property, including itself in perpetuity.

Other models of political change, however, as well as other modes of study are organized through an embrace of institutional temporalities that concede impermanence. Fugitive modes of study may not resemble institutions at all and, instead, are organic constellations of analysis that might emerge through struggle. The picket line, the blockade, and encampments can be sites of study, as can migration and the escape from slavery.[3] In *Parable of the Sower*, Octavia Butler (2000) allegorizes the challenge of adapting fleeting and fugitive modes of study to emplaced institutional forms. Lauren Olamina's "earthseed" philosophy organizes a divergent group of people fleeing Southern California, but the group loses coherence once they form the emplaced Acorn campus. The wider symbolic register of Butler's novel invokes a longer genealogy of fugitivity, which is distinctly described in Stefano Harney and Fred Moten's "undercommons" formulation (2013). The geographies of encounter in these modes of escape have been a site for the development of ways of knowing and infrastructures of living that cut across the categories of colonial-racial capitalism and thus present possibilities of the practice and gains of alternative study (King 2019). Examining Black and Indigenous world-making movements inspires us to draw on decolonial theory to disrupt the dichotomous categories of modernity and coloniality, such as "social versus natural," "human versus animal," and "space versus time." These disruptions are necessary to attend to the more-than-human relations in the alternative institutions that have been embedded with these world-making movements (Mignolo 2011; Quijano 2000).

The investigation of alternative institutions invites us to rethink our understanding of forms of organized practice for study along three axes (table 1).

---

3. There are many examples of this, including No More Deaths, where organizers have studied with migrant people to build together a praxis of migration across national borders attentive to human and more-than-human activities (Smith 2017). Another example is the Occupy Wall Street encampment in New York City, which fostered a critical analysis of how people are connected by debt and forged, first, the Rolling Jubilee and then the Debt Collective.

Table 1. Schematic for Analyzing Alternative Institutions

	Liberal-capitalist-statist modernity	Divergent/insurgent tendencies
Mode of organization	Durable, deep rooted, fixed	Fugitive, nomadic, maroon communities
	Permanence	Obsolescence
	Autocratic, vertical, arborescent	Democratic, horizontal, rhizomatic
	Centralized	Decentralized
	Expansive, growth	Static, degrowth
	Mediated control and management of means of production (e.g., funding and physical space)	Producers directly controlling and managing means of production
	Complying with the laws, policies, and practices of dominant institutions	Diverging, reconstituting, subverting, and eluding the laws, policies, and practices of dominant institutions
Mode of study	Hierarchical (students receive knowledge and evaluation from teachers)	Horizontal (students and teachers make knowledge and evaluations collaboratively)
	External motivations for learning (grades, credits, shame/honor affective economy)	Internal motivations for learning (curiosity, desires)
	Knowledge as commodity (property)	Knowledge as communist object (commons/usufruct)
Mode of political transformation	Resistance within dominant	Prefiguration of alternative beyond it
	Reform	Revolution
	Globally focused	Locally focused

The term orients us to an institution's mode of organization, its mode of study, and its mode of political transformation. These axes provide a schema for grasping the dynamics not only of alternative institutions, but of mainstream institutions as well. Within each axis are several additional dimensions that allow for a more precise analysis of the character of a given formation. This table collects some of the above-mentioned tensions that striate alternative institutions, as well as others that we elaborate further through our case studies. The groupings within each mode do not imply a value judgment of good or bad, nor does the order of the different modes imply a linear or hierarchical sequence. We are distinguishing these as ideal type categories for analytical purposes, but in reality, they are much messier and complexly intertwined. The middle column is labeled as liberal-capitalist-statist modernity because these descriptions have been aligned with the dominant world-making process, though we recognize that some of these descriptors can be repurposed to make different worlds. The righthand column is labeled divergent/insurgent tendencies as these descriptions frequently describe alternative movements; these may not, however, always be deployed to upend the dominant order. For example, neoliberalism seeks to mix centralization and decentralization in its variations of liberal-capitalist modernity. Even the most politically radical institutions can have characteristics from both columns in the same way that the most politically reactionary can.

We begin with a case study on the Jefferson School of Social Science, a Communist-supported labor school in Manhattan that operated from 1944 to 1956, and several of its affiliate institutions in Harlem. We follow this with a consideration of Dechinta Centre for Research and Learning, a land-based "experience" for research and postsecondary education led by northern Indigenous communities in Denendeh, Northwest Territories, Canada. Finally, we offer a brief conclusion that expands the Marxian vocabulary hewing to our schema after the Jefferson School example by placing it in conversation with decolonial theory on land-based education. This illustrates the flexibility of our approach to understanding alternative institutions and an attention to the ways of knowing that guide the institutions we study. It also allows us to reflect on the forms of solidarity possible in undertaking this work, particularly as white settler academics ourselves.

The Jefferson School of Social Science

The Jefferson School of Social Science emerged from the Popular Front's strategic collapse of outward political differences within the American Left. The school formed in 1944 from a merger of the New York Workers School and the School for Democracy. The Workers School, founded in 1923, offered training and courses for Communist Party USA (CPUSA) members, as well as a curriculum for trade unionists (Gettleman 1993). By contrast, the School for Democracy, "a liberal school for adults" (Dodd 1963, 148), had formed in 1941 as an offshoot of the New York Teachers Union, which had been expelled from the American Federation of Teachers (AFT). Some tolerance in the US state for leftist political activity during the war made it so that outwardly liberal but inwardly socialist institutions could operate openly.

There was another significant social force in the emergence of the Jefferson School. Black Left organizing also surged in this period, highlighting a grassroots investment in forms of adult education that had otherwise been latent in the School of Democracy and in the Workers School. The National Negro Congress, the Southern Negro Youth Conference, and Harlem residents raised funds to start the George Washington Carver School in Harlem in 1943 (Dolinar 2012). When the Carver School abruptly closed, the Jefferson School stepped in to absorb its debts and the Carver School's attention to the study of Black culture ("Minutes of the Executive Committee" 1947).

The Jefferson School's emergence at the intersection of Communist, liberal, and Black Left tendencies in New York illuminates its initial widespread appeal and offers insight into its mode of organization. It implemented a durable organizational structure, similar to a mainstream university; there was a board, a director, a layer of senior leadership, faculty, staff, and students. Despite these layers—and except for students—the school was a union shop from wall to wall. All permanent workers were members of the SCMWA (later UPWA) Local 555, the union that achieved the first collective bargaining contract for university faculty in the country in 1943. Jefferson School contracts stipulated standard uniform pay rates; all faculty made $55 per week, for instance. They also provided provisions for making temporary faculty permanent employees and job protections for pregnancy and childbirth, among other benefits ("Memorandum of Personnel Practice" 1945). Despite the verticalist organizational structure, the faculty worked to make governance decisions (sometimes with students), to manage curriculum, and to perform other matters by committee and in dialogue. One "self-criticism" session discussed, for instance, that teaching must be directed toward the "every-day language of working people" and that classes should take part in "collective" projects (*Report of the All-School Self-Critical Conference* 1953, 7–8).

The Jefferson School's desire for legibility as a regular higher education institution was guided by opportunities to receive federal funding through the GI Bill, but its ambitions to be a politically distinct parallel to the higher education system undergirded its mass appeal. From 1944 until 1956, the school enrolled 120,000 students at its main building in Manhattan and thousands more in extension courses in 10 neighborhood branches (Gettleman 2002). Most Jefferson School students were women (at times up to 70 percent, according to the school's figures, and up to 90 percent in the FBI records), and with dedicated recruitment schemes, the school enrolled

Black and Puerto Rican students at higher rates than they were represented in New York City's population (Hines 2022, 160). Some of these students were interested in the Communist Party, but many others sought out forms of education that they could not find within the traditional university system. One alarmed reporter exclaimed, "A majority of the students, far from being union toughs, imported bomb tossers or hardened social wreckers are, instead, run-of-the-mine young Americans between seventeen and twenty-five years old" (C. Thompson 1949).

Soon the appeal of the school to women, Black people, and students from "regular" universities came to be seen by the federal government as a threat. As enrollments skyrocketed, US Attorney General Tom H. Clark declared the school "subversive" in 1947, a designation the school's leaders would fight until its 1956 closure (Gettleman 2008). Over 100 university faculty nationwide signed on a petition to the government stating that "any attempt to suppress the teaching of Marxism in such an institution as the Jefferson School of Social Science represents a serious threat to all free inquiry." This argument did not prevail.

The Jefferson School's mode of study helped to solidify its distinctive coalition and suggests a political horizon beyond the limits of its organizational form. An attention to Marxism, anti-imperialism, feminism, and race defined its curriculum. Courses emphasized anti-imperial approaches to society, art, and science, while foregrounding the exploitation of Black people, women, and workers. Faculty produced study guides associated with courses that were affordable and available in the school's bookstore for purchase. One on "The Women Question" answered 65 questions theoretical ("How did the rise of imperialism affect the status of women?") and practical ("How does the occupational distribution of Negro women compare with that of white women?") and offered a list of 38 women leaders to study (Epstein and Wilkerson 1953). Another popular choice advised students on "How to Study."

The pedagogical method emphasized the horizontal generation and sharing of knowledge. Gwendolyn Bennett's flagship course at the Carver School situated the development of Black art and literature as part of a social and political struggle. Bennett's pedagogy suggests that Black cultural workers were engaged in a struggle for democracy and peace *with* working people, and she solidified this by bringing several important Black cultural workers to class to meet with her students (Hines 2022, 154–55; see Heatherton 2022,

166–68). This effort to tend to the knowledge made by and with working people, rather than training and credentialing student subjects, highlights the Jefferson School's philosophy of education.

This approach to study suggests an institutional commitment toward viewing knowledge as a "communist object," and the efforts to share the work of the school with those beyond its student body signals this (Thoburn 2010). Enrolling in classes required a marginal fee ($5 or $6), but scholarships were available to those who could not pay. The institution also reached a wider nonstudent public with frequent lectures and cultural events. These included performances by Woody Guthrie and Pete Seeger, dramatic readings of Langston Hughes's poetry, as well as social events, like square dances. There was a lounge, Club Jefferson, for drinks and food, the bookstore, and a library with 40,000 volumes and, according to the school's librarian, Henry Black, "completely normal" relations with public, academic, and governmental institutions (Ring 1985).

The successes of the Jefferson School—and the insurgent possibility offered by the school—resulted from its ability to mimic the "completely normal" that its pedagogy, curriculum, and mission otherwise sought to undo. It activated purged faculty looking for work; enrolled students, mainly women, working people, and people of color, otherwise excluded from the mainstream system; and shared the knowledge produced within the institution in forms legible to a wide coalition beyond the school. The Jefferson School embraced a reformist tendency as it resisted and recast the terms of standard academic life with an anti-imperial, anticapitalist politics.

Dechinta Centre for Research and Learning

Dechinta Centre for Research and Learning (née Dechinta Bush University) was founded in 2009, as a project for "Indigenous land-based education, research, and community programs rooted in Northern Indigenous knowledge and values."[4] The Dechinta Centre emerged in the historical context of postindustrial, neoliberal capitalism, which was reimagining itself through crisis during and after the "global economic meltdown" of 2008. In the world of higher education, this economic crisis punctured the postwar myth of "the Edu-Deal"—that a college education was a path for individuals

4. Dechinta Centre for Research and Learning home page, accessed December 19, 2024, https://www.dechinta.ca/.

to gain secure jobs—which had been used to justify individual and family investments in tuition and taking on student debt as a means toward class ascension (Caffentzis 2010). In contrast to either a neoliberal imaginary of self-entrepreneurial higher education or a nostalgic return to the Fordist "golden age," Dechinta opened horizons of radical imagination toward exodus from the colonial-capitalist higher education system.

"Indigenous land-based education" for decolonization is at the core of the project's mission, and it shapes Dechinta's modes of organization, study, and political transformation. This mission is seen in how a main organizer, Glen Coulthard (Yellowknives Dene First Nation), describes the project's historical contexts of emergence and intervention. Framing the modes of life of the Yellowknives Dene as well as of other Indigenous peoples as based on "social relations that are embodied by land and place," Coulthard highlights how "colonization involved a violent separation of our peoples from those social relations of land" (Coulthard and Simpson 2014). This "violent separation" is a historical and ongoing process that combines settler-colonial land dispossession and individualizing assimilationist education—as seen in the Indian residential schools in Canada and Indian boarding schools and industrial schools in the United States (Hamilton 2021; Newland 2024)—as linked aspects of the "primitive accumulation" that destroys Indigenous ways of life and enables the expansion of the modernist colonial, racial-capitalist world-making project. As a means for countering the latter, Dechinta's Indigenous land-based education "promotes true self-determination and decolonization for Indigenous peoples in the North," for Indigenous resurgence, by working with Indigenous "elders from our community—and other community members and knowledge holders—in order to re-embed students in the social relations" that are grounded in reciprocal relations with the land.

The organization of Dechinta is based in the durable, deep-rooted relations to the land of the Yellowknives Dene people. Coulthard's concept of "grounded normativity" frames the project's norms as embedded in reciprocal relationships to the land, as well as in opposition to settler-colonial, statist-capitalist modes of relating with the land, which define jurisdiction in terms of centralized sovereign authority, fixed borders, and property ownership (Coulthard 2014; Pasternak 2017). In contrast with the modernist colonial dichotomy of nature versus society, Indigenous cosmologies frame people as part of the land and the land as an extension of the people. One of

Dechinta's founders, Erin Ballentyne, says that the Dene word *dè* is often translated as land but that "land is not sufficient enough a word," as *dè* "is a living reciprocal relation of land, water, air, animals and humans" and "is our most honored teacher" (2014, 68).

This decolonial, Indigenous organizing approach is seen in Dechinta's mode of governance, as their radically democratic horizontalist practices disrupt modernist colonial hierarchies. Every night at Dechinta, all participants join a "governance circle" with directly democratic discussions and decision making about the center's activities, values, relationships, and conflicts (Coulthard and Simpson 2014). These discussions include children, elders, professors, and students and implement horizontalist principles that destabilize hierarchies of adults over children, of academic experts over novices, and those of hetero-patriarchy, white supremacy, settler colonialism, and capitalism.

Dechinta's founders are explicitly opposed to capitalist development, as Coulthard argues: "For our [Indigenous] nations to live, capitalism must die" (Coulthard 2013). But they have their own visions of growth, in a way that is "localized and decentralized," because land-based education must emerge from particular lands and knowledge holders (Coulthard and Simpson 2014). Coulthard calls for a movement of "truly resurgent, decolonizing, land-based education" through establishing "a network of these types of educational practices, on territories across Canada, on every Indigenous peoples' territory," normatively grounded in other Indigenous peoples' lands, nations, and struggles for resurgence, while interlinked with each other through Indigenous person-to-person, nation-to-nation relationships. Another Dechinta faculty participant, Leanne Betasamosake Simpson (Michi Saagiig Nishnaabeg, Alderville First Nation), speaks of this "Indigenous internationalism" in terms that invoke the perspectives of decolonial, Indigenous thought systems, to see the nations of Indigenous peoples as enmeshed with their more-than-human lands: "With our complex ways of relating to the plant nations, animal nations, and the spiritual realm, our existence has always been inherently international regardless of how rooted in place we are. We have always been networked. We have always thought of the bush as a networked series of international relationships" (Simpson 2017, 56). Simpson discusses this Indigenous internationalism in relation to her own background as Nishnaabeg and a member of the Alderville First Nation. When visiting the Dene people at Dechinta, she has contributed in a way "that honored the ethics, politics, and histories of both nations," such as through a "Michi Saagiig Nishnaabeg political practice" of "territorial acknowledgment" that "shows respect for Dene sovereignty, self-determination, and governance" (Simpson 2017, 64). Participants from different Indigenous communities are mutually transformed by this learning while also remaining oriented by their distinctive land-grounded cultures, struggling for Indigenous resurgence while resisting settler-colonial capitalism.

This struggle motivates the Dechinta organizers' long-term vision for their land-based education project: seeing it as integral to movements of "resurgence" of Indigenous ways of life (Ballentyne 2014, 74; Simpson 2017, 194). Looking forward, they see this project as part of broader ecological movements to save the planet. Through their many classes that teach about how to live sustainably with the land—such as hunting, fishing, gathering food, making living structures, building canoes—they are prefiguring and building an alternative, ecologically sustainable world-making project. By teaching these practices of Indigenous grounded normativity via reciprocal relationship with the land, they shape the students into ecological activists and promote sustainable Indigenous futures against settler-colonial capitalism's destruction of the earth.

Dechinta's modes of study combine hierarchy and horizontality. Everyone is seen as having important knowledge, but the teachers are valued for bringing particular kinds of knowledge to the classes. For instance, Indigenous elders bring traditional Indigenous forms of knowledge, and academics offer knowledges developed through academic disciplinary practices. At the same time, children are understood to have valuable knowledge and act as teachers themselves. Further, with a more-than-human, Indigenous, decolonial view of agency and epistemology, the actors who participate in knowledge creation include the other-than-human beings of the land, plants, and non-human animals (Simpson 2017, 150).

Dechinta's organizers and participants grapple with tensions from trying to survive within colonial capitalism while resisting it and creating Indigenous alternatives to it. These tensions play out in how students earn credits from the University of Alberta for courses, and how Dechinta has resource-sharing partnerships with the University of Alberta, University of British Columbia, Aurora College, and Collège Nordique Francophone. They take money from state-supported and regulated universities to make Dechinta free for students, which is a means for decommodifying knowledge. From the Indigenous view, with "land as pedagogy," knowledge is seen as a way of relating, rather than as a thing that's produced; through transformative learning in land-based education, the participants change their ways of relating with each other and the land, as meaning is derived "through a compassionate web of interdependent relationships that are different and valuable because of difference" (Simpson 2017, 156). There is no road to the Dechinta Centre, so the participants must fly in a seaplane that lands on the lake near the camp. As a space withdrawn from the cash economy, the participants are pushed to think about what they really need and to break their attachments to the capitalist practices of buying and selling by learning to survive through living on the land with Indigenous traditional practices (Ballentyne 2014, 78). For Indigenous students, part of their motivation to participate are their desires to reconnect with and support their Indigenous communities' ways of life, against their destruction by and assimilation into settler-colonial capitalism.

In addition to decommodifying knowledge, Dechinta takes land out of capitalist circuits of commodification. Dechinta's mode of political transformation combines resistance to the colonial-capitalist world-making project with both prefiguring and building alternatives beyond it. One form of resistance is through rerouting the flows of capital away from capitalist institutions, including universities, and toward alternative, resistant Indigenous land-based education spaces like Dechinta (Ballentyne 2014, 69). Another form of prefigurative resistance is how Dechinta removes Indigenous students, at least temporarily, from the capitalist settler-colonial education system and engages them in a land-based education project that can shape them as anticapitalist, anticolonial people becoming more grounded in Indigenous ways of life.

Dechinta takes a more revolutionary than reformist perspective on its approach to political change. It rejects the "colonial politics of recognition" within liberal-capitalist institutions (Coulthard 2014). The strategic question around credits, however, suggests that it is still playing the game in order to appropriate resources from the normal universities, akin to the "criminal relationship" of the "undercommons" (Harney and Moten 2013). They nevertheless try to minimize their dependence on the university's recognition and resources as much as possible, through building up their own autonomous land-based capacities, and they refuse to believe in "credits" as a route to transformation.

Conclusion

Our brief descriptions of the Jefferson School and Dechinta only gesture toward the analytical possibilities of considering alternative institutions via their modes of organization, study, and political transformation. Even if schools have conflicting philosophical underpinnings—the Jefferson School had been poised to reform the terms of colonial modernity, while Dechinta takes a more active decolonial stance—distinctive points of connection are made visible only when decentering the dominant system of higher education. Even so, the similarities and differences between these cases (and others) might be construed from a critical analysis of their political-economic contexts and how school organizers figure their institution's relationships to dominant institutional practices and forms. There have been many approaches to theorizing the relationship between dominant and alternative institutions—including Gramsci's "hegemony" and "counter-hegemony," and Deleuze and Guattari's "major" and "minor," among many others. Yet, one future direction for research on alternative institutions is to study how organizers and participants themselves theorize this relation. In M. E. O'Brien and Eman Abdelhadi's novel *Everything for Everyone,* a variegated set of communes with unique philosophical orientations form a confederation for study and survival, some even within the husks of what had once been universities (O'Brien and Abdelhadi 2022). By thinking across alternatives, we, researchers and organizers, may find cause to recognize the coalitional networks forming to constitute a distinctive system on the edges of the mainstream higher education system. How might modes of study, modes of organization, and modes of political transformation interface with one another beyond, between, against, and through the existing state-supported system? To what degree do alternative institutions invite us to reconstruct our sense of the sites, spatio-temporalities, and practices that constitute education?

References

Abdelhadi, Eman. 2024. Interview in "Palestine Solidarity Encampments Are a Rehearsal for Liberatory Self-Governance." *Movement Memos,* podcast, hosted by Kelly Hayes, May 23. https://truthout.org/audio/palestine-solidarity-encampments-are-a-rehearsal-for-liberatory-self-governance/.

Ballentyne, Erin Freeland. 2014. "Dechinta Bush University: Mobilizing a Knowledge Economy of Reciprocity, Resurgence, and Decolonization." *Decolonization: Indigeneity, Education and Society* 3 (3): 67–85.

Borges, Sónia Vaz. 2019. *Militant Education, Liberation Struggle, Consciousness: The PAIGC Education in Guinea Bissau 1963–1978*. Studia Educationis Historica, vol. 4. Frankfurt am Main: Peter Lang.

Butler, Octavia E. 2000. *Parable of the Sower*. New York: Warner.

Caffentzis, George. 2010. "University Struggles at the End of the Edu-Deal." *Mute*, April 15. https://www.metamute.org/editorial/articles/university-struggles-end-edu-deal/.

Ciccariello-Maher, George. 2017. *Decolonizing Dialectics*. Durham, NC: Duke University Press.

Coulthard, Glen Sean. 2013. "For Our Nations to Live, Capitalism Must Die." *Nations Rising*, November 5. https://www.nationsrising.org/for-our-nations-to-live-capitalism-must-die/.

Coulthard, Glen Sean. 2014. *Red Skin, White Masks: Rejecting the Colonial Politics of Recognition*. Minneapolis: University of Minnesota Press.

Coulthard, Glen Sean, and Leanne Simpson. 2014. "Leanne Simpson and Glen Coulthard on Dechinta Bush University, Indigenous Land-Based Education and Embodied Resurgence." *Decolonization: Indigeneity, Education and Society*, November 26.

Dodd, Bella V. 1963. *School of Darkness*. New York: Devin-Adair Company.

Dolinar, Brian. 2012. *The Black Cultural Front: Black Writers and Artists of the Depression Generation*. Jackson: University Press of Mississippi.

Epstein, Irene [Eleanor Flexner], and Doxey A. Wilkerson, eds. 1953. *Questions and Answers on the Woman Question*. New York: Jefferson School of Social Science.

Gallardo, Raúl Romero, and Xavie Gálvez. 2023. "The Rebel Education of the Zapatistas." *Funambulist*, no. 49 (August 17). https://thefunambulist.net/magazine/schools-of-the-revolution/the-rebel-education-of-the-zapatistas.

Gettleman, Marvin E. 1993. "The New York Workers School, 1923–1944." In *New Studies in the Politics and Culture of U.S. Communism*, edited by Michael E. Brown, Randy Martin, Frank Rosengarten, and George Snedeker, 261–80. New York: Monthly Review Press.

Gettleman, Marvin E. 2002. "'No Varsity Teams': New York's Jefferson School of Social Science, 1943–1956." *Science and Society* 66 (3): 336–59.

Gettleman, Marvin E. 2008. "Defending Left Pedagogy: U.S. Communist Schools Fight Back against the SACB (Subversive Activities Control Board) . . . and Lose (1953–1957)." *Convergence* 41 (2–3): 193–209.

Givens, Jarvis R. 2021. *Fugitive Pedagogy: Carter G. Woodson and the Art of Black Teaching*. Cambridge, MA: Harvard University Press.

Hall, Stuart. (1983) 2016. *Cultural Studies 1983: A Theoretical History*. Edited by Jennifer Daryl Slack and Lawrence Grossberg. Durham, NC: Duke University Press.

Hamilton, Scott. 2021. *Where Are the Children Buried?* Report to the National Centre for Truth and Reconciliation Winnipeg: University of Manitoba, National Centre for Truth and Reconciliation. https://nctr.ca/records/reports/.

Harney, Stefano, and Fred Moten. 2013. *The Undercommons: Fugitive Planning and Black Study*. Wivenhoe, UK: Minor Compositions.

Heatherton, Christina. 2022. *Arise! Global Radicalism in the Era of the Mexican Revolution*. Oakland: University of California Press.

Hines, Andy. 2022. *Outside Literary Studies: Black Criticism and the University*. Chicago: University of Chicago Press.

King, Tiffany Lethabo. 2019. *The Black Shoals: Offshore Formations of Black and Native Studies*. Durham, NC: Duke University Press.

Loggins, Jared A., and Andrew J. Douglas. 2021. *Prophet of Discontent: Martin Luther King Jr. and the Critique of Racial Capitalism*. Athens: University of Georgia Press.
Melamed, Jodi. 2011. *Represent and Destroy: Rationalizing Violence in the New Racial Capitalism*. Minneapolis: University of Minnesota Press.
"Memorandum of Personnel Practice." 1945. *Jefferson School of Social Science Records, 1942–1956*. Microfilm. Archives Division, Wisconsin Historical Society.
Menand, Louis. 2021. *The Free World: Art and Thought in the Cold War*. New York: Farrar, Straus and Giroux.
Meyerhoff, Eli. 2019. *Beyond Education: Radical Studying for Another World*. Minneapolis: University of Minnesota Press.
Mignolo, Walter. 2011. *The Darker Side of Western Modernity: Global Futures, Decolonial Options*. Durham: Duke University Press.
"Minutes of the Executive Committee of the Board, Wednesday, April 16, 4 p.m." 1947. *Jefferson School of Social Science Records, 1942–1956*. Microfilm. Archives Division, Wisconsin Historical Society.
Newland, Bryan. 2024. *Federal Indian Boarding School Initiative Investigative Report*. Vol. 2. Washington, DC: US Department of the Interior.
O'Brien, M. E., and Eman Abdelhadi. 2022. *Everything for Everyone: An Oral History of the New York Commune, 2052–2072*. Brooklyn: Common Notions.
Pahnke, Anthony. 2018. *Brazil's Long Revolution: Radical Achievements of the Landless Workers Movement*. Tucson: University of Arizona Press.
Pasternak, Shiri. 2017. *Grounded Authority: The Algonquins of Barriere Lake against the State*. Minneapolis: University of Minnesota Press.
Poulantzas, Nicos. 1975. *Political Power and Social Classes*. Translated by Timothy O'Hagan. London: NLB.
Quijano, Aníbal. 2000. "Coloniality of Power, Eurocentrism, and Latin America." *Nepantla: Views from the South* 1 (3): 533–80.
Report of the All-School Self-Critical Conference. 1953. New York: Jefferson School of Social Science. Jefferson School of Social Science Records and Indexes, Tamiment Library, New York University.
Rickford, Russell John. 2016. *We Are an African People: Independent Education, Black Power, and the Radical Imagination*. Oxford: Oxford University Press.
Ring, Daniel F. 1985. "Two Cultures: Libraries, the Unions, and the 'Case' of the Jefferson School of Social Science." *Journal of Library History (1974–1987)* 20 (3): 287–301.
Shepherd, Lauren Lassabe. 2023. *Resistance from the Right: Conservatives and the Campus Wars in Modern America*. Chapel Hill: University of North Carolina Press.
Simpson, Leanne Betasamosake. 2017. *As We Have Always Done: Indigenous Freedom through Radical Resistance*. Minneapolis: University of Minnesota Press.
Singh, Vineeta. 2023. "In the University (Archive) But Not of It: The Foundation of the Hampton Institute and the Forgetting of Abolition Democracy." *Critical Ethnic Studies* 8 (2). https://doi.org/10.5749/CES.0801.07.
Slate, Nico. 2022. "'The Answers Come from The People': The Highlander Folk School and the Pedagogies of the Civil Rights Movement." *History of Education Quarterly* 62 (2): 191–210.
Smith, Sophie. 2017. "Introduction: No More Deaths." *South Atlantic Quarterly* 116 (4): 852–62.

Thoburn, Nicholas. 2010. "Communist Objects and the Values of Printed Matter." *Social Text* 28 (2): 1–30.

Thompson, Craig. 1949. "Here's Where Our Young Commies Are Trained." *Saturday Evening Post*, March 12.

Thompson, John B. 1991. "Editor's Introduction." In *Language and Symbolic Power*, by Pierre Bourdieu, edited by John B. Thompson, translated by Gino Raymond and Matthew Adamson, 1–31. Cambridge: Polity Press.

Wilson, Ralph, and Isaac Kamola. 2021. *Free Speech and Koch Money: Manufacturing a Campus Culture War*. London: Pluto.

Athletics

Wayne L. Black

College athletics has always held a peculiar, if not hypocritical, position in higher education. On a momentous day, February 5, 2024, a National Labor Relations Board (NLRB) regional office in Boston made a historic ruling. They declared that Dartmouth College's men's basketball team were employees and could form a union (Lederman 2024). This ruling was a seismic shift in the college athletics landscape. A month later, the players made it official in a decisive 13–2 vote. The players had unionized, marking a significant shift in how society views college athletics.

Institutions have extorted financial, political, and economic capital from so-called amateurs for nearly 200 years, but beyond the Dartmouth union, the last decade has produced significant cracks in that classification. In 2019, California Governor Gavin Newsom signed Senate Bill 206, which gave California college athletes economic rights to their name, image, and likeness (Anderson 2019). With this, Newsom sent a clear message to the National Collegiate Athletics Association (NCAA): the amateurism model needed to change. The NCAA, the largest college athletics association, has long dictated how society views college athletics (Howe, Black, and Jones 2023). The NCAA is responsible for coining and propagating myths about student athletes being "amateurs" while generating billions in revenue for institutions (Byers and Hammer 1995; Staurowsky and Sack 2005). The NCAA has purveyed myths about college athletics as being primarily about fair play, high morals, degree attainment, and playing for the love of the game, effectively establishing a social norm that college athletics is uncompensated amateurism.

Amateurism is and will continue to be a hotly debated topic when discussing college athletics, but it is impossible to discuss without examining its connection to commercialization. An important period for the establishment of amateurism in college athletics followed World War II (Thelin 1994). This eddy later connected to higher education's growing adoption of the neoliberal ideals transforming the US economy (Boggs et al. 2019). The tension between amateurism and commercialization, however, is at the heart of discourse about money making in college athletics, starting with the landmark 1984 Supreme Court case *NCAA v. Board of Regents of the University of Oklahoma* (Benedict and Keteyian 2014). The NCAA wanted to control television rights to protect live attendance, but the US Supreme Court ruled that the NCAA violated the 1890 Sherman and 1914 Clayton Antitrust Acts, designed to prohibit cartels from stopping free trade. Free trade is a crucial concept to neoliberalism, and since World War II, higher education has become part of academic capitalism, which centers on profits over people (Jessop 2018).

Immediately following the ruling, institutions began creating super conferences to generate revenue, which laid the foundation for the rampant commercialization of today's college athletics. Conferences in the NCAA Power 5 are the wealthiest athletics institutions with the most resources because of media rights deals (Gaul 2016; Nocera and Strauss 2018), while other institutions have since sought to realign conferences to attempt to gain the same level of revenue.[1] In 2021, the University of Texas and the University of Oklahoma announced that they would leave the Big 12 to join the Southeastern Conference (SEC). This sent shockwaves through college athletics because Texas and Oklahoma were founding Big 12 members with their own lucrative media rights deals. This legacy did not matter: joining the "prestigious" SEC would mean more money from television matchups (Lederman 2021). A year later, University of California, Los Angeles and University of Southern California announced that they would depart the Pac-12 for the Big 10 Conference, another financially driven move (Hatch 2022).

College athletics' commercial expansion has brought critical questions about the role of athletics in higher education. Exploitation is rampant throughout college athletics. Black college athlete exploitation is most discussed in these terms, particularly at Power 5 institutions. Football and basketball are inextricably intertwined with race in higher education and American history. Black students could not attend white institutions, so historically Black colleges and universities (HBCUs) were created during the nineteenth century (Lovett 2011). HBCUs were the only spaces where

1. The Power 5 conferences are the ACC, Big 10, Big 12, Pac-12, and SEC.

Black athletes could participate in college football and basketball. During the twentieth century, HBCUs regularly beat all-white college teams in football and basketball, despite not having social or political capital (Hawkins et al. 2015). HBCU athletics were the pinnacle of Black athletic and academic excellence. Following the *Brown v. Board of Education* decision, however, historically white universities began enticing Black athletes to attend and play sports at their state-funded and federally supported institutions (Cooper, Cavil, and Cheeks 2023).

White universities were legally compelled to allow Black students to attend their universities, but shortly after integration, the commercialization of college athletics rapidly expanded. Between 1945 and 1970, higher education experienced a golden era where access to a college degree, and thus social mobility, was expanded (Thelin 2004). Historians tell this story but often fail to mention how this expansion was a method for capital accumulation. HBCUs were robbed of athletic talent, as Black athletes were persuaded to pursue higher education at historically white universities. In exchange for their labor, Black athletes received hostile and racist campus environments, which frequently still view them primarily as athletic labor (Kalman-Lamb and Silva 2023). Black college football and men's basketball players generate revenue at Power 5 institutions while graduating at lower rates than other college athletes. Not receiving any economic compensation—including in the form of a credential—has been the most visible form of exploitation in college sports for over 50 years (Edwards 2017).

Hypocrisy fuels college athletics' position within higher education. Amateurism, commercialization, and exploitation power this peculiar relationship. The recent decisions about unionization and name, image, and likeness suggest that a wider public no longer accepts amateurism, while raising questions about athlete rights, exploitation, and purpose in the face of evergrowing television deals for schools, conferences, and the NCAA. During the pandemic, college athletes voiced their concerns about players' economic rights and college athletics' role in social justice amid the disproportionate impacts of COVID-19 and police brutality against Black people (Black, Ofoegbu, and Foster 2022). Still, even with a growing interest in social justice and college athletics, the question of the meaning of college athletics within higher education remains unsettled.

Since the nineteenth century, athletics has had a peculiar material and symbolic meaning for higher education. Indeed, college athletics was known as a place for amateurs, but commercialization blurred the lines between amateurism and exploitation. Also, a wide public debate has raged for decades over whether athletics' purpose in higher education is an educational activity or a commercial cartel (Thelin 2004). Yet, given its significant draw on resources within colleges, from donors, and from wider investment in the form of television contracts, college athletics is unquestionably a political arena, one that is based essentially on exploitation. This political framing effectively sublates the ongoing debate of amateurism and commercialization and instead foregrounds questions about how material freedom, liberty, and justice exist within such an exploitative space. Addressing these concerns is essential for faculty, students, parents, policymakers, and activists who wish to reimagine athletics as a space for the common good instead of individualized exploitation.

College Athletics as a Political Arena in Higher Education

College athletics is unquestionably a political arena as students, faculty, presidents, and other activists are positioned to control amateurism and commercialization. As an organizational theorist, I define politics as how power is developed, distributed, and maintained within societies and how that power affects social consciousness and decision making (Shafritz, Ott, and Jang 2016). Mass political misinformation erodes public trust and confidence in society, including in higher education and college athletics (Bauer-Wolf 2017). Thus, viewing athletics through a political lens centers a socially committed perspective for defining athletics' material meaning in higher education.

Political gamesmanship has always underpinned college athletics. The industrialization of the United States during the nineteenth century laid the foundation for steady state support of college athletics' commercialization, largely through its regulatory commitment to amateurism (Smith 1990). Public cries for government interference and regulation throughout the twentieth century linked government politics to amateurism (Thelin 1994), and this eventually evolved into twenty-first-century political attempts by social movements and reformers to disrupt and dismantle this exploitative social system (Smith 2011).

These political dynamics around amateurism, commercialization, and exploitation are informed by the long political economic history of the university. Colonialism, enslavement, and global disenfranchisement allowed institutions like Harvard and Yale to accumulate capital in the US political system (Thelin 2004). American higher education is inextricably linked to slavery, as historian Craig Steven Wilder (2013) has written. This deeper history of the entanglement of universities with a racialized form of labor exploitation—not to mention other means for exploitation, as well as other forms by which exploitation can occur (gender, for instance)—has had resonance in the framing of conditions of twenty-first-century college athletes. Critical scholars have compared college basketball and football especially to slavery and plantations (Hawkins 2010). Scholars levied these critiques because Black male college athletes in Power 5 football and basketball were very clearly being exploited out of educational promises after being recruited from their communities with promises of education and opportunity (Cooper 2016). Comparing college athletics to slavery and plantation politics helped awaken a new wave of activism among scholars and athletes aimed at liberating Black men from oppressive economic conditions (Cooper, Macaulay, and Rodriguez 2019).

Sensationalized comparisons between college athletics and slavery helped bring attention to scandals and bring justice to some in college athletics. The issue, however, is that athletics scholars have often failed to include women in the comparison. The parallels to slavery drawn throughout the twentieth and twenty-first centuries have mainly pointed to economic exploitation of Black men (Nocera and Strauss 2018). Gender was rarely included in sports analysis, painting college athletics inequities for only Black men (Bruening 2005). Black women's experiences were underresearched until recently, when scholars such as Joy Gaston Gayles, Akilah Carter-Francique, and Tomika Ferguson laid a foundation to grasp the political dimensions of Black women's experiences with exploitation in college athletics (Conyers 2014). Black women were integral to slavery and the subsequent abolition, so any social comparison to slavery or plantation politics must include Black women's role in shaping those politics and social contexts.

Comparing college athletics to slavery helped bring public awareness to the issues that *some* Black college athletes experience, but as evidenced by gender exclusion, it created a monolithic consciousness of amateurism, commercialization, and exploitation. These monolithic views of college athletics have been reinforced by historians who chronicle college athletics history only through elite institutions. For instance, as Ronald A. Smith points out, "There has been no attempt to deal with two important nineteenth and twentieth-century questions in sports and in the larger society—the questions of gender and race" (Smith 1990, xi). A few historians have since foregrounded gender or race in college athletics history, such as Welch Suggs's *A Place on the Team: Triumph and Tragedy of Title IX* (2006) and Lane Demas's *Integrating the Gridiron: Black Civil Rights and American College Football* (2010). These powerful histories document how gender and race were foundational for shaping the structural form of college athletics. Still, like Smith's, these histories focus on elite institutions, fail to analyze the role of important groups of athletes (like Black women), and do not cover the full gamut of sports included in many athletics departments.

Failing to include gender or race in history limits how amateurism, commercialization, and exploitation are understood within athletics. Many people write about college athletics and college athletes, but few politicize college athletes' agency in recognizing their political position within college athletics and society (Weems and Kluch 2023). Throughout a segregated Jim Crow South during the nineteenth century, Black college athletes mobilized against political attacks by state and federal governments while representing white institutions (Martin 2010). College athlete activists, such as John Carlos and Tommie Smith, helped bring attention to global issues by protesting during the 1968 Olympics (Edwards 2017). Athlete activism declined during the late twentieth and early twenty-first century, as athletes did not want to risk losing potential access to higher education, which civil rights freedom fighters had gained (Bryant 2019). This concern about maintaining access to an increasingly competitive higher education system could explain why player movements during that time did not garner scholarly attention. But in 2020, the world was reminded that college athletes are political actors (Black, Ofoegbu, and Foster 2022). As Black people were murdered by police, and political uprisings continued throughout the global pandemic, college athletes joined together to protest these injustices. This was the latest extension of a wave of college activism that started in 2015, following the University of Missouri's strike against racism (Tompkins 2017).

This uprising made a significant contribution to the study of college athletics in higher education. In 2022, Joy Gaston Gayles addressed higher education's uncertain times during her Association of Higher Education presidential address. Gayles challenged scholars to unearth the truth about higher education and to ask critical questions about education's true meaning by naming oppressive ideologies (Gayles 2023). While speaking to higher education generally, her background as a foundational scholar for the critical study of college athletics made this a particularly important invitation for this subfield specifically. Indeed, it reminded me of what I see as the growing relevance of texts that encourage reflection on the longer social and political history of race, class, and gender, made prominent by figures like Cedric Robinson, Steven Osuna, Robin D. G. Kelley and others (Kelley 2003; Osuna 2017; Robinson 2000). When brought to bear on college athletics, this study of the Black radical tradition suggests an interest in class consciousness and the movements to end racialized oppression within college sports, as well as greater attention to the political demands of college athletes beyond the Power 5 conferences and the largest revenue-generating sports. Exploring how college athletes make meaning and develop their political consciousness becomes central to athletics' role in higher education. Importantly, this political consciousness must extend beyond neoliberal solutions and work to create a consciousness that improves society for all college athletes, not a privileged few.

References

Anderson, Greta. 2019. "Calif. Governor Signs Bill on Athletes' Rights." *Inside Higher Ed*, September 30. https://www.insidehighered.com/quicktakes/2019/10/01/calif-governor-signs-bill-athletes-rights.

Bauer-Wolf, Jeremy. 2017. "Lost Trust in College Sports." *Inside Higher Ed*, October 30. https://www.insidehighered.com/news/2017/10/31/ncaa-president-public-losing-trust-big-time-sports.

Benedict, Jeff, and Armen Keteyian. 2014. *The System: The Glory and Scandal of Big-Time College Football*. New York: Anchor.

Black, Wayne L., Ezinne Ofoegbu, and Sayvon L. Foster. 2022. "#TheyareUnited and #TheyWantToPlay: A Critical Discourse Analysis of College Football Player Social Media Activism." *Sociology of Sport Journal* 39 (4): 352–61.

Boggs, Abigail, Eli Meyerhoff, Nick Mitchell, and Zach Schwartz-Weinstein. 2019. "Abolitionist University Studies: An Invitation." *Abolition Journal*, August 28. https://abolitionjournal.org/abolitionist-university-studies-an-invitation/.

Bruening, Jennifer E. 2005. "Gender and Racial Analysis in Sport: Are All the Women White and All the Blacks Men?" *Quest* 57 (3): 330–49.

Bryant, Howard. 2019. *The Heritage: Black Athletes, a Divided America, and the Politics of Patriotism*. Boston: Beacon.

Byers, Walter, and Charles H. Hammer. 1995. *Unsportsmanlike Conduct: Exploiting College Athletes*. Ann Arbor: University of Michigan Press.

Conyers, James L., Jr. 2014. *Race in American Sports: Essays*. Jefferson, NC: McFarland.

Cooper, Joseph N. 2016. "Excellence beyond Athletics: Best Practices for Enhancing Black Male Student Athletes' Educational Experiences and Outcomes." *Equity and Excellence in Education* 49 (3): 267–83.

Cooper, Joseph N., J. Kenyatta Cavil, and Geremy Cheeks. 2023. "The State of Intercollegiate Athletics at Historically Black Colleges and Universities (HBCUs): Past, Present, and Persistence." *Journal of Issues in Intercollegiate Athletics* 7 (1): 22.

Cooper, Joseph N., Charles Macaulay, and Saturnino H. Rodriguez. 2019. "Race and Resistance: A Typology of African American Sport Activism." *International Review for the Sociology of Sport* 54 (2): 151–81.

Demas, Lane. 2010. *Integrating the Gridiron: Black Civil Rights and American College Football.* New Brunswick, NJ: Rutgers University Press.

Edwards, Harry. 2017. *The Revolt of the Black Athlete.* Urbana: University of Illinois Press.

Gaul, Gilbert M. 2016. *Billion-Dollar Ball: A Journey through the Big-Money Culture of College Football.* New York: Penguin.

Gayles, Joy Gaston. 2023. "Humanizing Higher Education: A Path Forward in Uncertain Times." *Review of Higher Education* 46 (4): 547–67.

Hatch, Brianna. 2022. "'There's So Many Questions': Sports-Realignment Shocker Could Mean a Sea Change for Higher Ed." *Chronicle of Higher Education*, July 1, sec. News. https://www.chronicle.com/article/theres-so-many-questions-sports-realignment-shocker-could-mean-a-sea-change-for-higher-ed.

Hawkins, Billy. 2010. *The New Plantation: Black Athletes, College Sports, and Predominantly White NCAA Institutions.* Basingstoke: Palgrave Macmillan.

Hawkins, Billy, Joseph Cooper, Akilah Carter-Francique, and J. Kenyatta Cavil, eds. 2015. *The Athletic Experience at Historically Black Colleges and Universities: Past, Present, and Persistence.* Lanham, MD: Rowman and Littlefield.

Howe, Jonathan E., Wayne L. Black, and Willis A. Jones. 2023. "Exercising Power: A Critical Examination of National Collegiate Athletic Association Discourse Related to Name, Image, and Likeness." *Journal of Sport Management* 37 (5): 333–44.

Jessop, Bob. 2018. "On Academic Capitalism." *Critical Policy Studies* 12 (1): 104–9.

Kalman-Lamb, Nathan, and Derek Silva. 2023. "'Play'ing College Football: Campus Athletic Worker Experiences of Exploitation." *Critical Sociology* 50 (4–5): 863–82.

Kelley, Robin D. G. 2003. *Freedom Dreams: The Black Radical Imagination.* Boston: Beacon.

Lederman, Doug. 2021. "Update: Texas and Oklahoma Say They'll Leave Big 12." *Inside Higher Ed*, July 25. https://www.insidehighered.com/quicktakes/2021/07/26/update-texas-and-oklahoma-say-theyll-leave-big-12.

Lederman, Doug. 2024. "Dartmouth Men's Basketball Players Vote to Unionize." *Inside Higher Ed*, March 5. https://www.insidehighered.com/news/students/athletics/2024/03/05/dartmouth-mens-basketball-players-vote-unionize.

Lovett, Bobby L. 2011. *America's Historically Black Colleges and Universities: A Narrative History from the Nineteenth Century into the Twenty-First Century.* 1st ed. America's Historically Black Colleges and Universities Series. Macon, GA: Mercer University Press.

Martin, Charles H. 2010. *Benching Jim Crow: The Rise and Fall of the Color Line in Southern College Sports, 1890–1980.* Urbana: University of Illinois Press.

Nocera, Joseph, and Ben Strauss. 2018. *Indentured: The Battle to End the Exploitation of College Athletes.* New York: Portfolio/Penguin.

Osuna, Steven. 2017. "Class Suicide: The Black Radical Tradition, Radical Scholarship, and the Neoliberal Turn." In *Futures of Black Radicalism*, edited by Gaye Theresa Johnson and Alex Lubin, 21–38. London: Verso.

Robinson, Cedric J. 2000. *Black Marxism: The Making of the Black Radical Tradition*. Chapel Hill: University of North Carolina Press.

Shafritz, Jay M., J. Steven Ott, and Yong Suk Jang. 2016. *Classics of Organization Theory*. 8th ed. Boston: Cengage Learning.

Smith, Ronald A. 1990. *Sports and Freedom: The Rise of Big-Time College Athletics*. New York: Oxford University Press.

Smith, Ronald A. 2011. *Pay for Play: A History of Big-Time College Athletic Reform*. Urbana: University of Illinois Press.

Staurowsky, Ellen J., and Allen L. Sack. 2005. "Reconsidering the Use of the Term Student-Athlete in Academic Research." *Journal of Sport Management* 19 (2): 103–16.

Suggs, Welch. 2006. *A Place on the Team: The Triumph and Tragedy of Title IX*. Princeton, NJ: Princeton University Press.

Thelin, John R. 1994. *Games Colleges Play: Scandal and Reform in Intercollegiate Athletics*. Baltimore: Johns Hopkins University Press.

Thelin, John R. 2004. *A History of American Higher Education*. Baltimore: Johns Hopkins University Press.

Tompkins, Joe. 2017. "'It's about Respect!' College-Athlete Activism and Left Neoliberalism." *Communication and Critical/Cultural Studies* 14 (4): 351–68.

Weems, Anthony J., and Yannick Kluch. 2023. "Resisting Resistance: Activism in/and the Political Economy of Intercollegiate Athletics." *Journal of Issues in Intercollegiate Athletics* 16 (2): 6.

Wilder, Craig Steven. 2013. *Ebony and Ivy: Race, Slavery, and the Troubled History of America's Universities*. New York: Bloomsbury.

B

Board of Trustees

Asheesh Kapur Siddique

Boards of trustees might seem like a strange, arcane formality of university organization, detached from the day-to-day realities of the academy as experienced by faculty, students, and staff. Yet, because they hold the power to determine budgets, faculty appointments, and tuition rates, trustees are the power centers of the modern university, shaping the conditions and possibilities in which the rest of campus life unfolds. As recent events have shown, when the work of trustees enters the spotlight, it is clear that these bodies serve to thwart academic freedom and social justice. In 2021, the University of North Carolina at Chapel Hill Board of Trustees made national headlines after they denied a tenured professorship to the journalist Nikole Hannah-Jones, overruling the support of faculty, after a lobbying campaign by conservative politicians who despised Hannah-Jones's groundbreaking reporting on the history of American slavery and racism (Killian and Ingram 2021). Trustees at American universities between 2003 and 2023, in their capacity to set tuition rates, more than doubled the cost of attending college at both public and private institutions (Kerr and Wood 2022).

Trustees were not always so powerful. In early modern Europe, universities were administered by those who taught and researched under their auspices. While state and ecclesiastical officials often had some influence over academic affairs, in general, faculty held enormous powers of governance and exercised them on the basis of seniority. But in the establishment of universities in the North American colonies of the seventeenth-century English empire, the practice of faculty governance came to be challenged. Both Harvard College (founded in 1636) and the College of William and Mary developed administrative structures in which external boards of supervisors—distinct from faculty—held major decision-making powers. When in 1650 Harvard obtained a charter of incorporation from the Massachusetts colonial government, the college fell under the rule of a corporation comprising a president, five fellows, and a treasurer, who were collectively empowered to "choose such officers and servants for the College," to "remove" them, and to make "orders and by-laws" for the institution's governance ("Harvard Charter of 1650" [1650] 2020). The Royal Charter (1693) issued to the College of William and Mary similarly placed the governance of the institution under the auspices of "trustees nominated and elected" by legislators in the assembly of the colony of Virginia.

These colonial-era boards of trustees held considerably more institutional power than their counterparts at universities on the other side of the Atlantic Ocean. "In contrast to the external boards that were responsible for the overall supervision of universities in Britain and northern Europe but allowed faculty to enjoy substantial autonomy in most matters of internal governance," the historian Larry Gerber (2014, 14) observes, "external governing boards in colonial American colleges . . . exercised significantly greater control over a wide range of issues." Indeed, as Gerber points out, these boards of trustees sought to execute their vision for the university through "a new administrative innovation: the strong college president, who was appointed by and reported to the external board, not to the faculty." Faculty in early American colleges and universities thus found themselves competing for authority with trustees, often mediated through the trustees' chief delegate in the figure of the university president.

The inherent tension between trustees and faculty that resulted from this arrangement was not lost on social observers in the early United States. "The trustees of a college are entitled by virtue of their office, to advise, instruct and direct its faculty in respect to its instruction and the administration of its discipline," observed Jasper Adams, president of Charleston College, in an 1838 lecture "On the Relation Subsisting between the Board of Trustees and Faculty of a University." At the same time, Adams (1838, 149–50) continued, trustees "have, with few exception[s], almost no qualifications which peculiarly fit them for the practical administration of those institutions." University trustees, he stated, "consist without much discrimination of eminent lawyers, clergymen, and physicians," along with "successful agriculturalists, manufacturers, merchants, and other substantial classes of the community"; but "the qualifications which have given them eminence and success in the professions and branches of business . . . have imparted to them no peculiar fitness" to "inspire" students "with the love of virtue, and the enthusiasm of learning." Adams summarized, "However distinguished in the line of their several pursuits and professions," trustees were "no more qualified and entitled to advise and direct a college faculty . . . than the client is to advise and direct his lawyer, or the patient his physician."

Nevertheless, by the time Adams spoke, the power of trustees in the young American nation had come to be protected by law. The imperial understanding articulated in the colonial-era charters to universities that trustees, not faculty, were the nerve centers of institutional governance now came to be affirmed as a guiding principle for the public administration of higher education in the new democracy. In *Trustees of Dartmouth College v. Woodward* (17 US 518 [1819]), the US Supreme Court ruled that the state of New Hampshire had violated the Constitution's Contract Clause when it had sought to replace the trustees of Dartmouth College, a private corporation, by giving the governor control of trustee appointments. By holding that corporate institutions were governed not by the sovereign public bodies that granted them charters but by the trustees named in the text of the charters, the decision enshrined considerable autonomy for institutions of higher education to govern their own affairs. But the decision also put on firm footing within US law the idea that *trustees—not* faculty—were the legitimate rulers of the university (Kaufman-Osborn 2023).[1] While freeing private universities from the stranglehold of state control, the *Dartmouth* decision also effectively disempowered faculty by affirming the executive authority of trustees over the institution. As Adams would go on to point out, since trustees did not need to have any particular knowledge of universities to govern over these institutions' affairs, educators were cast out of the realm of higher education administration.

Who composed these boards of trustees? Notwithstanding Adams's gloss on their dominance by businessmen and lawyers, relatively few systematic surveys seem to have been taken to answer this question prior to the early twentieth century. But when studies of university trustees began to emerge, the results demonstrated that Adams had indeed been prescient when observing that the "substantial classes" who ruled the American polity and economy also ruled its institutions of higher education. A 1917 survey found that those employed in the fields of business and law occupied the majority of seats on college and university boards at state colleges as well as at pri-

1. In this regard, Clyde W. Barrow (1990, 13) has urged the importance of "draw[ing] an empirical distinction between physical 'possession' of the means of mental production by faculties and the legal 'ownership' of these tools by private and public governing boards."

vate institutions across the country. The survey's author, Scott Nearing, concluded from his research that American higher education was a system of "plutocratized education," one "owned and largely supported by the people but dominated by the business world" (1917, 299). Subsequent early twentieth-century inquiries reported similar findings. A 1927 analysis by George S. Counts found that university boards were largely made up of "owners of enterprises" with "direct control over the economic resources of the community" (51–61). A survey published nearly a decade later of the composition of boards of trustees at 20 institutions across the country between 1860 and the mid-1930s affirmed the same: while in 1860, the author found, bankers, "business men," and lawyers composed about "one-half of board members," by 1930 "the percentage had risen to 73.6" (McGrath 1936, 264).

The Progressive Era's social theorists cast a keen and critical eye on university trustees, arguing that they made the American university into an instrument of capitalism. In 1918, Thorstein Veblen—who had been forced to resign from the economics faculty at both the University of Chicago (1906) and Stanford University (1909) over extramarital affairs—penned a powerful analysis, *The Higher Learning in America: A Memorandum on the Conduct of Universities by Business Men*. According to Veblen (2015, 78–80), the American university had undergone a transformation in the personnel of its rulers in the aftermath of the Civil War, "a wide-reaching substitution of laymen in the place of clergymen on the governing boards," a "substitution of businessmen" in whose "hands" "discretionary control in matters of university policy" had now been placed. A culture in which "business success is by common consent, and quite uncritically, taken to be conclusive evidence of wisdom even in matters that have no relation to business affairs" had transformed the university into an institution ruled by those "who have proved their capacity for work that has nothing in common with the higher learning." The "sole effectual function" of these "governing boards of businessmen," Veblen wrote, was "to interfere with the academic management" of universities, a subject "outside their competence and outside the range of their habitual interest." Upton Sinclair (1923, 27) echoed the sentiment in a self-published skewering of American education that appeared in the early 1920s: The "same men" who "serve J. P. Morgan and Company as directors in the coal trust, the steel trust, the railroad trust . . . serve also on the boards of schools, colleges, and universities throughout the United States." In Sinclair's estimation, "You could not tell a chart of the Columbia [University] trustees from a chart of the New York Central Railroad" (27).

The overlap between corporate power and educational governance as embodied in boards of trustees inspired postwar critics of American democracy to direct their scrutiny toward college campuses as sites of elite control and social reproduction. In 1947, psychologist Hubert Park Beck sought to update the study of the demographic and professional composition of trustees at 30 major research universities. He found that the "men who control our universities" were largely lawyers and businessmen, with "educational experts" themselves almost entirely "excluded from membership on boards controlling educational policy" (1947, 56). Those who held a "commanding role in the business world" (74), Beck noted, also commanded higher education from their dominance of university boards. For sociologist C. Wright Mills (1956, 217), the rule of universities by the wealthy combined with postwar cooperation between scientific research and the military (what he called "the militarization of science") solidified the social role of campuses as training grounds for a "power elite" that had come to rule American society and subvert the promise of democracy.

While the McCarthyite caricature of university faculties being dominated by the political Left proliferated in the postwar era, bolstered by conservative reactions to the campus activism of the sixties and seventies, the reality of higher ed governance is different. Boards of trustees have not only generally remained in firm control of major functions of university administration—including control of appointments of presidents and administrators, and the ability to set tuition. They have also continued to be dominated in their membership by figures from business and corporate law, with less than 10 percent of seats on boards held by faculty or higher education administrators (Scott 2018, 72). And the actual behavior of boards of trustees has consistently affirmed that Veblen, Beck, and Mills were correct to warn that these bodies work to decimate democracy in higher education. Much of the discourse around the public role of universities has focused on the issue of academic freedom, and trustees thwarting faculty appointments on ideological grounds often motivates news coverage of their role, as seen, for example, with the 2021 decision of University of North Carolina trustees to deny Hannah-Jones a tenured faculty position; and by Florida Governor Ron DeSantis's 2023 remaking of the boards of trustees of the state's public universities into an extension of his reactionary war on diversity, stocking them with rightwing political appointees, who have eliminated policies intended to address racial inequalities in admissions and campus life. The reactionary capacity of trustees remains alive and well (Hodgson and Kumar 2023; Robertson 2021).

At the same time, other significant actions by boards of trustees that rarely command headlines are no less detrimental to the future of democracy. As the bodies responsible for approving university budgets and appointments, trustees exercise authority over the issues at the heart of the current crisis of American higher education—student debt (since charters empower trustees to set tuition rates) and hiring (since charters empower trustees to exercise oversight over administrative and academic appointments, favoring the expansion of the former and the transformation of the latter from tenure-stream positions into precarious contracts). Trustees have played a pivotal role in approving skyrocketing increases in tuition and fees, which have in turn forced students and families to take on crippling loans to fund college education (Patel 2019); and by adopting an austerity-driven approach to approving new tenure-line faculty hiring, and favoring the creation of poorly compensated (and thus, from their perspective, "cheaper") contingent positions, they have fueled the academic jobs crisis (Berlinerbrau 2023). The same group of business and financial leaders who, through their control of for-profit corporations, facilitated the *gigification* of the American labor market from the midseventies onward have also, through their dominant position in university governance, enabled a contiguous proliferation of precarious employment in the academy.

A common response to the crisis created by trustee power has been to agitate for greater faculty representation in board membership (Ehrenberg, Patterson, and Key 2013). Yet, even the involvement of faculty as trustees has not prevented boards from interfering in academic freedom. In 2021, for example, the Linfield University Board of Trustees fired its own "faculty trustee," Daniel Pollack-Pelzner, a tenured professor of English with full voting rights on the board, after he spoke up about sexual assault and harassment committed by several of the Linfield trustees against other members of the university community (AAUP 2022). The Pollack-Pelzner case suggests that in a key way, boards of trustees are structurally reactionary to the point that they may be impossible to democratize or reform. What may be the more potent—though most politically contentious and difficult to achieve—solution to the multiple crises of academic freedom, debt, and precarious employment that trustees have fueled would be to take a cue from the Progressive Era critics of corporatized higher education: the reassertion of faculty governance and the corresponding neutering of the power of these boards to make consequential decisions for universities. Such a shift—a return, in a sense, to the medieval tradition of faculty as scholars and administrators, adjusted to contemporary norms of democratic decision making—would be at once the most traditional and most radical solution to the contemporary crisis of the American university.

References

AAUP (American Association of University Professors). 2022. "Academic Freedom and Tenure: Linfield University (Oregon)." American Association of University Professors, April. https://www.aaup.org/report/academic-freedom-and-tenure-linfield-university-oregon.

Adams, Jasper. 1838. "On the Relation Subsisting between the Board of Trustees and the Faculty of a University." In *The Introductory Discourse, and Lectures Delivered Before the American Institute of Instruction, at Worcester, (Mass.) August, 1837*, 141–58. Boston: James Munroe.

Barrow, Clyde W. 1990. *Universities and the Capitalist State: Corporate Liberalism and the Reconstruction of American Higher Education, 1894–1928*. History of American Thought and Culture. Madison: University of Wisconsin Press.

Beck, Hubert Park. 1947. *Men Who Control Our Universities: The Economic and Social Composition of Governing Boards of Thirty Leading American Universities*. New York: Columbia University Press.

Berlinerbrau, Jacques. 2023. "They've Been Scheming to Cut Tenure for Years. It's Happening." *Chronicle of Higher Education*, February 1, sec. The Review. https://www.chronicle.com/article/theyve-been-scheming-to-cut-tenure-for-years-its-happening.

Counts, George S. 1927. *The Social Composition of Boards of Education: A Study in the Social Control of Public Education*. Chicago: University of Chicago Press.

Ehrenberg, Ronald G., Richard W. Patterson, and Andrew V. Key. 2013. "Faculty Members on Boards of Trustees." *Academe*, May–June. https://www.aaup.org/article/faculty-members-boards-trustees.

Gerber, Larry G. 2014. *The Rise and Decline of Faculty Governance: Professionalization and the Modern American University*. Baltimore: John Hopkins University Press.

"Harvard Charter of 1650." (1650) 2020. Transcription, Harvard University Archives Research Guides. Harvard Library. Last updated December 1, 2020. https://guides.library.harvard.edu/c.php?g=880222&p=6323072.

Hodgson, Ian, and Divya Kumar. 2023. "While Facing Protests, Florida's New College Trustees Do Away with Diversity Office." *Miami Herald*, March 1.

Kaufman-Osborn, Timothy V. 2023. *The Autocratic Academy: Reenvisioning Rule within America's Universities*. Durham, NC: Duke University Press.

Kerr, Emma, and Sarah Wood. 2022. "A Look at 20 Years of Tuition Costs at National Universities." *U.S. News and World Report*, September 13.

Killian, Joe, and Kyle Ingram. 2021. "PW Special Report: After Conservative Criticism, UNC Backs Down from Offering Acclaimed Journalist Tenured Position." *NC Newsline*, May 19.

https://ncnewsline.com/2021/05/19/pw-special-report-after-conservative-criticism-unc-backs-down-from-offering-acclaimed-journalist-a-tenured-position/.

McGrath, Earl J. 1936. "The Control of Higher Education in America." *Educational Record* 18 (2): 259–72.

Mills, C. Wright. 1956. *The Power Elite*. New York: Oxford University Press.

Nearing, Scott. 1917. "Educational Research and Statistics: Who's Who among College Trustees." *School and Society* 6 (141): 297–99.

Patel, Vimal. 2019. "How Rising College Costs and Student Debt Contribute to a Social-Mobility 'Crisis.'" *Chronicle of Higher Education*, July 8, sec. News. https://www.chronicle.com/article/how-rising-college-costs-and-student-debt-contribute-to-a-social-mobility-crisis/.

Robertson, Katie. 2021. "Nikole Hannah-Jones Denied Tenure at University of North Carolina." *New York Times*, May 20, sec. Business. https://www.nytimes.com/2021/05/19/business/media/nikole-hannah-jones-unc.html.

"Royal Charter." 1693. Special Collections Research Center Knowledgebase, College of William & Mary. Accessed December 11, 2024. https://scrc-kb.libraries.wm.edu/royal-charter.

Scott, Robert A. 2018. *How University Boards Work*. Baltimore: Johns Hopkins University Press.

Sinclair, Upton. 1923. *The Goose-Step : A Study of American Education*. Pasadena, CA: Published by the author.

Veblen, Thorstein. 2015. *The Higher Learning in America: A Memorandum on the Conduct of Universities by Business Men*. Edited by Richard F. Teichgraeber. Baltimore: Johns Hopkins University Press.

B

Budget

Juan Pablo Pardo-Guerra

Universities are complex organizations. From their ostensible origins as institutions devoted primarily to instruction, they have grown into multifaceted organizations involved in a wide range of activities, from state-of-the-art research and local community outreach to incentivizing diversity, developing real estate, and amassing sometimes considerable investment portfolios. Universities are far from the Gothic buildings that many associate with their not-too-distant past. Today, they are closer in form to the multidivisional corporation, with a multiplicity of units loosely integrated under a single organizational roof.

Like modern corporations, the ecosystem of units, departments, and auxiliary operations of universities is often coordinated through a relatively mundane technology: spreadsheets. Sitting far from classrooms, quads, dining halls, laboratories, and library shelves, spreadsheets encode the relations that underly much of the institution's operation. They contain student enrollments, schedules of events, faculty evaluations, lists of applicants, lists of employees, information on subscriptions, templates for reporting activity to funding agencies, and much more. Spreadsheets constitute, in a material sense, a truer representation of the university than the one presented in the glossy brochures dutifully produced by marketing departments.

One set of spreadsheets is particularly critical: those that encode the budgets for the institution. Tracking flows of students, credits, dollars, people, and debts, these devices regulate how moneys and resources are distributed across schools, departments, units, and accounts. Their underlying budget models (which are the general philosophies through which specific budgets get built) are not merely practical ways of dealing with moneys. At the core, they are devices of governance that shape how universities engage with the world, how staff and faculty experience their professional lives, how capital investments are planned and executed, and how students are trained and supported. By putting a price on the many components of the university—

from buildings to labor—these devices determine, too, the implicit values of different kinds of knowledge. In pricing the organization in its totality, they set, in concrete ways through both affordances and constraints, the possible futures for the organization. Budgets and their models might not be the heart of the modern university, but they are certainly close to being mimeographs of their soul.

How do budgets work in higher education? How do they constrain? What do they enable? In this brief chapter, I explore the current state of budgetary practices in the sector and the importance of studying these devices for understanding the future of academics and higher education.

A Primer on Budgets

Research on the history of budgetary practices in higher education is relatively sparse. Like other aspects of organizational planning and operations that occur in the background and are not directly connected to the core practices of teaching and research, budgets are somewhat invisible, despite their critical role.[1]

At the most abstract level, a university budget is an agreement on how to balance revenues and expenses. "The budget" is neither a single instrument nor document but rather a federation of interconnected accounts, rules, heuristics, and forecasts that regulate the allocation of resources in different units in corresponding fiscal periods. The top-level budget can be understood as a concatenation of individual unit-level budgets. These are often delegated, implying that some decisions are not made centrally but left in the hands of units. Every year and in some institutions, for example, departments must estimate how much funding they will have available for such things as stationery, student support, staff salaries, lectureships, seminars, and faculty stipends. Some discretion is afforded (buying less paper for the photocopier); but not all is fungible and allowed (hiring a professor with money for staff support is, quite often, a difficult trick of alchemy).

1. Some generalist introductions to budgets have been published over time, reflecting interest on behalf of administrators and faculty members in understanding how moneys are distributed. Three recent books are excellent examples: Smith (2019a, 2019b) and Comrie (2021). While lacking the historical depth that some might be interested in (they present university budgets as extensions of broader business accounting and budgeting practices), they provide a welcome introduction to how budgeting works on the ground.

Budgets are linked by their positions in the overall operating *budget hierarchy*. While often independently managed, department budgets depend on school or college budgets, which themselves fall within the budgets of higher-level organizational units. The collection of all budgets corresponds to what is known as the *consolidated budget*, which represents the revenues and expenditures for the university in its entirety. These numbers are often made public as an itemized statement showing how much is received and spent in broad categories (instruction, research support, student aid, and so forth). Expenditures for universities, excluding expenses associated with medical schools and hospitals, tend to be quite similar, with about 45 percent going to salaries and wages, 15 percent to benefits, 10 percent to operations and maintenance, and 30 percent to other expenses.

Each element in this hierarchy is built through a budgeting process—what is known as the *budget model*—that specifies what kind of decisions can be taken to allocate expenditures in relation to projected revenues. These models represent different ways of governing the resources of universities. Moneys and resources can be allocated in various ways. One, for example, involves a centralized process of negotiation where each unit must justify all its expenditures (called *zero-based budgeting*). This model, as Dean O. Smith (2019a, 52) notes, "hampers long range planning," making it an uncommon practice in the sector. Another approach, called *incremental budgeting*, sets future budgets as slight increases (or decreases) with respect to past allocations, with "next year's budget [depending] on the prior year's budget" (Smith 2019a, 49). Also called *history and mystery models*, these budgetary allocation practices peg future disbursements to whatever was decided in the past, allowing for greater predictability into the future but, equally, fewer incentives for increased performance or greater operative efficiencies. Such models are quite common across the world. For example, in countries where higher education is heavily supported by the state, the moneys that units receive are tied to whatever is negotiated in the national budgeting process, often incrementally.

Other approaches, like *formula-based budgeting*, determine distributions through specific metrics such as enrollment levels, credit hours, numbers of students taught in laboratories, and so forth. These approaches create incentives while also increasing the complexity of the budgeting process. *Activity-based models* and *responsibility-centered models* return revenue to its source: The tuition generated by a unit, for example, is returned to it, minus a tax used by the administration to run core infrastructures and services. Moneys in these models are more fungible than in other budgetary practices: Funds are not earmarked according to history or formulas but can be used creatively by each unit in achieving their goals. Pure models are rare. More often than not, universities combine various budget models across their operations.

Budget models also account for specific constraints on how funds can be used. Endowments in universities are an example. Though these might seem to be readily available moneys that institutions can use in times of crisis (or, indeed, to remedy historical inequalities to which they have contributed over time), the way endowments are defined and held "in the books" limits their use: Most endowments are "restricted" accounts that can be used only for specific purposes delineated in the gift agreement. Accounting classifications like those that dictate whether an account is restricted or unrestricted determine how revenues received by institutions can be used, further complicating the process of allocation.

In addition to considering possible expenditures, budget models must consider how restrictions placed on funds allow or disallow cross-subsidies in operations. State and federal funds usually exclude payments for alcohol and tobacco, for example, making it necessary to hold these in different accounts than other funding sources. Restrictions can become more complicated. California's Assembly Bill 1887, for example, forbids the use of state funds for travel to states with discriminatory laws (the list includes Alabama, Kansas, Kentucky, Mississippi, North Carolina, South Dakota, Tennessee, and Texas), unless certain requirements are met.

These numerous restrictions are important enough to merit being encoded into the structure of universities' systems of accounting under what is known as the Chart of Accounts. Funds held by institutions aren't simply sitting in one large pile in some bank but are distributed across a panoply of accounts, numbered according to their possible use. The University of California, Berkeley, a quite typical case, works with nine account categories, ranging from assets and liabilities to intercampus transfers. Each account is identified with a number indicating its higher-order category (1XXXXX for assets, 2XXXXX for liabilities, and so forth), with the remaining numbers pointing at the restrictions the account has. The account 59002 at UC Berkeley, for example, is used to record internal campus expenses for building maintenance (think: The account you would charge a department for a lightbulb), whereas 59008 serves for recharges for travel. (The digit 5 indicates that these are expenses.) Combined with other information (for example, the department, project ID, program code, and accounting code), these account numbers are the basis for so-called chart strings, sequences of codes that allow tracking how moneys were spent from the account at high levels of granularity.

Budgets are not destiny, though, at least not on the ground. A well-organized budget might seem so precise as to run seamlessly, but this is not the case. Systems of accounting and budgeting philosophies require implementation. With this comes considerable work of interpretation by financial analysts and fund managers. Some moneys might not seem fungible *in theory*, and the work of budgeting within units often involves seeing how funds can be moved across categories to balance the books and cover expenses. While the challenge for administrators is traceability and auditability, for units, it is the production of fungibility: making moneys available in ways not contemplated by relatively rigid budgeting techniques.

Budgets as Instruments of (Counter)accountability

One key aspect of budgets is the degree to which they have enabled greater transparency in higher education, if at all. Discursively, budget models are often presented as instruments of transparency, following the same path taken with other modern technologies of governance. Responsibility-centered management—a budgeting approach that has gained considerable traction in US higher education—is particularly notable in this regard, preaching transparency as a basis for its overall legitimacy.

Yet budgets are neither simple nor altogether transparent. As mentioned above, universities often operate under mixes of different budgeting techniques, with some elements of the organization managed through responsibility-centered logics, others through incremental budgeting, and others through discretionary and bilateral negotiations between units and the central administration. Linked and spread out across thousands of accounts, these multiple logics generate a complex network of interdependencies that requires work and expertise to disentangle. That is why, as in other large organizations, budgets are also obfuscating technologies: Although theoretically tractable and transparent in principle, they are somewhat opaque in practice. This poses important avenues for rethinking the kinds of work that keep higher education institutions operating and adapting to their environments.

Precisely because of this complexity, budgets depend on large numbers of professional staff who devotedly keep the accounts of their units and make possible the movement of moneys (and the financing of projects) across the institution. Some of these positions have suffered losses to automatization, with processing of claims and budgeting of projects increasingly falling on the desks of instructors and faculty. But even in these circumstances, the operation of the budget depends on many staff members who understand the affordances and flexibilities in the Chart of Accounts, expenses processing systems, procurement platforms, and the budget more generally. They are the keepers of the spreadsheets and devices that make the budget possible.

This critical organizational middleware is often ignored in discussions about budgets—making it an attractive topic for both future research and on-the-ground organizing. A history of budgets need not focus only on how different families of models have taken hold of higher education, thus stressing managerial decisions taken at the top; but, perhaps more importantly, can also examine the praxis of budgeting within institutions, the way staff expertise is nurtured, preserved, or transformed.

What do we gain by studying the process of budgeting within units?

Budgets as Politics

In how budgets allocate resources, they are "political thing[s]. [They reflect] the outcome of a series of negotiations over what activities should be funded and at what levels" (AAUP 2004). Budgets determine priorities. Budgets constrain the kinds of things that can be paid for, actively shaping the flow of resources across and between units in the modern university. In how they are designed, budgets thus materialize specific normative expectations of universities as organizations, educational spaces, and sites for the generation of knowledge.

This is clear in how different budget models represent distinct management philosophies. The four budget models presented above can be mapped onto two larger ways of allocating resources: central administration management and revenue-centered, or responsibility-centered management.

Central administration management, as its name suggests, coordinates the allocation of resources—primarily tuition and state support in the case of public universities—through campus management. Models like zero-based and incremental budgeting correspond to this strategy, giving full control over resources to the university's managers. This makes the relations between individual units and the central administration significant in shaping how moneys are distributed and places the locus of power closer to the administrative core.

As Frederick S. Hills and Thomas A. Mahoney (1978) argue, these ways of budgeting alter how departments and units grow in moments of abundance and of scarcity. Studying the finances of the University of Minnesota, Hills and Mahoney find that departments with greater levels of political power, measured as participation of the unit's faculty in the university's governance structures (the local University Senate) and presence in outside advisory boards, tended to receive more discretionary resources in times of scarcity than departments with fewer powerful connections. As they note, "power is an influence utilized more as a protective force during periods of scarcity than as an exploitive force during periods of abundance" (458), with the strategies of discretionary resource allocation shifting during moments of austerity and abundance, although always tilted toward the coalitions of powerful subunits on campus. The role of subunit power in shaping allocations was also highlighted in work by Jeffrey Pfeffer and Gerald R. Salancik (1974), who found that those deemed more powerful were allotted greater resources.

A different kind of power politics is at play in so-called responsibility-centered models, which entail generating competition for revenue between units. This is done through models that make explicit the cost of services and materials for individual units—from telephone lines to the cost of instruction—that can be combined to produce new outputs (externally funded research, student credit hours, greater graduation rates, novel teaching programs) in various ways. Units are seen as points of revenues and expenses, driving their allocations. An academic department, for example, might be evaluated in terms of how much revenue it generates in the form of students taught, measured as the number of student credit hours it delivers over the course of a year. Associated with a particular "slice" of student tuitions and earmarked state revenue, these student credit hours become a measure of how successful a department is at attracting "customers" and determines the level of support that the unit will obtain the following fiscal year.

Unlike more mechanical models that constrain how funds are spent, units can invest these allocations entrepreneurially: They may hire more part-time instructors, or invest in more student support services, or hire more tenure-track faculty, as long as the costs do not exceed the allocations. Introduced into the world of higher education in the 1970s, these budget-modeling techniques incentivize "entrepreneurial" (Clark 1998) activities on campuses, with departments seeking to attract greater incomes by out-competing others for revenue-oriented metrics.

Despite their focus on entrepreneurial activity and greater organizational flexibility, responsibility-centered models exacerbate the inequalities within and across units. This is partly because the revenues of units under responsibility-centered management are more sensitive to external shocks than under other budgeting approaches, creating incentives for overinvestments in the short term but making long-term planning uncertain. This may be one reason the selection of specific budget models seems to have little effect on the educational performance of institutions, with volume of overall state support a much more important variable (Kelchen et al. 2024). Because these kinds of models tie resources to measures such as student enrollments and major numbers that universities have little control over in the long run, they lead to strategies that minimize fixed costs (like tenure-track positions) and maximize flexibility in costs (through, for instance, employing contingent instructors; Cross and Goldenberg 2003) at the demerit of educational stability. Depending on how these models are calibrated, they may also create inequalities between units. Models that give greater value to majors than to enrollments, for example, affect "service" departments that have lower capacity for transforming their students in classrooms into majors and degrees.

Budget models are also political in a broader sense, of course, encoding the contract between universities and society at large (Dougherty and Natow 2015). It is no coincidence that older generations of budgeting practices tended to rely on incremental models: there was an assumption, at least on paper, that state support would continue to grow along with student enrollments. These were models for abundance that never really contemplated future turbulence. And they generated investments in faculty and staff that are now facing duress. As budgeting practices and revenues change, some fields that may have once had healthy finances now face cuts, furloughs, and terminations. Newer generations of budgeting techniques like activity-based budgeting and responsibility-centered management start from an assumption of scarcity and austerity that must be dealt with by harnessing market-like mechanisms of competition. And though they are means of dealing with austerity, they are hardly mechanisms for challenging the politics of scarcity in higher education.

This is precisely what makes budgets so fundamentally vexing, particularly in universities and other institutions of higher education. Every budget model is an assumption about the future, a prospective bet of what funding will be like in years to come. But that future is unknown, a mere projection on spreadsheets, and one that often fails to materialize. There is, at the end of the day, no "correct" model, particularly in the kinds of ecologies with fractured politics and interests that define universities. What might work for the medical school may not work for a history department. What might serve the interests of a lab-based field may simply not reflect the constraints of a social science. As in politics more generally, there is no unique unambiguous solution. The best model may not be the one that perfectly aligns revenues and expenses, but may be one that reflects the collective, if contested, vision of what the university *ought* to be.

References

AAUP (American Association of University Professors). 2004. "Financial Exigency, Academic Governance, and Related Matters." American Association of University Professors, April. https://www.aaup.org/report/financial-exigency-academic-governance-and-related-matters.

Clark, Burton R. 1998. "The Entrepreneurial University: Demand and Response." *Tertiary Education and Management* 4 (1): 5–16.

Comrie, Andrew C. 2021. *Like Nobody's Business: An Insider's Guide to How US University Finances Really Work*. Cambridge: Open Book.

Cross, John G., and Edie N. Goldenberg. 2003. "How Does University Decision Making Shape the Faculty?" *New Directions for Higher Education* 2003 (123): 49–59.

Dougherty, Kevin J., and Rebecca S. Natow. 2015. *The Politics of Performance Funding for Higher Education: Origins, Discontinuations, and Transformations*. Baltimore: Johns Hopkins University Press.

Hills, Frederick S., and Thomas A. Mahoney. 1978. "University Budgets and Organizational Decision Making." *Administrative Science Quarterly* 23 (3): 454–65.

Kelchen, Robert, Justin Ortagus, Kelly Rosinger, Dominique Baker, and Mitch Lingo. 2024. "The Relationships between State Higher Education Funding Strategies and College Access and Success." *Educational Researcher* 53 (2): 100–110.

Pfeffer, Jeffrey, and Gerald R. Salancik. 1974. "Organizational Decision Making as a Political Process: The Case of a University Budget." *Administrative Science Quarterly* 19 (2): 135–51.

Smith, Dean O. 2019a. *How University Budgets Work*. Baltimore: Johns Hopkins University Press.

Smith, Dean O. 2019b. *University Finances: Accounting and Budgeting Principles for Higher Education*. Baltimore: Johns Hopkins University Press.

C

Campus

Davarian L. Baldwin

When it comes to the idea of a college campus, we mostly imagine a series of ivory towers, a city on a hill, elevated and isolated from the real world. The very meaning of the word *campus*—Latin for "a field"—suggests that this physical geography of learning exists in a state of nature, distinct from the society it serves (Turner 1984, 4). And yet throughout its history, the US campus, as a built environment, stands as the physical embodiment of the social hierarchies and political economy of its times, as a repository of the nation's horrors and even its liberatory possibilities.

Both as a physical form and as a set of ideas, the campus operates as a key fulcrum in the management of land, labor, and social relations across the changing vectors of the US capitalist economy. The campus has been particularly adept at stabilizing the imbalances between national claims to democratic equality and the financial realities of exclusivity, through the racialization of higher education space. In demands on the campus to hold these seeming contradictions, however, the space has also remained a site of struggle for building out the architecture of a freedom not yet achieved.

From the beginning, US higher education spaces have been shaped by what architectural historian Paul Venable Turner (1984, 3) calls, "the collegiate ideal." While continental European universities focus on academic concerns, US colleges and universities followed the model of English universities, where students and teachers cloister in shared spaces of both learning and living. The collegiate ideal then requires a campus that includes residential, dining, and recreational facilities alongside classrooms. So even if situated in the middle of bustling cities, the US campus has been designed and imagined as a self-contained world unto itself.

Arguably, the most iconic representation of the collegiate ideal in the United States is Thomas Jefferson's "academical village" design at the University of Virginia. The campus lays out a stunning network of green spaces surrounded by dormitories, hotels, and classrooms, all leading to a majestic rotunda (Bruce 1920). But this campus genius loci, its architectural ethos of a self-contained learning community, was actually an extension of the slave economy that made it possible.

Like the US colonial era more generally, the academical village was largely built by enslaved Black laborers rented from local landowners. And once UVA opened, these same enslaved workers transitioned to maintaining the campus buildings and serving the daily needs of administrators, faculty, and students. In short, the broader political economy of human bondage held together this enlightened microcosm of free thinking, personal development, and critical inquiry (McInnis and Nelson 2019; Wolfe 2020). And the sociopolitical contours that built and maintained this iconic campus pervaded the physical footprint of US higher education from the very beginning.

Historian Craig Steven Wilder (2013, 17–25) points out that the earliest European campuses in the Americas were structures designed to mark and secure the edges of their competing empires. The British followed the lead of Spain and France to build out colleges, like Harvard and William and Mary, that could train colonial administrators, maintain control over colonists, and advance Indigenous conquest through Christian rule.

College campuses were just as important to the colonial garrison as its armories and forts. Cannons, moats, and palisades flanked classrooms and boardinghouses. It is telling that the first brick structure on Harvard Yard was the Indian School, where Native students were trained into submission through English-language lessons, clothing, and etiquette instruction. The ultimate goal of converting Indigenous students to day laborers and homesteaders served both the maintenance of the colonial campus and the desire for colonial expansion (Wilder 2013, 26–28).

The slave economy underwrote all this campus infrastructure, especially as merchants and traders began to supplant the authority of the British colonial administration in the mid-eighteenth century. Their wealth—accumulated from the market in human bondage—funded construction, filled endowments, and influenced the culture of campuses at institutions like Columbia, Penn, and the College of New Jersey (Princeton) (L. M. Harris, Campbell, and Brophy 2019).

Donated lands became an extension of the college campus, where schools leased subdivided plots and their enslaved workers to tenants as a lucrative real estate investment. Enslaved people also served as collateral to both develop and preserve college campuses. In 1838, Georgetown faced the threat of closing and sold 272 enslaved people just to stay afloat. When the nation witnessed the westward push of cotton agriculture, Georgetown's Jesuit brethren transported enslaved Black people to establish Saint Louis University, the first college west of the Mississippi. Wilder makes clear that the early US campus stood as a "monument to slavery" (2013, 137).

Yet even the overwhelming might of the colonial college could not fully extinguish what might be called the contraband campus, resilient learning spaces of refuge for the enslaved. Black religious organizations worked in direct defiance of US higher education by building liberal arts colleges like Wilberforce (Ohio), Morris Brown (Georgia), and Lane (Tennessee) (Gasman 2007). Architectural scholar Kenrick Ian Grandison (1999) describes how these campuses were typically embedded within Black communities, buildings circled with their backs to the public, not as a form of exclusion but for self-defense against the violent white hostility to their very existence.

Oak trees, kitchen tables, and open fields served as clandestine landscapes of literacy and debate before largely Black women converted these spaces into contraband campuses behind enemy lines. For example, Mary Peake provided a space of refuge for the enslaved who quit the plantation before the Emancipation Proclamation, teaching any Black student she could until the space became the Hampton Agricultural and Industrial School in Virginia (Singh 2018, 30–34). But in the hands of Union General Samuel Armstrong, Hampton's postemancipation culture of manual labor training became a direct rebuke of Peake and her vision of the campus as a site of Black self-determination. Raised among missionaries in the US colonial theater of Hawaiʻi, Armstrong converted Hampton into a training ground for building Black servitude in a world without slavery. Hampton included basic education but seemed to prioritize field studies in crop cultivation and "domestic sciences" for women (Singh 2018; Talbot 1904).

Every aspect of the campus was embedded with living the habits of work. A ringing bell organized the regimented patterns of campus life from morning inspection and chapel to 12-hour "work study" periods and night school, all under the strict supervision of white instruction (Singh 2018, 53–56). The presumption of an inherent Black "delinquency" legitimized the manual education model of the Hampton campus, which would get reproduced at other schools, like Booker T. Washington's famed Tuskegee Institute.[1] The profound irony is that just as African Americans were largely being prepared for agricultural servitude, the nation underwent a steady process of industrialization that inspired different changes in the college campus.

As early as the mid-nineteenth century, textile manufacturers, like Abbott Lawrence, made significant donations to build engineering and science schools at Harvard and small liberal arts colleges, including Amherst and Bowdoin. The students produced here would increase the efficient refinery of cotton brought from the slave South into profitable finished goods. This technical turn was capped off by the founding of the Massachusetts Institute of Technology in 1861, as the United States transitioned from a farm to factory nation (Wilder 2013, 285–87). Yet mass production required more than a cadre of scientists and engineers, and the campus also became the training ground for a more expansive higher education.

The Morrill Land Grant Acts of 1862 and 1890 have been celebrated for democratizing education by building public universities. But the new schools also provided industrialists with the public resources to retrain largely white workers for a new industrial economy. And until recently, there was no discussion of how these new campuses were enshrined in American colonialism while reinforcing Jim Crow segregation.

The Morrill Act worked by distributing what were called public domain lands to states that could then be used for constructing a campus or sold to build the financial endowments of these new public universities. But the 10.7 million acres for this project were actually Indigenous lands, confiscated through seizure or suspect land treaties. This federal policy took place just as white homesteaders were moving west to expand the American empire. We have failed to fully engage what education studies scholar Sharon Stein calls "the material entanglements" between campus building and colonial expansion after the Civil War (2017, 4; Lee and Ahtone 2020). Schools, from MIT to the University of California, built their endowments on this colonial act of land theft.

The 1890 version of the act extended land grants to the former Confederate states. To their credit, lawmakers included a clause prohibiting racial

1. Reinhold Martin (2021) includes the important chapter "Bricks and Stones," which lays out a stark physical contrast between the landscapes of Tuskegee compared with elite liberal arts colleges built in Philadelphia.

discrimination in admissions. Instead of enforcing the integration of land-grant schools, however, the act provided additional funds to southern states so they could build separate and underfunded Black colleges. With this decision, the federal government used college campus building to help reinforce Jim Crow segregation six years before the "separate but equal" doctrine of *Plessy v. Ferguson* became law of the land (A. Harris 2021; Spivey 1978; Wennersten 1991).

By the late nineteenth century, rapid industrialization brought sweeping social transformations to an increasingly urban America. For the country's educated elite, demands that higher education reach a broader public were seen as part of this changing society and inspired a rigorous backlash expressed in the shape and design of the campus. At the turn of the twentieth century, not only were white women fighting for their right to vote, but they also demanded a seat at the table of the country's most elite schools. Instead of allowing direct entry, trustees across the Northeast supported the creation of affiliate "sister" schools like Barnard (Columbia), Radcliffe (Harvard), and Mount Holyoke (Dartmouth). Spatially, these women's colleges consisted of distinct buildings on campus or separate campuses nearby. Faculty from the men's schools offered instruction, and the women maintained their student life in an arrangement that didn't challenge traditional concerns about the dangers of "coeducation" (Horowitz 1993).

At the same time, the spatial location and architectural design of new campuses served as critical responses to a changing world. The pastoral retreat ethos of lush green campuses acquired even greater value amid the period of urban industrialization. The quasi-rural learning environments, filled with fresh air and open space, were meant to serve as a balm from the foul smell, commercial life, and so-called dangerous ethnic amalgams sullying the nation's cities (Severino 2005).

Newer institutions went even further by modeling the medieval enclosure design of British institutions like Oxford University and Trinity College in Scotland. In an age of change, the revival of Gothic architecture represented a new school's desire to project an image of age, permanence, respectability, and social conservatism. The planned design of Trinity College, on what was once the outskirts of Hartford, Connecticut, best captures this Gothic revival. Renderings depict opulent campus quadrangles filled with green courtyards and surrounded by brick facades on all sides, with spires atop tall towers on each corner of the quads. Already built on top of a hill, the campus also required visitors to breach imposing outer walls to even witness the interiors of campus life (Knapp and Knapp 2000; Weaver 1967). Trinity never finalized all the walls, but its plans became a model for the redesign of Princeton and the construction of schools like the University of Chicago, with its notorious quadrangle fortress draped in stone gargoyles (Turner 1984, 219).

But the ethos of enclosure didn't stop at architectural design. Higher education leaders used restrictions on campus residency as a mechanism to regulate the ethnic and class demographic of the student body. Amid the second revival of the Ku Klux Klan and calls for 100 percent Americanism in US cities, students at Trinity created a "Movement for Americanization" resolution, and administrators followed with their own "alien residence policy" to address what many considered an "undesirable element." The new residency mandate required all students to live in dormitories, which created an economic barrier for the working-class families who couldn't afford to board on campus. And for the white ethnic students that could still afford to attend, leaders argued that residency separated them from their local environment (Dougherty n.d., n.p.).

Campus facilities also became a powerful weapon of enclosure to combat changing social conditions beyond the gates. Even before its 1892 rebuild, UChicago grew its endowment largely through real estate acquisitions in the surrounding Hyde Park neighborhood. By subsidizing housing for faculty, students, and local professionals, UChicago inflated property values of the land that served as its primary economic base. The high land value also provided an economic boundary from European immigrant communities near campus (Bachin 2004; Boyer 2015). But the rapid increase of African Americans during the Great Migration posed an even greater perceived threat to the property values of campus real estate.

In response, the university financially backed the Hyde Park and Kenwood neighborhood associations and their use of racially restrictive covenants, gaining popularity across the country. These legally binding agreements—to prevent the sale to, lease to, or occupation of property by targeted racial groups—kept African Americans at bay from the real estate so central to UChicago's economic viability. Black Chicagoans ridiculed these covenants as "the University of Chicago Agreement to get rid of Negroes" (*Chicago Defender* 1937; also see Bachin 2004, 53–57). The University of Texas also deployed its campus facilities to bolster segregation both on and off campus.

This flagship public university used its Texas Memorial Stadium and new parking, athletic fields, and open space to buffer the already separate campus zone of women's facilities from the growing Black East Austin neighborhood nearby (Winling 2018, 59).

The Great Migration continued to change the literal complexion of the country at midcentury. And during the period of "white flight" to the suburbs, colleges and universities were too big and slow to follow. Most schools bunkered down and devised ways to hold the fort in the face of the so-called urban crisis of Black and Latinx inmigration amid economic divestment from cities.

By 1959, UChicago helped coordinate 14 urban universities into a lobbying force that successfully pushed for a significant change to the Federal Housing Act of 1949, which bolstered efforts at racial segregation. Dubbed the "112 credits program," this initiative triggered a two-to-one federal matching grant for any urban renewal program on or near a college or university campus up to five years before the program even began (Winling 2011). City schools from Johns Hopkins to the University of Colorado Denver used this program to turn their campuses into barricaded zones of learning to stem the tide of Black and brown residents living nearby. By 1964, there were at least proposals for 154 projects supported by the 112 program, involving 120 college campuses and 75 hospitals (Ashworth 1964; Baldwin 2021a; Klotsche 1966; McKee 2016).

The campus became the friendly face of urban renewal, where higher education's bulldozers demolished neighborhoods and established islands of campus buildings and vacant lots around city schools. In 1969, the University of Pennsylvania used the credits program to start displacing approximately 600 low-income African American families to build its University City Science Center, the nation's first inner city research park (Carlson 1999; Wolf-Powers 2022). But these acts of displacement also sparked critical student and community-led activism that made the campus a vital site of struggle.

Grassroots activism and postwar demands for another round of workforce training brought more working-class students, women, and students of color onto college campuses. They immediately powered historic free speech and antiwar demands alongside the creation of Black, ethnic, and women's studies programs (Biondi 2014; Ferguson 2012). At the same time, these new students joined the fight against higher education's violent acts of demolition and displacement in surrounding neighborhoods. Protestors shouted "Gym Crow!" in 1968 after learning that Columbia planned to build a school gymnasium in Morningside Park that would have served as a physical barrier between the campus and Harlem (Bradley 2009; Sokol 2013). The next year Penn students and community groups protested and even managed to broker a deal for scattered-site low-income housing in the area targeted for the Science Center (Carlson 1999). But the promises were never kept (see also Cole 2020).

While more students gained access to elite white universities, nothing compared to the role that city and community colleges played in reshaping the concept of the campus. City colleges had long been hotbeds of intellectual debate and political agitation for working-class youth, at least since City College of New York was dubbed "Harvard of the Proletariat" in the 1930s. But few could foresee the transformative capacity of these neighborhood schools when Black students on Chicago's West Side seized control of Crane Junior College and renamed it Malcolm X Community College in 1968. What was once a school that failed to transition its Black students to four-year colleges became a campus of community service, with increased student aid programs and a "prison annex" to educate incarcerated residents. Students also helped rethink campus safety by pushing to hire unarmed workers from a Black-owned security firm in place of Chicago Police Department officers (Cohen, Brawer, and Kisker 2014; Singh 2018, 117–22).[2]

Such reimaginings, about the function of a campus, were capped off by the Black and Puerto Rican student-led victories to combine existing free tuition practices with an open admissions policy by 1970. Organizers reasoned that the public college campus should help correct for a segregated and inferior secondary school system by providing the bridge instruction to prepare all citizens for social mobility (Biondi 2011; Reed 2023). These examples capture the vision of a people-powered campus that has been largely lost to us.

2. We must also consider the expansive visions of HBCUs and local institutes. Howard University faculty and students formulated the Black University, a higher education campus directed toward the total Black community. Both the Communiversity in Chicago and Atlanta's Institute of the Black World rethought the function and boundaries of the campus by bridging the gaps between scholars, activists, and local residents in service to the broader Black freedom struggle (see Yeboah 2021; Kelley 2016; Rickford 2016, 168–218).

In the following decades, mainstream campuses became largely fortified islands of wealth amid a sea of poverty, while community and city colleges limped along with paltry resources, despite their innovations. But by the nineties, we witness an important sea change marked by a Back to the City movement, with renewed public interest in urban life. College campuses were reimagined as "anchors" with sustained physical footprints that could help bring economic stability and even revitalization to divested communities. This new approach to campus development happened while schools were looking for new revenue streams amid shrinking direct federal and state funding to higher education. The "bell towers" of the college campus were targeted as the new "smokestacks" for cities (Birch, Perry, and Taylor 2013; Haar 2011, 149; Perry and Wiewel 2015). Therefore, campus infrastructure had to be retrofitted to serve as an economic engine.

By the early twenty-first century, colleges campuses witnessed an explosive rise in noneducational facilities, where classrooms were increasingly overshadowed by offices for real estate, fundraising, policing, and technology transfer. University lobbyists leaned heavily into the 1980 Bayh-Dole Act, allowing schools to obtain the intellectual property rights for research sponsored by federal funding and make its licensing available to the private sector. This monetization of campus laboratories bolstered the financial power of already tax-exempt campus land, through higher education's 501c3 nonprofit status. Titans in the dominant knowledge economy of pharmaceuticals, software, health services, and military defense flocked to campuses because of their power to reduce overhead costs through tax-free facilities, cheap student research labor, and continued federal funding for research and development that could be brought to market (Baldwin 2021a; Rooksby 2016).

The growing financial value of the campus, in today's knowledge economy, has become a lucrative industry in itself. Real estate developers, like Wexford Science and Technology, calculated the benefits of building on tax-exempt land and working exclusively on campus projects. Their "knowledge communities" reap substantial rewards by mixing spaces of academic-industry collaboration with luxury housing, storefronts, classrooms, retail, and laboratories. This expanding physical footprint is also secured by the "extraterritorial expansion" of campus police forces, which are usually armed, increasingly hold jurisdiction over neighborhood blocks, and yet largely evade public oversight (Baldwin 2021a; McKee 2023; Wolf-Powers 2022). The financial and spatial redesign of the campus profits developers, brings industry and jobs back to cities, and fills the coffers of university budgets. But what about the primarily Black, brown, and poor residents living on the periphery of these campuses, left to press their noses on the glass of prosperity and only brought back to clean the floors, cook the food, or secure the perimeters?

Many on the outside still take pride from living near magisterial campuses filled with ivory-covered Gothic buildings and sleek, glassy research facilities. But the campus tax-exempt status sucks funds from city budgets for schools and other public services. Campus expansion raises housing costs, which can displace longtime residents in the neighborhoods of color that surround the gates. Higher education's dominant control over labor can also lower wage ceilings and suppress collective bargaining efforts for entire cities. Campus police forces surveil and profile residents, bolstered by public authority but directed by these profit-driven university interests (Baldwin 2023a). In short, greater swaths of local communities are being turned into a campus at great costs.

The growing faith in the campus as an economic growth engine has also gone global. A once quaint model of "study abroad" is now overshadowed by exporting US campus brands onto international lands. The provocatively named Education City in Doha, Qatar, and the human rights, labor, and academic freedom controversies surrounding NYU's franchising of its campus in Shanghai and Abu Dhabi help demonstrate the worldwide consequences of the city-as-campus design (Chen 2018; Kamola 2019; Vora 2018). At the same time, international schools like Erasmus University are partnering with local and regional government actors and other nonprofits to build a "cultuurcampus" in the heart of the largely immigrant community on Rotterdam's South Bank. Under the educational cover of claiming to "civilize" the "non-Dutch," this project exploits the vulnerability of marginal neighborhoods, who are struggling to survive in the remnants of a city's once vibrant port economy (Klerk 2022).

Yet the consolidation of power through the urban form of the campus has also made its built environment a growing target of resistance and reimagining. Indigenous scholars and activists have developed a "land back" policy in response to the historic Morrill Act (Red Shirt-Shaw 2020). After unearthing higher education's role in slavery and urban renewal, African

Americans are building out visions of reparations (Baldwin 2020). Residents and even legislatures are demanding various forms of compensation for tax-exempt campus lands, primarily through payments in lieu of taxes (PILOTs). Progressive planners and public advocates argue that all campus expansions must come under the oversight of community-based planning and zoning boards (Baldwin 2023b). Activists and labor groups call for campus police abolition, by divesting from armed patrols and investing in the campus services of housing and food alongside living-wage jobs and trauma care as more effective forms of safety (Baldwin 2021b).

The 2024 protests around US complicity in Israel's destruction of Gaza further amplifies the broad-ranging consolidation of power that converges within the campus form. Demands for a ceasefire in Gaza are tied to growing calls of "disclose and divest" for university endowments invested in Israeli and war-related production supporting the genocide. Students sit within encampments protesting, praying, eating, and learning—hence building their own vision of campus life through practice. These displays of peace have been met with overwhelming campus and city police force, not only to stomp out student dissent but also to clear ground for the most important season of fundraising: graduation (Burga and Popli 2024). To further emphasize the degree to which the global is local, growing US demands to "boycott, divest, and sanction" Israeli higher education expose the manifold ways in which universities in and beyond the United States enforce intellectual censorship, support military training and weapons research, and participate in settler-colonial land dispossession in the Middle East and across the world (Wind 2024). There is no turning back to the myth of the isolated ivory tower.

For so long campuses were imagined as monastic "cathedrals of learning." But in fact, this built environment has always been fully embedded in social life, as a garrison of empire, a fortress of enclosure, a factory of extraction, and yes, a landscape of new possibilities. We miss the very function of higher education by holding on to the myth of the campus as simply an ethereal training ground for the future, when in fact it remains the pervasive staging ground for society's current conditions.

References

Ashworth, Kenneth H. 1964. "Urban Renewal and the University: A Tool for Campus Expansion and Neighborhood Improvement." *Journal of Higher Education* 35 (9): 493–96.

Bachin, Robin F. 2004. *Building the South Side: Urban Space and Civic Culture in Chicago, 1890–1919*. Chicago: University of Chicago Press.

Baldwin, Davarian L. 2020. "The Reparations Movement in Higher Education." *Thinking Republic*, October 11. https://www.thethinkingrepublic.com/being-counted/the-reparations-movement-in-higher-education.

Baldwin, Davarian L. 2021a. *In the Shadow of the Ivory Tower: How Universities Are Plundering Our Cities*. New York: Bold Type.

Baldwin, Davarian L. 2021b. "Why We Should Abolish the Campus Police." *Chronicle of Higher Education*, May 19. https://www.chronicle.com/article/why-we-should-abolish-campus-police.

Baldwin, Davarian L. 2023a. "'Educational Purposes': Nonprofit Land as a Vital Site of Struggle." *Nonprofit Quarterly*, July 26. https://nonprofitquarterly.org/educational-purposes-nonprofit-land-as-a-vital-site-of-struggle/.

Baldwin, Davarian L. 2023b. "'Just Protecting the University Property': Campus Policing as Extraterritorial Expansion." In *Cops on Campus: Rethinking Safety and Confronting Police Violence*, edited by Yalile Suriel, Grace Watkins, Jude Paul Matias Dizon, and John Joseph Sloan III, 33–40. Seattle: University of Washington Press.

Biondi, Martha. 2011. "'Brooklyn College Belongs to Us': Black Students and the Transformation of Public Higher Education in New York City." In *Civil Rights in New York City: From World War II to the Giuliani Era*, edited by Clarence Taylor, 161–81. New York: Fordham University Press.

Biondi, Martha. 2014. *The Black Revolution on Campus*. Berkeley: University of California Press.

Birch, Eugenie, David C. Perry, and Henry Louis Taylor Jr. 2013. "Universities as Anchor Institutions." *Journal of Higher Education Outreach and Engagement* 17 (3): 7–15.

Boyer, John W. 2015. *The University of Chicago: A History*. Chicago: University of Chicago Press.

Bradley, Stefan M. 2009. *Harlem vs. Columbia University: Black Student Power in the Late 1960s*. Urbana: University of Illinois Press.

Bruce, Philip Alexander. 1920. *History of the University of Virginia, 1819–1919: The Lengthened Shadow of One Man*. 5 vols. New York: Macmillian.

Burga, Solcyré, and Nik Popli. 2024. "Protestors Are Calling on Universities to Divest from Israel: Here's What That Means." *Time*, May 2. https://time.com/6974063/divestment-explained-campus-protest-israel.

Carlson, MacKenzie S. 1999. *A History of the University City Science Center*. Exhibit. University Archives and Records Center, University of Pennsylvania, September. https://archives.upenn.edu/exhibits/penn-history/science-center/.

Chen, Michelle. 2018. "The Labor Abuse that Went into NYU's Abu Dhabi Campus." *Nation*, July 26.

Chicago Defender. 1937. "Building Ghettoes," October 7.

Cohen, Arthur M., Florence B. Brawer, and Carrie B. Kisker. 2014. *The American Community College*. 6th ed. Jossey-Bass Higher and Adult Education Series. San Francisco: Jossey-Bass.

Cole, Eddie Rice. 2020. *The Campus Color Line: College Presidents and the 1960s Struggle for Black Freedom*. Princeton, NJ: Princeton University Press.

Dougherty, Jack. n.d. "Uncovering Unwritten Rules against Jewish and Black Students at Trinity College." In *On The Line: How Schooling, Housing, and Civil Rights Shaped Hartford and Its Suburbs*. Trinity College, book-in-progress. https://ontheline.trincoll.edu/uncovering-unwritten.html.

Ferguson, Roderick A. 2012. *The Reorder of Things: The University and Its Pedagogies of Minority Difference*. Minneapolis: University of Minnesota Press.

Gasman, Marybeth. 2007. *Envisioning Black Colleges: A History of the United Negro College Fund*. Baltimore: Johns Hopkins University Press.

Grandison, Kenrick Ian. 1999. "Negotiated Space: The Black College Campus as a Cultural Record of Postbellum America." *American Quarterly* 51 (3): 529–79.

Haar, Sharon. 2011. *The City as Campus: Urbanism and Higher Education in Chicago*. Minneapolis: University of Minnesota Press.

Harris, Adam. 2021. *The State Must Provide: Why America's Colleges Have Always Been Unequal—and How to Set Them Right*. New York: Ecco.

Harris, Leslie M., James T. Campbell, and Alfred L. Brophy, eds. 2019. *Slavery and the University: Histories and Legacies*. Athens: University of Georgia Press.

Horowitz, Helen Lefkowitz. 1993. *Alma Mater: Design and Experience in the Women's Colleges from Their Nineteenth-Century Beginnings to the 1930s*. Amherst: University of Massachuchusetts Press.

Kamola, Isaac. 2019. *Making the World Global: U.S. Universities and the Production of the Global Imaginary*. Durham, NC: Duke University Press.

Kelley, Robin D. G. 2016. "Black Study, Black Struggle." *Boston Review*, March 1. http://bostonreview.net/forum/robin-d-g-kelley-black-study-black-struggle.

Klerk, Marianne. 2022. "Davarian Baldwin: 'De cultuurcampus op Zuid is symbool voor de groeiende macht van universiteiten in steden.'" *Vers beton*, November 23. https://www.versbeton.nl/2022/11/davarian-baldwin-de-cultuurcampus-op-zuid-is-symbool-voor-de-groeiende-macht-van-universiteiten-in-steden.

Klotsche, J. Martin. 1966. *The Urban University and the Future of Our Cities*. New York: Harper and Row.

Knapp, Peter J., and Anne H. Knapp. 2000. *Trinity College in the Twentieth Century: A History*. Hartford, CT: Trinity College.

Lee, Robert, and Tristan Ahtone. 2020. "Land-Grab Universities." *High Country News*, March 30. https://www.hcn.org/issues/52-4/indigenous-affairs-education-land-grab-universities/.

Martin, Reinhold. 2021. *Knowledge Worlds: Media, Materiality, and the Making of the Modern University*. New York: Columbia University Press.

McInnis, Maurie Dee, and Louis P. Nelson, eds. 2019. *Educated in Tyranny: Slavery at Thomas Jefferson's University*. Charlottesville: University of Virginia Press.

McKee, Guian A. 2016. "The Hospital City in an Ethnic Enclave: Tufts-New England Medical Center, Boston's Chinatown, and the Urban Political Economy of Health Care." *Journal of Urban History* 42 (2): 259–83.

McKee, Guian A. 2023. *Hospital City, Health Care Nation: Race, Capital, and the Costs of American Health Care*. Philadelphia: University of Pennsylvania Press.

Perry, David C., and Wim Wiewel. 2015. *The University as Urban Developer: Case Studies and Analysis*. Hoboken, NJ: Taylor and Francis.

Red Shirt-Shaw, Megan. 2020. "Beyond the Land Acknowledgement: College 'LAND BACK' or Free Tuition for Native Students." Policy and Practice Brief, Hack the Gates. https://img1.wsimg.com/blobby/go/1e1bb38b-fdda-4ae1-93d8-f4102272ee48/downloads/Redshirt-Shaw_Landback_HTGreport.pdf?ver=1674240385450.

Reed, Conor Tomás. 2023. *New York Liberation School: Study and Movement for the People's University*. Brooklyn: Common Notions.

Rickford, Russell John. 2016. *We Are an African People: Independent Education, Black Power, and the Radical Imagination*. Oxford: Oxford University Press.

Rooksby, Jacob H. 2016. *The Branding of the American Mind: How Universities Capture, Manage, and Monetize Intellectual Property and Why It Matters*. Critical University Studies. Baltimore: Johns Hopkins University Press.

Severino, Carol. 2005. "Greenery vs. Concrete and Walls and Doors: Images and Metaphors Affecting an Urban Mission." *Metropolitan Universities* 6 (2): 103.

Singh, Vineeta. 2018. "Which Neither Devils nor Tyrants Could Remove: The Racial-Spatial Pedagogies of Modern U.S. Higher Education." PhD diss., University of California, San Diego.

Sokol, Samantha. 2013. "NYC That Never Was: A Gym in Morningside Park Sparks 1968 Columbia University Protests and Shutdown." *Untapped New York*, October 8.

Spivey, Donald. 1978. *Schooling for the New Slavery: Black Industrial Education, 1868–1915*. Westport, CT: Greenwood Press.

Stein, Sharon. 2017. "A Colonial History of the Higher Education Present: Rethinking Land-Grant Institutions through Processes of Accumulation and Relations of Conquest." *Critical Studies in Education* 61:1–17.

Talbot, Edith Armstrong. 1904. *Samuel Chapman Armstrong: A Biographical Study*. New York: Doubleday.

Turner, Paul Venable. 1984. *Campus: An American Planning Tradition*. Cambridge, MA: MIT Press.

Vora, Neha. 2018. *Teach for Arabia: American Universities, Liberalism, and Transnational Qatar*. Stanford, CA: Stanford University Press.

Weaver, Glenn. 1967. *The History of Trinity College*. Vol. 1. Hartford, CT: Trinity College Press.

Wennersten, John R. 1991. "The Travail of Black Land-Grant Schools in the South, 1890–1917." *Agricultural History* 65 (2): 54–62.

Wilder, Craig Steven. 2013. *Ebony and Ivy: Race, Slavery, and the Troubled History of America's Universities*. New York: Bloomsbury.

Wind, Maya. 2024. *Towers of Ivory and Steel: How Israeli Universities Deny Palestinian Freedom*. London: Verso.

Winling, LaDale. 2011. "Students and the Second Ghetto: Federal Legislation, Urban Politics, and Campus Planning at the University of Chicago." *Journal of Planning History* 10 (1): 59–86.

Winling, LaDale. 2018. *Building the Ivory Tower: Universities and Metropolitan Development in the Twentieth Century*. Politics and Culture in Modern America. Philadelphia: University of Pennsylvania Press.

Wolfe, Brendan. 2020. "Slavery at the University of Virginia." *Encyclopedia Virginia*. Virginia Humanities, December 7. https://encyclopediavirginia.org/entries/slavery-at-the-university-of-virginia/.

Wolf-Powers, Laura. 2022. *University City: History, Race, and Community in the Era of the Innovation District*. Philadelphia: University of Pennsylvania Press.

Yeboah, Amy. 2021. "Howard University and the Challenge of the Black University: A Conversation with Andrew Billingsley and Greg E. Carr." *Black Scholar* 51 (3): 25–38.

C

Classroom

Richard Simpson

The classroom is the single most important space in the university. It is the site of both knowledge production and subject formation, two primary functions of nation-state governance within a democracy.

Yet the resounding importance of this discursive space is equal to its status as a seemingly unspeakable subject. Few scholars write about their teaching or learning practices, and accounts of disciplinary and university histories rarely include focus on what occurs inside the classroom. The fields that do inventory its challenges—primarily rhetoric and composition—are delineated as the providers of "service" courses, which are often taught by graduate students or those holding nontenure appointments.[1] Indeed, pedagogy distinguishes the technical and vocational components of the profession. Put more simply, teaching is labor. That this work, or humanist knowledge production, is necessarily collaborative opposes the idea of the singular intellectual, and given that the history of this labor has never been written down in most disciplines, one begins to wonder if the discomfort of sharing classroom practices is structural to the profession's class consciousness.[2]

In addition to discounting how teachers collaborate with students to develop modes of literary, cultural, and humanist forms of analysis, the silence surrounding classroom practice elicits an empty signifier capable of taking on any number of local meanings while nonetheless serving as every university's equally venerated setting; it also opens the door for those outside to create fantasies, perhaps inevitably of the negative and conspiratorial kind.

1. The use of *class* to designate a group or distribution of students underlies its modern use to delineate social divisions. Raymond Williams finds that the earliest use of *class* in English belongs to the seventeenth century and holds a "special association with education," as it was most often used in schools just prior to becoming a general word for a group or division. The modern sense of *class* to refer to a social formation slowly emerged between 1770 and 1840 among the Industrial, American, and French Revolutions (1983, 60).

2. A recent exception placing the classroom at the center of literary studies and its professional development is Buurma and Heffernan (2021).

The omission of the material fact of labor in the classroom further elides opportunities for lateral interventions premised on teaching as a form of knowledge production as well as the way forms of production are intrinsically pedagogical. In this chapter I address alternative genealogies, modes of analysis, and directions of research and practice that emerge from this premise of the American classroom's complete and ongoing debt to the educative value of labor production.

In postrevolutionary America, an ideology suturing acts of learning to sites of labor casts educative value as inherent within assiduous work, specifically engagement with the earth and the necessity and worth of cultivating soil as instructive of the highest possible ethic and sense of selfhood (Eisinger 1947; Kulikoff 1992; Sturges 2011). This first classroom matriculated a yeoman farmer whose agrarian practice instituted scientific knowledge, social morality, and economic stability for the new nation (Appleby 1982; Smith 2007; Sweet 2002). Thomas Jefferson's *Notes on the State of Virginia* (1785) elevated this individual into a national hero and popularized stadial farming as the natural calling of American citizenry, in that its "deposit for substantial and genuine virtue" would be the most effective means to align personal independence, economic opportunity, and social interests as the basis for equality among autonomous citizen-producers (Hardt 2007). This figure of the yeoman farmer initiated an American affinity between labor and learning that engendered spatial practices as social pedagogies. We must therefore differentiate the idea of the classroom from the space of the schoolroom in the nineteenth century, given that the latter was antithetical to the primary educative environments in this era.

Landscapes built to produce socially necessary educative value used a decisively georgic aesthetic in which poetically depicted procedures of labor function as a teaching device (Lilly 1919).[3] Within a georgic mode, one's relationship to the environment explicitly stages a pedagogical method, not only in that cultivating land demonstrates scientific principles, but in that the very act of transforming the environment establishes an ethical and political identity in relation to it and therefore an identity in relation to others. This early georgic republic of farmers established a conception of civiliza-

3. The construction of pedagogical landscapes has a much longer international history that predates the United States. For discussions of planning and architecture as educational instruments outside the American context, see Mukerji (2014); and Panofsky (1957).

tion that relied on the development of an internal coherency and independent agency that arises from within, rather than being imposed by a higher authority (Cohen 2009; Upton 2008). Yet this learning process remains susceptible to environmental influence in that the earth's productive properties are not only the basis of human existence, but also, by persistently absorbing past human labor, its social invention and the foundation of future productivity. In this moment when American life was predominantly agricultural, nature was not yet an object asserted against the idea of culture, and this georgic ideology facilitated cities that did not yet represent a counterprinciple to the country but rather were viewed as a protraction of rural life's educative properties. The urban is as pedagogical as the agrarian. The ideologue of the yeoman farmer is the architect of the "academical village." Jefferson designed the site plan for the University of Virginia in 1805 as a self-contained community, foregrounding education, health, and morale as integral to its spatial arrangement, establishing a decisive break from the image, structure, and purpose of all previous American colleges of the colonial era (Woods 1985).

This use of space for instruction, an environment signifying a lesson, model, or ideology, is lately focused on the function of memorials, statues, and monuments; however, early nineteenth-century georgic sensibilities and the innately edifying value of "cultivation" expanded this practice beyond isolated objects, experimenting with entire landscapes that would, in time, determine the distinctly American body of higher education. The earliest classroom formations emerge in the Jacksonian era, in which the georgic ethos of agricultural work and rural economy animated city life through the horticultural practices of the urban elite, who hoped to dissociate their wealth accumulation from the kind found among Europe's landed aristocracies (Thornton 1989). The educative values of this morality of cultivation—self-discipline, virtue, and mental fortitude—motivated an "experimental garden," the most popular and influential pedagogical environment of the first half of the nineteenth century (Dal Co 1979; French 1974).

The Massachusetts Horticultural Society designed Mount Auburn Cemetery to orchestrate visitors through a programmed sequence of winding pathways adapted to the local topography and punctuated by burial plots, marked with varying styles of tombstone (Linden-Ward 1989). The lessons of this environment were enacted through the sensory experience emerging from one's encounter with bodies collectively woven into the grounds.

Just as the first American factory—established six miles away at Waltham—interlocked independent trades, reducing them to supplementary operations in the production of textiles, this experimental garden suspended and held together a mass of individual bodies in collaborative practice, a quantity forging a new quality of collective intelligence, which takes sensuous objective form as an infrastructure that educates. The horticulturalists demonstrated the intrinsic pedagogical capacity of production, as this landscape's corporeal embodiment extended the manufacturing process into a new social mechanism aimed at reforming the urban elite's subjectivities. This homeopathic approach to self-improvement did not achieve its goal, yet Mount Auburn inspired replication within all major cities in North America, influencing the midcentury park movement and, subsequently, the spatial form established to represent the colleges of the 1862 Land Grant Act.

Despite the Morrill Act's stated intent to promote the "practical education of the industrial classes," the act—signed in the same year as the Homestead Act and the Pacific Railroad Act, two additional enormous land grants that aimed to coordinate vast expanses of land acquired through brutal displacement of Native societies in the West—offered very little to the farming and industrial classes in terms of education (Act of July 2, 1862, Pub. L. No. 37-108). The scientific curriculum promoted by the legislation was dismissed as "book farming" by most Americans, who still found experience and labor the best and only teachers (Rudolph 1990, 259; Thelin 2011, 75–79).[4]

Yet the legislation attracted the nation's leading landscape architect, who, having just completed the four-year construction and planting of Manhattan's Central Park, now turned to design a forceful response to opposing theories of social progress surfacing in the wake of the necessity for specialized education within an industrial economy and its subsequent division between mental and manual labor. A month after visiting Amherst, Frederick Law Olmsted drafted *A Few Things to Be Thought of before Proceeding to Plan Buildings for the National Agricultural Colleges* (1866), presenting not only a philosophy of the land grant college as an intervention into the impending hierarchy setting in between rural and urban occupations, but also a site plan designating a "method of training that would accord with the philosophy" (Roper 1973, 310; Scholl and Gulwadi 2015). Again, a spatial

4. Education historian Frederick Rudolph summarizes the 1862 Land Grant Act as legislation that "gave political recognition to the yeoman farmer on the eve of his displacement" (1990, 250).

arrangement was advanced to establish a "method of training." Olmsted's intent to resolve—through positing landscape architecture as a productive force—the rupture of country and city, to protect the rural population and its way of life from historical obsolescence, has received much less attention than how his design principles, abstracted from their political reaction to capitalist industrialization, would come to define what only later would be referred to as a campus. With these pedagogical elements separated out, campus, much like classroom, would come to demarcate a super-sensible enclave, and an entire American landscape tradition would follow its course over the twentieth century and into our own time, meaning many different things at different moments with quite different values being brought into question.

For example, the first spatial ensemble to be constructed with a progressive education curriculum and at the scale of an entire city that we would today retroactively identify as a campus is Leland Stanford Junior University. As Olmsted went to work on drafts of the layout in 1886, Leland Stanford, in support of a Senate bill to legalize cooperation, began to publicly contend that employment is not a gift to the working class, but rather a service the worker pays for in the form of the profit kept by the employer. Stanford drafted the Cooperation Bill as a direct response to an insurmountable antagonism between an industrial oligarchy and the rising militancy of an international labor movement. He argued that the recent global upsurge in direct action taken by workers was, in effect, a new sign of intelligence, one critical result of industrial technology's ability to increase workers' wide-scale collaboration. Cooperation and worker ownership provided a third way between capitalism and socialism, yet the greatest benefit of this economic organization was societal, in that cooperative principles ensured each individual's actions were not a function of moral character, but rather one's placement within society (Stanford 1887). In a cooperative, differences among individuals are ignored or eliminated at the peril of science, industry, and the general welfare of the population. Not only would increased production and employment alone justify this legislation, but by emphasizing differences, cooperation involved another dimension: It would create a more intelligent people. Education is grasped here not as an adjunct to an economic system, but as a defining feature of organized labor production.

The bill did not pass the Senate floor; however, the urban project on which the Stanfords' had expended their entire fortune began construction one year later, designating worker cooperation as an integral component of its entire mission: "We have provided for thorough instruction in the principles of co-operation. We will have it instilled into the student's mind that no greater blow can be struck at labor than that which makes its products insecure" (Bancroft 1952; Stanford 1987). Courses in cooperation were part of the original curriculum. Yet, the spatial arrangement of the university city became the primary means of conveying these labor principles and of creating a space to make the future formation of a currently unavailable collective subjectivity possible. Among other features, the monumental use of the quadrangle, or "main quad"—a design element that had never been used in American education and whose only American predecessor is the parallelograms designed for Robert Owen's cooperative utopian community of New Harmony—unified and interlocked all university buildings into a comprehensive urban plan.

Not only is the spatial syntax of the American campus a direct product of the principles of cooperation, the internal structure, identity, and classroom practice of the profession in the early decades of the twentieth century were beholden to principles of free labor and the guild. As Taylorist automation upheaves American traditions of craft labor, the self-managing systems developed by the artisan class are displaced and extended in the process of modernizing higher education through the rhetoric of liberal humanism. Christopher Newfield shows that the American university instituted liberal humanism by prolonging a number of nineteenth-century free labor principles to characterize modern academic labor: the practice of experiential knowledge; the value of self-development; support for autonomous individual agency; labor practices free from commerce; and work as a process involving enjoyment (2004, 48–56). By espousing labor based on autonomy and aesthetic practices—self-directed work evaluated by affiliated practitioners and premised on training and cultivating younger colleagues in collaborative settings—university professors established working conditions that assimilated antimanagerial theories of free labor. The earlier experiments of urban classrooms now give way to those in schoolrooms, and the site-specific educative qualities of craft labor—themselves iterations of eighteenth- and nineteenth-century georgic sensibilities—provide the raw material of John Dewey's (1938, 40) experiential philosophy of education: "A primary responsibility of educators is that they not only be aware of the general principle of the shaping of actual experience by environing conditions, but that they also recognize in the concrete what surroundings are conducive to having experiences that lead to growth. Above all, they should know how to utilize the surroundings, physical and social, that exist so as to extract from them all that they have to contribute to building up experiences that are worth while." Dewey introduces a theory and practice that criticizes the traditional schoolroom's idea of learning as the acquisition of information, skills, and credentials that have been already worked out, so as to ensure the future will be just as the past. Yet experiential learning is not progressive in itself. For Dewey, only the action of *situating* the purpose, method, and subject matter of experience has educative potential (1938, 22). The unforeseen, idiosyncratic, and differentiated possibilities of experience within an educative environment are its primary virtues, and the work to alchemize that unique situation is among its contributions to the necessarily continual critique and reinvention of the democratic project.

In the subsequent "golden age" of the university, federal public policy fueled the growth of basic research, and the institution gave way to bureaucratic organizational structures, while providing affordable and accessible mass education through liberal arts meant to prepare a diverse citizenship capable of engaging national and international problems.[5] New approaches to humanist study and the development of theory significantly altered what was taught in the classroom as well as how it was taught. By the 1960s, intellectual energy had shifted to examine how the classroom functions as a representation of consciousness to maintain capital and nation-state governance. Early studies of this process challenged liberal education doctrines that identified schools as forces of democracy, instead noting their impact on social management and reproduction of labor relationships through delivering norms and expectations to future workers in their youth (Apple 1979; Bowles and Gintis 1976). Later, the materiality and formal structure of the classroom pulled focus as a powerful instructive mechanism in its own right, regardless of how radical the course reading list might be:

> The hierarchical relationship between teacher and taught is inscribed in the very lay-out of the lecture theater where the seating arrangements—benches

5. Yet Jodi Melamed (2011) identifies a "racial liberalism" at work in this era, which frames anti-racial discourse as an organizing strategy for US capitalist hegemony following the war that enables institutions like the American university to idealize, imagine, and anticipate but never achieve their espoused egalitarian and liberal values.

> rising in tiers before a raised lectern—dictate the flow of information and serve to "naturalize" professorial authority . . . These decisions help to set the limits not only on what is taught but on *how* it is taught. Here the buildings literally reproduce in concrete terms prevailing (ideological) notions about what education *is* . . . In this case, the frames of our thinking have been translated into actual bricks and mortar. (Hebdige 1997, 12–13)

The question of how to distinguish pedagogical practices that embody capitalist ideologies from those that function in alternative or oppositional relation to capitalist production became a vital framework for applied research in the early 1980s and 1990s. Critical pedagogy directs attention to operations of power in and through the production of values, identities, and social relations and draws questions toward exactly how and why knowledge gets constructed in the classroom, and how and why some constructions are legitimated and celebrated, while others are denied and diminished.[6]

Yet the desire for a classroom that can engage and create new public spheres and political formations that compelled this era's search for a critical pedagogy was perhaps nowhere more successful than in Santa Clara county, where university administrators expanded campus aesthetics to develop new manufacturing regions free of working-class and racial associations, while aligning partnerships with government and private industry in the form of "industrial parks" (Lowen 1997; O'Mara 2005; Washburn 2005). The American geography of academia—generated in direct response to class inequality—now enabled a new corporate culture to declare its presence, and the schoolroom once again became overshadowed by the pedagogical capacity of urban space, as ubiquitous corporate campuses provided the groundwork for Silicon Valley, the first transnational urban formation unique to the era of neoliberalism (Harvey 1989, 160).

Today the idea of the smart city occasions the dominant paradigm of urban futurity, in which mechanisms of learning, understanding, and reasoning are internalized within space through technologies that synchronize urban processes and infrastructures to improve resource efficiency, distribution of services, and urban participation as a way to stem mounting envi-

6. The term *critical pedagogy* was first used in Henry Giroux's 1983 *Theory and Resistance in Education: A Pedagogy for the Opposition*; however, the practice emerges from a long historical legacy of educational movements that aspire to link classroom practices to democratic principles and specifically to the interest of oppressed communities. Maxine Greene (1986) provides an account of the particularly American tradition of critical pedagogy.

ronmental and political crises (Picon 2015). Here urbanism becomes an interactive technology that achieves real-time monitoring, automates decision making, and optimizes consumption and communication patterns to establish sustainability and efficiency as the pinnacle of urban design. This networked architecture relies on citizens interacting with sensing technologies to communicate with and respond to computational environments (Gabrys 2014). Space becomes "smart" through the extraction of and value generation from data created by user activity to mobilize social cooperation as a productive force. What the idea of the smart city confirms—in its orientation of "data supply" as labor—is that the engine of its productive topologies is living knowledge, intelligence, experience, and subjectivity. A smart city is a classroom achieved by investing landscape with pedagogical agency, not only in the way citizens socially create information to reveal patterns of knowledge in the city, but also in the way this use then designs material infrastructure, subject formation, and modes of governance, initiating new georgic modalities into twenty-first-century urbanism.

The classroom, then, is never solely shaped by social and cultural practices but is also firmly embedded in production processes and world economic activity. It is now impossible and detrimental to separate pedagogical practice, the governance of universities, and the educative agency at work in the social formations of contemporary cities. Indeed the political gains that follow from the collective power of academic workers to withhold their labor by striking—in response to precarious labor contracts, unlivable wages, attacks on academic freedom and faculty unions, and other assaults on those in the teaching profession—reveals the extent to which the university, and specifically the work performed in the classroom, makes possible this institution's primary function to matriculate students and to produce degrees that draw millions of dollars in tuition, accreditation, tax designations, and federal and state government grants (Dyke and Bates 2019; Entin 2005; Fuelling 2023). Strengthening interunion alliances among university and industry workers provides increasingly effective tactics to alter the financial, administrative, and labor operations of the neoliberal university.

Yet in addition to affiliations that come from situating educators within the material conditions of labor and the working class, it is equally necessary to insist on broader visions of social change that emerge when we identify how labor and the working class is and always has been the source of knowledge production. Pedagogy links classroom practice to this process and history within capitalism, which is increasingly perceptible, no longer in minor or marginal experiments on the edge of town, but in the classroom structures of the smart city and in globalized urbanization itself. How might the spatial relationships that produce learning—and threaten the security of current regimes of professionalization, as much as the privatization of algorithmic infrastructures does, by recognizing knowledge making as a collective, embodied, situated, and environmental practice—be named and socialized as a critical function of advanced education?

In this context, pedagogical practice is a direct means of politicizing and historicizing the classrooms and institutions we aim to transform. Attending to how classroom practices absorb the socialization, value, and wealth of collective labor's experiential methods of learning provides access to entire histories of occluded futures, ruptures, and missed opportunities that invoke comparative precursors to the present moment. These early urban classrooms also warrant attention to index conceptualizations of the relation between spatial form and knowledge production explicitly conceived in their spatial practice, as well as to situate the recurring necessity to construct pedagogical landscapes as technologies that align forces of production to class formation, regardless of their ideological intention and idealist anticipation, as the means of addressing the most urgent social crises of their time.

What these classrooms announce and advance is the way labor relationships produce knowledge. In identifying the educative quality of production, we direct attention to how value-as-knowledge takes social form. Specifically, designating a space as pedagogical puts educative value into a geography that is also an educating object producing the means of knowledge creation. The very idea of the "classroom," "campus," "smart city," and so on is then significant as a momentary time stamp in which a mode of production is imagined and realized at once as a concrete material form *and* a social-spatial practice. Such landscapes articulate a collective production process materialized into an object of production. Certainly these spaces are gripped within a structure of exploitation in and as capital; yet they allow us to identify the stakes involved in their pedagogical logic, which includes sensitivity to the emergence of radically different economic arrangements.

Restoring the materiality of pedagogy—the work done in the classroom—to the center of discussions of higher education requires such work to be integrated into contemporary learning environments that articulate urban space, not solely monuments, as a *site* of knowledge production. Critical studies of the classroom must then not only acknowledge teaching and learning as situated collective activities, but also examine how the labor of knowledge making is situated within global sites and circulations of labor practices, which now open toward collaborations beyond class and beyond the classroom that are no less pedagogical.

References

Apple, Michael W. 1979. *Ideology and Curriculum*. New York: Routledge.

Appleby, Joyce. 1982. "Commercial Farming and the 'Agrarian Myth' in the Early Republic." *Journal of American History* 68 (4): 833–49.

Bancroft, Hubert Howe. 1952. *History of the Life of Leland Stanford*. Oakland: Biobooks.

Bowles, Samuel, and Herbert Gintis. 1976. *Schooling in Capitalist America*. New York: Basic Books.

Buurma, Rachel Sagner, and Laura Heffernan. 2021. *The Teaching Archive: A New History for Literary Study*. Chicago: University of Chicago Press.

Cohen, Benjamin R. 2009. *Notes from the Ground Science, Soil, and Society in the American Countryside*. New Haven, CT: Yale University Press.

Dal Co, Francesco. 1979. "From Parks to Region: Progressive Ideology and the Reform of the American City." In *The American City: From the Civil War to the New Deal*. Giorgio Ciucci, Francesco Dal Co, Mario Manieri-Elia, and Manfredo Tafuri, translated by Barbara Luigi La Penta, 143–292. Cambridge, MA: MIT Press.

Dewey, John. 1938. *Experience and Education*. New York: MacMillan.

Dyke, Erin, and Brendan Muckian Bates. 2019. "Educators Striking for a Better World: The Significance of Social Movement and Solidarity Unionisms." *Berkeley Review of Education* 9 (1). https://doi.org/10.5070/B89146423.

Eisinger, Chester E. 1947. "The Freehold Concept in 18th Century American Letters." *William and Mary Quarterly* 4 (1): 42–59.

Entin, Joseph. 2005. "Contingent Teaching, Corporate Universities, and the Academic Labor Movement." *Radical Teacher*, no. 73, 26–32.

French, Stanley. 1974. "The Cemetery as Cultural Institution: The Establishment of Mount Auburn and the 'Rural Cemetery' Movement." *American Quarterly* 26 (1): 37–59.

Fuelling, Mathias. 2023. "Blow It Up." *Verso*, February 16. https://www.versobooks.com/blogs/news/5563-blow-it-up.

Gabrys, Jennifer. 2014. "Programming Environments: Environmentality and Citizen Sensing in the Smart City." *Environment and Planning D: Society and Space* 32 (1): 30–48.

Giroux, Henry. 1983. *Theory and Resistance in Education: A Pedagogy for the Opposition*. South Hadley, MA: Bergin and Garvey.

Greene, Maxine. 1986. "In Search of a Critical Pedagogy." *Harvard Education Review* 56 (4): 427–41.

Hardt, Michael. 2007. "Jefferson and Democracy." *American Quarterly* 59 (1): 41–78.

Harvey, David. 1989. *The Condition of Postmodernity: An Enquiry into the Origins of Cultural Change*. Oxford: Blackwell.

Hebdige, Dick. 1997. *Subculture: The Meaning of Style*. New York: Routledge.

Kulikoff, Allan. 1992. *The Agrarian Origins of American Capitalism*. Charlottesville: University Press of Virginia.

Lilly, Marie Loretto. 1919. *The Georgic: A Contribution to the Study of the Vergilian Type of Didactic Poetry*. Baltimore: John Hopkins University Press.

Linden-Ward, Blanche. 1989. *Silent City on a Hill: Landscapes of Memory and Boston's Mount Auburn Cemetery*. Columbus: Ohio State University Press.

Lowen, Rebecca. 1997. *Creating the Cold War University: The Transformation of Stanford*. Berkeley: University of California Press.

Melamed, Jodi. 2011. *Represent and Destroy: Rationalizing Violence in the New Racial Capitalism*. Minneapolis: University of Minnesota Press.

Mukerji, Chandra. 2014. "Space and Political Pedagogy at the Gardens of Versailles." *Public Culture* 24 (3): 509–34.

Newfield, Christopher. 2004. *Ivy and Industry: Business and the Making of the American University, 1880–1980*. Durham, NC: Duke University Press.

O'Mara, Margaret Pugh. 2005. *Cities of Knowledge: Cold War Science and the Search for the Next Silicon Valley*. Princeton, NJ: Princeton University Press.

Panofsky, Erwin. 1957. *Gothic Architecture and Scholasticism: An Inquiry into the Analogy of the Arts, Philosophy, and Religion in the Middle Ages*. New York: Meridian.

Picon, Antoine. 2015. *Smart Cities: A Spatialised Intelligence*. London: Wiley.

Roper, Laura Wood. 1973. *FLO: A Biography of Frederick Law Olmsted*. Baltimore: Johns Hopkins Press.

Rudolph, Frederick. 1990. *The American College and University: A History*. Athens: University of Georgia Press.

Scholl, Kathleen G., and Gowri Betrabet Gulwadi. 2015. "Recognizing Campus Landscapes as Learning Spaces." *Journal of Learning Spaces* 4 (1): 53–60.

Smith, Henry Nash. (1950) 2007. *Virgin Land: The American West as Symbol and Myth*. New York: Vintage; Boston: Harvard University Press. Citations refer to Harvard University Press edition.

Stanford, Leland. 1887. "Labor and Capital: Views of Senator Stanford of California." *New York Tribune*, May 14.

Stanford, Leland. 1987. "Address of the Signing of the Deed, 26 November 1885." In *Stanford University: The Founding Grant with Amendments, Legislation, and Court Decrees*. Stanford, CA: Stanford University Press.

Sturges, Mark. 2011. "Enclosing the Commons: Thomas Jefferson, Agrarian Independence, and Early American Land Policy, 1774–1789." *Virginia Magazine of History and Biography* 119 (1): 42–74.

Sweet, Timothy. 2002. *American Georgics: Economy and Environment in Early American Literature, 1580–1864*. Philadelphia: University of Pennsylvania Press.

Thelin, John R. 2011. *A History of American Higher Education*. Baltimore: Johns Hopkins University Press.

Thornton, Tamara Plakins. 1989. *Cultivating Gentlemen: The Meaning of Country Life among the Boston Elite, 1785–1860*. New Haven, CT: Yale University Press.

Upton, Dell. 2008. *Another City: Urban Life and Urban Spaces in the New American Republic*. New Haven, CT: Yale University Press.

Washburn, Jennifer. 2005. *University Inc.: The Corporate Corruption of American Higher Education*. New York: Basic Books.

Williams, Raymond. 1983. *Keywords: A Vocabulary of Culture and Society*. New York: Oxford University Press.
Woods, Mary N. 1985. "Thomas Jefferson and the University of Virginia: Planning the Academic Village." *Journal of the Society of Architectural Historians* 44 (3): 266–83.

C

Critical University Studies

Rana M. Jaleel, Isaac Kamola, and Heather Steffen

The term *critical university studies* (CUS) identifies a strand of scholarship within the humanities and humanistic social sciences that examines the social role higher education plays in reproducing labor and capital. The field grew out of a body of work written during the 1990s and early 2000s, often by activist scholars engaged in campus organizing and unionization efforts. The term *critical university studies* was later developed as an effort to understand this work as constituting a recognizable scholarly field.

Because CUS remains a field in formation, we provisionally define it through key texts, questions, and debates, as well as the institution building and professionalization that take place around the term. We include both scholars who have embraced the name critical university studies as a marker of their intellectual contributions and those who critique the field, and we consider potential avenues for future work under the heading of CUS.

Field Formation

During the 1990s and early 2000s, union organizing within higher education, especially among contingent faculty and graduate students, inspired a growing body of work that turned critical attention to the corporatization and neoliberalization of US higher education (e.g., Johnson, Kavanagh, and Mattson 2003; Martin 1998). Such work focused on student debt, the rise of contingent faculty, and contemporary labor organizing across the landscape of higher education (e.g., Bousquet 2008; Readings 1996; Slaughter and Leslie 1997; Washburn 2005). Ex-AAUP president Cary Nelson's early, pre-Zionist work, including *Manifesto of a Tenured Radical* (1997a) and *Will Teach for Food: Academic Labor in Crisis* (1997b), might be productively understood as a throughline or blueprint for this moment. As a founding work in CUS, even as this scholarship predates that nomenclature, it centers the casualization of academic labor and the burgeoning academic labor movement. The CUS framework thus explicitly brought together disparate scholarship on academic labor and capitalism. For example, with the advent of the term, the privatization of science research funding (Lieberwitz 2005) could be considered under the same umbrella as scholarship theorizing academic labor as socially reproduced and contested "mental labor" (Ross 2000). This emerging body of scholarship was largely created at the intersections of, and often outside, academic disciplinary debates.

The idea of naming a field *critical university studies* was seemingly first broached at a series of conferences organized at the University of Minnesota. Following an unsuccessful graduate student union drive and a clerical workers' strike that yielded few concessions from the administration, graduate workers at Minnesota organized "Re-thinking the University: Labor, Knowledge, Value Conference" (2008), "Re-working the University: Visions, Strategies, Demands Conference" (2009), and "Beneath the University, the Commons" (2010). These conferences brought together graduate student unionists, scholars of higher education, faculty, university staff, undergraduate students, and others to discuss and theorize the state of higher education. At the 2009 conference, the term *critical university studies* was developed by the collective of conference attendees, and in 2011, it was used in print for the first time as the title of a panel at the Modern Language Association convention, co-organized by Heather Steffen and Jeffrey J. Williams.

In 2012, Williams's *Chronicle of Higher Education* essay "Deconstructing Academe: The Birth of Critical University Studies" became the first publication to use *critical university studies* as a term and propose it as a field. In this piece, Williams defined CUS as critical because it "focuses on the ways in which current practices serve power or wealth and contribute to injustice or inequality rather than social hope" and as a wide-ranging area of studies to emphasize its "cross-disciplinary character, focused on a particular issue," one that promiscuously draws on "research from any relevant area to approach the problem." Williams (2012) draws an analogy between CUS and critical legal studies, arguing that, like CLS's relationship to the law, CUS understands the university as deeply enmeshed within—not outside—social structures of power. Just as CLS "wished to show that the law was not neutral or impartial, but served dominant social and economic interests," Williams frames CUS as challenging the assumption that the university is a "neutral institution for the public good." In doing so, Williams's vision of CUS "foregrounds [the university's] politics, particularly how it is a site of struggle between private commercial interests and more public ones." One goal of CUS is to theorize the post-1970s trend away from state-backed support for public education and toward a neoliberal, increasingly privatized model of higher education.

The CUS framework encompasses the literature, broadly defined, of the 1990s and early 2000s that addressed academic capitalism and university corporatization. These critics paid special attention to the interplay between corporate and university governance logics and brought organizational questions into conversation with a reinvigorated and rapidly growing body of work focused on precarity. Marc Bousquet and Christopher Newfield, for example, contributed early on to the emerging and expansive CUS framework. Bousquet's work developed in tandem with graduate employee activism within the Modern Language Association and branched into a series of articles demystifying and deconstructing key terms in academic labor discourse. Bousquet's inquiries culminated in 2008 with the landmark book *How the University Works: Higher Education and the Low-Wage Nation*. Rather than treating the problems of academic labor as external to the operations of the university and subject to the whims of a separate market, Bousquet analyzes academic labor as part of a system of exploitation. For Bousquet, the university is a system of profit designed to mass produce highly trained low-wage workers: ABD (all but dissertation) graduate students, contingent faculty, and student workers are all similarly being trained to meet the labor needs of an increasingly proletarianized knowledge-based economy. Bousquet's analysis famously renders the PhD holder not as the success story of a university system dedicated to training the next generation of scholars, but as the "waste product" of the academic labor system. As Bousquet (2008, 21) puts it: "Under casualization [of academic labor], it makes very little sense to view the graduate student as potentially a 'product' for a 'market' in tenure-track jobs. For many graduate employees, the receipt of a Ph.D. signifies the end, and not the beginning, of a long teaching career. Most graduate students are already laboring at the only academic job they'll ever have—hence, the importance for organized graduate student labor of inscribing the designation 'graduate employee' in law and discourse." Far from indicating system failure, ABDs are a crucial component of the academic labor system, even more so than PhDs. They are cheap, disposable workers capable of filling teaching slots throughout the higher education landscape, from research universities (as graduate student workers) to community colleges (as adjuncts and full faculty members).

Student and faculty organizing against the decimation of the public education project also inspired Newfield. Attuned particularly to program cuts and tuition hikes in the University of California system and informed by his long history of service within UC's governance structure, Newfield's *Unmaking the Public University* (2008) argues that the dire political and financial straits in which public universities now find themselves cannot be explained by economic downturns or necessary restructuring. Instead, the dismantling of public education is part of a conservative project designed to short circuit the democratizing effects of public education across US society. Newfield understands public higher education to be largely responsible for the expansion of a multiracial middle class in the mid-twentieth century. The creation of such a middle class resulted in considerable public support for the university, making it difficult for antitax activists to justify defunding these popular institutions. To overcome this, throughout the 1990s and early 2000s, conservatives manufactured the *culture wars*—a term into which "campus hate-speech codes, school prayer, Afrocentric school curricula, abortion, politically correct language, family values, affirmative action, the racial distribution of intelligence, deconstructionist literary criticism, sexual harassment policy, the Great Books, hardcore pornography, publicly funded art, and many other fractious things" could be gathered and opposed (Menand 1995; see also Bérubé and Nelson 1995).

For Newfield, the culture wars—and their attempt to radically redefine the meanings of social equality and the role of the state—should be understood as the opening salvo in the economic attack on higher education. They delegitimized the institution to justify defunding it. Newfield's subsequent book, *The Great Mistake: How We Wrecked Public Universities and How We Can Fix Them* (2016), maps the "devolutionary cycle" that intensified following this initial onslaught. Once the university was no longer perceived as a public benefit, it became financially dependent on external donors and increasingly higher tuition, justifying further state budget cuts and expanded reliance on student debt. These changes lessened the quality while increasing the private cost of higher education, further validating cuts in public funding and spreading social distrust toward the institution. In Newfield's view, the university, once the core of a culturally egalitarian middle class, became an institution that reproduced a highly educated low-wage workforce, forming the foundation of a highly inegalitarian and plutocratic economy.

In the decade since the inception of critical university studies, the term has been adopted for institution building and professionalization across disciplines and national borders. Johns Hopkins University Press in the United States and Palgrave in the UK both host CUS book series. Dozens of articles include "critical university studies" in their titles, and numerous campus reading groups, online reference guides, and course syllabi have been organized around the term. The website Advancing Critical University Studies across Africa collects CUS resources from across the continent and the globe.[1] From 2007 to 2022, Newfield and Michael Meranze ran the influential blog *Remaking the University*, which hosted discussions of a broad range of issues concerning university life and policy, including funding sustainability, academic freedom, academic labor, and the future of the humanities.[2] But CUS has not been without its critics.

Responses to Critical University Studies

While the term *critical university studies* originated as a framework for organizing scholarship on the increasing precarity of the academic profession, including its reliance on graduate and adjunct labor and the exploitation of its staff and service workers, this analysis has been criticized by those who see the CUS project as implicitly or explicitly idealizing a so-called golden age mid-twentieth-century democratic past from which the university subsequently devolved. For instance, Abigail Boggs and Nick Mitchell's "Critical University Studies and the Crisis Consensus" (2018) takes explicit aim at CUS-identified authors, among others, for a purported romanticization of the university as a newly imperiled public good, under threat and in crisis: "With the glossy patina of an ostensibly progressive liberal humanism, the crisis consensus invokes the university as the protector of time-honored and -tested values, one whose defense requires a temporality characterized simultaneously by urgency and nostalgia" (434). For Boggs and Mitchell, such a historical understanding (what they call "temporal positioning") of the university inadvertently limits the terrain of inquiry: If the university is newly under attack by capital and therefore must be urgently defended to preserve the public good, then the "methodological injunction"

1. "Welcome to Critical University Studies," ACUSAfrica, accessed January 19, 2024, https://www.acusafrica.com.

2. *Remaking the University*, renamed *Remaking II: Long Revolution*, accessed January 19, 2024, http://utotherescue.blogspot.com.

to "repair" the university becomes an intellectual requirement—one that positions "leftist knowledge formations, relationships, and counternormative practices of valuation" in the service of "notably non-leftist political imaginaries" (436). To demonstrate the possibilities opened by abandoning the crisis consensus, Boggs and Mitchell review works with an alternate, "abolitionist" perspective, sharpening attention to "the constitutive and sustaining force of capital accumulation" as a context and driver for the development of today's higher education systems (450). In contrast to CUS's call to rescue the university as a threatened public good, Boggs and Mitchell contend, "an abolitionist approach would question the imperative to save the university, starting with the question of what is the university to be saved or what parts of it are worth saving" (462).

Coined by Eli Meyerhoff in his *Beyond Education* (2019), the term *abolitionist university studies* (AUS) names scholarship that emphasizes the university's role in perpetuating racial colonial capitalist regimes of power and that begins from the insight that "one of the defining features of the university in the U.S. context is the accumulation of lands, lives, resources, and relationships" (Boggs et al. 2019). The foundational AUS text, "Abolitionist University Studies: An Invitation," co-authored by Boggs, Meyerhoff, Mitchell, and Zachary Schwartz-Weinstein (2019), shifts the historical focus of CUS from the post–World War II university to emphasize the land grant/grab university's inception in the years after the putative end of US slavery (Lee and Ahtone 2020). This explicit turn to abolition and abolitionist practices—rooted in the Black radical tradition, which aims to end slavery in all its guises, even in the wake of juridical emancipation—suggests a fundamental dismantling and building anew. AUS scholarship seeks not only to open the workings of the university to political and economic critique, but expressly to "unearth the counter-memories of people who have been buried in the dominant histories" (Boggs et al. 2019, 4). To highlight the university's role in settler racial capitalism, AUS augments CUS's focus on the market relationships and injustices that define the university as a worksite. For AUS, the university is not only a site of labor exploitation but also an agent of extraction, accumulation, and dispossession—of value making beyond the wage relationship.

AUS centers the "post-slavery university" after 1865 rather than the massification of the mid-twentieth-century university. This periodization "emphasize[s] the unfinished work of the abolitionist movement by situating

US universities after the Civil War as continuous with a broader terrain of struggles pitting what W. E. B. Du Bois called the 'counter-revolution' of capital and property against abolitionism and Reconstruction" (Boggs et al. 2019, 4).

This historiographical shift enables abolitionist university studies' potential to address marginalized histories of labor, education, and knowledge production that are not always the focus of CUS. Like the decolonizing "scyborg" figure of la paperson's *A Third University Is Possible* (2017), AUS would consider the activist origins and subsequent disciplining of ethnic and gender studies as institutional departments and interdisciplinary fields (Nash and Owens 2015a) and the accompanying "adjunctification" of the profession (Schwartz-Weinstein 2016) as central to the study of contemporary US higher education. Other key nodes of what might be called AUS include investigations of the predation of universities on surrounding communities via tax breaks and real estate holdings afforded by their putative "nonprofit" status (Baldwin 2021); of the mutually beneficial relationships between universities and rightwing donor networks (Wilson and Kamola 2021); universities' participation in the ongoing project of settler-colonial land dispossession (Lee and Ahtone 2020; Stein 2022); and the global connections between universities and prisons, both military and civilian, and the gender and sexual politics of academic repression (Chatterjee and Maira 2014; Doyle 2015).

Futures

Whether AUS is truly a project separate from CUS or whether it is an analytic tendency within CUS remains to be seen.[3] CUS has always been a porous interdisciplinary inquiry premised, like AUS, on challenging the notion that the university is an unwavering conscript in the service of the public good. Differences and disputes in the study of "the" university, while at times rooted in profound theoretical disagreements, are as often the outcome of varying disciplinary investments and genealogies. For example, despite its portrayal in "Abolitionist University Studies: An Invitation," not

3. For a discussion that understands CUS as "draw[ing] from scholars who trace the origins of the American university to the slave trade, racial science, and Native American ethnic cleansing projects, as well as scholars who bring abolitionist and decolonial stances to highlight how the university continues to perpetuate state interests, carceral and settler logics, empire, and antiblackness," see Singh and Vora (2023, 40).

all CUS scholarship valorizes the post–World War II university as an unimpeachable golden age. Yet AUS's concern with the institutionalization of ethnic, gender, and other activist disciplines within the university as both radical tradition and part of a long history of academic colonial racial capitalism is a necessary intervention into the trajectory of much CUS scholarship focused on the university's changing relationship to capitalist accumulation. While CUS and AUS might privilege different historical periodizations and topical focuses, both tend to situate "the" university as their shared object of study. Both CUS- and AUS-identified work can do more to problematize the ways in which public land grant universities and elite private research institutions have become the implicit or explicit institutions being studied, while substantially less attention is paid to community colleges, smaller state and regional institutions, non-elite private colleges, technical schools, tribal schools, and HBCUs.

Future CUS and AUS scholarship might productively trace disciplinary and genealogical investments in the study of the university even as they continue to excavate the relationship between universities and labor. Such directions might engage other, parallel work on the university and public education that does not automatically travel under the banner of CUS or AUS. These may include progressive alternative educational projects and formats, such as the open school movement (Kohl 2009), community educational and outreach initiatives promoted by groups like the Black Panthers and the Young Lords (A. Nelson 2011), and the long history of public scholarship beyond the university charted in Roopika Risam's forthcoming work on "insurgent academics" (2023). Future work in CUS or AUS might also more explicitly engage with work in gender studies and queer studies that considers the place of gender and sex within the university. Explorations in this vein might follow the unevenness of disciplinary knowledge across public and private universities, as in Matt Brim's (2020) efforts to relocate queer studies from elite spaces to working-class peoples and places. New work might also engage more deeply with feminist studies' "pursuits of institutionalization alongside our rigorous critiques of the university, and our pleasures in the interdisciplinary and institutional 'travels' of women's studies' key analytics like intersectionality and transnationalism" (Nash and Owens 2015b, viii). Future work in CUS and AUS might also turn to scholarship from Indigenous perspectives, including histories of Indian schools and other weaponizations of government-sponsored education (Gram 2016), as well as analyses of the insurgent potential of pedagogical modes embedded in Indigenous philosophies and narratives (Grande 2015; Simpson 2007). Finally, CUS and AUS could offer more dedicated work on the relationship of US universities to universities abroad, following the lead of scholars like Neha Vora (2018), Isaac Kamola (2019), and Andrew Ross (2008). Beyond the relationships between universities in the US and elsewhere, CUS and AUS might broadly analyze local, regional, transnational, and international linkages between education projects and geopolitics. Existing work tracing the historical development of Middle Eastern studies or Asian studies, for example—including imperialist and anti-imperialist investments in area studies (Khalil 2016; Lanza 2017; Lockman 2016)—would provide a strong foundation.

When major US-based research institutions are not presumed to be the quintessential "university" to be studied, a fuller portrait of higher education can emerge. Such an orientation might bring us closer to the kind of study of universities that Andrew Ross wrote about in 2010: "To be effective advocates for the profession and for the cause of education, we need to recognize that our workplaces are subject to more than one gravitational force, and also that universities exert their own pull on other sectors" (Ross 2010). Following the pull of "the university"—across times, geographies, geopolitics, and sectors—certainly dispenses with the romance of an ahistorical, singular "university" while ceding neither the power nor the potential of universities to affect, for the better and for the worse, how we live and think and learn.

References

Baldwin, Davarian L. 2021. *In the Shadow of the Ivory Tower: How Universities Are Plundering Our Cities*. New York: Bold Type.

Bérubé, Michael, and Cary Nelson, eds. 1995. *Higher Education under Fire: Politics, Economics, and the Crisis of the Humanities*. New York: Routledge.

Boggs, Abigail, Eli Meyerhoff, Nick Mitchell, and Zach Schwartz-Weinstein. 2019. "Abolitionist University Studies: An Invitation." *Abolition: A Journal of Insurgent Politics*, August 28. https://abolitionjournal.org/abolitionist-university-studies-an-invitation/.

Boggs, Abigail, and Nick Mitchell. 2018. "Critical University Studies and the Crisis Consensus." *Feminist Studies* 44 (2): 432–63.

Bousquet, Marc. 2008. *How the University Works: Higher Education and the Low-Wage Nation*. New York: New York University Press.

Brim, Matt. 2020. *Poor Queer Studies: Confronting Elitism in the University*. Durham, NC: Duke University Press.

Chatterjee, Piya, and Sunaina Maira, eds. 2014. *The Imperial University: Academic Repression and Scholarly Dissent*. Minneapolis: University of Minnesota Press, 2014.

Doyle, Jennifer. 2015. *Campus Sex, Campus Security*. South Pasadena, CA: Semiotext(e).
Gram, John R. 2016. "Acting Out Assimilation: Playing Indian and Becoming American in the Federal Indian Boarding Schools." *American Indian Quarterly* 40 (3): 251–73.
Grande, Sandy. 2015. *Red Pedagogy: Native American Social and Political Thought*. Lanham, MD: Rowman and Littlefield.
Johnson, Benjamin, Patrick Kavanagh, and Kevin Mattson, eds. 2003. *Steal This University: The Rise of the Corporate University and the Academic Labor Movement*. New York: Routledge.
Kamola, Isaac. 2019. *Making the World Global: US Universities and the Production of the Global Imaginary* Durham, NC: Duke University Press.
Khalil, Osamah F. 2016. *America's Dream Palace: Middle East Expertise and the Rise of the National Security State*. Cambridge, MA: Harvard University Press.
Kohl, Herbert R. 2009. *The Herb Kohl Reader: Awakening the Heart of Teaching*. New York: New Press.
Lanza, Fabio. 2017. *The End of Concern: Maoist China, Activism, and Asian Studies*. Durham, NC: Duke University Press.
la paperson. 2017. *A Third University Is Possible*. Minneapolis: University of Minnesota Press.
Lee, Robert, and Tristan Ahtone. 2020. "Land-Grab Universities." *High Country News* March 30. https://www.hcn.org/issues/52-4/indigenous-affairs-education-land-grab-universities/.
Lieberwitz, Risa L. 2005. "Confronting the Privatization and Commercialization of Academic Research: An Analysis of Social Implications at the Local, National, and Global Levels." *Indiana Journal of Global Legal Studies* 12 (1): 109–52.
Lockman, Zachary. 2016. *Field Notes: The Making of Middle East Studies in the United States*. Stanford, CA: Stanford University Press.
Martin, Randy, ed. 1998. *Chalk Lines: The Politics of Work in the Managed University*. Durham, NC: Duke University Press.
Menand, Louis. 1995. "Mixed Paint." *Mother Jones*, March/April. https://www.motherjones.com/politics/1995/03/mixed-paint/.
Meyerhoff, Eli. 2019. *Beyond Education: Radical Studying for Another World*. Minneapolis: University of Minnesota Press.
Nash, Jennfer C., and Emily A. Owens, eds. 2015a. "Institutional Feelings: Practicing Women's Studies in the Corporate University." Special issue, *Feminist Formations* 27 (3).
Nash, Jennifer C., and Emily A. Owens. 2015b. "Introduction: Institutional Feelings: Practicing Women's Studies in the Corporate University." *Feminist Formations* 27 (3): vii–xi.
Nelson, Alondra. 2011. *Body and Soul: The Black Panther Party and the Fight against Medical Discrimination*. Minneapolis: University of Minnesota Press.
Nelson, Cary. 1997a. *Manifesto of a Tenured Radical*. New York: New York University Press.
Nelson, Cary, ed. 1997b. *Will Teach for Food: Academic Labor in Crisis*. Minneapolis: University of Minnesota Press.
Newfield, Christopher. 2008. *Unmaking the Public University: The Forty-Year Assault on the Middle Class*. Cambridge, MA: Harvard University Press.
Newfield, Christopher. 2016. *The Great Mistake: How We Wrecked Public Universities and How We Can Fix Them*. Baltimore: Johns Hopkins University Press.
Readings, Bill. 1996. *The University in Ruins*. Cambridge, MA: Harvard University Press.
Risam, Roopika. 2023. "Training for Insurgent Academics: Historicizing Current Trends in the Higher Ed Public Humanities." Webinar, June 28, 2023. Posted July 10, 2023, by the National Humanities Alliance, YouTube. https://www.youtube.com/watch?v=y6F9lOVc4T4.

Ross, Andrew. 2000. "The Mental Labor Problem." *Social Text* 18 (2): 1–31.

Ross, Andrew. 2008. "Global U." In *The University against Itself: The NYU Strike and the Future of the Academic Workplace*, edited by Monika Krause, Mary Nolan, Michael Palm, and Andrew Ross. Philadelphia: Temple University Press.

Ross, Andrew. 2010. "The Corporate Analogy Unravels." *Chronicle of Higher Education*, October 17. https://www.chronicle.com/article/the-corporate-analogy-unravels/.

Schwartz-Weinstein, Zach. 2016. "The Fantasy and Fate of Ethnic Studies in an Age of Uprisings: An Interview with Nick Mitchell." *Undercommoning* (blog), July 13. https://undercommoning.org/nick-mitchell-interview/.

Simpson, Audra. 2007. "On Ethnographic Refusal: Indigeneity, 'Voice' and Colonial Citizenship." *Junctures: The Journal for Thematic Dialogue*, no. 9, 67–80.

Singh, Vineeta, and Neha Vora. 2023. "Critical University Studies." *Annual Review of Anthropology* 52 (1): 39–54.

Slaughter, Sheila, and Larry L. Leslie. 1997. *Academic Capitalism: Politics, Policies, and the Entrepreneurial University*. Baltimore: Johns Hopkins University Press.

Soley, Lawrence C. 1995. *Leasing the Ivory Tower: The Corporate Takeover of Academia*. Boston: South End Press.

Stein, Sharon. 2022. *Unsettling the University: Confronting the Colonial Foundations of US Higher Education*. Baltimore: Johns Hopkins University Press.

Vora, Neha. 2018. *Teach for Arabia: American Universities, Liberalism, and Transnational Qatar*. Stanford, CA: Stanford University Press.

Washburn, Jennifer. 2005. *University Inc.: The Corporate Corruption of Higher Education*. New York: Basic Books.

Williams, Jeffrey J. 2012. "Deconstructing Academe: The Birth of Critical University Studies." *Chronicle of Higher Education*, February 19. https://www.chronicle.com/article/deconstructing-academe/.

Wilson, Ralph, and Isaac Kamola. 2021. *Free Speech and Koch Money: Manufacturing a Campus Culture War*. London: Pluto.

D

Debt

Eleni Schirmer and Jason Wozniak

American higher education has always been reliant on debt. Since the prerepublic era, the institution has never been fully funded by the state, relying instead on student tuition dollars, private donations, and debt financing to maintain operations and make capital improvements to campuses. Even during the so-called golden era of funding for public universities, roughly 1945–60, Congress authorized the federal government to lend money to students to attend college, rather than financing the institution itself. But the aid to students often didn't cover the full cost of operations and expenses. As a result, institutions took to charging tuition—putting students into debt—and pursuing other private financing options, such as taking on significant amounts of institutional debt. The shape of federal aid to higher education—meager subsidies for individual students—has meant that debt has accumulated on both sides of the ledger: on the backs of students and colleges' own books (Shermer 2021).

In the United States, universities have come under control of the contemporary financial elite. These actors have shaped universities in at least three ways: They lobbied for lower taxes; they led the financial institutions that advise and lend to universities; and they became members of university governing boards, putting them at the fiduciary helm of colleges. When the financial elite lobbied for lower taxes, they effectively called for a reduction in the amount of state aid available to fund universities, thus compelling universities to seek private funding. According to a recent survey on trends in educational funding, philanthropic support of education has sharply increased. Over the last fiscal year, total nonstate contributions have risen more than $6.6 billion, an increase of 12.5 percent. Of that total, 61 percent came from organizations, including corporations and foundations (Kaplan 2023, 6–7). While these contributions are often considered "gifts" they instantiate a debt. The university that receives is the university that owes a wealthy donor, corporation, or foundation a debt. Donors "expect their money to buy a voice in university affairs" (Chen and Corkery 2023) and increasingly want, and expect, to influence the hiring and firing of administration and faculty, dictate curricula, and shape university governance.

Second, these financial elite often lead the very financial institutions that advise or lend funds to universities. For example, upon becoming a University of California (UC) Board of Regents member in 2002, private equity billionaire Richard Blum brought in Lehman Brothers consultants to advise on UC borrowing. These consultants proposed that the UC system could increase its debt capacity from $1 billion to $11 billion by using general revenue bonds, as well as riskier methods like variable rate bonds and interest rate swaps. which would be backed by UC assets and future income, including tuition, but notably not by tax revenue. The board of regents adopted the policy, and UC bond borrowing jumped from $5 billion in 2003 to $14 billion in 2011 (Eaton 2022, 107). As sociologist Charlie Eaton notes, "UC's move toward general revenue bonds over state public works bonds shifted the orientation of UC executives away from popular democratic engagement via the state legislature and toward an autonomous governance relationship with financial markets" (2022, 107).

Finally, many of these actors sit on university boards of trustees—the very same boards who oversee setting tuition rates, salary schedules, and other materially consequential policies for universities. For example, Kenneth Jarin served as board chair for the Pennsylvania State System of Higher Education Board of Trustees from 2005 to 2011 and is a partner with Ballard Spahr, a finance firm that, among other things, "represents clients across public and private markets and throughout the capital stack in a wide range of complex debt and equity transactions."[1] Both the University of Pennsylvania and the University of Pittsburgh contracted Ballard Spahr in an effort to suppress their employees' unionization efforts (Wolfe 2019). There are many other similar examples. Indeed, the leaders of global financial capitalism now set the policies of universities, infusing a capitalist orientation into the mission of higher education. Debt is a central mechanism within a market-oriented education system.

This mechanism has simultaneously served as a tool for wealth generation for creditors and as a disciplining apparatus wielded against students

1. Ballard Spahr, "Finance," accessed December 19, 2024, https://www.ballardspahr.com/Services/Departments/Finance.

and faculty by the state. For instance, in the sixties, historically marginalized groups enrolled in campuses at higher and higher rates, partially in response to dominant policy ideologies that treated education as the remedy for racial and economic inequalities. Campuses became an important locus of social struggles, cultivating Black Power, antiwar, feminist, and Chicano liberation movements. The state responded to the growth of these movements by revoking the emerging vision of higher education as a public, liberatory institution. They imposed tuition to discipline student power movements. More recently, in spring 2024, student organizers protested their respective universities' financial investments in Israeli weapons and defense, used to accelerate the ongoing destruction of Palestinian life. The student encampments drew critical attention to the connections between the political economy of universities in the United States and genocide abroad. Almost immediately, a group of Republican congresspeople proposed a bill that would exclude student protestors from receiving student debt relief.

As the California Faculty Association notes, as the public higher education student population became darker between 1985 and 2017, the funding got lighter (CFA 2017). Cuts to funding were in part, as Melinda Cooper (2017), Charlie Eaton (2022), and others have shown, key to a larger neoliberal project, often influenced by neoconservative values, to transform higher education in the late twentieth century. Put differently, as students came from increasingly more racially diverse backgrounds, student debt loads increased.

Conservatives and political elites were deeply concerned with new access to higher ed and the revolutionary fervent it sowed (Ferguson 2017). These fears were evinced in statements offered by groups like the Trilateral Commission, which in their *Crisis of Democracy* (Crozier, Huntington, and Watanuki 1975), argued that there was *too much* democracy on college campuses. They were also evinced in the 1971 memo "Attack on American Free Enterprise System," popularly referred to as the Powell Memo, a letter sent by Nixon adviser Justice Lewis F. Powell Jr. to the Chamber of Commerce. The Powell Memo warns that Marxist radicals were indoctrinating students in anti-American (read anticapitalist, anti-imperialist) values and calls for corporate and conservative forces to take a more active role in the war of ideas. Assuming tighter control of higher education policies and priorities was paramount. Conservative leaders, including Ronald Reagan, Milton Freidman, and James Buchanan to name but a few, recognized that decreases in state funding and subsequent increases in both individual and institutional debt loads provided a potent means of disciplining universities and education toward market prerogatives. Debt instantiated an emphasis on human capital formation and return-on-investment logics—and tamped down revolutionary politics. As a gift to capital, student debt imposes more work on students and faculty, robs them of free time they might otherwise use to participate in political organizing, and disincentivizes participation in strikes or other forms of civil disobedience (Gouzoulis 2023).

As such, the increase of student and institutional debt in the neoliberal era should be conceived of as a process of evolving intensification within the American political economy. Although debt has long been a force in higher education, today's era marks an intensification of its powers never seen before.

Over the past four decades, declining state funding, soaring tuition, and flagging postgraduation wages have triggered a $1.7 trillion student debt crisis. The average student leaves college with tens of thousands of dollars of debt, much of which is dischargeable by neither death nor bankruptcy (Cooper 2017). This burden is not equally shared. Black students assume larger and more costly loans than white borrowers; women, on average, carry more student debt than men (Jiménez and Glater 2020; Miller, Nelson, and Dice 2017; Seamster and Charron-Chénier 2017). As scholars and activists rightly note, the student debt crisis is thus a matter of racial, class, and gender justice. A decade of mobilizing has moved student debt from a closeted, individual problem to a public and politicized one. Today's conversation is not about whether to cancel student debt but how much should be canceled and for whom.

Still far less attention has been paid to the other debt crisis in higher education: institutional debt. In the absence of adequate public funding, public universities have increasingly turned to debt financing to fund operations and, especially, capital development projects. Between 2003 and 2016, institutional debt at public and community colleges more than doubled, rising from $73 billion to $151 billion (Eaton et al. 2016). Interest payments on this debt have nearly doubled. Rising student debt is connected to rising institutional debts in critical ways, as significant portions of student tuition services institutional debts. In some cases, students' tuition dollars—that is, pending student debt—have served as collateral for universities' own debt financing (Meister 2009). In an era of declining state and federal revenue for public higher education, credit-rating agencies consider student tuition to be a more reliable source of funding than state appropriations, further solidifying the connections between student debt and institutional debt.

While debt financing may solve universities' short-term cash-flow problems, its long-term political implications are unclear. To date, there is little awareness of the impact of universities' debt financing on organizational priorities, much less on educational inequalities. The relative obscurity of debt financing has contributed to its enshrinement as a university governance tool and a site beyond governing boards, where a financial elite can exercise their power on the operations of universities. Nevertheless, few students, faculty, or staff are aware of the influence of institutional debt on their campuses, much less how movements might resist its command.

What Is Institutional Debt and Why Does It Matter?

In the United States, rising levels of institutional debt at public higher education institutions have been the consequence of the long-term reduction of state funding for public higher education (Mitchell, Leachman, and Saenz 2019). This shift is part of a larger project of economic and political reorganization, what economic sociologist Wolfgang Streeck refers to as the transition from tax states to debt states, whereby public services are no longer financed through tax revenues but through debt (Streeck 2014). As state funding has declined, colleges and universities increasingly finance operations formerly funded by the state, such as building construction and maintenance, as well as fringe benefits. Therefore, state budget cuts to higher education not only reduce public aid but also increase institutions' costs in noneducational arenas. Typically, universities take on debt through a version of municipal bonds, issued by the state or local government and, increasingly, by universities themselves. These bonds pledge that universities will repay their debt, plus interest and fees, to the private financial institutions that secure this financing.

The costs of debt cut into universities' educational spending. As state appropriations fall, universities are forced to cut expenses and increasingly debt finance operations. This, in turn, obliges universities to pay additional debt service expenses (i.e., interest and fees), further drawing down the state appropriation away from educational spending. For example, in 2008 the Commonwealth of Massachusetts stopped financing auxiliary buildings, such as dorms and student recreation centers. Further disinvestment occurred in 2016, when Massachusetts governor Charlie Baker made deeper cuts to capital project funding by slashing state support for academic buildings from nearly 100 percent to 50 percent or below.[2] At Salem State, a public university in Massachusetts, a capital project to build new health and science facilities stands to receive just 37.7 percent of its funding from the state. As a result, the campus will incur more debt to cover the remaining portion. Already debt service payments compose close to 10 percent of the institution's operating budget; in fiscal year 2020, the university paid approximately $17 million in debt service out of an operating budget of $180 million. This sum represents funds that are *not* spent on instructional costs, such as secure, high-paying instructional jobs, needed educational services, or affordable student tuition (Gonsalves and Levy 2021). For these reasons, we consider university debt payments as imposing instructional harm on students and educators.

More than just a financial burden on campuses' budgets, institutional debt constitutes an often invisible power relationship. First, debt determines budget priorities. Debt covenants stipulate payment order: creditors first, everyone and everything else last. Workers get paid, programs get staffed, and tuition gets sets only *after* private creditors have been paid. Bond repayment is almost always prioritized over spending on education or employees, an arrangement often mandated by law.

Second, credit institutions gain an outsized—and largely invisible—role in university governance. With decreased public funding, an institution's access to resources depends on its ability to secure low-interest loans, which, in turn, is a function of its credit rating. As such, credit-rating institutions, private financial institutions that are neither democratically elected nor appointed by elected representatives, have tremendously consequential disciplinary power over universities' priorities. Credit-rating agencies, rather than university community members' needs, dictate the terms on which educational resources will be distributed. This means that credit-rating agencies shape not only the institutions we work in but also the variety and quality of the educational experiences that we offer and that students experience.

2. Department of Capital Assets Management and Maintenance, Commonwealth of Massachusetts, Public Records Request no. 20-283 (January 13, 2021).

Credit-rating agencies are concerned, above all, with a university's ability to generate revenue and secure high returns on investments—*not* a university's pedagogical or community commitments, much less its labor practices or knowledge production. Moody's, a preeminent credit-rating institution, for example, prioritizes a university's branding strength. As it stipulates in its *Higher Education Rating Methodology*, "A strong brand name and reputation allow a university to compete effectively for tuition revenue, private gifts, research grants, faculty and staff, and government support. Market profile, therefore, provides the foundation for a university's long-term financial health and credit rating" (Moody's Investor Services 2019). Moody's prioritization of "brand strength" contributes to the growing trends of universities' advertising budgets (Cellini and Chaudhary 2020). Similarly, Moody's evaluates the degree to which a university is encumbered by government regulations, such as requiring legislative approval to set tuition. As it explains, "Government regulations, political pressure, or a university's mission may limit a university's ability to leverage its brand" (Moody's Investor Services 2019).

Additionally, Moody's appraises the level to which institutions are beholden to democratic governance regimes, such as faculty senates, or labor contracts. As the rating methodology states, "A university's flexibility to increase revenue, and/or reduce expenses, enables it to adapt to changes in its operating environment." Public universities may be subject to regulation of enrollment numbers or tuition and fees that can limit their ability to translate market strength into revenue growth. As major local or regional employers, universities may also face public or political pressure to "maintain staffing during economically challenging times to limit negative economic effects" (Moody's Investor Services 2019). In the eyes of Moody's, a university's capacity to react to economic conditions and events is a function of its market profile, labor costs (including financial commitments related to unionization and tenure), capital intensity, and political environment. That is, from a credit-rating perspective, stronger labor unions, robust internal democratic governance, and legislative decision making all threaten an institution's ability to prioritize creditor repayment. These factors reduce an institution's credit score.

In short, the influence of credit-rating agencies shape universities not only as places of employment but also as providers of education. Their predominant concern with returns on investment shapes universities' educational offerings. By incentivizing universities to maximize revenue streams, for example, they push institutions to shift increasingly toward revenue-generating models of instruction, over and above educational, research, and service needs. Universities offer coursework and programs that bring in the most money for the university, regardless of their benefit to the wider community. This constitutes one of the instructional harms of debt financing.

The rules of debt extract universities' resources, by way of interest and fees, and de-democratize their operations. Matters of significant public concern—such as staffing levels, program offerings, wages, and tuition—are privately determined, often well before the formal budgeting process even begins. The financial imperatives of debt financing distort the instructional missions of universities and threaten academic freedom, by reducing funds for teaching and research as well as by increasing incentives for universities to hire more precarious workers, reduce tenure protections, and prioritize revenue-generating fields over and above other disciplines.

Debt and the Neoliberalization of the University

Institutional debt is a key mechanism of what scholars and activists have identified as the ongoing neoliberalization of the university. This project has several defining features, including the intensification of work exploitation, the shifting of funding from public to private sources, and the ideological project to change the soul and mission of higher education. Institutional debt plays a part in each.

The intensification of work is best represented by ongoing adjunctification and the broader loss of labor rights. Adjuncts are woefully underpaid. At community colleges, for example, adjunct pay can run as low as $1,000 per course. Recent data show that nearly 25 percent of adjuncts receive public assistance, while 40 percent struggle to cover basic household expenses. By design, these faculty members have no job security and few basic labor rights. Yet credit-rating agencies like Moody's prioritize fiscal "flexibility," recognizing that an institution's ability to unilaterally reduce instructional expenditures (that is, faculty compensation) increases the likelihood that creditors will be paid. The proliferation of adjunct positions allows for this reduction to take place en masse and without regard for time-consuming and costly processes like due process (Valbrun 2020).

Additionally, debt plays an important role in the neoliberal shift in reliance from public to private sources of funding. Adjusting for inflation, between 2008 and 2018, state funding for two- and four-year institutions dropped by $6.6 billion nationally (Mitchell, Leaman, and Saenz 2019). This shifting of funding from public sources (state tax dollars) to private sources (individual students) has not only expanded students' debt, but it has also accelerated the financialization of higher education by pushing colleges and universities to take on institutional debt to maintain or develop their campuses. Institutional debt thus has quietly facilitated this transition in a manner largely hidden from the potentially critical eyes of the public (including faculty, staff, students, parents, and community members). The shift, however, has not come without consequences. As highlighted above, the power relations of institutional debt service push colleges and universities to prioritize concerns with return on investment over and above public educational aims.

This return-on-investment mentality trickles down to students' educational expectations, inflicting instructional harm. It reduces the project of education to a means of increasing individuals' market value and future earnings. Debt is thus a critical tool in the ongoing ideological project to change the soul and mission of higher education from a collectively held public good to a private asset with solely economically measurable returns. This, of course, has real effects on the production of knowledge within the academy, whether through the degree programs students choose to pursue or the faculty research that is supported and funded. Perhaps the most relevant example is the ongoing proliferation of business degrees conferred as the nation approaches a massive shortage of teachers, social workers, rural dentists, and family practice doctors (García and Weiss 2019; Lin, Lin, and Zhang 2016; NCES 2019).

In the absence of robust public funding, debt directs the potential of universities, as well as the students and faculty in them, uniquely toward debt service. University, student, and faculty growth—whether through new coursework, programs, facilities, or services—is nurtured or neglected based on the institution's capacity to pay debt. Debt, in other words, accelerates the austerity policies that hollow out university infrastructure, reduces the quality of educational interactions on college campuses, and harms instruction.

Possibilities for Future Exploration

Institutional debt financing is more than a symptom of the neoliberal university; it is a key driver of that project. One of the central aims of critical university studies should be to bring institutional debt to public light and to invite broad public discussion of its machinations and effects. Such research must never suffice, however. Research and knowledge production must contribute to and strengthen organizing efforts that seek to challenge existing creditor-debtor economic and power relations. To this end, we offer the following questions for discussion among researchers, activists, and educators:

- In places like West Virginia, Kansas, Puerto Rico, and elsewhere, debt-inspired austerity measures are sweeping campuses. How might an immediate moratorium on university debt service halt the pending cuts to faculty, programs, and student services? If universities were able to retain funds presently allocated for debt service, would jobs, programs, and student services be spared?
- How and under what conditions might the federal government assume the debts of public universities? What type of movements would be needed to cancel that debt if it were publicly held?
- What might creditor-debtor relations look like if lending conditions were collectively bargained? What if, for example, universities paid creditors last rather than first? Has covenant payment order ever been successfully challenged in courts of law or through social movements? What legal and contractual frameworks might movements build from to advance these calls?
- How do creditor-debtor relations on campuses play out beyond the United States? What would a comparative international analysis of institutional higher education debt reveal? For example, in countries with larger welfare commitments to public higher education, does institutional debt have less influence over governance and institutional priorities? How do institutions of international financial capitalism, such as the IMF, the World Bank, and other international creditors, influence domestic higher education spending priorities?

It is our hope that these questions and others generated by our chapter inspire a rethinking of how higher education is funded and governed.

References

CFA (California Faculty Association). 2017. *Equity Interrupted: How California Is Cheating Its Future*. Sacramento, CA: CFA.

Cellini, Stephanie, and Latika Chaudhary. 2020. "Commercials for College? Advertising in Higher Education." Brookings Institute, May 19. https://www.brookings.edu/articles/commercials-for-college-advertising-in-higher-education/.

Chen, David W., and Michael Corkery. 2023. "A New Playbook for College Donors: Power Politics." *New York Times*, December 13. https://www.nytimes.com/2023/12/13/us/universities-donors-penn-harvard.html.

Cooper, Melinda. 2017. *Family Values: Between Neoliberalism and the New Social Conservatism*. Brooklyn: Zone.

Crozier, Michel, Samuel P. Huntington, and Jōji Watanuki. 1975. *The Crisis of Democracy: Report on the Governability of Democracies to the Trilateral Commission*. New York: New York University Press.

Eaton, Charlie. 2022. *Bankers in the Ivory Tower: The Troubling Rise of Financiers in US Higher Education*. Chicago: University of Chicago Press.

Eaton, Charlie, Jacob Habinek, Adam Goldstein, Cyrus Dioun, Daniela García Santibáñez Godoy, and Robert Osley-Thomas. 2016. "The Financialization of US Higher Education." *Socio-Economic Review* 14 (3): 507–35.

Ferguson, Roderick. *We Demand: The University and Student Protests*. Berkeley: University of California Press, 2017.

García, Emma, and Elaine Weiss. 2019. "The Teacher Shortage Is Real, Large, Growing, and Worse than We Thought." Economic Policy Institute, March 26. https://www.epi.org/publication/the-teacher-shortage-is-real-large-and-growing-and-worse-than-we-thought-the-first-report-in-the-perfect-storm-in-the-teacher-labor-market-series/.

Gonsalves, Joanna, and Rich Levy. 2021. "Why Should I Care about My University's Capital Debt?" *MSCA Perspective*, April.

Gouzoulis, Giorgos. 2023. "Personal Debt Makes Workers Afraid to Strike." *Jacobin*, February 19. https://jacobin.com/2023/02/wage-earner-household-debt-strike-union-decline.

Jiménez, Dalié, and Jonathan D. Glater. 2020. "Student Debt Is a Civil Rights Issue: The Case for Debt Relief and Higher Education Reform." *Harvard Civil Rights–Civil Liberties Law Review* 55 (1): 131–98.

Kaplan, Ann E. 2023. *CASE Insights on Voluntary Support of Education (United States): 2022 Key Findings*. Washington, DC: Council for Advancement and Support of Education.

Lin, Vernon W., Joyce Lin, and Xiaoming Zhang. 2016. "U.S. Social Worker Workforce Report Card: Forecasting Nationwide Shortages." *Social Work* 61 (1): 7–15.

Meister, Bob. 2009. "They Pledged Your Tuition (An Open Letter to UC Students)." The Council of UC Faculty Associations, Davis, CA.

Miller, Kevin, Raina Nelson, and Sarah Dice. 2017. *Deeper in Debt: Women and Student Loans* Washington, DC: American Association of University Women. https://www.aauw.org/resources/research/deeper-in-debt/.

Mitchell, Michael, Michael Leachman, and Matt Saenz. 2019. "State Higher Education Funding Cuts Have Pushed Costs to Students, Worsened Inequality." Center on Budget and Policy

Priorities, October 24. https://www.cbpp.org/research/state-budget-and-tax/state-higher-education-funding-cuts-have-pushed-costs-to-students.
Moody's Investor Services. 2019. *Higher Education Rating Methodology*. New York: Moody's.
NCES (National Center for Education Statistics). 2019. "Bachelor's Degrees Conferred by Postsecondary Institutions, by Field of Study: Selected Years, 1970–71 through 2017–18." Digest of Education Statistics, NCES. https://nces.ed.gov/programs/digest/d14/tables/dt14_322.10.asp.
Seamster, Louise, and Raphaël Charron-Chénier. 2017. "Predatory Inclusion and Education Debt: Rethinking the Racial Wealth Gap." *Social Currents* 4 (3): 199–207.
Shermer, Elizabeth Tandy. 2021. *Indentured Students: How Government-Guaranteed Loans Left Generations Drowning in College Debt*. Cambridge, MA: Harvard University Press.
Streeck, Wolfgang. 2014. *Buying Time: The Delayed Crisis of Democratic Capitalism*. New York: Verso.
Valbrun, Marjorie. 2020. "CUNY Layoffs Prompt Union Lawsuit." *Inside Higher Ed*, July 5.
Wolfe, Emily. 2019. "Anti-union Firm Paid $240K by Pitt during Faculty and Grad Student Unionization Efforts." *Pittsburgh City Paper*, May 23.

D

Degree

Christopher Newfield

The terms *college degree* and *university degree* refer to the bachelor's degree, most commonly a BA (Bachelor of Arts) or BS (Bachelor of Science). These degrees certify successful completion of a field of undergraduate study, as much marketing, business, or health administration as chemistry, Arabic language, fine art, or sociology. The normal degree period in the West is three or four years, over which time knowledge in the primary subject areas is meant to accumulate and deepen, and facility with its use to increase.

The term *bachelor's degree* finds a first instance in 1386, earned by "one who has taken the first or lowest degree at a university, who is not yet a master of the Arts."[1] *Bachelor* referred during the late medieval and early modern periods to "a junior or inferior member, or 'yeoman,' of a trade-guild, or City Company." A bachelor's degree candidate was a kind of guild apprentice, and the degree signified completion of the apprenticeship in but not mastery of the trade or craft developed by study in the university. The bachelor's degree was a gateway to mastery, but that would be achieved through a variety of postgraduate activities, especially work.

A degree official confirms the successful completion of the requirements of a course of study. *Course* is a complex word, and academic courses combine several of its meanings.[2] The course of study has meant an "onward movement or travel, esp. in a particular path or direction." A course is an "action, process, or progress," "progress onward or through successive stages, esp. over time." A course is not only a channel external to the person but is at the same time "a line of (personal) action, way of acting, mode of behaviour," as in a "course of conduct," here a way of acting in the process of learning. A course is "a series or sequence," and more specifically, since 1560,

1. *Oxford English Dictionary*, "Bachelor," accessed December 20, 2024, https://www.oed.com/dictionary/bachelor_n?tab=meaning_and_use&tl=true#30461713.

2. *Oxford English Dictionary*, "Course," accessed December 20, 2024, https://www.oed.com/dictionary/course_n1?tab=meaning_and_use#8123968.

"a series of lectures, lessons, or instructional sessions in a particular subject; (chiefly British) a prescribed or planned curriculum or program of instruction in an academic subject, a vocational or practical skill, etc., esp. leading to an examination or qualification." A *course* in the United Kingdom is a North American *major*: it refers to the full series of classes, lectures, or modules in the Britain-based academic world, while a North American course is just one of many term-length sets of classes that compose the *major* (or minor). Whether called a course or a major, the degree certifies the successful completion of an organized forward movement in a particular direction through a planned curriculum or program.

The course, or major, is an apprenticeship, so what does its degree certify apprenticeship in? A bachelor butcher, baker, or candle-stick maker learned all aspects and stages of these trades. There were dozens, even hundreds of crafts, nearly all complex, or "skilled" as we would say now—Broderers, ironmongers, dyers, joiners, wheelwrights, saddlers, and scriveners, as well as mariners, actuaries, traders, and other merchants.[3] Education in a trade did not aim at some other trade: One might learn some accounting to run an embroidery workshop, but the quality of a Broderer's training was measured by the quality of their shop's embroidery, not of its accounting. Similarly, a BA certified a completed apprenticeship in studying, learning, or thinking, not in a readiness for later work in which some of the knowledge acquired might be used.

The content or subject of a BA degree was variable: the degreed graduate had finished their tutelage in how to think about organic chemistry or the history of art or, more recently, about IT network administration or health-sector business management. Each guild apprenticeship was organized around characteristic practices or combinations (overlapping with other trades that did not eliminate distinct trade identities). These involved "learning by doing," but so did a college degree: One learned thinking by doing thinking, across a range of forms—writing, calculation, reading, interpretative and quantitative analysis, laboratory experimentation, archival and other forms of information retrieval and evaluation—that were verified methods of producing new knowledge and practicing it. The college degree, from its origin, marked completion in an apprenticeship in thinking

3. "Database of Companies and Guilds," City of London, Livery Committee, accessed December 20, 2024, https://liverycommittee.org/about/livery-companies-and-guilds/livery-companies-database/.

and learning about some thing or things. Put more pointedly, undergraduate students were apprentice scholars, researchers, or intellectuals, developing general but powerful capabilities that could be applied to a range of topics and settings. Mastery would come in one of those later settings, supplied by activity in a workplace, a profession, a doctoral program, over long periods of practical experience. The North American emphasis on college major and the UK emphasis on university course distract from the nature of the bachelor/undergraduate apprenticeship in learning and thinking and learning to think.

The admission of the bachelor's degree into a low level of a guild of thinkers has always had a whiff of pointlessness. The early systematic theorization of the modern Western university occurred in reaction to one such firestorm of accusation, in Prussia during the late eighteenth and early nineteenth centuries. The charge that universities taught nothing useful was made in 1808 by an involved observer, Friedrich Niethammer, who described them as obsessed with "money and profit" and with getting more "technical and mechanical know-how" enfolded in professional training that would produce still greater profits (Reitter and Wellmon 2021, 15).

Two elements of this then-novel university theory are important here. First, a degree demonstrated that the undergraduate scholar had learned both how to think and how to translate thinking into action. Philosopher J. G. Fichte wrote, "The point of studying is not, after all, to enable someone to spend his whole life spouting off what he had learned for an exam years before. The point is for him to be able to apply what he has learned to the situations and predicaments that come up in life, and thus transform what he has learned into action: . . . the ultimate goal is not knowledge but the art of using knowledge" ([1807] 2017, 72). Second, the degree represented a social, public, collective benefit. To cite Fichte again, "The demand that every person ought to cultivate all of his talents equally contains at the same time the demand that all of the various rational beings ought to be cultivated equally" ([1807] 2017, cited in Schmidt 2013, 166). These ideas were always contested and often marginalized in later years, and yet the modern college degree stems from this view that the craft of thinking and learning includes the application of thinking to all "the situations and predicaments" that societies face.

A long line of "degree" theorists opposed the splitting of knowledge from use. In John Henry Cardinal Newman's landmark nineteenth-century text, *The Idea of the University,* he identified the university with "liberal" rather than "useful" learning, which has given rise to the false contrast in which liberal knowledge is allegedly useless. Newman in fact wrote, "Those rather are useful, which bear fruit; those liberal, which tend to enjoyment." This is usually interpreted to refer to the pleasures of liberal study "for its own sake," tied to a British version of higher learning that leads to ethical self-possession, or in ambitious Kantian terms, to *Bildung*, or self-development that produces an ability to combine aesthetic, practical, and pure reason. But having a degree in "enjoyment" is better understood as signaling a capacity for the self-sufficient *use* of knowledge, that is, "use not determined by external or superior forces" (Newfield 2003, 55). Newman shared with his political opposite, Karl Marx, an interest in what the latter called use-value: Enjoyment was the "absence, the non-necessity, of the accumulation of additional value," of surplus value. The university degree focused not on useless knowledge but on noncommodified knowledge. Noncommodified knowledge could and regularly did lead to use. But its development would unfold according to its own tendencies and the practices of the knowledge workers involved, rather than being controlled by other forces, such as government, corporate sponsors, or philanthropists.

Coming from a completely different social position, W. E. B. Du Bois demanded a similar effect of degree completion in *The Souls of Black Folk* ([1903] 1996, ch. 7): The "Negro college . . . must maintain the standards of popular education" that allow "the sovereign human soul" of every Black American "to know itself and the world about it; [to seek] a freedom for expansion and self-development [and to] love and hate and labor in its own way, untrammeled alike by old and new." A degree indicated a unity of accumulated multidimensional knowledge and the personal formation that afforded the graduate the free—uncoerced—use of that knowledge.

The perceived value of a university degree has always been at the mercy of disputes about its content. Internal conflicts about curriculum have been permanent features of academic life. Sometimes these spill over into local or national politics, as has been frequent in the United States since the 1960s. Today's curricula are radically different from those of the eighteenth- and nineteenth-century period of foundational theory and went through four epochal shifts:

1. the replacement of classical foundations with a wider range of majors, including English and other modern languages in addition to Greek

and Latin, as well as the natural and physical sciences, as well as elective courses, pioneered by Charles Eliot, president of Harvard University from 1869 to 1909;

2. the advent of professional schools in the early twentieth century and, later, undergraduate departments in professional subjects like business administration;
3. the development of general education courses as a supplement to the major, accelerated by the publication of *General Education in a Free Society* (Harvard Committee 1945); and
4. the racial and international diversification of teaching materials in the arts, humanities, and social sciences through the civil rights movement and the "canon wars" of the 1980s.

The constant feature of all these disputes and their results was the idea of the degree as the systematic exposure of each student to a range of subjects, methods, skills, and perspectives—or, in the British course, the latter three across one subject—that would be sufficiently integrated to allow the college graduate to grasp the diversity and complexity of knowledge while being able to apply and continuously learn new knowledge across the full range of "situations and predicaments that come up in life."

The expansion of both industrial capitalism and postgraduate education after 1900—doctoral study and academic and professional masters—put contradictory pressure on the college degree. On the one hand, organized degree courses exposed students to current knowledge in a systematic way, accelerating their learning even as university research accelerated the expansion of knowledge itself. The major, or course, allowed—and the degree expressed—the effectiveness of structuring and integrating knowledge to reduce duplication and reinventing the wheel. On the other hand, corporate executives, politicians, and the popular culture of capitalism encouraged the general application of process engineering and return-on-investment metrics of value. Frederick Taylor's widely influential "scientific management" broke production processes down into small units so that each could be optimized, and by 1920 some influential university presidents—Henry S. Pritchett of MIT was one leading example—wanted to apply this method of disaggregation to reengineer their universities along industrial lines (Veblen [1918] 2015). The industrial analogy suggested that degrees should be designed and operated by a professor who would not "produce any longer by his own initiative" but by orders from management (Barrow 1990, 70). Over the course of the twentieth century, the general impulse to design education for business raised the issue of whether universities should insist on the power of the degree "bundle" of subjects, methods, skills, and perspectives, or instead unbundle them, the better to eliminate the "lower-value" subjects and methods and focus on those most valued by business and other interests.

Over the course of the twentieth century, the growth of mass higher education increased political and corporate interest in cheap higher education. An unbundled degree promised to be a cheap degree, fully standardized, stripped of expensive overheads like buildings and live instructors, delivered through information and communication technology, and generally simplified through commodification. An early unbundled quasi-degree was the correspondence course, in which materials and gradable assignments were delivered through the post, then completed and returned through the post for grading (Noble 2001). This "distance learning" was televised in the 1960s and then digitalized in the 1990s. Describing what would become the all-online Western Governors University, Utah Governor Mike Leavitt predicted that "an institution of higher education will become a little like a local television station" (Noble 1998). A similar focus on the degree as the outcome of a content delivery process recurred during the global promotion of massive open online courses (MOOCs) in the early 2010s, when administrators' unquenchable desire for cost savings overrode missing evaluations of pedagogical effectiveness (Rivard 2013). Something similar happened in the mid-2020s with machine learning and large language models when (over)sold as "generative artificial intelligence." Once again, the core features of a degree—active learning over time in relation to multiple subjects, methods, skills, and perspectives that are gradually integrated and put to use through the continuous labor of the student—are eclipsed by the technology of the delivery system. With chat-style writing assistants, the technology may help bypass thinking itself (Terry 2023).

In the United States, colleges have been under pressure to instill practical workplace skills since at least the late nineteenth century. Many US colleges and universities began as trade schools for accounting, sales, and secretarial careers. Job pressure increased after World War II, as college became a mass institution; after the 1950s, as human capital theory taught that "learning equaled earning," suppressing the public benefits of higher education; after the 1960s, as the concept of the postindustrial information society linked technical degrees directly to corporate profit and national wealth; after the 1970s, as US global economic dominance faded, and corporations looked to shift training costs to colleges and shrink noncommercial subjects; after the 1980s, as the culture wars targeted the university's broad intellectual, racially integrative, and democratizing missions; and after the 1990s, as finance, health, and digital technology eclipsed all other sectors.

Business demanded workforce-ready graduates, and politicians in the Reagan and Clinton eras were happy to enforce these demands. While a three- or four-year college education generated a range of *general skills* that applied to a wide range of activities, most growth was in jobs that required either little college or *specific skills* that could be taught in shorter and narrower modules. The latter could allegedly be addressed with *microcredentials*, like certificates or badges, and developed in coding camps and other alternatives to the multiyear commitment of a bachelor's degree. The explosion of tuition costs and student debt made shorter and cheaper minidegrees attractive, particularly to lower-income students, returning students, and students from marginalized or oppressed communities who had never been admitted in high proportions to higher education in the first place.

Non-elite universities responded to these issues by further massifying the normative college degree (larger classes, less professorial contact) and by further vocationalizing the curriculum, a trend that was far along by the early 2010s (Menand 2011). As public colleges moved "downmarket" to look more like short-term or online credentialing programs, they were more likely to be compared to them and to be found slower and more expensive. The public prominence of the idea of unbundling degrees into discrete skills signaled the weakened independence of universities in relation to commerce, not their validity as substitutes for full-time three- to four-year courses of study. By 2020, when the COVID-19 pandemic closed universities across the world and pushed education online, the unbundled credential had come to judge the degree, not vice versa. One practical effect was that confidence in the value of a college degree reached new lows (Brenan 2023; Tough 2023).

The pandemic's negative effects on student learning and satisfaction, however, partially reversed the drift toward digital and unbundled college. Much of society relearned the lesson that learning is social and collaborative, and that online alternatives increase passivity, surveillance, learning loss, alienation, and in some cases, mental health problems (e.g., Bird, Castleman, and Lohner 2022; Mervosh 2023). In the 2020s, college degrees were also more widely evaluated for their contribution to social justice, which included demands that student debt be canceled, affordability and access be equalized for students of color, public college tuition be reduced or returned to zero, and funding and quality not be cut at accessible institutions as they had been throughout the twenty-first century. Linking the degree to social justice could build on both radical social movement demands and historic university theory, which, in its late eighteenth-century phase, had tied university degrees to the transformation of collective human powers—to repeat Fichte's phrase, "that all of the various rational beings ought to be cultivated equally."

College degrees can be improved. They could be made more sequential, coherent, and explicit about and diverse in the methods taught; more hospitable to racialized, low-income, and first-generation students; and better able to join the liberal and the practical arts. High-quality higher learning is compatible with affordable access for all interested members of the entire society. Degrees can best be fixed if they are not blamed for problems in the labor market, capitalist economy, corporate management system, banking and private equity, national politics, social media, or public information systems. Higher learning can be made universally available to whoever wants it, but only if the degree's powers are understood as clearly as its limits. These powers include knowledge-based self-determination—in one of the only venues in modern society able to sustain this capacity's difficult development.

References

Barrow, Clyde W. 1990. *Universities and the Capitalist State: Corporate Liberalism and the Reconstruction of American Higher Education, 1894–1928*. Madison: University of Wisconsin Press.

Bird, Kelli A., Benjamin L. Castleman, and Gabrielle Lohner. 2022. "Negative Impacts from the Shift to Online Learning during the COVID-19 Crisis: Evidence from a Statewide Community College System." Working paper, Annenberg Institute at Brown University. September 21. https://www.edworkingpapers.com/ai20-299.

Brenan, Megan. 2023 "Americans' Confidence in Higher Education Down Sharply." Gallup, July 11. https://news.gallup.com/poll/508352/americans-confidence-higher-education-down-sharply.aspx.

Du Bois, W. E. B. (1903) 1996. *The Souls of Black Folk*. New York: Penguin Classics.

Fichte, J. G. (1807) 2017. "A Plan, Deduced from First Principles, for an Institution of Higher Learning to Be Established in Berlin, Connected to and Subordinate to an Academy of Sciences." In *The Rise of the Research University: A Sourcebook*, edited by Louis Menand, Paul Reitter, Chad Wellmon, 67–103. Chicago: University of Chicago Press.

Harvard Committee. 1945. *General Education in a Free Society: Report of the Harvard Committee.* With an introduction by James Bryant Conant. Cambridge, MA: Harvard University Press.

Menand, Louis. 2011. "Live and Learn." *New Yorker,* May 30. https://www.newyorker.com/magazine/2011/06/06/live-and-learn-louis-menand.

Mervosh, Sarah. 2023. "Math Scores Dropped Globally, but the U.S. Still Trails Other Countries." *New York Times,* December 5. https://www.nytimes.com/2023/12/05/us/math-scores-pandemic-pisa.html.

Newfield, Christopher. 2003. *Ivy and Industry: Business and the Making of the American University, 1880–1980.* Durham, NC: Duke University Press.

Noble, David F. 1998. "Digital Diploma Mills: The Automation of Higher Education." *Monthly Review* 49 (9). https://monthlyreview.org/1998/02/01/digital-diploma-mills/.

Noble, David F. 2001. *Digital Diploma Mills: The Automation of Higher Education.* New York: Monthly Review Press.

Reitter, Paul, and Chad Wellmon. 2021. *Permanent Crisis: The Humanities in a Disenchanted Age.* Chicago: University of Chicago Press.

Rivard, Ry. 2013. "Udacity Project on 'Pause.'" *Inside Higher Ed,* July 18. http://www.insidehighered.com/news/2013/07/18/citing-disappointing-student-outcomes-san-jose-state-pauses-work-udacity.

Schmidt, Alexander. 2013. "Self-Cultivation (Bildung) and Sociability Between Mankind and The Nation: Fichte and Schleiermacher on Higher Education." In, *Ideas of Education: Philosophy and Politics from Plato to Dewey,* edited by Christopher Brooke and Elizabeth Frazer, 160–77. London: Routledge.

Terry, Owen Kichizo. 2023. "I'm a Student: You Have No Idea How Much We're Using ChatGPT." *Chronicle of Higher Education,* May 12. https://www.chronicle.com/article/im-a-student-you-have-no-idea-how-much-were-using-chatgpt.

Tough, Paul. 2023. "Americans Are Losing Faith in the Value of College: Whose Fault Is That?" *New York Times,* September 5. https://www.nytimes.com/2023/09/05/magazine/college-worth-price.html.

Veblen, Thorstein. (1918) 2015. *The Higher Learning in America: A Memorandum on the Conduct of Universities by Business Men.* Edited by Richard F. Teichgraeber III. Annotated ed. Baltimore: Johns Hopkins University Press.

D

Discipline

Vineeta Singh

Disciplines are not just descriptive labels; they are also productive projects. They produce knowledge, experts, and the notion of expertise itself. They also color the way academics see the world; how we shape subjects and objects; how we frame problems; and how we inhabit our own subjectivity as scholars separate from what we study. Following Eli Meyerhoff's invitation to recognize education as one "mode of study" among many, one "way of composing the relations among collected means of studying" among many (Meyerhoff 2019, 14), disciplinarity represents something akin to an ongoing primitive accumulation of knowledge: the separation of the student from the means of studying.

If there is anything like an academic consensus on what constitutes a discipline, it is based on distilling academic practice into the core elements that are shared across academic divisions: a proper object of study; specialized terminology to analyze it; a canon (and its contestation); a common methodology to make meaning of this canon; and an intellectual community to maintain standards of how methods are practiced. Self-narratives of specific disciplines also feature Great Men, purposes, and ideals that birth and shape their pursuit of truth. Such formulaic or hagiographic definitions risk eliding how disciplines also index the organization of resources, authority, and labor in the university as well as other sites of capitalist extraction and accumulation. As much as they are intellectual projects, disciplines are also institutional (organizational, bureaucratic) projects that arrange labor in space and across time. We tend to think of disciplines' intellectual projects as productive labor (producing knowledge and the experts who refine it) and their institutional projects (teaching work and the amorphous conglomeration of service tasks) as reproductive labors. What might be illuminated if we switch these labels and ask what the intellectual project of disciplinarity reproduces and what its institutional project produces?

From the medieval period in Europe through the early twentieth century in the North Atlantic, when academics spoke of discipline, they most often meant a shared practice, that is, methodology. As the early universities of continental Europe brought together teachers and students in metropolitan centers, knowledge workers seeking protection from the arbitrary exercise of state violence began to define their intellectual community (or faculty) by shared labors, as well as beginning to identify which scholars were not part of their intellectual community by citing distance from these tools of making knowledge. Command of methodology and access to professional networks carved out academics' subjectivity and conferred the authority embedded in the *discipular* tradition, passing knowledge from master to pupil.

In addition to continuity, disciplinarity has also denoted hierarchy: within and through the transmission of knowledge from master to pupil; between the various disciplines, which early on divided into higher and lower faculties; and most fundamentally in the separation of knower from the body of knowledge they study. Conventional pedagogical practices, from the lecture to the oral defense, and rank-differentiated regalia embody this hierarchical organization of the disciplinary world (Reitter and Wellmon 2021, 8). Indeed, pedagogy itself was hierarchy (note: the etymological root of *pedagogy* combines the words for boy/child and guide). This paternalistic schema lends itself well to imperial and capitalist world-making projects because they impose an artificial scarcity as they reify knowledge, making it amenable to the epistemology of property. Disciplinarity authorized academics' work as legitimate, authoritative, and most importantly, universalizable. The desire for universalizing also meant an embrace of the quantifiable and a distrust of slippery subjective realities. Michel Foucault stresses that all science (a broad term for knowledge-production practices) exhibits a will to order: "The sciences," he writes, "always carry within themselves the project, however remote it may be, of an exhaustive ordering of the world; they are always directed, too, toward the discovery of simple elements and their progressive combinations; and at their center they form a tableau in which knowledge is displayed as a system contemporary with itself" ([1966] 1994, 74). Disciplines putatively impose order on chaos but in fact produce both chaos and order as properties. The episteme of disciplinarity is the discovery of the order inherent in the world. The disciplinary lens hides its production as a transparent rendering of the world. While specific disciplines produced truths about the world, disciplinarity functioned as part of the white man's burden. The natural sciences were helpmeets of the colonial project. The knowledge they produced justified the subjugation of Indigenous populations across the globe. The need to reproduce the disciplines also served as justification for expanding colonial projects and legitimizing colonial states (Wilder 2013).

The modern research university, as embodied in the institutions of late nineteenth-century Germany and shortly after in the United States (see, for example, Johns Hopkins), has served as the blueprint of how to organize the productive labors of knowledge production as well as the putatively reproductive labors of teaching and service to the institution and to the discipline for modern US universities and colleges. This iteration of the university, with its tripartite hierarchy of research, teaching, and service, presents disciplinarity's intellectual project as its productive labor and its institutional project as its reproductive labors. The value the modern university places on professionalization became evident in the faculty's turn to the rhetoric of professionalization in their self-representation (e.g., Barrow 1990). The modern disciplines coevolved with the professional ideals of tenure, shared governance, and academic freedom. As university governance became more centralized through the twentieth century, disciplines were pitted against each other to compete for increasingly limited resources distributed by central administration.

Although academic common sense seems to think of the post–World War II boom in area studies as the origin of interdisciplinarity, philologist Roberta Frank has written that interdisciplinarity was "common coin in the social sciences" already, and "by the late 50s, the idea even seemed old hat" (1988, 73). Frank traces the history of the term *interdisciplinary* to a surprisingly specific time and place: "born in New York City in the mid-1920s, most likely at the corner of 42nd and Madison . . . in the corridors of the Social Science Research Council as a kind of bureaucratic shorthand for what the council saw as its chief function" (73). The intellectual history of area studies has chronicled how geopolitical concerns and corporate philanthropy valued "real-world application" over "pure sciences." This "real-world" orientation required the integration of innovations from multiple disciplines. Funders were eager for synergistic applications of disciplinary tools to new objects of study outside their conventional domain.

In contrast to this additive interdisciplinarity, the emergence of the interdisciplines through formations like the Third World Liberation Front at San Francisco State University proposed an epistemic break with the schema of disciplinarity itself. Historian and Black studies scholar Vincent E. Harding connected this rejection of "artificial barriers of the academic disciplines" to the anticolonial revolutionary's rejection of all sorts of boundaries erected to uphold the social systems we call national, political, economic, and social. The interdisciplines serve as a way of reorienting student, faculty, and staff labor to a different kind of productivity, directed toward serving *the community*—a contentious term, as it is defined primarily by a separateness from the university and cannot survive scrutiny from a labor studies lens (e.g., Mitchell 2015). These students saw that the knowledge the academy could produce about their lives (think Moynihan Report) consistently misrepresented their lives and the histories of their communities. But they did not contain their critique to disciplinary findings. They turned their analytical lens on disciplinarity itself, concluding that this misrepresentation was overdetermined by the prevalent ways of organizing knowledge production in higher education. As Joshua Myers writes, Black studies is founded on the radical belief that "asking what produces the lie, rather than what constitutes the lie, is a more necessary response than simply refusing the lie" (2022, 3).

The interdisciplines did not just reject the specific development of the disciplines that had laid the foundation of the military-industrial complex (the "academic-military-industrial complex" in the first draft of President Eisenhower's speech), but also questioned the utility of disciplinarity itself. If the early formation of the disciplines was driven by faculty coalescing around refining specific methodologies, the protagonists in the birth of the interdisciplines were students, and the point of crystallization was the rejection of what had become the "proper objects" of the disciplines.

The interdisciplinarity Frank describes requires the attribution of a proper object to each discipline, such that the interface of these disciplines can create interdisciplinarity. There, interdisciplinarity means borrowing tools from one discipline to study the object "proper" to another. The interdisciplines eschew proper objects. Women's studies, for instance, is not properly the study of women, and not even of patriarchy, but the study of all the questions and problems that coalesce around the sign of gender (see Wiegman 2012). Neither is Black studies reducible to "Black *content*"; rather, as the writers of the Lumumba Zapata Coalition for a Third World college argue in their manifesto demanding engagement with previously neglected histories and a recalibration of the mainstream curriculum through the introduction of whiteness studies, Black studies serves as a lens to provincialize Euro-American thought. It provides a lens that must necessarily be turned on whiteness and Manichaeism of all sorts marshaled under the sign of race. Where the drive of a discipline is toward reductionism, the interdiscipline is formed in rejection of this reductionism, which is incompatible with the complexity of human life, queering (i.e., rendering strange) disciplinarity itself.

The interdisciplinary mode of study demonstrates how, paradoxically, true community service praxis requires dissolving the stultifying distinction between university/expertise and community. This interdisciplinarity also requires a break with the institutional project of disciplinarity, a break with the hierarchy, the authority, the imposition of order, and the fetishization of novelty that characterizes disciplinarity itself. The interdisciplines are meant to disrupt the hierarchy of disciplinarity by bringing in types of expertise not validated by the academy. Black feminist literary scholar Toni Cade Bambara theorized that the promise of the interdisciplines would be fulfilled when the fields were taught by "those grandmothers, those on the corner hardheads, those students, those instructors, whoever happens to have the knowledge and expertise we desire, regardless of the number of or absence of degrees, publications, titles, honors" (1969, 21). As previous research on ethnic studies and academic multiculturalism has demonstrated, much of this epistemic challenge was domesticated with depoliticized initiatives for "inclusion" that expanded the reach of the university rather than conceding its monopoly on authorizing knowledge (see Ferguson 2012; Melamed 2011). Today, an Ethnic Studies 101 lecture hall might not look terribly different from one for Physics 101. Fifty years after the Third World Strike at SF State, it can seem easier to see how the institution has transformed the promise of ethnic studies rather than how the interdisciplines have disrupted the institution from within. Yet, the university still houses "decolonial desires" that subvert the machinery of the institution to produce ephemeral assemblages and networks "transforming what and whom the university can be for" (la paperson 2017; Boggs et al., n.d.).

In the Bayh-Dole era, during the rise of academic capitalism and neoliberal managerialism in the US university, the protagonist of the story of disciplinarity shifts from the student (now envisioned as a consumer rather than a knowledge worker) to the administrator (manager). Business interests dominate university boards and treat endowments as analogous to corporate portfolios (see Gordon 2006). This means both that the intellectual project of the discipline is reduced to the function of credentialization for the student, and that its institutional project becomes simply return on investment for the department and the student. Given the ballooning of tuition and student fees that has accompanied state disinvestment from public higher education, it is not surprising that students' abilities to pay off loans have become the central focus of popular discourse around majors and disciplines—or perhaps more accurately, the *rhetoric* of return on investment functions as an enticement for students to voluntarily generate debt-as-asset for others.

Bachelor's degrees in *interdisciplinary studies* (formerly integrated studies or general studies) then serve as enticements for "nontraditional students" while providing the institution a way of dissimulating neoliberal flexibility and austerity as pedagogical projects. Interdisciplinary/transdisciplinary and subdisciplinary majors are often designed and maintained by the faculty whose home disciplines are considered to be in some sort of perpetual crisis or PR nightmare aggravated by the rhetoric of return on investment (think: English, or more handwringingly, "the humanities"). The Modern Language Association, the premier disciplinary organization for some of these disciplines, describes these "proliferating niche majors" as an attempt to "carve up existing institutional bureaucracies in creative ways, sourcing instructors from multiple units or identifying cohorts of faculty members within existing departments" (Marx and Cooper, 2020). These flexible arrangements of teaching labor dovetail nicely with the university's preference for contingent labor. Such departments or programs cobbled together either by "elevating" adjuncts to term contracts or by pulling apart existing units and redistributing their faculty, serve the institution by creating alternative routes to graduation for students who cannot be retained in traditional major/degree pathways (an important measure for college rankings, which themselves are an important indicator of institutions' financial well-being). For such programs, staffed by teaching faculty and academic advisers, the institutional project *is* the intellectual project. We are tasked with crafting an academic veneer for a student support service. Yet these spaces also function as something of an undercommons, asking uncomfortable questions about disciplinarity, and modeling other ways of being in the university. By no means do we exist outside the trappings of disciplinarity. But without the structure of a traditional department, our teaching can allow us to explore what a future without the trappings of disciplinarity might allow our student colleagues to imagine. The intellectual project of interdisciplinary studies in the current moment could be the provincialization—or even abolition—of disciplinarity as intellectual and institutional projects. Knowing that disciplines are neither inevitable nor guaranteed, we continue to search for other ways of studying, engaging, and creating.

References

Bambara, Toni. 1969. "Realizing the Dream of a Black University (1969)." In *"Realizing the Dream of a Black University" and Other Writings, Part II*. https://cuny.manifoldapp.org/read/realizing-the-dream-of-a-black-university-other-writings-part-ii/section/e641fa52-0da7-4334-ba89-53232e8a0245.

Barrow, Clyde W. 1990. *Universities and the Capitalist State: Corporate Liberalism and the Reconstruction of American Higher Education, 1894–1928*. Madison: University of Wisconsin Press.

Boggs, Abigail, Eli Meyerhoff, Nick Mitchell, and Zach Schwartz-Weinstein. n.d. "Abolitionist University Studies: an Invitation." Abolition University. Accessed February 15, 2024. https://abolition.university/invitation/.

Ferguson, Roderick A. 2012. *The Reorder of Things: The University and Its Pedagogies of Minority Difference*. Minneapolis: University of Minnesota Press.

Foucault, Michel. (1966) 1994. *The Order of Things: An Archaeology of the Human Sciences*. New York: Random House.

Frank, Roberta. 1988. "'Interdisciplinary': The First Half Century." *Items* 6 (40): 73–78. https://oakland.edu/Assets/upload/docs/AIS/Issues-in-Interdisciplinary-Studies/1988-Volume-06/06_Vol_6_pp_139-151_Interdisciplinary_The_First_Half_Century_(Roberta_Frank).pdf.

Gordon, Lewis R. 2006. *Disciplinary Decadence: Living Thought in Trying Times*. New York: Routledge.

la paperson. 2017. *A Third University Is Possible*. Minneapolis: University of Minnesota.

Marx, John, and Mark Garrett Cooper. 2020. "Curricular Innovation and the Degree-Program Explosion." *Profession*, Winter 2020. https://profession.mla.org/curricular-innovation-and-the-degree-program-explosion/.

Melamed, Jodi. 2011. *Represent and Destroy: Rationalizing Violence in the New Capitalism*. Minneapolis: University of Minnesota Press.

Meyerhoff, Eli. 2019. *Beyond Education: Radical Studying for Another World*. Minneapolis: University of Minnesota Press.

Mitchell, Nick. 2015. "(Critical Ethnic Studies) Intellectual." *Critical Ethnic Studies* 1 (1): 86–94.

Myers, Joshua. 2022. *Of Black Study*. London: Pluto.

Reitter, Paul, and Chad Wellmon. 2021. *Permanent Crisis: The Humanities in a Disenchanted Age*. Chicago: University of Chicago Press.

Wiegman, Robyn. 2012. *Object Lessons*. Durham, NC: Duke University Press.

Wilder, Craig Steven. 2014. *Ebony and Ivy: Race, Slavery, and the Troubled History of America's Universities*. New York: Bloomsbury.

D

Diversity

p. s. kehal

Diversity and inclusion are among the most debated keywords in US higher education today. Known under many different phrases across the US sector when implemented as policies, programs, or initiatives—DEI (diversity, equity, and inclusion), JEDI (justice, equity, diversity, and inclusion), or IDEAL (inclusion, diversity, and equity in a learning environment), for instance—diversity and inclusion can be thought of as concepts and values. As concepts, they can change over time, and these changes reflect shifts in political, economic, and social contexts. As values, diversity and inclusion in the United States project a core idea today: Difference is an opportunity, and organizations should capitalize on this difference through inclusion. For example, higher education organizations could enroll more students from different backgrounds, hire faculty with different political philosophies, invite speakers onto campuses with different partisan affiliations, and create campus centers to bridge difference. These could all qualify as consistent with values of diversity and inclusion depending on the context and actors involved. Yet, diversity and inclusion are debated as concepts because they are politicized, or capable of transforming the very social fabric of one's life at the individual, organizational, and societal levels (Berrey 2015; Kennedy and Tadesse 2019).

With these implications, diversity and inclusion have supporters and resisters across the political spectrum. While diversity advocates argue that they are politically and partisanly neutral and target structures of inequality, critics allege that diversity is used to include only those who align with liberal to leftist positions, targeting conservative thought, communities, religions, and people for exclusion (Brint and German 2021; Glasener, Martell, and Posselt 2019). Similarly, those who criticize while advocating for diversity and inclusion, advocate for inclusion of difference but criticize diversity and inclusion in practice because they are insufficient to meet the scale of transformation needed (Grande 2018; Rodgers and Liera 2023). In these cases, when supporters or resisters invite speakers or hire faculty with different philosophies or ways of working in organizations, diversity and inclusion are contested as concepts because it can be unclear what values are being implemented. While diversity advocates and critics are not homogeneous in terms of background, in the United States, they share a nationalist focus and globalize diversity and inclusion when it benefits a shared nation-based position: bringing the global "best" to the United States, or "a race of the top."

When people debate the efficacy of diversity initiatives for inclusion in the United States, they have argumentative loops over the values associated with diversity and inclusion. Supporters of diversity lean on the history of social movements in the 1960s and 1970s, claiming that diversity and inclusion is what makes US higher education worthwhile—a multicultural democracy realized at last (Jayakumar, Garces, and Park 2018; Newfield 2005). Critics draw on a longer history of presumed "excellence" or "merit" that they feel defines US higher education from its "founding," arguing that contemporary efforts are nothing more than window dressing for including unqualified or unprepared people, who undermine this long-lasting US excellence (Geiger 2016; McNamee and Miller 2013). Even advocates who seek greater transformation draw on a longer history—from colonial invasion to present (Boggs et al. 2019; Grande 2018). In these common argumentative loops, people focus on or evade very different elements of US higher education (e.g., enrollments; hiring; labor, human, environmental rights) under the banner of debating diversity, making it difficult if not structurally impossible to reach a resolution. Debates on diversity become topics of analyses themselves, producing more discourse about diversity without any necessary commitment to making it a material reality in enrollments, hiring, and labor rights, for instance (Bell and Hartmann 2007; byrd 2019; Kezar and Posselt 2019).

These loops are possible because those who debate diversity typically dehistoricize diversity and inclusion as concepts. Instead, they contemporize them as values, focusing on a specific historical trajectory of inclusion and treating diversity and inclusion as normative nationalist values (e.g., 1960s onward). When individuals dehistoricize diversity and inclusion as concepts, they can evade how administrators, faculty, and donors imbued particular values into diversity and inclusion as the US university system grew from its emergence in the late 1860s (Ris 2021; Veysey 1965). While campuses existed before the 1860s in what is currently the United States, such as colonial colleges, from the 1860s to the 1940s, new campuses were created, and old campuses were reorganized around particular values of labor and output (Barrow 1990; Boggs et al. 2019; Du Bois 1973). Until the 1950s and 1960s, administrators and faculty made campuses to explicitly serve white male students, predominantly of Christian background, even as Black people, women, non-Christian people, and people from working-class backgrounds gradually entered the growing system (Brubacher and Rudy 1968; Gerber 2014; Karabel 2005; Synnott 2010; Thelin 2004; Wechsler 2014). From the 1860s until the mid-1900s, then, diversity and inclusion as concepts represented a threat, and to counteract this threat, administrators and faculty valued white male individuals of an elite social pedigree for inclusion (Stulberg and Chen 2011). At that time, colleges and universities were meant to prepare individuals to be leaders of the white patriarchal society; educating individuals who were not white men—and mostly of Christian background—was therefore inconsistent with the purpose of higher education. These values, to prefer white men and train them to be leaders, were implemented in the types of coursework offered, the research norms being developed, and the enrollment and hiring policies at colleges and universities (Gerber 2014; Ross 1991; Synnott 2010; Thelin 2004; Veysey 1965). As the historical narrative goes, antiracist desegregation movements and gender integration efforts from the 1940s to the 1970s challenged these campus values until finally reversing them (Malkiel 2016; Stulberg and Chen 2011; Teddlie and Freeman 2002). By the end of the 1970s, though desegregation and integration had been abandoned, the idea of diversity as a source of educational benefit and multicultural inclusion took ascendence. The calculus had been switched: Diversity and inclusion as concepts represented not threat but opportunity, and administrators, faculty, and campus actors should value people of all backgrounds, not only white male individuals, for inclusion. In this orientation of opportunity, colleges and universities that were segregated for white men could "reap the social benefits of being perceived as progressive, diverse organizations, while simultaneously functioning to maintain the status quo" (Rodgers and Liera 2023, 445). Administrators encouraged people to self-commodify their racial identity as an opportunity for self-advocacy, all while bringing people with marginalized backgrounds from across the globe into an enclosure for extraction (Gerrard, Sriprakash, and Rudolph 2022).

For a nation founded on colonizing the lands of numerous Indigenous nations now collectively called the United States, and a nation that practiced chattel slavery and state-protected white and male supremacy, this reversal was a welcomed change in values. When thinking of diversity and inclusion as concepts rather than as static values circulating among higher education actors, diversity and inclusion are tools for organizational survival, or "technologies" enabling university leaders to "constantly [refine] to acquire the latest innovation" and be both "revolutionary and traditional" (Ferguson 2012, 12; Johnson 2020). In this perspective, organizational leaders reorder values through diversity and inclusion and adapt their organizations to new conditions while holding on to core ideals and structures (Garbes 2021; Hamilton, Nielsen, and Lerma 2023; Kirton and Guillaume 2019; Noon 2018). This strategic reordering is critical, since policymakers and university leaders, with supportive citizenry, built US higher education through colonization, slavery, and white male domination (Boggs et al. 2019; Ross 1991; Wilder 2013). Colleges and universities have changed in fundamentally important ways over the decades: Student, staff, and faculty bodies' demographic compositions have more variation in background, more degrees and topics for study exist, and more organizational types of colleges and universities operate. Yet, it is a theoretical and empirical question whether US higher education as a structure and as individual campuses still hold on to colonization, slavery, and white male domination as core ideals (Dancy, Edwards, and Davis 2018; Jones 2023; Rocha Beardall 2021).

For instance, many colleges and universities, such as land-grant institutions, still hold in their endowments the money and lands they received during westward expansion. To this day, they continue to profit off this expropriation and exploitation of Indigenous people and their ways of being (Lee and Ahtone 2020). Relatedly, in terms of the logics of colonialism and imperialism, the organizational and cultural norms of contemporary higher education organizations are quite reflective of those of slave plantations (Sacks 1987; Squire, Williams, and Tuitt 2018). But beyond organizational structures and norms, university leaders' contemporary decision making continues to reify white male domination through diversity and inclusion. The COVID-19 pandemic revealed how administrators could use diversity and inclusion to continue a legacy of exploiting women and nonwhite people, for example. In June 2020, higher education administrators debated the potential long-lasting effects of declining fall enrollments if professors provided exclusively online instruction during a global health pandemic requiring physical distancing. The dean of the College of Liberal Arts and Sciences at the University of Iowa, a public research institution, indicated that being an online university would not fulfill their institutional mission (Miller 2020). As a result, faculty had to opt out of in-person teaching, and the dean encouraged one such faculty member—who was diagnosed with an autoimmune condition—"to think about trying to manage [those concerns] because—as an underrepresented minority, a woman of color—you have a tremendous impact to students if you can overcome some of that anxiety and fear" (Miller 2020). In this case, university leaders used diversity and inclusion for organizational labor purposes. While these may not universalize people's experiences at all colleges and universities, they are illuminating: The values of diversity and inclusion may have shifted to value nonwhite and nonmale people and communities, but the concepts remain tools to maintain the university. In the context and history of US racial and colonial capitalism, university officials use diversity and inclusion to accumulate more individuals and resources for extraction—marginalized people and their value to the organization. As racial capital, this immunocompromised professor was valuable enough to include to show the university as "diverse." Colonial dispossession in this case happened in two ways: the professor's presence was needed to maintain the colonial university, but their life was not necessary to maintain, and they could be exposed to higher chances of premature death.

Yet, diversity and inclusion as concepts may be undergoing another shift in values. In the 2023–24 academic year, pro-Palestinian and antiwar student movements created encampments across US campuses in an effort to have their institutions divest materially and academically from Israel. When the newest phase of the Nakba—the name for the decades-long Zionist strategy to eliminate Palestinians—began in October 2023, university leaders sent messages empathizing with Israeli and Jewish victims, at times conflating the two. In these instances, and subsequent ones, leaders barely if at all acknowledged Palestinian loss and harm, let alone acknowledging the disproportionate murder of Palestinian life and society. At the University of North Carolina at Chapel Hill, this erasure and evasion was so extreme that Palestinian students and advocates filed a federal civil rights complaint about the racism they experienced (Killian 2024). After continued disregard for Palestinians and the genocide they were enduring, students launched their encampments.

While many claimed this activism was illegal and violated campus polices, students and advocates justified their activism on two grounds: basic human ethics to end a genocide, and the values of diversity and inclusion. For the latter case (the former is beyond this chapter's scope), advocates challenged universities to live up to their stated ideals: How could they be committed to diversity and inclusion, especially on a global stage, if they were materially contributing to a genocide through investments in weapons manufacturers and companies that enabled the Nakba? Rather than engaging in this question, university leaders used state, campus, and national police repression to shut down these encampments and protests. In fact, university leaders invoked their values of diversity and inclusion to justify this repression: claims that Jewish students felt unsafe on campus, which intentionally created Jewish students as a monolith around a political position and ignored the fact that Jewish students were part of the student movements. While administrators strategically used diversity and inclusion to justify their actions, they also leaned into rightwing attacks on diversity and inclusion by framing all pro-Palestinian and antiwar advocacy as equivalent to or relying on antisemitism.

University leaders' carceral response explicitly exposed a fissure that has been implicitly recognized in US higher education: Diversity and inclusion as concepts serve colonial and imperial interests through US higher education. The contemporary political context on campuses exposed the "silent" nationalist, colonial, and imperial fissures in diversity and inclusion as concepts. In August 2024 in preparation for the new academic year, New York University updated their diversity and inclusion policies to explicitly make Zionists a protected class. In doing so, university leaders made Zionist "an identity meriting protection under Title VI of the Civil Rights Act of 1964, rather than a political ideology used to justify apartheid and genocide" (Palestine Legal 2024).

These fissures are not new, as various traditions of university studies have increasingly named the United States' colonial and imperial interests (Chatterjee and Maira 2014; Rocha Beardall 2021; Stein 2018). What was new was the disregard among administrators and faculty of pretending otherwise; university leaders' values of diversity and inclusion included not challenging US colonialism and imperialism. To the extent that university actors challenge US colonialism, it is confined domestically, as leaders create new relationships with Indigenous tribes, nations, communities, and people. But this approach has been strongly critiqued by many Indigenous communities native to North America for being superficial, focused on representation and, in some cases, continuing colonization (Coulthard 2014; Grande 2015; Hunt 2014).

In this shifting terrain, diversity and inclusion are unlikely to disappear as concepts for university leaders, even as they negotiate the values they associate with them to suppress Palestinians and Palestine. On one hand, a rightwing reactionary movement against diversity has led college and university leaders to retreat from their commitments to diversity, and to antiracism and transgender inclusion specifically, a trend that was already underway in many contentious political contexts (antonio and Clarke 2011; Glasener, Martell, and Posselt 2019; Okechukwu 2019). On the other hand, college and university leaders in safer political contexts have capitalized on diversity and inclusion in labor terms: not compensating students of color as they experiment with new forms of inclusion (i.e., antiracist community spaces) before appropriating it for themselves (i.e., as an inclusive university initiative for prospective students); reframing inclusion efforts as part of professors' on-campus service obligations; and implementing privatizing practices at all levels of workers, namely nontenure line staff (Berrey 2014; Kezar, DePaola, and Scott 2019; Lerma, Hamilton, and Nielsen 2019; Miller 2020). While this could be considered inconsistent with diversity and inclusion as colloquially understood in the United States, in a historicized context, these practices of inclusion and exploitation are consistent with how university leaders have used the concept of diversity and inclusion.

By considering how people in empowered positions—whether in higher education or other industries—use diversity and inclusion differently as concepts or values, a diversity and inclusion "advocate" and "critic" are not normative statuses. Instead, they are political positions associated with political goals. In some cases, advocates and resisters rework diversity and inclusion to return higher education to its segregated ways of being, and in other cases, advocates and resisters seek to create a higher education that has not yet emerged. Whether DEI in practice translates into diversity, equity, and inclusion or diversity, equity, and imperialism, the key distinction between political actors is the values they imbue into the concepts of diversity and inclusion.

References

antonio, anthony lising, and Chris Gonzalez Clarke. 2011. "The Official Organization of Diversity in American Higher Education: A Retreat from Race?" In *Diversity in American Higher Education*, edited by Lisa M. Stulberg and Sharon Lawner Weinberg, 87–103. New York, NY: Routledge.

Barrow, Clyde W. 1990. *Universities and the Capitalist State: Corporate Liberalism and the Reconstruction of American Higher Education, 1894–1928*. Madison: University of Wisconsin Press.

Bell, Joyce M., and Douglas Hartmann. 2007. "Diversity in Everyday Discourse: The Cultural Ambiguities and Consequences of 'Happy Talk.'" *American Sociological Review* 72 (6): 895–914. https://doi.org/10.1177/000312240707200603.

Berrey, Ellen. 2014. "Breaking Glass Ceilings, Ignoring Dirty Floors: The Culture and Class Bias of Diversity Management." *American Behavioral Scientist* 58 (2): 347–70. https://doi.org/10.1177/0002764213503333.

Berrey, Ellen. 2015. *The Enigma of Diversity: The Language of Race and the Limits of Racial Justice*. Chicago: University of Chicago Press.

Boggs, Abigail, Eli Meyerhoff, Nick Mitchell, and Zach Schwartz-Weinstein. 2019. "Abolitionist University Studies: An Invitation." *Abolition Journal*, August 28. https://abolitionjournal.org/abolitionist-university-studies-an-invitation/.

Brint, Steven, and Komi T. German. 2021. "The University of California Drifts toward Conformism." *New Discourses*, March 8. https://newdiscourses.com/2021/03/university-california-drifts-toward-conformism-representation-academic-freedom/.

Brubacher, John, and Willis Rudy. 1968. *Higher Education in Transition: A History of American Colleges and Universities*. Rev. and enlarged ed. New York: Harper and Row.

byrd, derria. 2019. "The Diversity Distraction: A Critical Comparative Analysis of Discourse in Higher Education Scholarship." *Review of Higher Education* 42 (supp.): 135–72.

Chatterjee, Piya, and Sunaina Maira, eds. 2014. *The Imperial University: Academic Repression and Scholarly Dissent*. Minneapolis: University of Minnesota Press.

Coulthard, Glen Sean. 2014. *Red Skin, White Masks: Rejecting the Colonial Politics of Recognition*. Minneapolis: University of Minnesota Press.

Dancy, T. Elon, II, Kirsten T. Edwards, and James Earl Davis. 2018. "Historically White Universities and Plantation Politics: Anti-Blackness and Higher Education in the Black Lives Matter Era." *Urban Education* 53 (2): 176–95.

Du Bois, W. E. B. 1973. *The Education of Black People: Ten Critiques, 1906–1960*. Edited by Herbert Aptheker. New York: Monthly Review Press.

Ferguson, Roderick A. 2012. *The Reorder of Things: The University and Its Pedagogies of Minority Difference*. Minneapolis: University of Minnesota Press.

Garbes, Laura. 2021. "When the 'Blank Slate' Is a White One: White Institutional Isomorphism in the Birth of National Public Radio." *Sociology of Race and Ethnicity* 8 (1). https://doi.org/10.1177/2332649221994619.

Geiger, Roger L. 2016. *The History of American Higher Education: Learning and Culture from the Founding to World War II*. Princeton, NJ: Princeton University Press.

Gerber, Larry G. 2014. *The Rise and Decline of Faculty Governance: Professionalization and the Modern American University*. Baltimore: Johns Hopkins University Press.

Gerrard, Jessica, Arathi Sriprakash, and Sophie Rudolph. 2022. "Education and Racial Capitalism." *Race Ethnicity and Education* 25 (3): 425–42. https://doi.org/10.1080/13613324.2021.2001449.

Glasener, Kristen M., Christian A. Martell, and Julie R. Posselt. 2019. "Framing Diversity: Examining the Place of Race in Institutional Policy and Practice Post-Affirmative Action." *Journal of Diversity in Higher Education* 12 (1): 3–16. https://doi.org/10.1037/dhe0000086.

Grande, Sandy. 2015. *Red Pedagogy: Native American Social and Political Thought*. 10th Anniversary ed. Lanham, Md: Rowman and Littlefield.

Grande, Sandy. 2018. "Refusing the University." In *Toward What Justice? Describing Diverse Dreams of Justice in Education*, edited by Eve Tuck and K. Wayne Yang, 47–65. New York: Routledge.

Hamilton, Laura T., Kelly Nielsen, and Veronica Lerma. 2023. "'Diversity Is a Corporate Plan': Racialized Equity Labor among University Employees." *Ethnic and Racial Studies* 46 (6): 1204–26. https://doi.org/10.1080/01419870.2022.2089049.

Hunt, Sarah. 2014. "Ontologies of Indigeneity: The Politics of Embodying a Concept." *Cultural Geographies* 21 (1): 27–32.

Jayakumar, Uma M., Liliana M. Garces, and Julie J. Park. 2018. "Reclaiming Diversity: Advancing the Next Generation of Diversity Research toward Racial Equity." In *Higher Education: Handbook of Theory and Research*, vol. 33, edited by Michael B. Paulsen, 11–79. Cham: Springer International. https://doi.org/10.1007/978-3-319-72490-4_2.

Johnson, Matthew. 2020. *Undermining Racial Justice: How One University Embraced Inclusion and Inequality*. New York: Cornell University Press.

Jones, Angela. 2023. "Cisgendered Workspaces: Outright and Categorical Exclusion in Cisgendered Organizations." *Social Problems*, April 26, spad017. https://doi.org/10.1093/socpro/spad017.

Karabel, Jerome. 2005. *The Chosen: The Hidden History of Admission and Exclusion at Harvard, Yale, and Princeton*. Boston: Houghton Mifflin.

Kennedy, Michael D., and Merone Tadesse. 2019. "Towards a Theory and Practice of Diversity and Inclusion in Globalizing US Universities: Transformational Solidarities of Knowledge Activism." *Youth and Globalization* 1 (2): 254–81. https://doi.org/10.1163/25895745-00102004.

Kezar, Adrianna J., Tom DePaola, and Daniel T. Scott. 2019. *The Gig Academy: Mapping Labor in the Neoliberal University*. Baltimore: Johns Hopkins University Press.

Kezar, Adrianna J., and Julie R. Posselt, eds. 2019. *Higher Education Administration for Social Justice and Equity*. New York: Routledge.

Killian, Joe. 2024. "Students for Justice in Palestine Files Civil Rights Complaint against UNC-Chapel Hill." *NC Newsline* (blog), April 10. https://ncnewsline.com/2024/04/10/students-for-justice-in-palestine-file-civil-rights-complaint-against-unc-chapel-hill/.

Kirton, Gill, and Cécile Guillaume. 2019. "When Welfare Professionals Encounter Restructuring and Privatization: The Inside Story of the Probation Service of England and Wales." *Work, Employment and Society* 33 (6): 929–47. https://doi.org/10.1177/0950017019855229.

Lee, Robert, and Tristan Ahtone. 2020. "Land-Grab Universities: Expropriated Indigenous Land Is the Foundation of the Land-Grant University System." *High Country News*, March 30. https://www.hcn.org/issues/52.4/indigenous-affairs-education-land-grab-universities.

Lerma, Veronica, Laura T. Hamilton, and Kelly Nielsen. 2019. "Racialized Equity Labor, University Appropriation and Student Resistance." *Social Problems* 67 (2): 286–303. https://doi.org/10.1093/socpro/spz011.

Malkiel, Nancy Weiss. 2016. *"Keep the Damned Women Out": The Struggle for Coeducation.* Princeton, NJ: Princeton University Press.

McNamee, Stephen J., and Robert K. Miller Jr. 2013. *The Meritocracy Myth*. 3rd ed. Lanham, MD: Rowman and Littlefield.

Miller, Vanessa. 2020. "If Students Don't Return, Iowa Universities Face More Severe Budget Cuts, Leaders Say." *Cedar Rapids (IA) Gazette*, June 19, sec. Education. https://www.thegazette.com/subject/news/education/university-of-iowa-in-person-classes-online-fall-semester-20200619.

Newfield, Christopher. 2005. *Unmaking the Public University: The Forty-Year Assault on the Middle Class.* Cambridge, MA: Harvard University Press.

Noon, Mike. 2018. "Pointless Diversity Training: Unconscious Bias, New Racism and Agency." *Work, Employment and Society* 32 (1): 198–209. https://doi.org/10.1177/0950017017719841.

Okechukwu, Amaka. 2019. *To Fulfill These Rights: Political Struggle over Affirmative Action and Open Admissions*. New York: Columbia University Press.

Palestine Legal. 2024. "Palestine Legal Statement on NYU's New, Draconian Student Conduct Policies." Palestine Legal, August 29. https://palestinelegal.org/news/2024/8/29/palestine-legal-statement-on-nyus-new-draconian-student-conduct-policies.

Ris, Ethan W. 2021. "What's Future Is Epilogue: The Uses of Higher Education History." *American Journal of Education* 127 (4): 657–68. https://doi.org/10.1086/715035.

Rocha Beardall, Theresa. 2021. "Settler Simultaneity and Anti-Indigenous Racism at Land-Grant Universities." *Sociology of Race and Ethnicity* 8 (1): 197–212. https://doi.org/10.1177/23326492211037714.

Rodgers, Aireale J., and Román Liera. 2023. "When Race Becomes Capital: Diversity, Faculty Hiring, and the Entrenchment of Racial Capitalism in Higher Education." *Educational Researcher* 52 (7): 444–49. https://doi.org/10.3102/0013189X231175359.

Ross, Dorothy. 1991. *Origins of American Social Science*. Cambridge: Cambridge University Press.

Sacks, Karen Brodkin. 1987. *Caring by the Hour: Women, Work, and Organizing at Duke Medical Center*. Urbana: University of Illinois Press.

Squire, Dian, Bianca C. Williams, and Frank Tuitt. 2018. "Plantation Politics and Neoliberal Racism in Higher Education: A Framework for Reconstructing Anti-Racist Institutions." *Teachers College Record* 120 (14): 1–20.

Stein, Sharon. 2018. "Higher Education and the Im/possibility of Transformative Justice." *Critical Ethnic Studies* 4 (1): 130–53.

Stulberg, Lisa M., and Anthony S. Chen. 2011. "A Long View on 'Diversity': A Century of American College Admissions Debates." In *Diversity in American Higher Education*, edited by Lisa M. Stulberg and Sharon Lawner Weinberg, 51–62. New York: Routledge.

Synnott, Marcia Graham. 2010. *The Half-Opened Door: Discrimination and Admissions at Harvard, Yale, and Princeton, 1900–1970*. New Brunswick, NJ: Transaction.

Teddlie, Charles, and John A. Freeman. 2002. "Twentieth-Century Desegregation in U.S. Higher Education: A Review of Five Distinct Historical Era." In *Racial Crisis in American Higher Education: Continuing Challenges for the Twenty-First Century*, rev. ed., edited by William A. Smith, Philip G. Altbach, and Kofi Lomotey, 77–102. Albany: State University of New York Press.

Thelin, John R. 2004. *A History of American Higher Education*. Baltimore: Johns Hopkins University Press.

Veysey, Laurence R. 1965. *The Emergence of the American University*. 3rd ed. Chicago: University of Chicago Press.

Wechsler, Harold S. 2014. *The Qualified Student: A History of Selective College Admission in America*. New York: Routledge.

Wilder, Craig Steven. 2013. *Ebony and Ivy: Race, Slavery, and the Troubled History of America's Universities*. New York: Bloomsbury.

E

Ed Tech

Annie McClanahan and Louise McCune

In the mid-1960s, mainstream macroeconomist William J. Baumol became interested in a surprising topic: the problem of "the starving artist." In a canonical essay, "On the Performing Arts: An Anatomy of Their Economic Problems," Baumol and his co-author William G. Bowen concluded that musicians were paid poverty wages because "the live performing arts" was unable to implement transformative "technological economies" (Baumol and Bowen 1965, 495). A follow-up essay in 1967 extended this analysis by dividing all economic activities into two types: "technologically progressive activities," in which technological innovations and economies of scale allowed "output per man hour" to increase progressively, and "nonprogressive" activities, "which by their very nature, permit only sporadic increases in productivity" (Baumol 1967, 415–16). In the later essay, Baumol's key example of a "nonprogressive" activity wasn't violin playing but teaching: "Despite the invention of teaching machines," Baumol noted, "there still seem to be fairly firm limits" to productivity growth in education, which meant it would persistently lag "productivity in the remainder of the economy" (416).

For more than half a century, Baumol's theory of technological stagnation has been used by orthodox economists and policy experts to explain the rising costs of higher education and health care (see Baumol 2012). Here, we focus on the "teaching machines" of the twenty-first century, from Learning Management Systems (LMSs) to algorithms that track student "outcomes." Our primary emphasis is on how these innovations in ed tech affect what Baumol describes as the "productivity" of instructional labor. We begin with the massive open online course, or MOOC, whose brief efflorescence in the early 2010s sparked the interest of critical university studies scholars in ed tech as a site of analysis and struggle. We suggest that the failure of the MOOC helped pave the way for the current boom in online education (OLE). OLE, we contend, is intensifying preexisting processes like adjunctification and is likely to have particularly adverse effects on historically excluded, first-generation, and at-risk students. It also will increase the economic "productivity" of teaching by enabling economies of scale and providing an alibi for other austerity measures; by providing a mechanism for the capture of instructors' intellectual property; and by rationalizing, deskilling, and even fully automating the labor of teaching.

Educational technology is not itself a new phenomenon: Audrey Watters notes we are currently at the tail end of roughly "75 years of computing, almost 60 years of computer-assisted instruction, at least 40 years of the learning management system, more than 25 years of one-to-one laptop programs, [and] a decade (give or take a year) of mobile learning" (Watters 2017, n.p.). Yet these innovations—from the "closed circuit televisions" mentioned by Baumol in the 1960s, to the "word processing" innovations of the 1980s, to the development of LMSs in the 1990s—were largely perceived and described as *tools*: They might transform pedagogy and curriculum but would not fundamentally shift the economic model of higher education. That changed with the rise of the MOOC—open access, asynchronous online courses that could be offered to students across the country and around the world. *Remote*, or *distance*, education had been around for a long time—for-profit correspondence schools date back to the late nineteenth century, and University of Phoenix launched the first online college program in 1989 (Noble 2001; Smith et al. 2023). Unlike these modalities, however, the MOOC would allow a single instructor to teach tens of thousands of students at once via online video streaming, enabling precisely the economies of scale Baumol thought were impossible in a "nonprogressive" sector like education. Stanford professor Sebastian Thrun's 2011 MOOC "Introduction to Artificial Intelligence"—a no-credit, free course offered through Stanford's website and ultimately taken by 150,000 students from around the world—promised to "disrupt" higher ed so extensively that the *New York Times* rather peremptorily declared 2012 "The Year of the MOOC," and Thrun left his university job to cofound an ed-tech start-up focused on developing more MOOCs (Srivas 2016).

A lot of ink was spilled between 2011 and 2013 on what MOOCs promised or portended. A meta-analysis of MOOC discourse notes two key themes in what Richard Grusin aptly named "MOOC mania": a sense of "economic crisis [leading to] calls for increased faculty productivity" and "a vision of online education as a solution to problems of access and affordability" (Grusin 2013; Rhoads et al. 2015, 404). Those same themes would appear in critiques of MOOCs as "an academic labor policy" intended to make the professoriate more precarious by "'solv[ing]' the problems of education through computational automation," as Ian Bogost (2013, n.p.) put it. Yet entrepreneurs and investors quickly got cold feet—although hundreds of universities rushed to produce MOOCs between 2011 and 2014, by 2013 Thrun announced he was "pivoting away" from the MOOC model, largely because the promise of "access" had run aground on the reality that only around 5 percent of students were actually completing the courses (Cottom 2013). Universities themselves, in turn, began to realize that offering their product for free (albeit in watered-down and scaled-up form) might not be a great business model. During the very same years scholars and others were worrying about the threat of MOOCs as a technology of automation, most universities were solving the labor-cost problem in a far more familiar way—by hiring more and more adjunct and part-time instructors—while also raising tuition to ever-greater heights (see Coalition on the Academic Workforce 2010; Cawley 2020).

Between 2010 and 2020, then, the most significant transformation in ed tech was not a radical "disruption" but simply a rapid increase in the use of ed-tech tools developed by private vendors. While "Decade of the For-Profit LMS" might sound less sexy than "Year of the MOOC," that would probably be a more accurate way to describe the innovations of this period. In the 1990s, campuses had designed and built their own LMSs, admissions management software, online bulletin boards, and even email clients. In the early 2000s, however, watershed revisions to federal education policy allowed public universities (as well as K–12 schools) to outsource these services to for-profit companies (Burch 2021; Greene 2021; Watters 2017). Immense amounts of private equity and venture capital were sloshing around the tech sector in those years, and higher ed quickly became the fastest-growing new market for tech. Soon, colleges and universities were spending billions of dollars annually on LMSs and other technology and digital services. Today an estimated $20 billion is spent each year on higher ed tech, while tens of billions more are paid to third-party vendors of enrollment management and online program management (OPM) software (Hamilton et al. 2022; Marcus 2021; Protopsaltis and Baum 2019; Smith et al. 2023).

Critical university studies scholars have described these arrangements between not-for-profit colleges and universities and for-profit vendors as a form of "privatization by obfuscation," referring to the omissions and occlusions that screen the intercessions of private profit from the awareness and agency of those who might otherwise oppose them (Hamilton et al. 2022, 4). In our experiences researching ed-tech contracts at our institution, University of California, Irvine, we found obfuscation in the institutional protocols that govern campus adoption of learning management tools as well as in the contracts themselves. After a months-long FOIA process, we were able to review campus- and systemwide contracts with Respondus, Perusall, YuJa, Gradescope, Ed Discussion, and Turnitin and learned that most purchases were approved by a very small number of noninstructional staff, with no faculty input, and that they were often completed without the requisite step of negotiating a full contract with the vendor. Put simply, these private-public partnerships are being brokered in decision-making silos removed from shared governance. Moreover, although the university claims contracts are reviewed to ensure privacy protections, most of the contracts we reviewed suggested no serious attempt to ensure that student and faculty data and Intellectual Property (IP) are not being used for private profit. Indeed, data extraction is central to the business model of what Ben Williamson calls "Big EdTech": Once anonymized, the metadata captured can easily be sold, used for marketing, or fed back into algorithms for improving the for-profit tech. Williamson thus notes that the incredibly high valuations of the biggest private ed-tech companies derive not from subscription and user fees but instead from the commercial value of user data and IP generated and collected through the platform (Williamson 2022).

Privatization and data extraction aren't the only concerns with ed tech of this kind. Another issue is student privacy, especially with various forms of monitoring, tracking, and surveillance software. Much of the first wave of critical university studies scholarship (and activism) on ed tech focused on Turnitin, a "plagiarism detection" software first developed in the early 2000s and now integrated into virtually all university LMSs (see Purdy 2009; Twomey 2009). Turnitin's Terms of Service require students and instructors to permanently hand over their IP rights: as Sean Morris and Jesse Stommel explain, "Every essay students submit—representing hours, days, or even years of work—becomes part of the Turnitin database, which is then sold to universities . . . Turnitin has a 'non-exclusive, royalty-free, perpetual, worldwide, irrevocable license' to more than 734 million student papers" (Morris and Stommel 2017, n.p.).

Applications like Turnitin are also a form of surveillance, creating what the Conference on College Composition and Communication (CCCC) describes as a "hostile environment," and what other scholars have termed a "pedagogy of punishment" (CCCC 2013; Swauger 2020, n.p.). This punitive surveillance model has been further expanded by recent innovations in online *remote proctoring* of exams and standardized tests. Remote proctoring companies like ProctorU and Examity employ low-wage workers centralized in business process outsourcing (BPO) work centers in the underdeveloped world to monitor students taking exams and tests. Students are required to turn on their computer's webcam and be monitored (and recorded) throughout the exam. A 2022 court case determined that remote proctoring violated students' right to privacy (see Martin 2023). These concerns are even greater with automated proctoring, which (as one company describes it) uses "advanced A.I. software" to "detect abnormal student behavior that may signal academic dishonesty" (quoted in Kelley 2021). Relying on facial recognition software, motion detection, and biometric data, automated proctoring is an example of what Safiya Noble (2018) terms "algorithms of oppression," and Ruha Benjamin (2019), "The New Jim Code." Scholar Shea Swauger describes automated proctoring as a "racist technology calibrated for white skin" and recounts how "students with black or brown skin have been asked to shine more light on themselves when verifying their identities for a test" (2020, n.p.). Categorizing behaviors like stimming or staring into space as "abnormal," remote proctoring companies have also been charged with discrimination against disabled and neurodivergent test takers as well as against students wearing headscarves and those whose gender expression may not "match" their state-issued ID.

Student protests against online proctoring during COVID were so effective that in 2021, several universities canceled contracts with the vendors of these services; the US Senate even sent a letter of inquiry requesting detailed information about policies from the three largest automated proctoring companies (Kelley 2021; Swaak 2022). Yet the backlash against surveillance ed tech has largely not addressed the equally problematic use of surveillance tools for "softer" purposes, including monitoring student "wellness" and educational outcomes. Lindsay Weinberg has written powerfully about the surveillant use of data analytics, sensors, and other "smart campus" technology—from the "predictive analytics" used to track students' academic progress to "mental health apps" like WellTrack. She notes that these technologies ultimately institutionalize the very forms of inequality that universities claim to be redressing, whether by using machine-learning data to "nudge" students toward certain educational outcomes or by targeting historically excluded students for high levels of student debt (Weinberg 2021, 2023).

The massive—and massively profitable—investments of tech companies and venture capitalists in education-sector apps, LMSs, and data services show that for-profit tech has fully embedded itself in higher education. But this tech still did not lead to the kind of disruptive, labor-saving innovation that Baumol claimed could never happen in higher education (a view that the failure of MOOCs seemed to confirm). That kind of change would become possible only with the steady normalization—and then swift expansion—of OLE. David F. Noble predicted "the coming of the online university" in his 2001 book *Digital Diploma Mills: The Automation of Higher Education,* but the expansion of OLE in the first decade of the twenty-first century remained limited by the 1965 Higher Education Act (HEA), which defines the criteria for federal-aid-eligible "institutions of higher education" in part by specifying the amount and type of "regular substantive instruction" (RSI) they are required to provide (D. F. Noble 2001; Eaton, Howell, and Yannelis 2020). In 2006, revisions to the HEA broadened the definition of RSI, effectively lifting Title IX aid limitations on online programs. OLE in this period, however, was still limited primarily to for-profit colleges and universities: By 2012, more than half of students at for-profit institutions were studying online, compared to only 1 percent of those at nonprofit institutions (Cellini 2021). Online education in the for-profit sector enabled what scholars describe as "predatory inclusion," a process whereby historically underrepresented students achieve access to higher education but under far worse terms than more privileged students once did. Students attending for-profit online schools are more likely to be older, female, and nonwhite, and they experience significantly worse educational outcomes than those attending not-for-profit, in-person institutions (Protopsaltis and Baum 2019, 9; Smith et al. 2023). In 2018, the Trump administration's Department of Education loosened requirements on online education again—while these revisions were likely intended to help grow the for-profit sector, they ultimately formalized and legitimated OLE across all kinds of institutions (Protopsaltis and Baum 2019). Increasingly, OLE wasn't associated just with the widely maligned correspondence model or the manifestly predatory for-profit sector: By 2019, nonprofit public and private institutions enrolled two-thirds of fully online students, and OLE was "the fastest growing segment of postsecondary education" (Smith et al. 2023, 1; Eaton, Howell, and Yannelis 2023).

In 2020, the speed of OLE's growth went from fast to breakneck, as hundreds of millions of postsecondary students and teachers suddenly shifted in-person courses online during the COVID pandemic. More than 30 percent of college students took all their classes online in 2021–22, while 60 percent took at least one online course, doubling prepandemic numbers (NCES 2022, 2023; Venable 2023). Although these shifts were made on an emergency basis, they ultimately created a sea change, as institutions realized the opportunities for cost savings on everything from infrastructure to labor. Our institution, UC Irvine, recently announced in its strategic plan that it had a goal of "diversifying pedagogical options" by having at least 25 percent of regular academic-year courses offered in an exclusively online format by the end of this decade.

Many of the problems with ed tech described above have been exacerbated and amplified by the rapid rise of OLE. Online education's infrastructure is subtended by agreements between nonprofit institutions of higher education and for-profit OPM vendors: third-party, for-profit providers backed by private equity or venture capital that run 85 percent of all online programs for public universities (Hamilton et al. 2022). OPMs are typically revenue sharing, meaning that universities are directly funneling tuition dollars into companies backed by both venture capital and private equity investment. The federal government has called for greater oversight of OPMs, which are often managed outside the regular operations of the campus and without the intercession of faculty governance. A 2022 paper reviewing contracts between third-party OPM vendors and public universities specifies various mechanisms by which these agreements and their implementation exploit universities and postsecondary students for private gain, for instance, by prioritizing enrollment and revenue growth over student outcomes (Hamilton et al. 2022). OPMs are also often designed to target racially and economically marginalized students for online programs through marketing and recruitment campaigns. UC Berkeley's contract with their OPM 2U, for instance, stipulated that UCB give 2U access to all data for students who applied to UCB but who were not academically qualified—2U then used the student data UCB had sold them to market lower-ranked, high-cost online programs to those same students (Hall and Dudley 2019).

Processes of predatory inclusion also continue to shape trends in OLE. Black and Latinx students, Pell Grant recipients, and first-generation college students are concentrated in online programs, which are often framed explicitly as access expanding. Yet OLE tends to disproportionately disadvantage historically excluded and underresourced students, producing lower grades, affecting outcomes in future courses, and increasing the likelihood of dropping out (Baum and McPherson 2019). One study of student outcomes found that Black and Pell Grant–receiving students were more likely to end up in online courses than other students; these online students were significantly less likely to graduate on time and more likely to be delinquent on their student loans (Smith et al. 2023). Education scholars Di Xu and Ying Xu (2020, 352) have suggested that online education tends not to resolve but to "exacerbate educational inequities," while Spiros Protopsaltis and Sandy Baum (2019, 30) note that "moving vulnerable students online will widen attainment gaps rather than solving the seemingly intractable problem of unequal educational opportunity." One likely future for OLE will be the entrenchment of institutional hierarchies, which determine who is able to access smaller, in-person classes and who ends up being educated mostly or entirely online: Large public-serving institutions (from community colleges to research universities) will eventually offer more online courses than in-person ones, whereas elite private institutions and small liberal arts colleges will market themselves as providing a more personalized, "artisanal" in-person experience.

Almost all research on OLE outcomes emphasizes the difference between fully online courses and *hybrid* courses, which mix online and in-person instruction. Hybrid courses don't entirely mitigate the problems of OLE for vulnerable students—nor any of the other concerns described above around privacy and privatization—but most studies suggest that partially online courses in which students have consistent in-person interactions with the instructor produce significantly better outcomes than fully online, asynchronous courses. Hybrid courses, however, don't offer universities the cost savings and economies of scale that fully online courses do. With fully online courses, the 2,000-person lecture Baumol describes as a "disquieting" prospect can be quite easily achieved without the expense of building and maintaining a huge lecture hall. When offered across a statewide network of campuses, like the University of California system, fully online courses allow for other "efficiencies" too: Why have a Department of Classics or German on each UC campus when one campus can host classes taken by students across the system? Our institution, UC Irvine, now offers asynchronous online instruction not only for gen ed and large lecture courses but also for upper-division language instruction and majors-only seminars, and a growing number of courses are being offered via UC Online's "cross-campus enrollment" program.

OLE also promises to drastically reduce labor costs: once fully developed, an online course can be run without the university having to pay the instructor who developed it. Often, faculty are told that because they retain IP over curriculum, their course content can't be used without their permission. The reality, unfortunately, is more complex. Historically, a *teacher exception* has exempted primary, secondary, and postsecondary teachers from standard work-for-hire rules automatically granting IP to the employer, but this exception has been subject to significant erosion since it was first established in the midseventies. Indeed, universities have already been creating workarounds to faculty IP rights. On our campus, for instance, faculty are enticed to create online courses by being offered additional research funds, but to receive those funds, they must preemptively sign over their curricular IP rights. Other institutions have simply changed their policy on faculty curricular IP by fiat, as when Purdue University issued a memo claiming the right to all courseware and online material in perpetuity (Flaherty 2020; Scully 2004; Townsend 2003).

Online classes can be taught so easily without additional faculty labor that it's not even necessary for the instructor to be alive: In 2021, a student at Concordia University in Montreal discovered that the professor for the course he was taking online had died two years earlier. The dead faculty member's recorded lectures and curriculum provided the course content, while the grading was done by low-waged graduate student teaching assistants, or TAs (Kneese 2021). This example crystallizes the relationship between labor-saving technology and deskilling: the process whereby work is standardized, rationalized, and broken up into smaller components to increase productivity. Scholar Robert Ovetz connects labor deskilling to pedagogical "unbundling": "the differentiation of instructional duties that were once typically performed by a single faculty member into distinct activities performed by various professionals." Ovetz describes the process whereby "*teaching* is . . . deskilled into *assessment, measurement, and monitoring* while *learning* is . . . replaced by *competency of task completion*" (2020, 4, 6). The justification for deskilling is often pedagogical—the language of competencies, outcomes, pathways, standardization, multimodality, modularity, and perhaps worst of all, the masking of predatory inclusion as "expanding access." But the real aim of unbundling and deskilling is to increase productivity by turning the complex intellectual and emotional labor of teaching into a series of discrete, technologically mediated tasks and to reduce labor costs by shifting work to low-waged adjuncts and graduate students.

In some ways, the story of the TAs running the class of their dead professor from behind the scenes suggests that fears of *full* automation in higher ed may be somewhat misplaced. Instead, we might draw on Mary L. Gray and Siddharth Suri's idea of "ghost work": the low-waged, precarious outsourced labor that enables online infrastructure, from the precariously employed remote proctors watching students' webcams from call centers in India to the low-waged outsourced laborers in Bogotá and Medellín paid two dollars per hour to direct the "food delivery robots" that are now omnipresent on US campuses (Gray and Suri 2019; Rooholfada 2019). From this perspective, the real threat to university labor today might come not from new technological innovations but rather (as in the days of MOOC mania) from more familiar dangers, namely adjunctification and the exploitation of low-waged graduate students.

Yet this too may be too simple. As we write these pages, instructors everywhere are agonizing about how to respond to student use of automated writing systems like ChatGPT. But faculty are also likely to be receiving emails from ed-tech companies like Packback, a "digital TA," which uses those same AI language models to produce "instant, personalized feedback" on student writing, or Khanmigo, an AI-guided chatbot "tutor" developed by Khan Academy. A UC Berkeley chief operating officer, questioned in spring 2023 about how his campus would pay for the increases in graduate student instructor stipends following their historic strike, said that campuses would start "automating grading using machine-learning" to save on the labor costs of graduate student instructors (Markovich 2023). Once deskilling is complete, and teaching labor has been rendered fully interchangeable regardless of academic content, the result will be the automated "teaching machines" Baumol thought were impossible. If faculty and students don't organize together to stop these processes, even the lowest-waged teachers may find themselves—as workers facing automation always have—out of work.

References

Baum, Sandy, and Michael McPherson. 2019. "The Human Factor: The Promise and Limits of Online Education." *Daedalus* 148 (4): 235–54.

Baumol, William J. 1967. "Macroeconomics of Unbalanced Growth: The Anatomy of Urban Crisis." *American Economic Review* 57 (3): 415–26.

Baumol, William J. 2012. *The Cost Disease: Why Computers Get Cheaper and Health Care Doesn't.* New Haven, CT: Yale University Press.

Baumol, William J., and William G. Bowen. 1965. "On the Performing Arts: The Anatomy of Their Economic Problems." *American Economic Review* 55 (1–2): 495–502.

Benjamin, Ruha. 2019. *Race after Technology: Abolitionist Tools for the New Jim Code.* Princeton, NJ: Princeton University Press.

Bogost, Ian. 2013. "MOOCs and the Future of the Humanities." Ian Bogost blog. http://bogost.com/writing/moocs_and_the_future_of_the_hu/.

Burch, Patricia. 2021. *Hidden Markets: Public Policy and the Push to Privatize Education.* 2nd ed. New York: Routledge.

Cawley, Maggie. 2020. "I Don't Really Work Here: Part-Time Faculty and the Adjunctification of Higher Ed." Master's thesis, West Chester University, PA. https://digitalcommons.wcupa.edu/cgi/viewcontent.cgi?article=1214&context=all_theses.

CCCC (Conference on College Composition and Communication). 2013. "2013 Resolutions and Sense of the House Motions." CCCC, National Council of Teachers of English. https://cccc.ncte.org/cccc/resolutions/2013.

Cellini, Stephanie Riegg. 2021. "For-Profit Colleges in the United States: Insights from Two Decades of Research." In *The Routledge Handbook of the Economics of Education*, edited by Brian McCall, 512–54. London: Routledge.

Coalition on the Academic Workforce. 2010. "One Faculty Serving All Students." Issue brief. http://www.academicworkforce.org/CAW_Issue_Brief_Feb_2010.pdf.

Cottom, Tressie McMillan. 2013. "The Audacity: Thrun Learns a Lesson and Students Pay." Some of Us Are Brave: The Archive, November 19. https://tressiemc.com/uncategorized/the-audacity-thrun-learns-a-lesson-and-students-pay/.

Eaton, Charlie, Sabrina T. Howell, and Constantine Yannelis. 2020. "When Investor Incentives and Consumer Interests Diverge: Private Equity in Higher Education." *Review of Financial Studies* 33 (9): 4024–60.

Flaherty, Colleen. 2020. "IP Problems." *Inside Higher Ed*, May 18. https://www.insidehighered.com/news/2020/05/19/who-owns-all-course-content-youre-putting-online.

Greene, Daniel. 2021. *The Promise of Access: Technology, Inequality, and the Political Economy of Hope.* Cambridge, MA: MIT Press.

Gray, Mary L., and Siddharth Suri. 2019. *Ghost Work: How to Stop Silicon Valley from Building a New Global Underclass.* Boston: Houghton Mifflin Harcourt.

Grusin, Richard. 2013. "The Dark Side of the Digital Humanities—Part 2." Center for 21st Century Studies, *Thinking C21* (blog), January 9. https://www.c21uwm.com/2013/01/09/dark-side-of-the-digital-humanities-part-2/.

Hall, Stephanie, and Taela Dudley. 2019. "Dear Colleges: Take Control of Your Online Courses."

The Century Foundation, *Higher Education Report*, September 12. https://tcf.org/content/report/dear-colleges-take-control-online-courses/.

Hamilton, Laura T., Heather Daniels, Christian Michael Smith, and Charlie Eaton. 2022. "The Private Side of Public Universities: Third-Party Providers and Platform Capitalism." Berkeley Center for Studies in Higher Education, Research and Occasional Paper Series.

Kelley, Jason. 2021. "A Long Overdue Reckoning for Online Proctoring May Finally Be Here." Electronic Frontier Foundation, June 22. https://www.eff.org/deeplinks/2021/06/long-overdue-reckoning-online-proctoring-companies-may-finally-be-here.

Kneese, Tamara. 2021. "How a Dead Professor Is Teaching a University Art History Class." *Slate*, January 27. https://slate.com/technology/2021/01/dead-professor-teaching-online-class.html.

Marcus, Jon. 2021. "More Colleges and Universities Outsource Services to For-Profit Companies." *Hechinger Report*, January 8. https://hechingerreport.org/more-colleges-and-universities-outsource-services-to-for-profit-companies/.

Markovich, Ally. 2023. "Raises Won during Strike Have $38M Price Tag: How Will UC Berkeley Pay?" *Berkleyside*, March 14. https://www.berkeleyside.org/2023/03/14/uc-berkeley-cost-of-strike.

Martin, Hailey. 2023. "Unconstitutional Room Scans? The Fourth Amendment in the Digital Age," *University of Cincinatti Law Review* 91. https://uclawreview.org/2023/01/04/unconstitutional-room-scans-the-fourth-amendment-in-the-digital-age/.

Morris, Sean, and Jesse Stommel. 2017. "A Guide for Resisting Edtech: The Case Against Turnitin." *Hybrid Pedagogy*, June 15. https://hybridpedagogy.org/resisting-edtech/.

NCES (National Center for Education Statistics). 2022. "Table 105.50. Number of educational institutions, by level and control of institution: Academic years 2010–11 through 2020–21." Data table, Digest of Education Statistics. NCES, Institute of Education Sciences, US Department of Education. https://nces.ed.gov/programs/digest/d22/tables/dt22_105.50.asp.

NCES (National Center for Education Statistics). 2023. "Undergraduate Enrollment." Condition of Education. NCES, Institute of Education Sciences, US Department of Education. https://nces.ed.gov/programs/coe/indicator/cha.

Noble, David F. 2001. *Digital Diploma Mills: The Automation of Higher Education*. New York: Monthly Review Press.

Noble, Safiya. 2018. *Algorithms of Oppression: How Search Engines Reinforce Racism*. New York: New York University Press.

Ovetz, Robert. 2020. "The Algorithmic University: On-Line Education, Learning Management Systems, and the Struggle over Academic Labor." *Critical Sociology* 47 (7–8): 1–20.

Protopsaltis, Spiros, and Sandy Baum. 2019. "Does Online Education Live Up to Its Promise? A Look at the Evidence and Implications for Federal Policy." Center for Education Policy and Evaluation, George Mason University.

Purdy, James P. 2009. "Anxiety and the Archive: Plagiarism Detection Services as Digital Archives." *Computers and Composition* 26 (2): 65–77.

Rhoads, Robert, Maria Camacho, Brit Toven-Lindsey, Jennifer Berdan Lozano. 2015. "The Massive Open Online Course Movement, xMOOCs, and Faculty Labor." *Review of Higher Education* 38 (2): 397–424.

Rooholfada, Emma. 2019. "Kiwi Hires Colombian Students to Supervise KiwiBots." *Daily*

Californian (Berkeley), October 15. https://dailycal.org/2019/10/15/kiwi-hires-colombian-students-to-supervise-kiwibots.

Scully, Jed. 2004. "Virtual Professorship: Intellectual Property: Ownership of Academic Work in a Digital Era." *McGeorge Law Review* 35 (2): 227–76.

Smith, Christian Michael, Amber D. Villalobos, Laura T. Hamilton, and Charlie Eaton. 2023. "Promising or Predatory? Online Education in Non-Profit and For-Profit Universities." *Social Forces* 102 (3): 1–26.

Srivas, Anuj. 2016. "Sebastian Thrun, Modi, and the Forgotten Promise of MOOCs." *Wire*, April 26. https://thewire.in/business/sebastian-thrun-modi-and-the-forgotten-promise-of-moocs.

Swaak, Taylor. 2022. "Students Say Room Scans during Online Tests Are Invasive: Now a Judge Agrees." *Chronicle of Higher Education*, August 24. https://www.chronicle.com/article/students-say-room-scans-during-online-tests-are-invasive-now-a-judge-agrees.

Swauger, Shea. 2020. "Our Bodies Encoded: Algorithmic Test Proctoring in Higher Education." In *Critical Digital Pedagogy*, edited by Jesse Stommel, Chris Friend, and Sean Michael Morris, ch. 6. Mountain View, CA: Press Books.

Townsend Gard, Elizabeth. 2003. "Legal and Policy Responses to the Disappearing Teacher Exception, or Copyright Ownership in the 21st Century University." *Minnesota Intellectual Property Review* 4 (2): 209–83.

Twomey, Tyra. 2009. "What's the Deal With TurnItIn." In *Pedagogy Not Policing*, edited by Tyra Twomey, Holly White, and Ken Sagendorf, 149–56. Syracuse, NY: Graduate School Press, Syracuse University.

Venable, Melissa A. 2023. *2023 Online Education Trends Report*. Best Colleges, June. https://www.bestcolleges.com/wp-content/uploads/2023/06/2023-Online-Education-Trends-Report-compressed-v2.pdf.

Watters, Audrey. 2017. *The Monsters of Educational Technology 4*. Self-published ebook.

Weinberg, Lindsay. 2021. "Mental Health and the Self-Tracking Student." *Catalyst* 7 (1): 1–27.

Weinberg, Lindsay. 2023. "Smart Campus: Student Recruitment in the Age of Austerity." Talk at UC Irvine, June 6.

Williamson, Ben. 2022. "Big EdTech." *Learning, Media and Technology* 47 (2): 157–62.

Xu, Di, and Ying Xu. 2020. "The Ambivalence about Distance Learning in Higher Education." In *Higher Education: Handbook of Theory and Research*, vol. 35, edited by Laura W. Perna, 351–402. Cham: Springer.

Endowment

Dennis M. Hogan

Endowments are, at a basic level, easy to understand. An endowment is a permanent fund invested as capital to support the activities of a college, university, or other institution into perpetuity. The principal of the endowment (the original investment), is never to be diminished or depleted, while the profits on the investment can be either directed toward operating expenses or reinvested into the endowment to increase the principal and grow the capital.[1] The primary source of endowment capital is charitable gifts to universities and colleges made by alumni or other benefactors; these gifts are placed in trust for management by the trustees of the institution and for the benefit of its students, faculty, and other associated personnel. Richard Franz and Stephan Kranner observe that, compared to other kinds of trusts, university endowments have three "special characteristics." They include "(1) the permanent transfer of wealth from donors to the institution, (2) their perpetual time horizon, and (3) the special network a university enjoys through its stakeholders" (2019, 3). Unlike other forms of investment accounts, in which investments are managed by a third party for the benefit of the investor or other third party, and eventually withdrawn from management, the money contributed to a university or college endowment is never withdrawn. Endowments are not time limited: Colleges and universities assume they will continue to exist into perpetuity, and endowment capital is invested on that basis as well. Finally, universities grow, manage, and invest the endowment in part through the network of alumni, professors, students, trustees, and other associates and affiliates, which offers specific duties and opportunities for members of this network and can affect the growth and performance of the endowment. While college and university

1. The legal definition reads: "endowment. (1Sc) 1. A gift of money or property to an institution (such as a university) for a specific purpose, esp. one in which the principal is kept intact indefinitely and only the interest income from that principal is used" (Garner 2009, 608).

endowments exist in different forms throughout the world (and endowments as a perpetual income source have a long history), endowments have achieved a particular importance in the United States, where the role of private philanthropy in higher education is pronounced, and endowments play a large and important role. They also represent substantial stores of value: In 2023, the National Association of College and University Business Officers (NACUBO) surveyed 699 US institutions holding endowment funds; the value of these funds totaled $839 billion (NACUBO 2024b).

Although the concept may seem simple, analysis of the endowment presents several challenges. As Henry Hansmann wrote in 1990, it is easy to understand why colleges and universities would want to maintain some funds to preserve intergenerational equity—the idea that future students will derive the same educational benefits as current students—and to "serve as a financial buffer against periods of financial adversity, . . . help to insure the long-run survival of the institution's reputational capital, . . . protect the institution's intellectual freedom, and . . . assist in passing on values prized by the present generation" (39). By any measure, however, the largest university endowments, even in 1990, far exceeded the scope of what would be required to weather even catastrophic economic outcomes. As Hansmann outlines, endowment logic has taken on a life of its own, and by the end of the 1980s, the goal of accumulation for its own sake had become the consensus position among university boards and finance offices. This naturalized position was itself the product of historical developments. Many US colleges and universities founded in the eighteenth and nineteenth century had endowments, though at the time the term did not strictly refer to a permanent fund destined to be invested as capital. As Bruce A. Kimball and Benjamin A. Johnson (2012, 17) demonstrate, through the early twentieth century the sense of endowments included both financial resources and physical ones, like the land on which the university was located and the buildings in which university functions took place. These were permanent property intended to support the university but were not principally employed as capital. Over the course of the nineteenth century, universities did invest assets in secure instruments like bonds, but they were generally prohibited by law and custom from investing in equities and other high-risk instruments (Conti-Brown 2011, 717). Similarly, university fund-raising primarily raised money for operating expenses, but not investment (Kimball and Johnson 2012).

The latter part of the nineteenth century saw an explosion of philanthropic giving, as fortunes made during Reconstruction and the Gilded Age gave way to donations to higher education on a previously unprecedented scale (Rudolph 1990, 181–82); these included sizable gifts by magnates like Andrew Carnegie, John D. Rockefeller, and Leland Stanford (Kimball and Johnson 2012, 4–5). By the early twentieth century, however, universities and colleges—led by Harvard and its president, Charles William Eliot—began to understand that "the competition for academic distinction was a struggle to accumulate wealth" (2012, 9). By the 1930s, the contemporary understanding of endowment as a permanent invested fund had been established; from the 1920s through the 1960s, colleges and universities invested increasingly in securities, abandoning their previous conservatism in pursuit of higher returns; "by the late 1960s," as Christopher J. Ryan Jr. (2016, 169) writes, "a majority of university endowments had adopted a model of investing three-fifths of endowment funds in corporate stock and only two-fifths remained in bonds." Shortly thereafter, however, endowment managers began to adopt modern portfolio theory, which called for a greater diversification of assets to "maximize long-term total return" but entailing still greater risk (Ryan 2016, 171). Over the 1970s, a combination of economic headwinds and still-expanding government support for higher education reduced the importance of endowment growth in the overall higher education financial picture, but strong market performance in the 1980s brought the role of endowments back into the forefront—leading Hansmann to question the endowment business entirely (Kimball and Johson 2012, 3).

Henry Hansmann wrote at a time when endowment growth already seemed preposterously high, but he wrote just before a revolution in endowment management that was set to transform the industry. While Harvard had led the transition to permanent fund accumulation and the move to investments in stocks, Yale, led by endowment manager David Swensen, began a new phase in endowment management based on what has been called the "Yale model," or the "endowment model," of investing (Chambers and Dimson 2015, 10). A new application of portfolio theory (Ryan 2016, 171n49), this model substantial reshuffles asset mixes. As Josh Lerner, Antoinette Schoar, and Jialan Wang (2008, 214) write, the major asset classes of endowment investing include "equities, fixed income, real estate, alternatives (which includes hedge funds, commodities such as oil and timber, and private equity buyout and venture funds), and cash." Swensen's innovation was, in part, to massively increase the share of Yale's endowment devoted to alternative assets. Other wealthy private schools followed suit, reaping enormous endowment gains in the years between 1992 and 2007 (Lerner, Schoar, and Wang 2008, 208). The causes for this period of high returns were multiple: financial deregulation in the Reagan era freed up capital for investment, while innovative strategies like leveraged buyouts contributed to the rise of private equity (Eaton 2022, 59). A rising finance economy made fortunes that led to more donations to colleges and universities, increasing the principal of their endowments. Finally, elite colleges and universities, with their close relationships to financiers, acted as early investors in venture capital and private equity firms, positioning themselves to benefit from the largest and earliest gains in this sector. While the "endowment model" spread from Yale and other well-endowed elite universities to other schools and eventually other institutional investors, many of the most extraordinary returns were confined to schools that had adopted it early (Eaton 2022, 63–66). Nevertheless, the period before the Great Recession saw endowments perform better than ever before, largely thanks to the adoption of the endowment model and the growing tolerance for risk among endowment managers.

The economic downturn that began in 2008 hit university endowments hard before giving way to a new period of unprecedented growth. Between 2008 and 2009, college and university endowments lost 23 percent of their value, as the worsening economic picture affected all asset classes, and even highly diversified funds were not immune (Hill 2010, 589). During this time, as students and families struggled to afford college, universities too announced major cutbacks, affecting every aspect of university operations (Hechinger 2009). Amid growing fears about college affordability, some politicians began to call for more action from universities to spend down endowments to increase financial aid and mitigate the rising cost of college.[2] Nevertheless, the economic recovery (and the rising stock market, alongside another boom in venture and private equity valuations) initiated a second unprecedented period of endowment growth, with elite private

2. Iowa Republican Senator Chuck Grassley led this charge in Washington. See Grassley (2008).

colleges and universities again leading the way.[3] The 2017 Tax Cuts and Jobs Act, passed by a Republican Congress and signed into law by Donald Trump, reduced taxes on many Americans, especially corporations and the wealthy, but it also introduced, for the very first time, an endowment excise tax, which targeted the wealthiest universities measured by endowment per student (Bird-Pollan 2021, 1076). The tax was, to be fair, a political attack on a higher education sector perceived as hostile to Republicans, but it also appealed to a broadening political consensus that questioned university wealth accumulation. The COVID-19 pandemic, which initially threatened to wipe out huge portions of endowments, instead delivered massive growth, boosting the sector's overall fortunes. Since 2021, endowments have fallen slightly as stock market performance has slowed, but overall university and college endowments are in stronger financial positions than ever (NACUBO 2024a).

Despite this overall wealth, the real story of endowments is one of stark inequality among institutions. While the wealthiest institutions each have tens of billions of dollars in assets, most colleges and universities have endowments so negligible they are not even counted in the NACUBO survey. Among schools that do respond to the survey, distribution of endowment values is highly skewed: While the average value of endowments is $1.2 billion per institution, the median endowment is only $215.7 million (NACUBO 2024a). In 2023, 142 institutions held endowments valued at $1 billion or greater, representing just over 20 percent of colleges and universities surveyed. These institutions, however, held nearly $716 billion in assets, representing just over 85 percent of total endowment values. Altogether, the extreme inequality in distribution of endowment assets reflects other kinds of inequality across higher education, with institutions starkly divided by wealth; reputation; public and private status; racial, ethnic, and class composition of the student bodies; and academic and professional outcomes for students and graduates. When considered in terms of endowment per student, the inequalities grow starker still. Some of the largest endowments are held by public university systems, such as the University of Texas and the University of California. These systems serve vastly more students, however,

3. Between 2009 and 2022, the value of all endowments surveyed by NACUBO (2024a) grew from $306 billion to $839 billion. In just one year—2021—the endowment for Washington University in St. Louis grew 65 percent (Flory 2021), while Williams College's endowment reported a 49.9 percent annual return (Ingoe-Gerney 2021).

than elite private schools with similarly sized endowments, meaning that the school has fewer per student resources regardless of the actual size of the endowment. And this is the case for the best endowed and most prestigious public universities (which, as Christopher Newfield [2016, 115–22] has demonstrated, have turned increasingly to private philanthropy and endowment building as state appropriations have declined over the last several decades, with disastrous effects for the public school mission); most public schools do not have even these resources. Community colleges, which enroll 38 percent of all college students nationwide (AACC 2023), typically have minimal endowments or none at all (Hill 2010, 589). Similarly, HBCUs, Tribal colleges, and other minority-serving institutions do not appear among institutions with the largest endowments, and while some of the best-resourced historically Black colleges and universities, like Howard University, have established relatively healthy endowments, they are still smaller than those of primarily white institutions of comparable size and prestige (NACUBO 2024a). Tribal colleges and universities (TCUs) are less supported still, and while the federal government provided some endowment money, and land-grant status, to 29 TCUs, federal policies "deprived TCUs of the financial foundation that supported Morrill institutions [supported by land parcels], replacing it with a competitive grant-driven metric that limited the overall amount of funding available to support all TCUs" (McCoy, Risam, and Guiliano 2021, 172).[4] Years of unequal support for these institutions have taken a toll, and as a recent report from the United Negro College Fund and PGIM make clear, many private HBCUs rely to a much greater extent on federal funding than their predominantly white counterparts. HBCUs also allocate fewer resources to investment management; pursue more conservative investment strategies, resulting in lower risk but also in lower returns; and "have smaller alternatives allocations than non-HBCUs," meaning they invest less in venture capital, private equity, hedge funds, and natural resources—sectors that have driven strong returns but require both information and access to opportunities that are not public (UNCF and PGIM 2024, 6). Well-endowed primarily white institutions already benefit from wealth, status, and generous philanthropic networks, all factors reflected in college and university rankings. As Carolyn Brooks, executive director of the Association of 1890 Research Directors, which coordinates research

4. The Morrill Act established land-grant colleges and universities.

efforts among 17 historically Black land-grant institutions, has argued, such rankings, which consider quantifiable metrics like endowment value, further entrench hierarchies of wealth and prestige, to the advantage of a few (Brooks and Marcus 2015, 253).

Equity issues in endowments encompass not only contemporary problems of racial and class inequality and unequal access to pathways to success for students, but historical instances of wealth accumulation on the basis of slavery and Indigenous dispossession. The close economic connections of several US universities to slavery have been well documented and are an important area of ongoing research. Brown University's endowment was established in part through collections taken from wealthy planters in South Carolina, and the Brown family, alongside the entire economy of colonial Rhode Island, profited directly and indirectly from the slave trade (Brown University Steering Committee on Slavery and Justice 2006, 13–17). Harvard University, similarly, profited from "loans to Caribbean sugar planters, rum distillers, and plantation suppliers" (Presidential Committee on Harvard and the Legacy of Slavery 2022, 31). Harvard also accepted donations from traffickers in enslaved people, used the labor of enslaved people, and benefited from other economic ties with the slave economy in the United States and throughout the hemisphere through most of the nineteenth century.[5] Between 1817 and 1865, 4,000 enslaved people "lived and worked" at the University of Virginia (Svrluga 2024). The 1838 sale of 272 enslaved people by Jesuit priests helped save Georgetown University; recent research has shown that the profits from that sale also helped found the Loyola University of Maryland (President's Task Force Examining Loyola's Connections to Slavery 2024, 9–10). Still, as a result of the nineteenth-century practice of fund-raising for operating budgets and investing principally in tangible goods; the indifferent record keeping of university administrators; the fact that most large endowments grew principally from fund-raising and investments in the early twentieth century; and the large amount of research remaining to be done, direct connections between profits from slavery and money currently in specific endowment funds have only occasionally been conclusively established. There are exceptions, however: The University of Chicago, for example, as Caine Jordan, Guy Emerson

5. See the Presidential Committee on Harvard and the Legacy of Slavery (2022), especially chapter 3, "The Slavery Economy and Harvard," 31–57.

Mount, and Kai Perry Parker (2018, 169) have demonstrated, established the endowment for the Divinity School by taking out loans against a parcel of land donated by Stephen A. Douglas and purchased with profits from his plantation in Mississippi. As multiple scholars have conclusively shown, intimate ties with the slave economy helped to establish physical infrastructure, reputations, and relationships with leading families that would later be transformed concretely into endowment money.

Like universities that profited from slavery, US land-grant universities were established and endowed by acts of Indigenous genocide and dispossession. As Robert Lee and Tristan Ahtone have demonstrated, the Morrill Act, which established federal land banks to be given to states in trust for establishing public colleges and universities, depended on land previously occupied by, and stolen from, Indigenous nations (Lee and Ahtone 2020); in some cases, that land was set aside mere years after the dispossession of the people who had been living there (Palmer 2023, 1253). These parcels of land were only rarely used as the physical location of the new colleges and universities; usually, they were located hundreds or thousands of miles away from the states whose universities they belonged to. Rather, the land was used for speculation, sale, and resource exploitation: Profits from these land holdings were then converted into university buildings, faculties, and endowments; in all, "grants of land raised endowment principal for 52 institutions across the United States" (Lee and Ahtone 2020). Direct land management by universities continued for years or even decades, and in some cases, direct university management of Morrill Act parcels stolen from Indigenous people continues even today. A 2024 report by Lee and Ahtone highlights the ways in which some land-grant colleges and universities continue to exploit the resource wealth of these lands into the twenty-first century, including to produce fossil fuels, which contribute to global warming (Ahtone et al. 2024).

These histories, combined with the moral issues at stake in contemporary investment practices, the enormous value of the endowments held by the wealthiest colleges and universities, and the lack of transparency about how funds are administered and where they are invested, have made today's endowments frequent targets of political demands for divestment, distribution, and reparations by activists, community members, scholars, and students from within and beyond the academy. Many of the schools that have formally investigated their ties to slavery have used general endowment funds to establish special endowments to further racial justice work on campus or in the community or to offer reparations to the descendants of enslaved people with connections to the university (Moscufo 2022). Steps have more recently been taken in similar directions by institutions seeking to repair relationships with Indigenous people negatively affected by university actions at Morrill Act colleges and universities and other institutions that benefited from Indigenous genocide (Palmer 2023, 1252). Contemporary business practices of endowments have engendered repeated campaigns calling for divestment: The 1970s and 1980s divestment campaign targeting South Africa, undertaken in support of the decades-long movement against apartheid, is "hailed by some as the most successful divestment campaign to date" (Deeks 2017, 335; also see Apfel 2015, esp. 919–20). Since then, divestment movements have targeted endowments with holdings in the tobacco industry; in companies complicit in the genocide in Darfur (Rucker 2006); in fossil fuels and other companies and resources that contribute to climate change (Barron et al. 2023, 2); in weapons and firearms manufacturers (Jahnke 2015; Mauldin 2023); and in companies and entities that support or benefit from Israel's illegal occupation of Palestinian territory, among others (Alonso 2023). Moreover, the continued emphasis on alternative investments among endowment managers means that some university and college investment offices are not merely investors in publicly traded equities but have significant ownership stakes in companies and properties whose ethical status is up for debate.

These developments have produced some complications: Harvard University, for example, has come under fire for its ownership of farmlands in Brazil that human rights experts say have driven regional conflict and in some cases were stolen from Indigenous people and communities descended from Brazilian *quilombo* (maroon) settlements (GRAIN and Rede Social de Justiça e Direitos Humanos 2018). Activists and scholars have drawn connections between growing institutional investments in venture capital and private equity and the deleterious effects these sectors can have on the economy, affecting ordinary people in the United States and across the world (Phillips-Fein 2023). Though the South African divestment campaign was notably successful, and some endowments have made moves to limit or taper their investments in fossil fuels and other drivers of climate change, university leaders have generally resisted calls for divestment. University leaders fear a slippery slope: Agreeing to any particular call for divestment inevitably opens the door to further challenges from activist groups organizing around any number of causes.

The primary goal of endowment management, university leaders argue, should be securing enough growth to support the university into perpetuity, not using the endowment for political ends. From one point of view, this is sound logic: an investor who abandons the prime directive of profit seeking will not long remain successful, and as Daniel Apfel (2015) has argued, individual investors liquidating positions do little to promote sectoral, much less global, change, even if they "purify portfolios for the benefit of the investor" (917). Increasingly, however, divestment campaigns are framed as movements seeking to produce wider capital flight from an industry or practice and produce the economic conditions for political change. Ultimately, the fight over the ethical nature of college endowments is a fight over the ethical status of capitalism itself in a global system structured by class domination, imperialism, and white supremacy: If colleges and universities, nonprofits though they are, are in the business of using their money as capital, they will find few places to invest that are entirely free from ethical compromise.

References

AACC (American Association of Community Colleges). 2023. "Fast Facts 2023." AACC. https://www.aacc.nche.edu/wp-content/uploads/2023/03/AACC2023_FastFacts.pdf.

Ahtone, Tristan, Robert Lee, Amanda Tachine, An Garagiola, Audrianna Goodwin, Maria Parazo Rose, and Clayton Aldern. 2024. "Misplaced Trust: Stolen Indigenous Land Is the Foundation of the Land-Grant University System. Climate Change Is Its Legacy." *Grist*, February 7. https://grist.org/project/indigenous/land-grant-universities-indigenous-lands-fossil-fuels/.

Alonso, Johanna. 2023. "Pro-Palestinian Students Demand Divestment from Israel." *Inside Higher Ed*, December 6. https://www.insidehighered.com/news/students/free-speech/2023/12/06/divestment-top-issue-among-pro-palestinian-college-students.

Apfel, Daniel C. 2015. "Exploring Divestment as a Strategy for Change: An Evaluation of the History, Success, and Challenges of Fossil Fuel Divestment." *Social Research* 82 (4): 913–37. https://www.jstor.org/stable/44282147.

Barron, Alexander R., Rachel C. Venator, Ella V. H. Carlson, Jane K. Andrews, Junwen Ding, and David DeSwert. 2023. "Fossil Fuel Divestment in U.S. Higher Education: Endowment Dependence and Temporal Dynamics." *Elementa* 11 (1): 00059. https://doi.org/10.1525/elementa.2023.00059.

Bird-Pollan, Jennifer. 2021. "Taxing the Ivory Tower: Evaluating the Excise Tax on University Endowments." *Pepperdine Law Review* 48 (4): 1055–84. https://digitalcommons.pepperdine.edu/plr/vol48/iss4/6.

Brooks, Carolyn B., and Alan I. Marcus. 2015. "The Morrill Mandate and a New Moral Mandate." *Agricultural History* 89 (2): 247–62. https://doi.org/10.3098/ah.2015.089.2.247.

Brown University Steering Committee on Slavery and Justice. 2006. *Slavery and Justice.* Providence, RI: Brown University Steering Committee on Slavery and Justice. https://slaveryandjustice.brown.edu/sites/default/files/reports/SlaveryAndJustice2006.pdf.

Chambers, David, and Elroy Dimson. 2015. "The British Origins of the US Endowment Model." *Financial Analysts Journal* 71 (2): 10–14. https://doi.org/10.2469/faj.v71.n2.7.

Conti-Brown, Peter. 2011. "Scarcity amidst Wealth: The Law, Finance, and Culture of Elite University Endowments in Financial Crisis." *Stanford Law Review* 63 (3): 699–749. https://www.jstor.org/stable/41105411.

Deeks, Laura E. 2017. "Discourse and Duty: University Endowments, Fiduciary Law, and the Cultural Politics of Fossil Fuel Divestment." *Environmental Law* 47 (2): 335–427. https://www.jstor.org/stable/26491778.

Eaton, Charlie. 2022. *Bankers in the Ivory Tower: The Troubling Rise of Financiers in US Higher Education.* Chicago: University of Chicago Press.

Flory, Julie Hail. 2021. "Washington University Managed Endowment Pool Generates Record 65% Return." *St. Louis (MO) Source,* September 20. https://source.wustl.edu/2021/09/washington-university-managed-endowment-pool-generates-record-65-return/.

Franz, Richard, and Stephan Kranner. 2019. "University Endowments: A Primer." *CFA Institute Research Foundation Briefs,* July. https://doi.org/10.2139/ssrn.3485783.

Garner, Bryan A., ed. 2009. *Black's Law Dictionary.* 9th ed. St Paul, MN: West.

GRAIN and Rede Social de Justiça e Direitos Humanos. 2018. "Harvard's Billion-Dollar Farmland Fiasco." *GRAIN,* September 6. https://grain.org/article/entries/6006-harvard-s-billion-dollar-farmland-fiasco.

Grassley, Charles E. 2008. "Wealthy Colleges Must Make Themselves More Affordable." *Chronicle of Higher Education,* May 30. https://www.chronicle.com/article/wealthy-colleges-must-make-themselves-more-affordable/.

Hansmann, Henry. 1990. "Why Do Universities Have Endowments?" *Journal of Legal Studies* 19 (1): 3–42. https://www.jstor.org/stable/724411.

Hechinger, John. 2009. "College Endowments Plunge." *Wall Street Journal,* January 27. https://www.wsj.com/articles/SB123302147236318209.

Hill, Frances R. 2010. "University Endowments: A (Surprisingly) Elusive Concept." *New England Law Review* 44:581–600.

Ingoe-Gerney, Greer. 2021. "Endowment Sees 49.9% Annual Return in 2021 Fiscal Year." *Williams Record,* October 26. https://williamsrecord.com/458153/news/endowment-sees-49-9-return-in-2021-fiscal-year/.

Jahnke, Art. 2015. "University Will Not Divest from Firearms Manufacturers." *BU Today,* February 2. https://www.bu.edu/articles/2015/university-will-not-divest-from-firearms/.

Jordan, Caine, Guy Emerson Mount, and Kai Perry Parker. 2018. "'A Disgrace to All Slave-Holders': The University of Chicago's Founding Ties to Slavery and the Path to Reparations." *Journal of African American History* 103 (1–2): 163–78. https://doi.org/10.1086/696362.

Kimball, Bruce A., and Benjamin A. Johnson. 2012. "The Inception of the Meaning and Significance of Endowment in American Higher Education, 1890–1930." *Teachers College Record* 114 (10): 1–32. https://doi.org/10.1177/016146811211401007.

Lee, Robert, and Tristan Ahtone. 2020. "Land-Grab Universities." *High Country News,* March 30.

Lerner, Josh, Antoinette Schoar, and Jialan Wang. 2008. "Secrets of the Academy: The Drivers of University Endowment Success." *Journal of Economic Perspectives* 22 (3): 207–22. https://doi.org/10.1257/jep.22.3.207.

Mauldin, Lillian. 2023. "How a University Endowment Fund Is Upholding the Norms of Militarism." *Inkstick*, June 27. https://inkstickmedia.com/how-a-university-endowment-fund-is-upholding-the-norms-of-militarism/.

McCoy, Meredith, Roopika Risam, and Jennifer Guiliano. 2021. "The Future of Land-Grab Universities." *Native American and Indigenous Studies* 8 (1): 169–75. https://doi.org/10.5749/natiindistudj.8.1.0169.

Moscufo, Michela. 2022. "College Campuses See Growing Reparations Movement." ABC News, July 30. https://abcnews.go.com/US/college-campuses-growing-reparations-movement/story?id=87069082.

NACUBO (National Association of College and University Business Officers–Commonfund Institute). 2024a. "Final Endowment Market Values—Fiscal Years 1974 to 2023." Excel spreadsheet, NACUBO, February 15.

NACUBO (National Association of College and University Business Officers–Commonfund Institute). 2024b. "Presentation of Key Insights from the 2023 NCSE." *2023 NACUBO-Commonfund Study of Endowments*, NACUBO, February 15.

Newfield, Christopher. 2018. *The Great Mistake: How We Wrecked Public Universities and How We Can Fix Them*. Baltimore: Johns Hopkins University Press.

Palmer, Meredith Alberta. 2023. "Good Intentions Are Not Good Relations: Grounding the Terms of Debt and Redress at Land Grab Universities." *ACME: An International Journal for Critical Geographies* 22 (4): 1239–57. https://acme-journal.org/index.php/acme/article/view/2296.

Phillips-Fein, Kim. 2023. "Conspicuous Destruction." *New York Review*, October 19. https://www.nybooks.com/articles/2023/10/19/conspicuous-destruction-plunder-brendan-ballou/.

Presidential Committee on Harvard and the Legacy of Slavery. 2022. *The Legacy of Slavery at Harvard: Report and Recommendations of the Presidential Committee*. Cambridge, MA: Harvard University Press.

President's Task Force Examining Loyola's Connections to Slavery. 2024. *Final Report*. Loyola University Maryland. https://www.loyola.edu/_media/department/president/documents/loyola-md-connections-to-slavery.pdf.

Rucker, Philip. 2006. "Student-Driven Sudan Divestment Campaign Grows." *New York Times*, April 6. https://www.nytimes.com/2006/04/26/nyregion/studentdriven-sudan-divestment-campaign-grows.html.

Rudolph, Frederick. 1990. *The American College and University: A History*. Athens: University of Georgia Press.

Ryan, Christopher J., Jr. 2016. "Trusting U.: Examining University Endowment Management." *Journal of College and University Law* 42 (1): 159–212. https://www.nacua.org/docs/default-source/jcul-articles/volume-42/42_jcul_159.pdf?sfvrsn=c65e64be_12.

Svrluga, Susan. 2024. "Loyola University Maryland Says It Had Ties to an 1838 Sale of Slaves." *Washington Post*, January 18. https://www.washingtonpost.com/education/2024/01/18/loyola-university-maryland-slavery-georgetown-jesuits/.

UNCF (United Negro College Fund) and PGIM. 2024. *Investing in Change: A Call to Action for Strengthening Private HBCU Endowments*. UNCF and PGIM. https://cdn.uncf.org/wp-content/uploads/PGIM_UNCF_2023-Paper_v5.pdf.

E

Entrepreneurship

Jesse Goldstein

Entrepreneurship has become a ubiquitous part of the higher education landscape.[1] Research agendas, curricular changes, and even institutional priorities are all increasingly folded into the language—and logic—of entrepreneurship, with all it has come to stand for: innovation, risk taking, and market opportunities on the one hand, insecurity, investor pressures, and market discipline on the other. While on the rise for over a half century, and even longer at a few elite universities, only more recently have a wide range of higher education institutions embraced the idea of entrepreneurial universities (Gibb and Hannon 2006). University administrators tout entrepreneurial approaches to running the university as a proactive response to increasingly precarious institutional finances, and they embrace entrepreneurship as a curricular and research ideal. This can shape the experience of students, who see costs endlessly rise, while desirable postgraduation opportunities feel increasingly hard to come by. In this context, there is pressure to embrace entrepreneurship as a framework for crafting career success amid financial precarity.

Entrepreneurship reduces diverse aspects of higher education—including student achievement and broader institutional mandates to serve the public good—to questions of market success, with a focus on metrics such as postgraduation employment, institutional rankings, and the increasingly corporatized university's economic bottom line (Cerro Santamaría 2020). After putting the concept into historical and political economic context, I explore the evolution of entrepreneurship at universities and some of the ways the concept turns all aspects of university life toward market competition. In conclusion, I discuss how university communities can actively push back against these entrepreneurial tendencies.

1. Thanks to Gina Maggi for research assistance in preparing this chapter.

A History of Entrepreneurship and/in the University

As a concept, entrepreneurship is often traced through figures like Joseph Schumpeter (2010), who argued that entrepreneurs were necessary for capitalism's "creative destruction," facilitating economic growth through risk taking, self-discipline, and the rebellious joy of creativity. Toward the latter half of the twentieth century, Schumpeter's conception of the entrepreneur was reinterpreted as a general human condition by the economist Ludwig von Mises and popularized by figures like management consultant Peter Drucker, who embraced constant change in an effort to create a bold and exciting alternative to what was increasingly seen as boring and unfulfilling white-collar work (*Economist* 2009; Plehwe 2020). The popular embrace of entrepreneurship coincided with broader macroeconomic trends toward declining corporate rates of profit and a turn toward financial speculation, as well as the rise of neoliberalism.

Already we can see multiple layers to this term. It most explicitly refers to the risk taking and "innovation" involved with new business formation, a somewhat concrete activity. At the same time, however, entrepreneurship has been and continues to be cast as a broader ideal and subjectivity. In this sense, it is an orientation toward the world anchored by a presumption that all problems are market problems, and all market problems can be met with profitable solutions (Dardot and Laval 2017). Economic thinkers like Gary Becker and Frank Knight proposed theories of human capital, which Michel Foucault (2008) later conceptualized as an emergent subjectivity. Anyone and everyone can aspire to become an enterprising or entrepreneurial self by embodying a commercial spirit and constantly searching for profitable market opportunities. Entrepreneurs embrace risk and accept that market competition is the natural order of progress. In an entrepreneurial ecosystem (or university), there is no question that many will lose so that a few can win; this is simply the way of the ~~market~~ world (Plehwe, Slobodian, and Mirowski 2020).

With the rise of this enterprising subjectivity comes a growing sense that anyone can become entrepreneurial. To the extent that entrepreneurship simply stands in for positive character traits like creativity, problem solving, risk taking, and self-reliance, it is hard to find fault with the promotion of these ideals, and entrepreneurship can become one more thread in the broader landscape of self-improvement narratives (such as Maxwell 2000;

and Ries 2014). But that is not the full story. Entrepreneurship is as much about these positive character traits as it is about an embrace of market-based solutions, unbridled competition, and a willingness to accept precarious and uncertain conditions as a risk pool to compete within. The idea that anyone can be an entrepreneur conceals the variegated reality that not everyone enters the fray with the same affordances. Racialized, gendered, and classed differences dramatically shape individuals' conditions of entrepreneurial viability and success (Gill 2014; Komulainen et al. 2020). In higher education specifically, the freedom to embrace the uncertainties of entrepreneurship comes easier to debt-free students than those haunted by the anxieties—and responsibilities—of a future anchored by minimum monthly payments (Chen and Goldstein, n.d.).

A number of legislative changes in the latter half of the twentieth century helped usher in the embrace of entrepreneurialism by universities. As Annie McClanahan argues, the rise of human capital theory coincided with the promotion of the GI Bill and a midcentury economy in which college degrees (regardless of discipline) translated into a steadily rising premium for graduates entering a labor market that needed skilled employees. This helped justify public expenditures on education as economic development, and by the late 1960s, public universities were still relatively affordable, if not outright tuition free (McClanahan 2019). As hotbeds of countercultural and political activism, however, public universities became targets of conservative politicians as social welfare excesses being "wasted" on unprofessional, unkempt, and unappreciative youth. Imposing tuition on these large public universities would—conservative politicians argued—effectively turn students into consumers (instead of freeloaders, living large on taxpayer dollars) and therefore make them more concerned with the value of their education (Nations 2021). Critical university studies scholars such as Christopher Newfield (2016) see these disciplinary efforts ushering in a neoliberal era in which higher education was no longer seen as a public good. This positioning opened the door for all aspects of these institutions, from students to scholarship, to be differentially articulated within marketized logics.

During this time, broader macroeconomic trends toward deindustrialization and declining ranks of well-paid unionized jobs encouraged even more young people to turn toward college as a path toward economic security and the promise of middle-class life. But unionized blue-collar jobs weren't the only ones disappearing; the white-collar jobs that had lured students into higher education were also becoming increasingly scarce. The education premium that had been rising since the mid-twentieth century began to stagnate by the turn of the century, and by the 2008 financial crisis, it started to drop for the first time. Higher education institutions shifted blame away from the market or the university and onto individual students whose enterprising spirit must not be rising to the challenge (McClanahan 2019). In addition, student enrollment in public universities rose, yet federal support remained relatively constant (in inflation-adjusted dollars), which added to the pressure to find other sources of revenue.

These other sources included corporate partnerships and market-oriented innovation. In the 1980s a number of neoliberal market reforms, including the Bayh-Dole Act in 1980, the Stevenson-Wydler Act in 1980, the National Cooperative Research Act in 1984, and the Federal Technology Transfer Act in 1986, all helped create a university environment much more favorable to private-sector-oriented entrepreneurship (Berman 2012; Mirowski 2011). For instance, the Bayh-Dole Act allowed universities—and importantly, private companies—to retain rights to intellectual property developed from federally funded research (Washburn 2005). This opened up a new revenue stream for and attracted private investment in universities, which could serve as federally funded R&D incubators for private corporations. This outside investment began to affect the research priorities at universities, which shifted toward biotech and other applied STEM research.

In universities' pursuit of financial solvency, they have had to shift away from broader educational and cultural priorities toward those that lead to revenue (Croucher and Lacy 2022). This has come at the expense of deprioritizing "nonmarket" benefits, including liberal arts and cultural education, in favor of production-oriented STEM and business fields, meant to translate into a renewed education premium for college graduates.

Toward the Entrepreneurial University

University entrepreneurship orients creativity and risk taking toward market-focused "solutions," whether that market be of consumers (students are often cast in this light, as the university's consumers, purchasing a degree and an experience) or investors (who choose which entrepreneurial projects, and which entrepreneurs, are worthy of investment). Faculty and students alike are exhorted to embrace the spirit of entrepreneurship—an excitement for creativity, risk taking, and innovation. They are also asked to channel this energy into profitable endeavors, whether that means students pitching new business ideas, STEM faculty developing new intellectual property, or any member of the university demonstrating how a new project or even their very role offers the university a suitable "return on investment" (Harvey 2015).

As universities become increasingly entrepreneurial, they introduce greater competition, privatization of risk, and financialization of daily life into the cultural milieu of university life (Wilson 2017). Today, students can find a wide array of entrepreneurial opportunities on campuses: pitch competitions, hackathons, incubators, and accelerators, as well as courses and curricula explicitly focused on entrepreneurship. At Virginia Commonwealth University, there was recently an initiative (led by the provost, rejected by faculty) to include "entrepreneurial literacy" as a general education requirement.

For many students, the pursuit of an entrepreneurial dream may be superseding the American dream, as a shifting notion of oneself and of future possibility is anchored in the relentless pursuit of unlikely success and the acceptance of considerable personal risk, whether in the form of debt or the sting of competitive failure. Alexandra Robbins (2006) argues, in her book *The Overachievers,* that this competition morphed into an "overachiever culture" of perfectionism, which "increased intensity and narrowed ideals." The competition for admission into selective universities and for limited scholarship funds is only the beginning for some students, as university entrepreneurship programs and courses often pit students against one another for grades and other prizes. Yet competition is not reserved for students. It extends to professors, departments, and universities as they vie for top rankings in administration-imposed success metrics, such as national rankings, enrollment, endowments, employment, research funding, and publications (Joseph 2015; Levin, Martin, and Damián 2020; Mirowski 2014). Fewer desirable, secure faculty positions has led to increased competition for those roles, leading academics to find ways to entrepreneurially "brand" themselves and their ideas using avenues such as active profiles on social media and personal websites, in addition to traditional publishing routes (Burton and Bowman 2022).

Whereas full-time faculty have seen their relative ranks decrease, an increase in university administration has more than counterbalanced this shift.

As public funding decreases as a percentage of total revenue, universities increasingly migrate toward private and diversified sources of income. Private funders want their investments to be managed with the "efficiency" of enterprises, thus justifying the hiring of more administrative staff. In theory, these administrators are meant to cut costs and rationalize the operation of the university. Yet, the increase in administration—at "ten times the rate of full-time tenure track professors"—has increased costs, not in any small part because of the market-competitive salaries of administrators (Newfield 2016).[2] While entrepreneurial administrators will often exhort the need to act like a "lean start-up" as justification for firing their employees (or, in corporate speak, "the nonrenewal of contracts"), this rarely—if ever—results in a thinning of executive ranks, which are figured as under-resourced and overburdened. The 2023 restructuring of West Virginia University, led by career university president E. Gordon Gee under the heading of "academic transformation," is a perfect example of this double standard in action.

Entrepreneurship Reconsidered

A fundamental misconception about entrepreneurship filters down into the university experience. The entrepreneur is hailed as being an independent founder of a venture, with their success primarily dependent on their personal grit, determination, charisma, and drive. In reality, however, an entrepreneur's success is largely dependent on funding from investors (Goldstein 2018). This goes for students (the ability to afford tuition, unpaid internships, etc.), for faculty (funding for positions, research, etc.), and for the university itself (partnerships, donations, nonresident students, etc.). Tremendous inequities are built into entrepreneurial systems, however, and the university is no exception. Access to funding is highly inequitable, with preexisting racialized, classed, and gendered inequities shaping the field, creating a situation in which wealth and privilege tend to reproduce themselves in the name of meritocratic success (Seamster 2019). For instance, research has shown that in the world of start-ups, women and people of

2. Between 1975 and 2011, the number of full-time nonfaculty professional employees has increased 369 percent relative to 23 percent for full-time tenured and tenure-track faculty. See Curtis and Thornton (2014).

color are much less successful in securing venture funding than their white male counterparts.[3]

Throughout the labor market, there are stark differences between the ideal of the celebrated tech entrepreneur, awash in capital and world-shaping possibilities, and the reality of what Silvio Lorusso (2019) calls the entreprecariat: gig, freelance, and unemployed workers constantly pushed to, on the one hand, internalize blame for their economic insecurity and, on the other, to self-brand, self-innovate, and self-motivate to an increasingly elusive possibility of market success (Burton and Bowman 2022). The entrepreneurial university downplays these distinctions, spinning tales of the tech innovator while promising students that the credentials they are pursuing are a necessary means of escape. Ironically, many midtier universities who exalt the entrepreneurial ethos are in fact experiencing the institutional version of entreprecarity. They blame their faculty for flagging enrollments amid rising tuition costs and a supposed demographic drop in the college-aged population, while demanding innovative initiatives and the restructuring of programs deemed out of line with a "new and improved" vision of a university that can prepare students for the "jobs of the future" (Loher and Strasser 2019).

To fully appreciate the disciplinary and inequitable side of entrepreneurship, it is important to focus on the role of investors, who despite talk of socially and environmentally conscientious investing still make their investment decisions with a primary focus—and often a legally mandated fiduciary responsibility—to maximize returns. A typical innovation/start-up pathway involves entrepreneurs pitching to venture investors, who create a portfolio of high-risk investments and provide mentorship, support, and funds as long as a project remains promising, while knowing all along that many of their portfolio's entrepreneurs will fail, and that they are simply playing the odds. From the investor's perspective, as long as their larger portfolio performs well and a few entrepreneurs succeed, they can tolerate the disposal of the remainder.

Entrepreneurs must constantly perform for and prove themselves to an

---

3. In 2022, Black and Latino founders received 1 percent and 1.5 percent respectively of total US venture capital funding. Women-led teams received 1.9 percent, and only 0.1 percent went to Black and Latino women. The total amount of funding is also heavily skewed, with white male founders averaging over $210 million in total funding, and underrepresented founders averaging only $91.1 million (Ganesan et al. 2023).

investor class that holds major sway over their future; in the university context, even while administrators proclaim that they are entrepreneurial, or helping create an entrepreneurial university, what they don't say is that they are positioning themselves as the venture capitalists of the system. In this analogy, administrators are the investors presiding over the whole ecosystem with near complete control to determine which projects are funded, which faculty are celebrated, and which disciplines/departments are resourced (Berman 2012). In other words, the academic workplace of entrepreneurial subjects is one where an employer positions itself as an investor. Instead of holding a long-term responsibility for compensating faculty and staff fairly, university administrators treat the university itself as a competitive marketplace, asking their employees to consistently prove that they are worthy of investment.

Though entrepreneurship affects the higher education system writ large, it manifests in different ways across institutions, largely along funding lines. Elite private institutions with the largest endowments have traditionally attracted wealthy students to their top-ranked MBA programs and have seen expansions of these programs into undergraduate programs as well. Wealthy graduates in turn fund buildings, programs, competitions, and the like, while continuing to shift the culture of the liberal arts campus to a business- and science-oriented atmosphere (Newfield 2016). These directives are embraced by university administrators, whose ranks increasingly include economists with industry or government ties (Mirowski 2011). Meanwhile, their public, midtier counterparts struggle to make the same changes without the same level of funding. These schools have seen the greatest tuition hikes passed on to students who are less likely to be able to afford them (Indiviglio 2011). Students who decide to take on the debt necessary to attend these schools find themselves without the same resources available to their elite private counterparts, including access to alumni networks, which are critical to obtaining funding for ventures or securing high-paying jobs (Krishnan and Wang 2019). Here we see the cruel optimism of neoliberalism at work, with faculty, staff, and students asked to invest in institutions that may in fact be the prime barrier to their flourishing. Entrepreneurialism is positioned as a cure-all that privatizes and shifts risk onto the individual and ignores the sea change of precarity in the larger environment.

In the gaps created by the overwhelmed and underfunded public higher education system and increasingly expensive private options, many precarious students turn to for-profit schools, which are entrepreneurial businesses first and foremost. The growth of for-profit universities has increased since the 1970s. They function not only as entrepreneurial businesses that provide investors a suitable return, but also as adopters of entrepreneurial programs, like coding bootcamps, though frequently with far fewer resources (e.g., career counselors, alumni networks, etc.) and far more risk for their students (e.g., lack of accreditation, higher debt and rates of default, lower graduation rates; Cottom 2017). Here we see some of the starkest implementations of the risk-profit calculation inherent to entrepreneurial management: Executives see students in default as a source of profitability rather than a failure of their business model, as evidenced by their comments in earnings calls attended by analysts from their institutional investors (Shebanow 2019).

What's to Be Done?

University communities can and do confront these entrepreneurial imperatives in various ways, from assertions of faculty governance and academic freedom to labor organizing, undercommoning, and the development of explicitly noncompetitive ethics for creative endeavors, whether institutional, curricular, or research based. At its core, the institutional embrace of entrepreneurship is an effort to normalize precarity while collapsing all forms of creativity—whether that of students, faculty, staff, or administrators—into market-mediated forms. All sorts of labor and student organizing can—and does—push back against the austerity politics that often hides behind the entrepreneurial veneer. When faculty and staff are able to see themselves as workers with rights (as opposed to investments to be hedged and churned), they can demand increased compensation and workplace security, which cuts against institutional mandates for maximum flexibility and "lean" operations (Krause et al. 2008). Similarly, student debt struggles resist the entrepreneurial university by laying bare the stark difference between predatory and unforgiving loan agreements, which are anathema to the venture investments that fuel entrepreneurial ecosystems (and that give entrepreneurs the freedom to "fail forward"; Chen and Goldstein, n.d.).

In addition, assertions of academic governance and freedom are increasingly important as universities look to wrest control from faculty and establish their entrepreneurial agendas, whether that means creating deeper ties with corporate partners, demanding specific forms of grant-fundable research, or pressuring faculty to measure the success of their curriculum relative to reductive and self-justifying measures of postgraduation employment and earnings. Faculty unions, governance organizations (senates, councils), and professional organizations such as the American Association of University Professors (AAUP) play important roles in these struggles to maintain a broadly diverse and critical intellectual environment.

Last, students, staff, and faculty build vibrant intellectual communities and creative projects in various ways that resist entrepreneurial imperatives to reduce creativity to its market-mediated form. Whether conceptualized as undercommoning (Harney and Moten 2013), slow scholarship (Hartman and Darab 2012), or simply continuing to pursue critical and antisystemic work, many in the university community play an essential role in maintaining the vibrancy of nonentrepreneurial spaces, where risk taking, experimentation, and creative possibilities have been and continue to be so much more than what markets and their investors seek.

References

Berman, Elizabeth Popp. 2012. *Creating the Market University: How Academic Science Became an Economic Engine*. Princeton, NJ: Princeton University Press.

Burton, Sarah, and Benjamin Bowman. 2022. "The Academic Precariat: Understanding Life and Labour in the Neoliberal Academy." *British Journal of Sociology of Education* 43 (4): 497–512. https://doi.org/10.1080/01425692.2022.2076387.

Cerro Santamaría, Gerardo del. 2020. "Challenges and Drawbacks in the Marketisation of Higher Education within Neoliberalism." *Review of European Studies* 12:22.

Chen, V., and Jesse Goldstein. n.d. "Failing Forward."

Cottom, Tressie McMillan. 2017. *Lower Ed: The Troubling Rise of For-Profit Colleges in the New Economy*. New York: New Press.

Croucher, Gwilym, and William B. Lacy. 2022. "The Emergence of Academic Capitalism and University Neoliberalism: Perspectives of Australian Higher Education Leadership." *Higher Education* 83 (2): 279–95. https://doi.org/10.1007/s10734-020-00655-7.

Curtis, John W., and Saranna Thornton. 2014. "Losing Focus: The Annual Report on the Economic Status of the Profession, 2013–14." *Academe* 100 (2): 4–17.

Dardot, Pierre, and Christian Laval. 2017. *The New Way of the World: On Neo-Liberal Society*. Translated by Gregory Elliott. London: Verso.

Economist. 2009. "Remembering Drucker." November 19. https://www.economist.com/business/2009/11/19/remembering-drucker.

Foucault, Michel. 2008. *The Birth of Biopolitics: Lectures at the Collège de France*. Edited by Michel Senellart. Translated by Graham Burchell. New York: Palgrave Macmillan.

Ganesan, Vasanth, Ramya Mahalingam, Anil Nathan, Audrey Ware, and Allen Weinberg.

2023. "Underrepresented Start-Up Founders." McKinsey and Company, June 23. https://www.mckinsey.com/featured-insights/diversity-and-inclusion/underestimated-start-up-founders-the-untapped-opportunity.

Gibb, Allan, and Paul Hannon. 2006. "Towards the Entrepreneurial University?" *International Journal of Entrepreneurship Education* 4:73–110.

Gill, Rebecca. 2014. "'If You're Struggling to Survive Day-to-Day': Class Optimism and Contradiction in Entrepreneurial Discourse." *Organization* 21 (1): 50–67. https://doi.org/10.1177/1350508412464895.

Goldstein, Jesse. 2018. *Planetary Improvement: Cleantech Entrepreneurship and the Contradictions of Green Capitalism*. Cambridge, MA: MIT Press.

Harney, Stefano, and Fred Moten. 2013. *The Undercommons: Fugitive Planning and Black Study*. Wivenhoe, NY: Minor Compositions.

Hartman, Yvonne, and Sandy Darab. 2012. "A Call for Slow Scholarship: A Case Study on the Intensification of Academic Life and Its Implications for Pedagogy." *Review of Education, Pedagogy, and Cultural Studies* 34 (1–2): 49–60. https://doi.org/10.1080/10714413.2012.643740.

Harvey, Dan. 2015. "Entrepreneurial U, or *Bildung* in the Ruins." *South Atlantic Quarterly* 114 (3): 631–49. https://doi.org/10.1215/00382876-3130789.

Indiviglio, Daniel. 2011. "Obama's Student-Loan Order Saves the Average Grad Less Than $10 a Month." *Atlantic* (blog), October 26. https://www.theatlantic.com/business/archive/2011/10/obamas-student-loan-order-saves-the-average-grad-less-than-10-a-month/247411/.

Joseph, Miranda. 2015. "Investing in the Cruel Entrepreneurial University." *South Atlantic Quarterly* 114 (3): 491–511.

Komulainen, Katri, Päivi Siivonen, Kati Kasanen, and Hannu Räty. 2020. "'How to Give a Killer Pitch?' Performances of Entrepreneurial Narratives as Identity Models in Higher Education." *Entrepreneurship Education and Pedagogy* 3 (3): 214–35. https://doi.org/10.1177/2515127420908039.

Krause, Monika, Michael Palm, Mary Nolan, and Andrew Ross. 2008. *The University against Itself: The NYU Strike and the Future of the Academic Workplace*. Philadelphia: Temple University Press.

Krishnan, Karthik, and Pinshuo Wang. 2019. "The Cost of Financing Education: Can Student Debt Hinder Entrepreneurship?" *Management Science* 65 (10): 4522–54. https://doi.org/10.1287/mnsc.2017.2995.

Levin, John S., Marie C. Martin, and Ariadna I. López Damián. 2020. *University Management, the Academic Profession, and Neoliberalism*. Albany: State University of New York Press.

Loher, David, and Sabine Strasser. 2019. "Politics of Precarity: Neoliberal Academia under Austerity Measures and Authoritarian Threat." *Social Anthropology/Anthropologie Sociale* 27 (S2): 5–14.

Lorusso, Silvio. 2019. *Entreprecariat: Everyone Is an Entrepreneur. Nobody Is Safe*. Eindhoven: Onomatopee 170.

Maxwell, John C. 2000. *Failing Forward: Turning Mistakes into Stepping Stones for Success*. Harper Collins Leadership. Nashville, TN: Thomson Nelson.

McClanahan, Annie. 2019. "Serious Crises: Rethinking the Neoliberal Subject." *Boundary 2: An International Journal of Literature and Culture* 46 (1): 103–32.

Mirowski, Philip. 2011. *Science-Mart: Privatizing American Science*. Cambridge, MA: Harvard University Press.

Mirowski, Philip. 2014. *Never Let a Serious Crisis Go to Waste: How Neoliberalism Survived the Financial Meltdown*. London: Verso.

Nations, Jennifer M. 2021. "How Austerity Politics Led to Tuition Charges at the University of California and City University of New York." *History of Education Quarterly* 61 (3): 273–96. https://doi.org/10.1017/heq.2021.4.

Newfield, Christopher. 2016. *The Great Mistake: How We Wrecked Public Universities and How We Can Fix Them*. Critical University Studies. Baltimore: Johns Hopkins University Press.

Plehwe, Dieter. 2020. "Schumpeter Revival? How Neoliberals Revised the Image of the Entrepreneur." In *Nine Lives of Neoliberalism*, edited by Dieter Plehwe, Quinn Slobodian, and Philip Mirowski, 120–42. London: Verso.

Plehwe, Dieter, Quinn Slobodian, and Philip Mirowski, eds. 2020. *Nine Lives of Neoliberalism*. London: Verso.

Ries, Eric. 2014. *The Lean Startup: How Today's Entrepreneurs Use Continuous Innovation to Create Radically Successful Businesses*. New York: Crown Business.

Robbins, Alexandra. 2006. *The Overachievers: The Secret Lives of Driven Kids*. New York: Hachette.

Schumpeter, Joseph A. 2010. *Capitalism, Socialism and Democracy*. London: Routledge.

Seamster, Louise. 2019. "Black Debt, White Debt." *Contexts* 18 (1): 30–35. https://doi.org/10.1177/1536504219830674.

Shebanow, Alexander, dir. 2019. *Fail State*. San Francisco: Gravitas Ventures.

Washburn, Jennifer. 2005. *University, Inc: The Corporate Corruption of American Higher Education*. New York: Basic Books.

Wilson, Julie A. 2017. *Neoliberalism*. New York: Routledge.

F

Fiction

Jeffrey J. Williams

Where do we look for knowledge of the university? Usually to data, as well as to its history and to the tradition of the idea of the university. In fact, when we—that is, critics from the humanities in the United States—talk about the university, we tend to emphasize ideas. For instance, Bill Readings, in his oft-cited *The University in Ruins* (1996), diagnosed the problem with contemporary higher education as having come unmoored from its grounding ideas—"Reason," articulated by Immanuel Kant and roughly meaning the pursuit of knowledge for its own sake; and "national culture," adumbrated by Wilhelm von Humboldt—instead embracing the substanceless idea of "excellence," inspired by business management gurus like James Grunig. In contrast, Readings argues for "dissensus," a kind of postmodern reason, with the awareness that there is no definitive truth.

Another tradition that receives much less attention, however, is that of fiction and film. While they are often brushed aside as frivolous, their sheer number and popular footprint in American culture call for looking at both. To put it another way, we tend to deliver our ideas and critiques, but we might instead listen to what these other expressions tell us. Thus, in this chapter, I offer a kind of surface reading or broad description of mainstream US fiction and film.[1] In various ways, they speak to popular expectations, hopes, and suspicions about higher ed. To wit, those in high school likely derive their image of what college is like not from the data but from film, fiction, and other cultural representations of it. Or for older citizens, film and fiction might reinforce their impression of the questionable value of

1. I favor the term *description* over *surface reading*; see discussion of description in Marcus (2016). Still, rather than dispensing with critique, I mean something more like David Scott's argument in *Stuart Hall's Voice*, that a key to understanding is listening and seeking clarification rather than victory in argument. In addition, I should note that I focus on the specific case of US fiction and film because that is where I am located, and because it has gained prominence as the US university has become a dominant institution in the world since World War II. There are, of course, other traditions, and it would be useful to do a comparative study.

college and spur them to vote to cut public support. So, what can we draw from university fictions?

In broad outline, literary and filmic representations of the university tend toward two orientations: The literary tradition tends to center on those who work as academics, usually in midlife, whereas the filmic tradition gravitates to college-age characters and undergraduate life. They are often lumped together, but I find it useful to distinguish the former as *academic fiction*, which foregrounds those who work as faculty, typically professors but more recently adjuncts or graduate students as well, and often takes place off campus, in their homes or elsewhere, in contrast to *campus fiction* (or film), which foregrounds undergraduate experience and largely occurs on college grounds.[2]

The anglophone academic novel is typically seen as a quaint, coterie genre, akin to drawing room fiction, depicting the quirky interactions of a small world (in the title of David Lodge's 1985 novel). Most scholarly accounts read it as an offshoot of the British tradition of Oxbridge mysteries or novels of manners, like Dorothy Sayers's *Gaudy Night* (1937) and C. P. Snow's *The Masters* (1950) (see Showalter 2005). The academic novel has coalesced as a mainstream literary genre in the United States since around 1990, however, enlisting entries from prominent novelists including Paul Auster, Ann Beattie, Michael Chabon, Jennifer Egan, Percival Everett, Jonathan Franzen, Denis Johnson, Jhumpa Lahiri, Jonathan Lethem, Lorrie Moore, Richard Powers, Francine Prose, Richard Russo, Jane Smiley, Brandon Taylor, and Weike Wang, among others.

What does this fiction tell us? Contrary to the cliché that the university is an ivory tower removed from the world, it continually responds to the world, and the academic novel has changed accordingly. The genre has multiplied following the mass expansion of higher ed in the United States over the past 60 years, with college becoming a normal experience for a majority

2. See Williams (2012) for a full discussion of the number and types of recent fiction. The standard bibliographical surveys are Kramer (2004) and Conklin (2008). The critical field is thin; though that has started to change recently. Notably, Mark McGurl's *The Program Era: Postwar Fiction and the Rise of Creative Writing* (2009) calls attention to academic milieux in fiction since writers are now university trained, and they "write what they know"; I'd add that readers are university familiar, too. On film, Marez's *University Babylon* uncovers some of the history of film production on campuses, especially in California, and their racialized biases, as well as foregrounds lesser-known alternative films that show Hispanic, Indigenous, and other experience.

of Americans, with more than three-quarters attending some form of it since 1990. That means that writers are almost universally college educated now, and their readers probably have attended at least some college and are familiar with professors and higher ed. Academic experience is no longer special but *common culture*, for readers as well as writers.

To see it historically, college was an unusual experience in 1900, when only about 3 percent attended, or even in 1950, when about 10 percent attended some college, but now it has become part of everyday American life (Williams 2012, 576–77). Moreover, a college professor was a rare entity in 1900, about 1 in 3,200 of the population, whereas other professionals, like lawyers and ministers, were more prevalent, each about 1 in 600. To think of it experientially, most Americans would have encountered a lawyer, doctor, or minister, but unless they lived in a college town, they probably would not have had much contact with a college professor. By 2000, professors had outpaced most other professions, with about 1 in 200 a professor, whereas about 1 in 300 is a lawyer.

Thus, another thing recent academic fiction tells us is that the college professor has become a colloquial figure, a more accessible professional than, say, medical doctors, but more intriguing than schoolteachers. In some ways, contemporary academic fiction updates the bourgeois novel, offering a new version of an organization man with white-collar woes and midlife issues. It is a form of workplace fiction, showing its protagonists dealing with job pressures and management difficulties, as well as relationship issues with colleagues or partners. In addition to its personal imbroglios, it sometimes dramatizes debates in the culture wars, changes in science and technology, and, especially recently, the precarious conditions of academic labor.

We can start to see a shift in the importance of higher education in American fiction and film in the 1950s, with scientists becoming a more common figure, for instance, in Fred MacMurray's *The Absent-Minded Professor* (1961) and Jerry Lewis's *The Nutty Professor* (1963), as well as in science fiction and horror movies (although some scientists work in independent labs rather than in universities).[3] Besides the cluster around science, several noteworthy novels registered other aspects of life during midcentury, such

3. On the one hand, these fictional scientists express hope in scientific progress, although on the other, they show what Susan Sontag (1966) identified in "The Imagination of Disaster" as anxiety about nuclear weapons. In a striking counter to Sontag, Fredric Jameson (1971, 404–8) holds that the films also show "the mystique of the scientist" and their professional work conditions.

as Mary McCarthy's *Groves of Academe* (1952), which foregrounded politics during the McCarthy period; Bernard Malamud's *A New Life* (1961), which turned on the shift to national hiring, as a Jewish East Coaster is displaced to the Northwest; and Allison Lurie's *The War between the Tates* (1974), which puts the novel of divorce in an academic setting. Still, the academic novel was by and large a minor genre.

That changed around 1990. Don DeLillo's *White Noise* (1985) pioneers the shift, as it uses the academic novel to comment on contemporary American society, with its lingo, supermarkets, tourist sites, and blended families. The subsequent wave of fiction takes a few directions: One prominent strand includes comedies of hapless white males, such as Richard Russo's *Straight Man* (1995), Michael Chabon's *Wonder Boys* (1995), and more recently, Julie Schumacher's trilogy beginning with *Dear Committee Members* (2014). They follow the residual form of Kingsley Amis's *Lucky Jim* (1954), although they inject more contemporary concerns, for instance, about budget cuts and the shrinkage of the humanities. In a slightly different vein, Richard Powers's *Galatea 2.2* (1995), centering on a young, lovelorn male researcher, deals with conceptual issues about early computing and proto–artificial intelligence. In some sense, this wave conveys a romance of academic work: Professors have a good deal of work freedom, immune from the usual strictures of a desk job and able to follow their preoccupations. That image of freedom, and the presumed job security to follow it, might also prompt some public suspicion or resentment of professors.

Another strand that spiked through the 1990s includes novels that stage scenes from the decade's culture wars, including Ishmael Reed's *Japanese by Spring* (1993), John L'Heureux's *Handmaid of Desire* (1996), Francine Prose's *Blue Angel* (2000), Philip Roth's *The Human Stain* (2000), and Jane Smiley's *Moo* (1995), as well as David Mamet's discomfiting play *Oleanna* (1992). These often focus on the advent of literary theory, as well as on sexual and racial politics. They register the tension of the increasing number of women faculty—from about one-third of faculty in 1987 (the first year that the statistic appears in NCES reports) to more than half by 2018, albeit still fewer tenure-stream professors—as well as the institutionalization of feminism and affirmative action (NCES 2023). They suggest a contradictory view of academics: The fiction skewers the remove of academics, immersed in the obscure language of theory, but it also suggests the influence if not centrality of academe to US cultural politics.

Through the early 2000s, rather than "Lucky Jim," the image of the professor started shifting to "Unlucky Jim," with fiction foregrounding the degradation of academic jobs. Beginning with James Hynes's *Publish and Perish* (1997), it has become a major type now, featuring protagonists who work as adjuncts, graduate students, or other tertiary workers (for instance, as a driver for visiting speakers). Notably, a number foreground women, for instance, Susannah Moore's *In the Cut* (1995; made into a 2003 movie directed by Jane Campion, and with Meg Ryan), about a lecturer in New York; Michelle Huneven's *Blame* (2009), about a community college lecturer; and Christine Smallwood's *Life of the Mind* (2021), also about an adjunct in New York. Whereas midcentury novels assumed full-time jobs, and the plot often turned on tenure, these portray a world after tenure and its now almost-unimaginable job security.

This new academic novel also exhibits a wider range of identities, responding to demographic shifts in the United States, as well as to a more stratified system of academic jobs. For example, Jhumpa Lahiri's fiction spotlights Indian American graduate students, notably in the opening story of her Pulitzer-winning *Interpreter of Maladies* (1999), and Weike Wang's *Chemistry* (2017) centers on a Chinese American graduate student struggling with work in a biology lab. Alternatively, one of the protagonists of Tony Tulahimutte's *Private Citizens* (2016) is a poor white lab worker as well, whose adviser suggests he work as a landscaper, and Brandon Taylor's *Real Life* (2020) recounts the alienation of a poor black graduate student in his bio lab. These depart from humanities departments to other parts of the university multiplex and flesh out some layers of labor in universities, especially in STEM labs.

The latter three, as well as Smallwood's *Life of the Mind*, come from millennial authors and exhibit a new sensibility: Academe is no longer a cloister or place of hijinks, but a pressured workplace that fosters insecurity, alienation, and depression. That inverts the traditional image of higher ed, which assumes the positive launch of a career and one pathway to the American dream; rather, these show the thwarting of career. As Smallwood's protagonist reflects, "No one of Dorothy's generation would ever accrue the kind of power that [her adviser] had . . . Dorothy was like a janitor in the temple who continued to sweep because she had nowhere else to be but who had lost her belief in the essential sanctity of the enterprise" (143).

To be sure, the fiction varies a good deal, is of course not a pure reflection of social reality, and sometimes relies on stock types and carries inaccuracies, misunderstandings, or fantasies about academic life and work. Still, it suggests ways in which the university intertwines with American society and culture and gives some sense of the popular impression of life and work in higher ed.

If academic fiction tends toward midlife workplace tales, campus fiction and film tack to coming-of-age plots—or more exactly, the transition to adult standing, featuring college-age students (18–23) and their hijinks, relationships, and learning. Typically aimed toward a mass teen audience, they are often farcical and invoke stock types (nerds and socialites, frats and sororities, sensitives and prigs, etc.), but they also speak to the expectation of self-exploration and learning, and to varying degrees the negotiation of cultural difference and understanding others.

While campus experience might form a step in conventional bildungsroman—a chapter in Joyce's *Portrait of the Artist as a Young Man* or the middle part of Fitzgerald's *This Side of Paradise*—it has long held a significant place in film, even when college was rare. For instance, early films such as Harold Lloyd's *The Freshman* (1925) and Buster Keaton's *College* (1927) set out some standard motifs: College is social, less about scholarly learning, and little about job training, turning on relationships with friends, romantic and sexual partnering, dealing with others, and struggling with authority figures—hence, its frequent depiction of activities like parties, sports, and Greek events much more than classrooms.

That social motif continues in contemporary films such as *Animal House* (1978), *Back to School* (1986), *Road Trip* (2000), *Van Wilder* (2002), *White Chicks* (2004), *House Bunny* (2008), and so on, to name just a few mainstream ones with well-known actors. Even for those out of college, the lure of undergraduate life generates nostalgia, spurring a few films about middle-aged protagonists, for instance, *Old School* (2003), in which a group of midlife men form their own frat house, and *Neighbors* (2014), about a couple who reenlivens their marriage catalyzed by a frat house next door. These might seem vulgar, sexist, or simply frivolous, but they also convey a kind of romance of college, with the expectation that its main purpose is social. That sense is not wrong, however skewed: College tends to establish social affiliations that shape the rest of people's lives, carrying over to subsequent friendships, jobs, and marriages, as well as cultural interests and tastes (Armstrong and Hamilton 2013).

Overall, these films tend to represent majoritarian American culture, centering on white, hetero, male students, although a number of contemporary films foreground the cultural politics of race and gender, for instance, Spike Lee's *School Daze* (1988), *PCU* (1994), John Singleton's *Higher Learning* (1995), *White Chicks* (2014), *Monsters University* (2013), and *Dear White People* (2014). In these, college is not an ivory tower but a space for sorting out identity and negotiating cultural difference, usually turning on a conflict that results in a degree of understanding. They tend to internalize the expectation that a key part of education in college is diversity.

What do we take from this projection of diversity? In *University Babylon: Film and Race Politics on Campus*, Curtis Marez (2017, 29), quoting Sara Ahmed, finds that such affirmations of diversity usually offer "magical substitutes for structural transformations." Further, Marez holds that mainstream films reproduce racialized, heteropatriarchal, settler-colonial ideology, and he uncovers examples of film production on University of California campuses, such as *Conquest of the Planet of the Apes* (1972), to argue that they underwrite the "university-cinema-industrial complex." Marez presents a strong critique especially of racialization in film, and his book is an important one extending critical university studies to film. Still, I think that we should see these representations more dialectically: They present images of sociality, a space apart from work, negotiation of cultural tension, and political education at the same time that they present images of racialized, heterosexist, and classist ideology. That is, they are contradictory rather than just conveying a univocal ideology. Like most narrative art, they tend to stage the politics through a personal change rather than structural change, but does that entirely negate their efficacy? And is that change an emblem for the possibilities of larger change? Finally, I think that the question is less about the films per se and more about what their audiences do with them, which in fact might spur countercritical responses, as one survey reports.[4]

One dimension that these films gloss over is class. They typically assume

4. Citing a survey of African American students, Marez notes of one student: "College films make him want to attend university, thereby deconstructing the hierarchical opposition between white knowledge and Black ignorance" (2017, 20). In general, he confirms that how students use college film, even if problematic, is a major influence in their wanting to attend college.

the student as traditional college age in the midst of a full-time, four-year term, usually at a separate and manicured campus, when the truth is that most people without privilege go to college over several years at less than idyllic campuses and at a higher average age, work for a large part of it (an average of 30 hours a week at public colleges and universities; Mortensen 2002; Nathan 2005, 34), and do not attain a bachelor's degree. Though the films' image applies only to a minority of those privileged enough to attend, they tell us another colloquial view of college: the fantasy of leisure, a space apart, offering "an idyll on the threshold of decades of relentless work," as Nick Burns puts it (2024, 80). And, I would add, not only before work, but before one has to pay student debt. The impression of the traditional college student influences the politics of funding, among other things; for instance, it affects the perception of debt, as many assume that it applies only to young people, and they'll make their money back over the course of their careers, whereas most people have a more uneven trajectory, and debt can follow them into retirement age.

In addition to the romance of free time, these films hold out college as a space for transformative learning and sometimes a kind of political education. The scenes of learning tell us something about how students might perceive college: Their focus might be less on the classroom than on informal situations with peers. For instance, in *Road Trip*, the journey concludes with the brainy one of the group tutoring the main protagonist in the basics of the history of philosophy, enabling him to pass his final exam when they get back. Others in the group also learn personal lessons about how to assert oneself and, at one point, about race in the United States, when they stay at an affiliated African American fraternity. And *Higher Learning* centers on the education of various groups, black and white, on campus.

The lessons are also sometimes about political procedures. For instance, though problematic, *Animal House* portrays the loutish protagonists rallying together to pass their courses and fight against the powers that be, both the administration, personified by an uptight dean, a trope in these films, and a rich, snobby fraternity. Sketching the trajectory of an underdog overcoming the dominant, these films depict a species of class conflict, the less privileged struggling against powerful administrators allied with the wealthy. In *Animal House*, the victory comes through a formal appeal in front of a review board; similarly, *Accepted* (2006; with Justin Long, Jonah Hill, and Blake Lively) culminates in a board hearing, where the upstarts gain institutional legitimacy. The films assume remediation through liberal procedural channels rather than radical action or transformation, but still, they confer some value to democratic institutional forms. They might show a fantasy fulfillment, but they also suggest the justice of such struggle.

A few recent films portray a more sobering political education, for instance, the 2022 *Emily the Criminal*, whose protagonist, played by Aubrey Plaza, scrambles to make ends meet and pay her student loan debt working as a food delivery person. The experience of college is evacuated, leaving only crushing debt behind, with little better than gig jobs. Because of low pay, undependable hours, and shabby treatment, she quits, turning to an Amway-like credit card scam ring. The film shows that debt isn't just a bill but permeates people's lives and possibilities. It also helps us picture how the difficult-to-imagine figure of $1.6 trillion of college student loan debt translates to people's lives. The film counters the commonplace that there is a $1 million return on investment (ROI) from attending college; instead, for many, college in the current neoliberal scheme inducts them into a precarious underclass.

Popular campus films are no doubt a mixed bag, conveying ideology as well as social hope, fantasy fulfillment as well as substantive comment on the university. While they offer contradictory—if not incoherent—impressions of higher education, we should listen to them more. In *Stuart Hall's Voice*, David Scott proposes that we adopt the ethic of listening over that of critique. Scott does not dispense with critique but holds that it cannot cast off "conceits of omniscience" (2017, 5), and listening provides a key step toward better understanding—which might make our criticism stronger. Rather than seeing these popular films merely as mystified, what do they tell us? Furthermore, sometimes our criticism speaks for us, for our interests or positions, whereas it might help to try to glean the various constituencies that the university encompasses. To be sure, higher education enjoins a panoply of interests, including those of ordinary citizens, political figures, and parents, as well as faculty and students. To think of it another way, as I mentioned earlier, why is there so much conservative focus on the university at present? How can we understand that position, which might help us more effectively answer it? To add to our understanding, we should make the examination of fictive representations a part of critical university studies.

References

Armstrong, Elizabeth A., and Laura T. Hamilton. 2013. *Paying for the Party: How College Maintains Inequality*. Cambridge, MA: Harvard University Press.

Burns, Nick. 2024. "Student Debt in American Society." *New Left Review* 145:65–83.

Conklin, John E. 2008. *Campus Life in the Movies: A Critical Survey from the Silent Era to the Present*. Jefferson, NC: McFarland.

Jameson, Fredric. 1971. *Marxism and Form: Twentieth-Century Dialectical Theories of Literature*. Princeton, NJ: Princeton University Press, 1971.

Kramer, John E. 2004. *The American College Novel: An Annotated Bibliography*. 2nd ed. Latham, MD: Scarecrow.

Marcus, Sharon. 2016. "Erich Auerbach's *Mimesis* and the Value of Scale." *Modern Language Quarterly* 77 (3): 297–319.

Marez, Curtis. 2017. *University Babylon: Film and Race Politics on Campus*. Berkeley: University of California Press.

McGurl, Mark. 2009. *The Program Era: Postwar Fiction and the Rise of Creative Writing*. Cambridge, MA: Harvard University Press.

Mortensen, Tom. 2002. "'I Worked My Way through College. You Should Too': 1964 to 2002." *Opportunity* 125: 1–11.

Nathan, Rebekah, 2005. *My Freshman Year: What a Professor Learned by Becoming a Student*. New York: Penguin.

NCES (National Center for Education Statistics). 2023. "Table 315.10. Number of Faculty in Degree-Granting Postsecondary Institutions." Digest of Education Statistics, NCES.

Readings, Bill. 1996. *The University in Ruins*. Cambridge, MA: Harvard University Press.

Scott, David. 2017. *Stuart Hall's Voice: Intimations of an Ethics of Receptive Generosity*. Durham, NC: Duke University Press.

Showalter, Elaine. 2005. *Faculty Towers: The Academic Novel and Its Discontents*. Philadelphia: University of Pennsylvania Press.

Smallwood, Christine. 2021. *The Life of the Mind*. New York: Hogarth.

Sontag, Susan. 1966. "The Imagination of Disaster." In *Against Interpretation and Other Essays*, 209–25. New York: Farrar, Straus, Giroux.

Williams, Jeffrey J. 2012. "The Rise of the Academic Novel." *ALH* 24:561–89.

L

Legislation

Elizabeth Tandy Shermer

"The most important door that will ever open," President Lyndon Baines Johnson insisted, was "the door to education." The 1965 Higher Education Act (HEA), he insisted, was "the key which unlocks it," including for students at the Welhausen Mexican School, where he had been a teacher. Even then he knew "that college was closed to practically every one of those children because they were too poor" (Johnson 1965).

That vital part of his Great Society agenda seemed the culmination of decades of halting legislative steps toward federal support for higher education so the academy could grow and become more accessible. The first law most Americans learn about in school was the 1862 Land-Grant Agricultural and Mechanical College Act, better known as the Morrill Act. Almost a century later, Congress passed the 1944 Servicemen's Readjustment Act, the GI Bill of Rights for veterans that enabled 2.2 million to go to college. More young people enrolled after the 1958 National Defense Education Act provided loans for undergraduates, grants for graduate students, and direct support for subjects vital to defense. Seven years later, Johnson signed HEA, which prioritized established and developing campuses, their libraries, and the many students in need of tuition assistance.

Those well-known federal laws were far more complicated than the tidy narrative found in many college textbooks. All those legislative breakthroughs kept with the long-standing legal and cultural tradition of protecting an individual campus's autonomy and leaving higher education funding up to state legislatures, church authorities, and private donors. Those laws also shaped the country's astounding variety of postsecondary institutions, including small liberal arts colleges, sprawling state universities, wealthy private campuses, and online for-profits. Those separate acts also reflected the nation's changing workforce needs, as it became a leading manufacturer and superpower that has struggled to adapt to a new world order driven by financial industries, including student lending. The resultant student debt crisis also highlights how lawmakers embraced tuition assistance as a way to covertly enable young people of color, like those Johnson taught at Welhausen, to enroll, which actually reenforced the systemic inequities that LBJ promised HEA would vanquish.

The Morrill Act did not offer tuition assistance but still reflected how much congressional legislation has promised individual advancement, prioritized larger economic needs, limited federal authority, and bolstered white supremacy. This celebrated law permitted states to use profits from the sale of federal lands to endow a campus dedicated to practical training in agriculture, military science, and engineering, then called the mechanical arts. Vermont Republican Justin Morrill intended these land grants to be accessible to all but also emphasized agribusiness and industrial needs. That aim reflected how important the idea of individual opportunity and advancement has been in American history, as well as the needs of a country that had started to industrialize before the Civil War. New and growing cities as well as enterprises would need food, raw materials, and scientific know-how. The military would also be important as white settlers moved into new territories. Endowments would be created from the sale of some of that land, which researchers have shown to have been violently seized from Indigenous communities (Sorber 2018; also see R. Lee and Ahtone 2020).

Yet the Morrill Act did not guarantee that money would be available immediately nor force states to use this money. Legislatures did, of course, but that was carried out through state, not federal, laws. Some, like Massachusetts, directed funds to existing campuses that were not state schools, like the Massachusetts Institute of Technology, which had been chartered but not built yet. Lawmakers could also shift which campuses held this endowment, as Massachusetts lawmakers did. Most legislatures got far less per acre than they hoped (the average across the country was $1.65 an acre). Sales also took time. Forty years after Congress passed the law, University of California (UC) regents still held unsold land (Curti and Nash 1965, 60–86, esp. 78–80; Stadtman 1970, 45–47).

By then, Congress had also foreshadowed how federal legislation would codify the segregation that Johnson insisted HEA would help vanquish. Lawmakers passed the so-called Second Morrill Act in 1890, after years of fighting over whether more money was needed to aid these institutions. Negotiations were particularly tense that year over whether support would be denied to "a college where a distinction of race and color was made in the admission of students." States could offer a separate option, which captured the essence of the Jim Crow order quickly being constructed through local and state laws across the South after Reconstruction. Debate ended with a law promising "just and equitable" division of allocations to states. Legislatures' power nonetheless ensured that there was never equal support for schools, now called historically Black colleges and universities (HBCUs), started from this federal infusion (Harris 2021, 33–57).

The Roosevelt administration did not challenge the inequality built into state and national higher education laws but did redirect federal support toward tuition assistance. This strategy, like the Morrill Act, emphasized individual opportunity, reflected larger economic concerns, and limited federal authority. That policy shift reflected how important the nation's labor market was to New Dealers. Job creation was a critical goal of the federal loans and grants for construction and repair projects, for which only state schools were eligible. Federal officials did not force campuses to apply but required them to raise the matching funds, for which many campuses looked to local and state leaders, as well as to donors. Colleges also had a lot of power over the National Youth Administration (NYA) work-study program, which New Dealers designed to encourage 16- to 25-year-olds to go to or stay in school. Enrolling would keep them out of competition for jobs and off welfare rolls while they finished degrees. Credentials seemed certain to improve their chances for well-paying work, as well as the quality of the entire country's workforce, which, by then, needed more than the disciplines that the Morrill Act had privileged. New Dealers paid the salary of students working part time at a participating institution so that student workers could pay for tuition, books, and living expenses. But nonprofit public and private colleges chose whether to accept this aid, who received support, and what jobs they did. Federal officials set rules only about how needy a student had to be to receive this help, as well as how many hours they could work. Few of the 600,000 recipients earned enough to cover all college costs, but the majority excelled in a beloved program unceremoniously defunded during 1943 congressional budget battles.

That work-study experiment nonetheless shaped the more famous 1944 GI Bill's tuition assistance, which lawmakers also designed to keep unemployment down, limit the competition for jobs, and improve the economic mobility of the soldiers who had already served their country. The federal government sent enrolled veterans a small monthly "subsistence check" of

$50 for single and $75 for married GIs. Lawmakers openly discussed limiting that help on the assumption that wives would work and that veterans must be kept from living high on the hog on the taxpayers' dime. That money was supposed to cover living expenses while veterans were enrolled in participating campuses, which (unlike under the work-study program) received tuition payments directly from the Veterans Administration (Shermer 2021, 33–77).

None of those Roosevelt era experiments directly tackled the inequality already woven into American higher education. Widespread discriminatory admission practices kept African American, Jewish, Catholic, and women applicants from matriculating, a requirement for being considered for work-study or using their GI Bill benefits. An institution's eligibility for the small work-study experiment and the more expansive GI Bill did not require a public or private campus to desegregate or stop using the quota system. Both practices had kept the American student body overwhelmingly white, Protestant, and male since the Progressive Era, when for-profit schools were far more likely to admit the many citizens and immigrants excluded from academia. Congress made for-profits eligible for the GI Bill, which was still not enough to meet the unexpectedly large demand for this benefit. The federal government had just offered tuition assistance, which did not supply the revenue or labor necessary to rapidly expand campuses or their faculties to meet the needs of soldiers or civilians. Only public schools had been eligible for New Deal construction projects, which large established institutions (like the University of California) had an easier time securing. State allocations and private donations helped during the GI Bill's rollout but did not do enough. Classrooms were overcrowded, veterans lived in derelict military surplus, and campus admissions officers denied many GIs entrance before this first GI Bill expired in 1952 (Mettler 2005; Shermer 2021).

States did far more than Congress to meet the growing demand for college degrees, which seemed to guarantee economic prosperity for individuals and their communities in the Cold War's early years. Regional schooling traditions as well as business needs did a lot to shape how states expanded higher education. Public postsecondary options, for example, were more entrenched in the West, where the California legislature was still exceptional for the money spent even before the 1960 Donahoe Higher Education Act's passage. That law incorporated many elements of the UC regents'

Master Plan for Higher Education, which outlined a tuition-free system of community colleges, state colleges, and research universities. That state investment provided an opportunity for individuals to pursue degrees that then seemed to guarantee well-paying work as well as the educational infrastructure that pleased employers, especially those in the manufacturing sectors. Those industries relied on universities to meet research and workforce training needs far different from what Morrill had imagined Americans needing one hundred years earlier.

Lawmakers in other parts of the country were also eager to keep or attract profitable industries but did not necessarily fund public options robustly. Legislators, for example, founded the State University of New York (SUNY) system amid revelations about the quota system being used to deny veterans' admission during the GI Bill's rollout. Legislative support languished until the late 1950s, when New York was one of the first states to experiment with a student loan program to incentivize bankers to lend to students enrolling in public and private campuses. Other states followed as newly elected Governor Nelson Rockefeller used state allocations, tuition revenue, and a complicated construction fund to build new campuses for and merge financially strapped private schools (like the University of Buffalo) with SUNY. Rapid expansion seemed critical to keeping industry, attracting new investment, and retraining citizens for new jobs in a state that had already lost a lot of manufacturing investment to western and southern states. North Carolina Governor Luther Hodges actually admitted that he had not understood the importance of the state's colleges and universities until he tried to convince manufacturers to relocate. They expected a skilled labor force, which Hodges worked with the legislature to provide through more funding for community colleges, state colleges, and universities. Those allocations aided his office's effort to bolster the public and privately funded Research Triangle Park, connected to two public campuses and one private university (Shermer 2013, 184–224; 2021, 117–63).

States needed to experiment because federal efforts to fund higher education continually stalled in Congress. Lawmakers agreed to fund government support for scientific research, but the money available through the National Institutes of Health and National Science Foundation largely went to well-established public and private campuses. Neither Democrats nor Republicans could agree on directly funding colleges and universities, which raised questions about aiding segregated schools, funding private campuses (especially those with religious affiliations), threatening states' rights, and increasing federal taxes as well as expenditures (Clowse 1981; Urban 2010).

Those divides continued even after the Soviets launched their first satellite in 1957. Lawmakers spent almost a year negotiating the temporary 1958 National Defense Education Act (NDEA), which offered limited support for programs related to training young people for work in defense industries. Most Americans remain far more familiar with NDEA's small one-year loans for undergraduates and grants for graduate students, for which campuses had to apply. As with Roosevelt era legislation, all nonprofit campuses were eligible, including religious colleges and the segregated institutions that students of color had been increasingly fighting to integrate since the GI Bill's enactment. Staff also had a lot of power over tuition assistance, which Congress continually renewed for more than 50 years. Admissions and financial-aid officers determined which applicants received support; they used these programs to compile recruitment packages to compete with other schools for top students and athletes. Aspiring co-eds were especially unlikely to receive this help, because the targeted fields (math, science, and engineering) were aimed at male students, who could expect to find work in them after graduation (Shermer 2021, 117–63).

Employment concerns also shaped how lawmakers and the Johnson White House designed HEA, which, like so many state and federal laws, emphasized individual advancement, reflected broader economic needs, and protected campuses' authority. But this Great Society legislation seemed like dramatic direct investment in nonprofit campuses, which, per the 1964 Civil Rights Act, could no longer receive federal revenue if they discriminated on the basis of race, religion, or sex. The first three titles offered aid for institutions and their libraries, which included additional money for underresourced "developing institutions." Lawmakers nonetheless prioritized the fourth section's tuition assistance, which Johnson discussed at length in a signing statement. He promised this help "means that a high school senior anywhere . . . can apply to any college . . . and not be turned away because his family is poor." The president did not mention that campuses would decide which students received financial-aid packages, which could include a new work-study option, a small grant, a defense loan, or a new guaranteed student loan, which bankers made available to financial-aid officers to distribute. Federal officials did not force universities or financiers to participate in a program that promised bankers repayment, nor did they assure colleges or students that these loans would be available for fees that had gone up more than 90 percent since the first GI Bill had expired (Shermer 2021, 163–201; Graham 2011).

Lawmakers also did nothing to explicitly ensure equal opportunities to enroll. Segregationists still in Congress recoiled at desegregation, let alone integration. So HEA's architects, unlike NYA's director, covertly designed institutional support and tuition assistance to aid African Americans. Liberals hoped funding for "developing institutions" would go to HBCUs, which they rightly predicted would remain most welcoming to students of color, as they had since the Second Morrill Act's passage. Yet the limited state and philanthropic support for colleges meant a lot of institutions qualified. There was nothing to compel them or well-endowed universities to admit students of color, let alone women, in large numbers. Those battles had been and continued to be waged in the courts. Congress also did not infringe on the power financial-aid officers had over who received federal tuition assistance. White House insiders and their congressional allies had set rules only for work-study and grant options to benefit low-income students, who were then more likely to be from families of color (like the Welhausen students Johnson mentioned). Liberals had implicitly hoped that only middle-income white students would be offered guaranteed loans, whose interest charges left borrowers paying more, over time, for the same degrees as their wealthier peers. Those credentials were intended not just to improve the country's labor force, as Roosevelt era experiments had intended, but also to make access to education more equitable so that citizens of color could theoretically compete for the middle-class jobs that increasingly required a college degree (Shermer 2021, 163–201).

But HEA and its subsequent reauthorizations never erased wage and wealth gaps. Lawmakers focused far more on tuition assistance programs that did little to keep the overall cost of higher education down. For example, the first major congressional reauthorization, the 1972 Education Act, opened up federal tuition assistance programs to for-profits and included the now celebrated (then controversial) Title IX and Pell Grant programs. For-profits had remained more accessible to nontraditional students after the first GI Bill ended. They had even remained eligible for later educational benefits for veterans, even though they were excluded from NDEA and HEA. The 1972 revisions made for-profits eligible (with some restrictions) for civilian tuition assistance at a moment of economic crisis, when older Americans were looking for new job skills. Lawmakers did nothing to police institutions, which congressional investigations almost 20 years later revealed to have bilked many students for worthless degrees. Those graduates had included many women who needed the access to education that Title IX had seemed to ensure.

Equal opportunities were easy for lawmakers to promise but hard to enforce. That 1972 addition did nothing to force employers to pay college-educated women equally. Graduates of color also continued to face unequal treatment in the labor market despite the passage of the Civil Rights and Higher Education Acts. Lawmakers nevertheless still looked to tuition assistance to attack workplace inequities in the early 1970s. The new scholarships direct from the federal government for low-income students (now known as Pell Grants) were intended to covertly help students of color afford college. Financial-aid officers were not in charge of this tuition assistance. Lawmakers also incentivized campuses to admit these students by tying how much direct federal support a school could receive to the number of Pell recipients. But these grants were always small in comparison to the actual cost of attending college, which pushed many Pell awardees to borrow. And this program had no mechanism to ensure that a Pell recipient of color, like women promised equality through Title IX, would be paid equally after graduation. Presidents, senators, and representatives nevertheless continued to focus on tuition assistance, particularly student lending, for the next 50 years in subsequent HEA reauthorizations (Gladieux and Wolanin 1976; Shermer 2021, 202–41).

States were complicit in what became a student debt crisis that disproportionately affected students of color, especially women. Legislatures across the country cut higher education expenditures throughout the late twentieth and early twenty-first centuries, when the majority of voters wanted less taxing and spending. Colleges and universities were an easy target. "Every public official," as a college consultant explained in the new millennium, "knows that colleges and universities can raise tuition to compensate for state cutbacks." Federal legislation seemed to encourage colleges to look for ways to pay for themselves through reauthorizations passed to bolster tuition assistance programs and laws making it possible for campuses to profit off research, like the 1980 Bayh-Dole Act (Fergus 2018, 49–96; J. Lee and Clery 2004, 23; Mettler 2014; Shermer 2021, 242–88).

Political gridlock has kept state and federal lawmakers from adequately responding to public uproar over soaring college costs, unpayable student debts, and declining quality of higher education in the new millennium. There have been (as in decades past) politically controversial, halting steps focused on individual opportunity and workforce needs without treading on campus autonomy. Some legislatures have agreed on different versions of making community colleges free, waiving tuition for families making less than $125,000 or debt forgiveness programs, especially for those working in health care or education. Less help has come from Congress, which managed to replace the original student loan program with direct loans from the government through the budget reconciliation process in 2010. Lawmakers also paused student loan payments early in the COVID-19 pandemic, which was extended throughout the pandemic via executive orders. That is also how President Joe Biden promised to forgive a lot of federally held student debt in fall 2022, a process the Supreme Court derailed in a summer 2023 decision. But he notably broke with tradition of alluding to racial inequities in that effort and in the fall 2023 rollout of a new repayment plan promising much cheaper monthly payments. The president *openly* admitted that Americans of color owed more and had a harder time paying those debts off. But his statements and White House press releases, like Johnson's remarks upon signing HEA, did not even hint at the many ways state and federal higher education laws had contributed to inequities in the name of individual advancement, economic dynamism, states' rights, and institutional autonomy since the Civil War (Shermer 2021; Vogue and Sneed 2023; White House 2022, 2023).

References

Clowse, Barbara Barksdale. 1981. *Brainpower for the Cold War: The Sputnik Crisis and National Defense Education Act of 1958*. Westport, CT: Greenwood.

Curti, Merle, and Roderick Nash. 1965. *Philanthropy in the Shaping of American Higher Education*. New Brunswick, NJ: Rutgers University Press.

Fergus, Devin. 2018. *Land of the Fee: Hidden Costs and the Decline of the American Middle Class*. New York: Oxford University Press.

Gladieux, Lawrence E., and Thomas R. Wolanin. 1976. *Congress and the Colleges: The National Politics of Higher Education*. Lexington, MA: Lexington Books.

Graham, Hugh Davis. 2011. *The Uncertain Triumph: Federal Education Policy in the Kennedy and Johnson Years*. Chapel Hill: University of North Carolina Press.

Harris, Adam. 2021. *The State Must Provide: Why America's Colleges Have Always Been Unequal—and How to Set Them Right*. New York: Ecco.

Johnson, Lyndon B. 1965. "Remarks at Southwest Texas State College upon Signing the Higher Education Act of 1965." American Presidency Project, November 8. https://www

.presidency.ucsb.edu/documents/remarks-southwest-texas-state-college-upon-signing-the-higher-education-act-1965.

Lee, John, and Sue Clery. 2004. "Key Trends in Higher Education." *American Academic* 1 (1): 21–36.

Lee, Robert, and Tristan Ahtone. 2020. "Land-Grab Universities." *High Country News*, March 30. https://www.hcn.org/issues/52-4/indigenous-affairs-education-land-grab-universities/.

Mettler, Suzanne. 2005. *Soldiers to Citizens: The GI Bill and the Making of the Greatest Generation*. Oxford: Oxford University Press.

Mettler, Suzanne. 2014. *Degrees of Inequality: How the Politics of Higher Education Sabotaged the American Dream*. New York: Basic Books.

Shermer, Elizabeth Tandy. 2013. *Sunbelt Capitalism: Phoenix and the Transformation of American Politics*. Philadelphia: University of Pennsylvania Press.

Shermer, Elizabeth Tandy. 2021. *Indentured Students: How Government-Guaranteed Loans Left Generations Drowning in College Debt*. Cambridge, MA: Harvard University Press.

Sorber, Nathan M. 2018. *Land-Grant Colleges and Popular Revolt: The Origins of the Morrill Act and the Reform of Higher Education*. Ithaca, NY: Cornell University Press.

Stadtman, Verne A. 1970. *The University of California, 1868–1968*. New York: McGraw-Hill.

Urban, Wayne J. 2010. *More than Science and Sputnik: The National Defense Education Act of 1958*. Tuscaloosa: University of Alabama Press.

Vogue, Ariane de, and Tierney Sneed. 2023. "Supreme Court Blocks Biden's Student Loan Forgiveness Program." *CNN*, June 30. https://www.cnn.com/2023/06/30/politics/supreme-court-student-loan-forgiveness-biden/index.html.

White House. 2022. "Fact Sheet: 'President Biden Announces Student Loan Relief for Borrowers Who Need It Most.'" White House Briefing Room, August 24. https://www.whitehouse.gov/briefing-room/statements-releases/2022/08/24/fact-sheet-president-biden-announces-student-loan-relief-for-borrowers-who-need-it-most/.

White House. 2023. "Fact Sheet: 'The Biden-Harris Administration Launches the SAVE Plan.'" White House Briefing Room, August 22. https://www.whitehouse.gov/briefing-room/statements-releases/2023/08/22/fact-sheet-the-biden-harris-administration-launches-the-save-plan-the-most-affordable-student-loan-repayment-plan-ever-to-lower-monthly-payments-for-millions-of-borrowers/.

N

Noncitizen Student

Abigail Boggs

To write or think about the *noncitizen student* in the context of the US university is to consider the experiences of students enrolled in US institutions of higher education who do not have the legal status of a United States citizen. As such, they do not have the legal and political rights of full membership in the community, including voting and holding public office, and can be subject to denial of entry and deportation by the state. While the Constitution formally extends protections such as due process and equal protection to "all persons," rather than just citizens, the challenges of gaining admission to the country and then the experiences of persistent monitoring and living under the threat of expulsion and future denial of entry mean that life in the United States is substantially restricted for students without US citizenship. These challenges are exacerbated for students racialized as nonwhite and those who have traveled from countries the US government considers threats to its security (Cole 2008; Ngai 2004).

In fields such as American studies, Asian American studies, Latinx studies, sociology, history, and immigration studies, scholars use the terms *denizen*, *foreign-born person*, *alien*, and *noncitizen* to mark the grouping of people who are in the United States without the status of citizenship (Buff 2008; Lowe 1996; Ngai 2004; Paik 2020). Naomi A. Paik warns that the term *noncitizen* is imperfect in that it "defines a person by a status they lack and implicitly establishes citizenship as the norm" (168). I understand and appreciate this concern. Yet, tracing the convoluted and uneven history of how immigration law has conditioned the lives of students without citizenship puts pressure on the certainty with which the category *citizen* itself is discussed, along with many of the analytical terms through which higher education, migration, and national politics are studied (Kramer 2009). Understanding the processes and implications of displacement from what is presumed to be the "norm" of citizenship is a necessary aspect of contending with and contesting how such a status constrains the lives of the myriad groups of people it encompasses and the institutions, including the state and universities, with which they interact.

I offer the term *noncitizen student* to bring the study of higher education into necessary conversation with critical edges of immigration studies and, importantly, to stress the too often obscured and neglected ways in which the experiences of noncitizen students, as well as institutional desire and need for them, shape the history, practices, and politics of US universities and colleges. To study the US university with attention to noncitizen students requires grappling with the wide-ranging significance of the overlapping histories of higher education and immigration as tools of the state and capital in the international arena and in the very process of making and naturalizing the nation-state form.

History of the Noncitizen Student

Centering the noncitizen student puts into question a fundamental conceit of the study of higher education: that the sector's primary purpose is and has always been the reproduction of an educated citizenry and labor force for a single nation-state from within its own population. As Christopher Loss argues, during the Cold War US policymakers invested in higher education as a global education strategy, "convinced that higher education created prosperous, civic minded, psychologically adjusted democratic citizens worthy of special rights and privileges" (2012, 4). In an earlier era, he argues, "one of the major goals of the old-time denominational college, which dominated the nation's education landscape before the Civil War, was to train citizens for a life of public service in the new nation" (10). Tracing an even longer history of the contemporary university to the earliest era of British colonialism in the seventeenth century, Craig Steven Wilder illustrates that the work of these institutions was not just to support an existent empire, but to actually bring it into being through their function as "imperial instruments akin to armories and forts" and "as part of the colonial garrison with the specific responsibilities to train ministers and missionaries, convert indigenous peoples and soften cultural resistance, and extend European rule over foreign nations" (2013, 33).

Wilder's work has been widely influential, pushing the field of higher education studies and higher education institutions themselves to contend with their pasts, as they were fundamentally enabled through a mode of accumulation built on the labor and lives of enslaved people from Africa.

Less attention has been paid, however, to Wilder's discussion of how the earliest colleges and universities in the United States, namely Harvard, William and Mary, and Dartmouth, secured both land and funding through the assertion of a mission to directly educate Indigenous students.[1] Wilder's attention to this mission highlights how the university's work in producing and then reproducing the nation has aimed to assimilate noncitizens not only to the nation, but to the imperial project that undergirds it. For instance, Harvard's 1650 charter required the school to "educate the English and Indian youth of this country in knowledge and godliness," and many scholars trace William and Mary's history to efforts as early as 1612 to found a university to take Indian children and "traine them up with gentlenesse, teach them our English tongue, and the principles of religion" ("Harvard Charter" [1650] 2020; Johnson [1612] 1836, 18). While few Indigenous students attended any of these institutions during the British colonial period, the histories Wilder surfaces show that the institutions themselves were both materially and epistemologically organized around the domination of Indigenous peoples and lands. Today, these efforts can be read as a central technique through which colonial forces attempted to implement assimilation as a mode of elimination. This eliminative mode fostered accumulation in two ways: through the dispossession of land and through the incorporation of Indigenous youth into British culture and knowledge systems (Kazanjian 2014; Wolfe 2006). The Harvard and William and Mary charters predate the founding of the United States, so the students were of course not "noncitizens," but they were clearly youth from polities other than that of their instructors and their benefactors.

These cases make clear that people who do not belong to the governing polity most directly tied to educational institutions have never been wholly excluded from them. In fact, just the opposite is true. "Foreign" students were central to the missions and actual function of many of the most prestigious institutions of higher education in the United States from their very inception. That the student is not necessarily a citizen does not put into question the fact that institutions of higher education have long served the needs and interests of the empire, often underwritten with a Christian mis-

1. Wilder's most fundamental and most overlooked argument is that universities materially and epistemologically provided the organizing logic for the nation-state as a project of domination over other nations, peoples, and lands and that this logic continues to govern university operations in the present.

sion and in alignment with the development of capitalism. Rather, efforts to educate, convert, and civilize Indigenous students illustrate the deep history of students being selectively and conditionally incorporated, through their education as potential future citizens, future and current laborers, or ambassadors-in-training who will, it is assumed, return to their homes and proselytize their communities in the ways of their educators (Boggs 2023).

By the mid-nineteenth century new federal immigration laws and ideas about citizenship emerged as the US economy and government reorganized after formal emancipation. Public state-supported universities expanded significantly, tasked with developing knowledge projects to expand the means of capital accumulation and funded by the 1862 Morrill Land Grant Act, which expropriated land from tribal nations as "seed money for higher education" (Boggs et al. 2019; R. Lee and Ahtone 2020). While state and Christian boarding schools for Indigenous youth notoriously proliferated during this period, the new colleges and universities were generally not open to their enrollment. At the same time, exclusionary laws barring Chinese immigration through a broadly conceived ban on Chinese laborers included exemptions for categories of people of particular use for capital, including "merchants" and individuals traveling "for the purpose of study." As Madeline Hsu argues, this did not mean that would-be Chinese students crossed into the United States with ease. Rather, Chinese students were frequently detained and subjected to invasive medical exams and intense scrutiny of their travel documents (Hsu 2015, 36). That students remained technically exempt from the otherwise intensifying regime of racialized US immigration restrictions is testament to the value governmental officials and industrial leaders saw in their education.

With a brief deviation in 1921, students have remained an exceptional category in US immigration to the present, but the ways they are recruited, monitored, regulated, and policed has only intensified. Throughout the twentieth century and into the present, programs organized and funded by state, religious, and corporate philanthropic organizations made possible a pattern of recruitment of students from regions of the world otherwise excluded or severely restricted by US immigration law because students were imagined as "potential instruments of U.S. national power" (Kramer 2009, 781). From the late 1940s into the 1960s, programs recruited students from decolonizing countries in Africa and Asia that US forces saw as at risk of falling into communism. Such programs facilitated the US educations of

Kofi Annan and Barack Obama Sr., among others. During this period, there was a "mini cold war for students" based on "the full realization that an international exchange of students can be an immense source of good will and propaganda" (Von Eschen 1997, 131; see also Bu 2003; Ferguson 2012; Getachew 2020; Kramer 2009). By 1962, John W. Gardner of the Carnegie Corporation led a Presidential Commission that established the exchange of students as "a basic ingredient of the foreign relations of the U.S." (Elfin and Montague 1963, 59).

The Contemporary Noncitizen Student

The category of noncitizen student currently functions as an umbrella term steeped in legal logics, categorizations, and processes shaped by a range of governmental and institutional interests and anxieties. As such, it brings into relief the distinct but entwined relationships between several groups of people and the US government, US-based capital, and colleges and universities. Perhaps most obviously, it indexes students who travel to the United States for the purposes of study through the "international" or "foreign" student process after receiving an F visa from the US government, a category of student that has received much attention in higher education scholarship over the last three decades (Bevis and Lucas 2007; J. J. Lee 2007). *Noncitizen student* also encompasses students who have lived in the United States for any period of time without having gone through a formal immigration or visa process and are therefore classified as "undocumented" (Abrego and Negrón-Gonzales 2020; Terriquez 2014). The term can also signal people conscripted into US citizenship who understand their primary political affiliation to be to a polity, community, or group other than the United States, for instance, to a tribe (Simpson 2010; Volpp 2015). And, read capaciously, the category can include students who are technically citizens of the United States but who are often not recognized as such and are therefore denied substantive citizenship by the people enacting and enforcing laws and policies due to racialized conceptualizations of "the citizen" as presumptively white (Glenn 2002, 53).

Falling into the broad category of *noncitizen student* has a range of implications for students' daily lives and how they can imagine their futures. These implications are shaped by the restrictive legal terms under which the US government grants students on visas and undocumented students conditional access to both the country and the college or university in which they enroll. Processes for administering the presence of students on visas, what have been called F and M visas since 1952, have the longest history and are the most formalized, thus shaping the experiences of other noncitizen students. As noncitizens, students hoping to travel to the United States must first navigate the visa application and interview process in their home countries. This process is uneven and varies widely depending on relations between that country and the US government at that particular moment. To receive a visa in advance of traveling, the prospective student must persuade their interviewer that they are a bona fide student who desires an education in the United States but does not want to move to the United States permanently, since such an intention is one of the most frequently cited grounds for denial under section 214(b) of the 1952 Immigration and Naturalization Act (Boggs 2020). They must also demonstrate that they have the financial means to cover their first year of living and studying in the United States or they will be denied a visa due to their potential to become a "public charge," per section 212(a)(4) (USCIS 2025).

Should they be granted the visa, noncitizen students must then contend with uncertainty during their travel to the United States and throughout their stay. A visa does not guarantee admittance to the country or their ability to stay long enough to complete their education. Instead, upon arrival at the border, students' entrance can be approved or denied by a Customs and Border Protection agent. Once in the United States, students face constant monitoring by international student advisers, whose primary legal and professional responsibility is to maintain records that verify student status by vigilantly updating each Student and Exchange Visitor Information System (SEVIS) record. This computerized monitoring system was first implemented after September 11, 2001, but was imagined by Richard Nixon in 1969 to monitor Arab and Arab Americans in response to claims by Zionist lobbying groups that they were organizing on campuses and making connections to the Black Panther Party and Students for a Democratic Society (Hagopian 1975, 101). Currently, SEVIS records include 150 data fields that must be updated within 24 hours of any changes or failures to comply with visa stipulations, so they can be investigated by Immigration and Customs Enforcement (ICE). Between its initiation and 2018, SEVIS enabled the deportation of 256,087 students (Walsh 2019, 330). Through and beyond SEVIS, students are subjected to various forms of monitoring, including those that collect their biometric data, strictly limit their hours of work beyond their studies, and require regular surveillance of their academic performance by their university.

The policies and practices applied to students on visas not only shape their lives but also have expanding implications for other noncitizen students and campus life more broadly. For instance, when ICE visits a campus, all students (and faculty and staff) become newly exposed to the expanded domain of immigration enforcement. In 2007, this meant that a simple clerical error on an Iranian UC Santa Barbara student's SEVIS record led ICE to conduct an early morning raid of their apartment. While the Iranian student was able to provide paperwork to correct the issue, ICE officers arrested and detained their third-year undergraduate roommate, who could not provide documentation, accusing her of overstaying a visitor visa (Pike 2007).

The status of noncitizens also has financial implications for students and for universities. In response to the attrition of state funding for public higher education since the late 1960s, many state university systems have increased tuition and fees for nonresident students, that is, students who are from outside the state a public university system serves, such as California, Texas, or Washington, to fill gaps in their budgets left by the retrenchment of public funding. For instance, for the 2023 cohort at UC San Diego, in-state costs are around $40,000, while nonresidents pay an additional $32,574 for supplemental tuition. Despite living in a given state and being part of families that have paid state taxes, which go toward education, for potentially their entire lives, as noncitizens, undocumented students have been subjected to paying "nonresident" tuition. Over the last two and a half decades, 23 states have addressed this issue by providing in-state tuition to undocumented students, through the passage of legislation such as California's AB540, passed in 2001, or Arizona's Proposition 308, voted into law in 2022, but there is no guarantee that such policies will remain in place. In response to fears that the Trump administration would create a sudden decline in Chinese student enrollments, in 2018 the University of Illinois Urbana-Champaign reportedly took out a $424,000 insurance policy that provides $60 million coverage to secure itself.

Noncitizen Student Movements

Whether a noncitizen student is on a visa or undocumented, their status as noncitizen renders them especially dependent on and thus vulnerable to the various university workers with whom they interact, be they faculty, staff, or administration. Interviews with students regularly demonstrate a casual acceptance of differential and often exploitative treatment as simply "the cost of earning an American degree" (J. J. Lee 2007, 28). Exacerbated by systems of racial, gendered, classed, linguistic, and ableist inequity, students frequently work far beyond the terms of their contracts and can be subjected to various forms of harassment, sexual and otherwise. These abuses are compounded by the fact that the immigration status of noncitizen students has frequently been employed by university administrations to undermine student unionizing efforts, with threats that students who join a union will be reported to ICE as being out of status and thus potentially subject to deportation (Bittle 2017). Recently, noncitizen students have refused to be cowed by these threats. Instead, they have been at the forefront of organizing efforts calling out campus administrators for their callous abuse of student vulnerability in an effort to break strikes, and calling instead for solidarity with undocumented students and students of color (West 2020).

Noncitizen students organizing in the present build on a long, though often submerged, legacy of collective organizing by students in the past that disrupted the assimilatory intentions of the US state and capital, establishing lateral, transnational solidarities critical of the United States, capitalism, and even the statist mode of organizing the world. In 1941 students in Ohio and then New York formed the African Student's Association (ASA). While the participating students from decolonization nations in Africa were initially recruited to serve US interests in the region, for many, such as the ASA's second president, Kwame Nkrumah, an education in the United States only intensified their radical anticolonial positions (Kramer 2009; Laosebikan 2010). Founded by the American Friends of the Middle East (AFME) and funded by the CIA, the Iranian Student Association (ISA) formed in the immediate aftermath of the 1953 US-orchestrated coup in Iran, which installed the shah as dictator. By 1960, however, AFME withdrew support for the ISA "in dismay over student criticism" of the United States (Moradian 2022, 77). This work continues in the participation of noncitizen students in new formations, such as the Lausan Collective, which built from the Hong Kong Anti-Extradition Bill movement to create a platform for "critical left voice . . . connecting it with other liberatory uprisings across the world"; and the Chinese Students and Activists (CSA) Network, an organization that connects "Chinese (overseas) students" who work in solidarity with "the Chinese immigrant community, the Asian American community, working class people of color, Indigenous communities and white progressives and liberals to build something together."[2] Despite the clear intentions of various institutional bodies that arrange for the education of noncitizen students in the United States, the presence and efforts of these students agitates against those same interests and toward the rearrangement of the most basic categories and terms of nations, nationalism, states, and identities that organize and restrict political thought and freedom struggles.

References

Abrego, Leisy J., and Genevieve Negrón-Gonzales. 2020. *We Are Not Dreamers: Undocumented Scholars Theorize Undocumented Life in the United States*. Durham, NC: Duke University Press.

Bevis, Teresa Brawner, and Christopher J. Lucas. 2007. *International Students in American Colleges and Universities: A History*. New York: Palgrave Macmillan.

Bittle, Jake. 2017. "This University Suggested International Students Could Be Reported to ICE if They Unionized." *Nation*, October 5. https://www.thenation.com/article/archive/this-university-suggested-international-students-could-be-reported-to-ice-if-they-unionized/.

Boggs, Abigail. 2020. "Conditioned Inclusion: The Student Visa as History." *Abusable Past*, August 19. https://abusablepast.org/conditioned-inclusion-the-student-visa-as-history/.

Boggs, Abigail. 2023. "Educational Pasts, Enduring Colonial Presents: Indigenous Student Conscripts and the Foundation of the US University." *History of the Present*. 13 (2): 141–65.

Boggs, Abigail, Eli Meyerhoff, Nick Mitchell, and Zach Schwartz-Weinstein. 2019. "Abolitionist University Studies: An Invitation." *Abolition Journal*, August 28. https://abolitionjournal.org/abolitionist-university-studies-an-invitation/.

Bu, Liping. 2003. *Making the World Like Us: Education, Cultural Expansion, and the American Century*. Westport, CT: Praeger.

Buff, Rachel. 2008. *Immigrant Rights in the Shadows of Citizenship*. New York: New York University Press.

Elfin, Mel, and Constance Montague. 1963. "Foreign Students: Diplomas and Diplomacy." *Newsweek*, April 22.

Ferguson, Roderick A. 2012. *The Reorder of Things: The University and Its Pedagogies of Minority Difference*. Minneapolis: University of Minnesota Press.

Getachew, Adom. 2020. *Worldmaking after Empire: The Rise and Fall of Self-Determination*. Princeton, NJ: Princeton University Press.

Glenn, Evelyn Nakano. 2002. *Unequal Freedom: How Race and Gender Shaped American Citizenship and Labor*. Cambridge, MA: Harvard University Press.

Hagopian, Elaine. 1975. "Minority Rights in a Nation-State: The Nixon Administration's Campaign against Arab-Americans." *Journal of Palestine Studies* 5 (1–2): 97–114.

2. "About Lausan," Lausan Collective, accessed February 7, 2024, https://lausancollective.com/about/; "About Us," CSA Network, accessed February 7, 2024, https://www.csanetwork.org/about-us.

"Harvard Charter of 1650." (1650) 2020. Harvard Library. Last updated December 1, 2020. https://guides.library.harvard.edu/c.php?g=880222&p=6323072.
Hsu, Madeline Y. 2015. *The Good Immigrants: How the Yellow Peril Became the Model Minority.* Princeton, NJ: Princeton University Press.
Johnson, Robert. (1612) 1836. *The New Life of Virginia . . .* (London, 1612). In *Tracts and Other Papers Relating Principally to the Origin, Settlement, and Progress of the Colonies in North America,* vol. 1, no. 7, compiled by Peter Force, 18. Washington, 1836–1846.
Kazanjian, David. 2014. "'To See the Issue of His Exorbitant Practices': A Response to 'The Dispossessed Eighteenth Century.'" *Eighteenth Century* 55 (2–3): 273–82.
Kramer, Paul A. 2009. "Is the World Our Campus? International Students and U.S. Global Power in the Long Twentieth Century." *Diplomatic History* 33 (5): 775–806.
Laosebikan, Olanipekun Oladotun. 2010. "In Pursuit of the 'Golden Fleece': African Students and Higher Education in the United States, 1925-1959." *West Africa Review* 17:26–38.
Lee, Jenny J. 2007. "Neo-Racism toward International Students: A Critical Need for Change." *About Campus* 11 (6): 28–30.
Lee, Robert, and Tristan Ahtone. 2020. "Land-Grab Universities: Expropriated Indigenous Land Is the Foundation of the Land-Grant University System." *High Country News,* March 30. https://www.hcn.org/issues/52-4/indigenous-affairs-education-land-grab-universities/.
Loss, Christopher P. 2012. *Between Citizens and the State: The Politics of Higher Education in the 20th Century.* Princeton, NJ: Princeton University Press, 2012.
Lowe, Lisa. 1996. *Immigrant Acts: On Asian American Cultural Politics.* Durham, NC: Duke University Press.
Moradian, Manijeh. 2022. *This Flame Within: Iranian Revolutionaries in the United States.* Durham, NC: Duke University Press.
Ngai, Mae M. 2004. *Impossible Subjects: Illegal Aliens and the Making of Modern America.* Princeton, NJ: Princeton University Press.
Paik, Naomi A. 2020. *Bans, Walls, Raids, Sanctuary: Understanding U.S. Immigration for the Twenty-First Century.* Oakland: University of California Press.
Pike, Kaitlin. 2007. "Immigration Raid Challenged: Government Agents Arrest UCSB Student." *Santa Barbara (CA) Independent,* May 31. https://www.independent.com/2007/05/31/immigration-raid-challenged/.
Simpson, Audra. 2010. "Under the Sign of Sovereignty: Certainty, Ambivalence, and Law in Native North America and Indigenous Australia." *Wicazo Sa Review* 25 (2): 107–24.
Terriquez, Veronica. 2014. "Dreams Delayed: Barriers to Degree Completion among Undocumented Community College Students." *Journal of Ethnic and Migration Studies* 41 (8): 1302–23.
USCIS (US Citizenship and Immigration Services). 2025. "Students and Employment." Last updated January 24, 2025. https://www.uscis.gov/working-in-the-united-states/students-and-exchange-visitors/students-and-employment.
Volpp, Leti. 2015. "The Indigenous as Alien." *UC Irvine Law Review* 5 (289): 289–326.
Von Eschen, Penny M. 1997. *Race against Empire: Black Americans and Anticolonialism, 1937–1957.* Ithaca, NY: Cornell University Press.
Walsh, James P. 2019. "Education or Enforcement? Enrolling Universities in the Surveillance and Policing of Migration." *Crime, Law and Social Change* 71 (3): 325–44.
West, Charlotte. 2020. "Breaking: UC Santa Cruz Terminates Contracts for 54 Graduate Students." *Voices of Monterey Bay.* February 29. https://voicesofmontereybay.org/2020/02/27/international-students-take-charge-at-uc-santa-cruz/.

Wilder, Craig Steven. 2013. *Ebony and Ivy: Race, Slavery, and the Troubled History of America's Universities*. New York: Bloomsbury.
Wolfe, Patrick. 2006. "Settler Colonialism and the Elimination of the Native." *Journal of Genocide Research* 8 (4): 387–409.

P

Police

Grace Watkins and Yalile Suriel

Campus police are a fixture on college grounds in the United States. Squad cars with large university insignia decals patrol the streets on and near campus. Blue Light emergency call boxes dot the landscape, providing a direct line to emergency dispatch. Police headquarters with holding cells and interrogation rooms can be found among the campus classrooms, libraries, and dormitories. These features have become so ubiquitous as to be often overlooked. This effect is exacerbated by the common misconception that campus police are mere "rent-a-cops" or security guards. Rather, most campus police are now full-service departments with broad powers and jurisdiction. They are an integral part of the American university's disciplinary, risk management, and gentrification efforts.

According to the Bureau of Justice Statistics, "about two-thirds of the more than 900 U.S. 4-year colleges and universities with 2,500 or more students use sworn police officers to provide law enforcement services on campus" (Reaves 2015). These police officers are housed under various names, such as University Police Department or Department of Public Safety. As of 2011, among four-year institutions, an estimated 9 in 10 public colleges and 4 in 10 private colleges have had sworn police officers. They exist at predominantly white institutions (PWIs), HBCUs, religiously affiliated universities, and community colleges. The University of Pennsylvania (Heinzerling 2017) and the University of Chicago (Thompson 2019) maintain the largest private police forces in their states, with an estimated 120 and 100 officers, respectively. Campus police budgets often reach multimillions of dollars annually and have continued to grow as funding for academic departments and student support programs have been cut. Most sworn campus police officers are authorized to use sidearms (94%), chemical or pepper spray (94%), and batons (93%). In addition, over 100 departments are equipped with military-grade equipment, including assault rifles, grenade launchers, and even armored vehicles (Reclaim UC 2020).

In many cases, sworn campus police officers can patrol beyond campus boundaries. Seven in ten campus law enforcement agencies have memorandums of understanding or other formal written agreements with outside law enforcement agencies. As such, campus police jurisdiction can extend anywhere from a few miles off campus to an entire state (Baptiste 2015). These MOUs place thousands of people completely unaffiliated with the university under the jurisdiction of campus police. For example, at the University of Chicago, the campus police jurisdiction covers an area that includes the residences of 50,000 nonstudents living in nearby Hyde Park (Gold 2014). This broad jurisdictional authority is further complicated by the fact that campus police forces operate with little external oversight, as campus police are often not subject to public records laws. As a result, the powers and activities of campus officers are not fully legible to the surrounding communities that fall under their jurisdiction. This secrecy works in the favor of campus police.

The nature of campus policing has evolved since its invention almost 130 years ago (Bordner and Petersen 1983; Gelber 1972; Sloan 1992, 2023). In 1895, Yale University hired the first two campus officers to patrol the college grounds (Anbinder 2023). It was not until the postwar period, however, that campus policing became more widespread. Many institutions of higher education hired campus guards to keep up with the boom in student enrollment that resulted from the GI Bill helping veterans attend college. In the 1940s and 1950s, campus officers largely did not have formal police powers. Rather, they were housed in maintenance and groundskeeping departments and more closely resembled night watchmen. Officers carried out a range of custodial duties and the enforcement of student conduct codes, in addition to monitoring the campus grounds for signs of theft or property damage.

In the 1960s higher education was forever changed by the student protest movement. College students across the country organized large-scale protests against the Vietnam War, segregation, and several other social causes. Students grasped the potential for campuses to serve as bases for activism to transform society. Furthermore, as many schools became increasingly diverse, students also turned their attention to challenging university complicity in the reproduction of inequality (Angulo and Graham 2011; Bernstein 2012; Cain and Dier 2020; Huff 2010; Schrum 2012).

The louder the protests, the more severe the response of college administrators, the boards of trustees they reported to, and the various bodies of law enforcement that were called in to quash student demonstrations. These encounters continued to escalate until several fatal shootings in 1970 increased legislative and public pressure on university leaders to get their campuses under control. On May 4, 1970, the Ohio National Guard opened fire on antiwar protestors at Kent State University, killing four students and wounding nine others (Broadhurst 2010; Grace 2016; Means 2016; Simpson and Wilson 2016). Days later, city and state police officers opened fire on a women's dormitory at the historically Black Jackson State College during a protest, leaving two students dead and twelve others injured (Bristow 2020; Gasman and Tudico 2008; Spofford 1988). In the aftermath of this violence, President Richard Nixon established the President's Commission on Campus Unrest, headed by former Pennsylvania Governor William Scranton (Ferguson 2017). The Scranton Commission pushed institutions of higher learning to develop internal mechanisms to "improve [their] capability for responding effectively to disorder" and "strengthen [their] disciplinary process" (President's Commission on Campus Unrest 1970, 12). More importantly, schools were tasked with ensuring that "the once good, American institution of universities" would cease to be "combat zones" (12).

Administrators across the country began to consider the expansion of campus police as a way to reduce student protest or, at the very least, keep these protests out of national headlines. They envisioned police departments that would reside exclusively inside institutions of higher education and work alongside administrators to keep scandals in house. In other words, administrators were motivated not only by finding an alternative to the violence associated with municipal policing, but also by risk and reputational management. In the face of widespread student rebellions and pressure from lawmakers to keep students in line, colleges and universities entered the 1970s with a decision to make. Would they continue to operate under the previous model, in which universities had to rely on outside law enforcement to quell unrest? Or would institutions of higher education develop their own mechanism for student control?

The majority of schools chose the latter. The student protest movement sparked a transformation in campus policing. Virtually overnight, campus security units were transformed into large police departments with official power, weapons, and equipment. Many campus police forces doubled or even tripled in budget and manpower within a year of the Kent and Jackson State shootings. Campus police were moved from maintenance and grounds-keeping departments to report directly to high-ranking college administrators. The expansion of campus police was met, however, with significant opposition from many students and faculty. Some faculty members were concerned that campus police presented a threat to their academic freedom. Many students resented the intrusion into university space. Additionally, for the new wave of Black, Latinx, and Indigenous students, navigating a new police force added yet another layer to the mounting pressures of integration (Baldwin 2021; Ferguson 2017; Suriel 2021). Despite this pushback, campus police continued to grow.

Following the student protest movement, several subsequent events have catalyzed the professionalization of campus police into the departments they are today. The "tough on crime" policies and "crime wave" rhetoric of the 1980s and 1990s were influential in expanding campus departments. One particularly important development was the 1986 murder of 19-year-old Lehigh University student Jeanne Clery, which inspired the passage of the Jeanne Clery Disclosure of Campus Security Policy and Campus Crime Statistics Act in 1990. The Clery Act requires higher education institutions to disclose campus crime in a timely manner, as well as record and annually release reports of on-campus arrests (Sloan, Fisher, and Cullen 1997). The Clery Act provided campus police with an opportunity to expand their forces to help their institutions comply with federal law. In fact, campus police forces hired an average of two new officers to manage their new responsibilities under the act. Universities advertise their campus police forces as an integral part of their sexual assault prevention and crime reduction strategies to protect (especially) women students. Ample reports suggest, however, that campus police regularly ignore student reports of gender-based violence or botch their investigations, in addition to accounts of sexual misconduct from officers themselves (Watkins 2020).

The continued growth of campus police in the 1980s and 1990s can be seen as part of the broader participation of universities in the war on crime. Higher education has funded and fostered collaborations with numerous law enforcement and for-profit prison companies, as can be seen with Vanderbilt University Law School's partnership with CoreCivic. In addition, police science departments produce literature that promotes the expansion of the prison-industrial complex. Universities have also spent hundreds of thousands of dollars purchasing products made with prison labor (Chase and Suriel 2020).

Two more recent events—9/11 and the 2007 Virginia Tech mass shooting—went beyond previous efforts to militarize campus police departments. After 9/11, colleges and universities gained access to surplus military equipment through the US Department of Defense 1033 Program (Barrett 2020). The attack at Virginia Tech and the looming threat of future school shootings led to the further acquisition of military-grade weapons, increased officer manpower, and surveillance of the university community.

The presence of campus police forces affects university affiliates and non-affiliates alike. In particular, students of color, university service employees, and local residents frequently experience racist profiling and stops by campus police when walking across college grounds. In doing so, campus police create a racialized border around the university, treating students of color, staff, and residents from nearby neighborhoods as possible suspects rather than valued community members. The presence of campus police greatly affects how students of color experience college life, shaping and reinforcing conceptions of who "looks like" a student. Moreover, campus officers across the country have shot and killed Black people in recent years, especially students and local residents experiencing acute mental distress.[1]

The off-campus jurisdiction of campus police has served as a tool for gentrification as part of larger "urban renewal" projects. Many universities have bought land and buildings near campus and then increased their campus police patrols of these new acquisitions, pushing out working-class Black and brown residents in the process (Baldwin 2021; Cole 2021; Williams 2021).

Yet another way that campus police shape university life is through their surveillance and often violent suppression of student activism. Most recently, in spring 2024, students across the country were arrested by campus police for their involvement in protests in support of the Palestinian people. This is simply the most recent iteration of how campus police have histori-

1. In 2018, a campus police officer at the University of Chicago, Nicolas Twardak, shot and wounded a student named Charles Thomas, who was suffering from a mental health crisis; see Kartik-Narayan (2018). In 2015, a campus police officer at the University of Cincinnati, Ray Tensing, shot and killed Samuel Dubose, a 43-year-old Black man, after he was pulled over for a missing license plate off campus grounds; see Weingartner (2016).

cally responded to student activism, often with other local law enforcement. Students of color, queer and trans students, and leftist student organizers have been subjected to harsh crackdowns by campus police. Campus officers have been particularly involved in quashing student and staff labor union actions, such as the 2020 University of California COLA (cost of living adjustment) wildcat strikes (Gurley 2020; Maira and Sze 2012; Rodríguez 2012). During these encounters, campus police use the professionalization, legitimacy, and expanded jurisdictions they acquired in the latter half of the twentieth century to accomplish the objectives of the 1960s and 1970s—to suppress or at the very least to attempt to keep student protest out of national headlines.

At first glance, campus policing seems to be at odds with the educational mission of colleges and universities. The unique powers and abuses of campus police are obfuscated by higher education's reputation and status as protectors of the public good. In light of the longer trajectory of higher education, however, this contradiction seems deeply intertwined with the very structure of these institutions. Campus police is one of the most significant manifestations of the exclusionary and neoliberal features of contemporary higher education. Moreover, calls for transparency and accountability have often been met with resistance by campus police chiefs and university administrators (Newman 2015; O'Donoghue 2021; Parton 2019). At the heart of the matter is the fact that institutions of higher learning possess some of the largest private police forces in the world. Their existence serves to legitimize police as a provider of safety, while countless reports of violence, harassment, and surveillance by campus officers stand in stark contrast to this vision.

References

Anbinder, Jacob. 2023. "Locking the Gates: Yale University and the Police Power in the Post-Industrial City, 1959–1977." In *Cops on Campus: Rethinking Safety and Confronting Police Violence*, edited by Yalile Suriel, Grace Watkins, Jude Paul Matias Dizon, and John Joseph Sloan III, 55–76. Seattle: University of Washington Press.

Angulo, A. J., and Leland Graham. 2011. "Winthrop College in the Sixties: Campus Protests, Southern Style." *Historical Studies in Education* 23 (2): 113–28.

Baldwin, Davarian L. 2021. *In the Shadow of the Ivory Tower: How Universities Are Plundering Our Cities*. New York: Bold Type.

Baptiste, Nathalie. 2015. "Campus Cops: Authority without Accountability." *American Prospect*, November 2. https://prospect.org/api/content/091dccd9-e138-5287-9bc7-a0bbfebf869e/.

Barrett, Brian. 2020. "The Pentagon's Hand-Me-Downs Helped Militarize Police: Here's How." *Wired*, June 2. https://www.wired.com/story/pentagon-hand-me-downs-militarize-police-1033-program/.

Bernstein, Michael A. 2012. "'The Uses of the University': After Fifty Years: Introduction." *Social Science History* 36 (4): 473–79.

Bordner, Diane C., and David M. Petersen. 1983. *Campus Policing: The Nature of University Police Work*. Lanham, MD: University Press of America.

Bristow, Nancy K. 2020. *Steeped in the Blood of Racism: Black Power, Law and Order, and the 1970 Shootings at Jackson State College*. New York: Oxford University Press.

Broadhurst, Christopher J. 2010. "'We Didn't Fire a Shot, We Didn't Burn a Building': The Student Reaction at North Carolina State University to the Kent State Shootings, May 1970." *North Carolina Historical Review* 87 (3): 283–309.

Cain, Timothy Reese, and Rachael Dier. 2020. "Protests and Pushback: Women's Rights, Student Activism, and Institutional Response in the Deep South." *History of Education Quarterly* 60 (4): 546–80.

Chase, Robert T., and Yalile Suriel. 2020. "Black Lives Matter on Campus—Universities Must Rethink Reliance on Campus Policing and Prison Labor." *Black Perspectives* (blog), June 15. https://www.aaihs.org/black-lives-matter-on-campus-universities-must-rethink-reliance-on-campus-policing-and-prison-labor/.

Cole, Eddie. 2021. "The Racist Roots of Campus Policing." *Washington Post*, June 2. https://www.washingtonpost.com/outlook/2021/06/02/racist-roots-campus-policing/.

Ferguson, Roderick A. 2017. *We Demand: The University and Student Protests*. Oakland: University of California Press.

Gasman, Marybeth, and Christopher L. Tudico, eds. 2008. *Historically Black Colleges and Universities: Triumphs, Troubles, and Taboos*. New York: Palgrave Macmillan.

Gelber, Seymour. 1972. *The Role of Campus Security in the College Setting*. Washington, DC: US Government Printing Office.

Gold, Hannah K. 2014. "Why Does a Campus Police Department Have Jurisdiction over 65,000 Chicago Residents?" *Vice* (blog). November 12. https://www.vice.com/en/article/4w7p8b/why-does-a-campus-police-department-have-jurisdiction-over-65000-chicago-residents-1112.

Grace, Thomas M. 2016. *Kent State: Death and Dissent in the Long Sixties*. Amherst: University of Massachusetts Press.

Gurley, Lauren Kaori. 2020. "California Police Used Military Surveillance Tech at Grad Student Strike." *Vice*, May 15. https://www.vice.com/en/article/7kppna/california-police-used-military-surveillance-tech-at-grad-student-strike.

Heinzerling, Kelly. 2017. "With 120 Officers, Penn Has the Largest Private Police Force in Pennsylvania." *Daily Pennsylvanian*, October 8. https://www.thedp.com/article/2017/10/with-120-officers-penn-has-the-largest-private-police-force-in-pennsylvania.

Huff, Christopher A. 2010. "Radicals between the Hedges: The Origins of the New Left at the University of Georgia and the 1968 Sit-In." *Georgia Historical Quarterly* 94 (2): 179–209.

Kartik-Narayan, Ashvini. 2018. "The Fight over Chicago's Largest Private Police Force." *South Side Weekly*, July 16. https://southsideweekly.com/the-fight-over-chicagos-largest-private-police-force-university-of-chicago-ucpd/.

Maira, Sunaina, and Julie Sze. 2012. "Dispatches from Pepper Spray University: Privatization, Repression, and Revolts." *American Quarterly* 64 (2): 315–30.

Means, Howard. 2016. *67 Shots: Kent State and the End of American Innocence*. Boston: Da Capo.

Newman, Jonah. 2015. "Private Colleges Keep Police Policies and Procedures under Wraps." *Chicago Reporter*, August 25. http://www.chicagoreporter.com/private-colleges-keep-campus-police-policies-and-procedures-under-wraps/.

O'Donoghue, Julie. 2021. "21 Ways LSU Hid or Suppressed Information about Sexual Misconduct." *Louisiana Illuminator* (blog), March 10. https://lailluminator.com/2021/03/10/21-times-lsu-hid-or-suppressed-information-about-sexual-misconduct/.

Parton, Jon. 2019. "BYU Files Suit in Fight over University Police Public Records." *Courthouse News Service*, October 23. https://www.courthousenews.com/byu-files-suit-in-fight-over-university-police-public-records/.

President's Commission on Campus Unrest. 1970. *The Report of the President's Commission on Campus Unrest*. Washington, DC: US Government Printing Office.

Reaves, Brian A. 2015. *Campus Law Enforcement, 2011–12*. BJS Special Reports. Office of Justice Programs, Bureau of Justice Statistics. https://www.ojp.gov/library/publications/campus-law-enforcement-2011-12.

Reclaim UC. 2020. "How Much Money Does the University of California Spend on Its Police Departments?" *Reclaim UC* (blog), June 22. https://reclaimuc.blogspot.com/2020/06/how-much-money-does-university-of.html.

Rodríguez, Dylan. 2012. "Beyond 'Police Brutality': Racist State Violence and the University of California." *American Quarterly* 64 (2): 301–13.

Schrum, Ethan. 2012. "To 'Administer the Present': Clark Kerr and the Purpose of the Postwar American Research University." *Social Science History* 36 (4): 499–523.

Simpson, Craig S., and Gregory S. Wilson. 2016. *Above the Shots: An Oral History of the Kent State Shootings*. Kent, OH: Kent State University Press.

Sloan, John J., III. 1992. "The Modern Campus Police: An Analysis of Their Evolution, Structure, and Function." *American Journal of Police* 11:85.

Sloan, John J., III. 2023. "The End of In Loco Parentis and Institutionalization of Campus Policing." In *Cops on Campus: Rethinking Safety and Confronting Police Violence*, edited by Yalile Suriel, Grace Watkins, Jude Paul Matias Dizon, and John Joseph Sloan III, 1–16. Seattle: University of Washington Press.

Sloan, John J., Bonnie S. Fisher, and Francis T. Cullen. 1997. "Assessing the Student Right-to-Know and Campus Security Act of 1990: An Analysis of the Victim Reporting Practices of College and University Students." *Crime and Delinquency* 43 (2): 148–68. https://doi.org/10.1177/0011128797043002002.

Spofford, Tim. 1988. *Lynch Street: The May 1970 Slayings at Jackson State College*. Kent, OH: Kent State University Press.

Suriel, Yalile. 2021. "Campus Eyes: University Surveillance and the Policing of Black and Latinx Student Activism in the Age of Mass Incarceration, 1960–1990." PhD diss., Stony Brook University.

Thompson, Meghan. 2019. "University of Chicago Police History May Offer Lessons for Hopkins, Baltimore." *WTOP News* (Chevy Chase, MD), February 21. https://wtop.com/baltimore/2019/02/university-of-chicago-police-history-may-offer-lessons-for-hopkins-baltimore/.

Watkins, Grace. 2020. "The Crimes of the Campus Police." *Chronicle of Higher Education*, October 20, sec. The Review. https://www.chronicle.com/article/the-crimes-of-campus-police.

Weingartner, Tana. 2016. "Campus Cop on Trial for Shooting Death during Routine Traffic Stop." *NPR*, October 25, 2016, sec. Law. https://www.npr.org/2016/10/25/499224917/campus-cop-on-trial-for-shooting-death-during-routine-traffic-stop.
Williams, Teona. 2021. "For 'Peace, Quiet, and Respect': Race, Policing, and Land Grabbing on Chicago's South Side." *Antipode* 53 (2): 497–523. https://doi.org/10.1111/anti.12692.

Ranking

Jelena Brankovic and Stefan Wilbers

The term *ranking* (or, more often, *rankings*) is usually understood as a hierarchy of higher education institutions, which is expected to indicate differences in their quality as educational and scientific organizations. These rankings first emerged around the turn of the twentieth century and were initially produced by scientists and academic administrators, yet they rarely reached beyond academic circles. Today's college and university rankings, in contrast, are typically produced by media and data analytics companies, such as *U.S. News and World Report*, Quacquarelli Symonds (QS), and *Times Higher Education* (*THE*), and are a much more complex, far-reaching, and consequential enterprise. Their influence on administrators, faculty, students, policymakers, and the higher education sector as a whole—all over the world—has been extensively documented, studied, debated, and puzzled over (Brankovic, Hamann, and Ringel 2023).

But how have some seemingly simple lists come to be so important? Scholars writing about their history typically recognize two events as turning points. The first one is linked to the first college rankings published by *U.S. News*, back in 1983. Their success was such that, by the end of that decade, *U.S. News* rankings would become an annual publication, which they have remained ever since. The second turning point came in 2003, with the publication of the Academic Ranking of World Universities by Shanghai Jiao Tong University in China, commonly known as the Shanghai Ranking, followed by an ever-growing number of other annually published national and international rankings. Yet, seeing rankings and their history by focusing on a handful of examples, as successful as they are considered to be, obscures a story that is not only more interesting but also helpful in understanding the mechanisms behind the grip these lists have on higher education today. It is this story that we are interested in here.

Rankings and Status Competition in Higher Education: A History

We see rankings as a social operation that comprises four suboperations: comparison of performances, quantification, zero-sum visualization, and repeated publication (Werron and Ringel 2017). Contemporary college and university rankings incorporate all of them, and in so doing, they transform relatively stable status orders into *dynamic competitive fields* (Brankovic, Ringel, and Werron 2018). This ability to produce the effect of competition sets rankings apart from other evaluation methods, such as accreditation, ratings, or benchmarks. Of course, for rankings to trigger competitive behavior in higher education institutions, they must be—to some degree at least—considered by those institutions.

If university rankings and status competition are virtually inseparable today, this was hardly the case when the first rankings were being produced more than a century ago. The early attempts to rank higher education institutions in the United States are today associated with the work of James McKeen Cattell (1860–1944)—psychologist, editor of the journal *Science*, and a prominent figure in the American Association for the Advancement of Science (Godin 2007; Hammarfelt, de Rijcke, and Wouters 2017). Having been keenly interested in the advancement of science and the scientific profession, Cattell worked extensively on developing measures of "scientific merit" of individual scientists, which led him to produce rankings of institutions based on their share of "the top thousand scientific men" (Godin 2007, 699, 709).

Although Cattell (1910) had foreseen a potential in his rankings to serve practical purposes, including those related to informing student choice, there is no evidence that his rankings lived up to this ambition. The fact that Cattell's rankings were not widely circulated, however, does not mean that there was no interest in comparing and debating the quality of institutions in academic and administrative circles during his time. Neither does it mean that status-based differences between institutions had not been entertained. Or that prospective students did not care about college prestige and quality. Finally, it does not mean that the status of a college or a university was seen as permanently fixed and unchanging. All of these were present in some form, or to some degree, yet it would take decades before these would become seen as directly related to rankings.

Although the United States was certainly not the only country in which discussion on status distinctions, standards, and measurements of quality in higher education had been taking place by the 1980s, it is the first country in which university rankings had become regularly published and their presence in higher education stabilized. The US history is thus both a special case and an instructive story for understanding the complex interplay between rankings and status competition in higher education more generally.

Status Production through Classification and Comparison

One of the important debates in US higher education at the turn of the twentieth century revolved around defining "the standard American university" (Geiger 2005, 56). Standardization had been largely pursued in reference to ideal models and actively promoted by influential actors, such as the Carnegie Foundation for the Advancement of Teaching (CFAT), the Association of American Universities (AAU), and other professional organizations (Thelin 2011). Notable works contributing to this debate, which explicitly compared American universities, were *Great American Universities* by journalist Edwin Slosson (1910); Abraham Flexner's (1910) report on medical schools, commissioned by CFAT; and the classification of universities and colleges produced by Kendric Charles Babcock of the Bureau of Education (1911), at the request of the AAU. These works are revealing of the kinds of comparisons that central actors in American higher education at the time sought or considered meaningful in some way (Wilbers, Ringel, and Werron 2021).

As elsewhere, qualitative distinctions between colleges and universities, together with differences in prestige or wealth, had been an enduring feature of American higher education. These distinctions, however, had not been an object of systematic inquiry or nationwide public discussion until the early twentieth century. The works of Babcock, Flexner, and Slosson were a step in this direction, although they were more for orientation purposes than for making precise distinctions (Wilbers and Brankovic 2023). Even in Babcock's report, in which universities and colleges were grouped into discrete classes I–IV, the criteria used were qualitative and subject to different interpretations. But the classes were unambiguous in one important sense: the institutions Babcock put in Class I were seen as having the highest standards, and those in Class IV, the lowest. When some deans and college presidents learned about the study, they "were enraged by their school's classification," which led to the study never being officially published (Webster 1984, 506).

But classifications would not disappear with the interest in ranking institutions increasing. When Raymond Hughes ranked graduate departments in 1925, he included only those he thought were "doing graduate work of some distinction" (Hughes 1925, 3). *U.S. News* would in turn rely on the Carnegie Classification regarding which institutions to include in its rankings (Solorzano and Quick 1983). More recent descriptors, such as "Top 100" and "world-class" universities, further attest to the historical coevolution of classifications and rankings in the production of university status distinctions, which is hardly exclusive to the United States (Brankovic 2018; Morphew 2002). This speaks to the enduring interplay between classification, comparison, and status dynamics in higher education—of which rankings are a more recent expression.

Quantifying Status Distinctions

An important characteristic of the early twentieth-century comparisons was their focus on identifying qualitative distinctions between institutions of higher education. Vivid, dense descriptions and narrative accounts were given priority, while numbers had secondary importance. Slosson, for example, would even caution the reader not to put too much weight on numbers: "In presenting these diagrams and statistics I do not wish to be understood as giving them an exaggerated importance. The really important things are incommensurable and uncountable" (1910, 474). Another important feature of these studies, which complemented their qualitative character, was that they were based primarily on the personal insight of an individual of some authority, who would as part of the study personally visit all the institutions, conduct interviews, take notes, and judge the quality based on those observations.

The following decades would be marked by a gradual departure from the narrative style and personal insight, running parallel to a greater interest in chronicling higher education in more quantitative terms and using standardized data collection methods, such as surveys. Directory-style periodicals, such as *School and Society*, the *Educational Record*, and the *College Blue Book*, soon became the sites where data and key facts on American higher education were curated (Kunkel 1924; Kunkel and Prentice 1939). The rankings (and ratings) produced before the 1960s that did gain some attention (especially Hughes 1925, 1934; Keniston 1959), however, were based not on the available institutional data, but on the so-called reputation survey—a simple opinion survey distributed to the faculty and members of college and university administrations. Reputation survey was the method of choice also in the rankings produced by Allan M. Cartter for the American Council on Education (ACE) in 1966, although with one important caveat: seeing the limitations of such "subjective" data, Cartter analyzed how they correlated with "'objective' measures of quality" available at the time, such as spending per student or library resources (1966, 4).[1] During the 1970s, debating quantitative methods of comparing and ranking higher education institutions would become increasingly common among social scientists—an interest that continues (Wilbers and Brankovic 2023).

This "scientific turn" would, nonetheless, not render the "subjective" opinions of professional peers obsolete in future rankings. In fact, reputation surveys would remain the principal method behind many rankings, including later international ones, all the way to the present. In a way, its persistence attests to the enduring importance of peer judgment when evaluating higher education. Notably, it is more commonly a method of choice for commercial organizations, such as *U.S. News*, QS, and *THE*, which use it alongside "objective" data, such as citations, faculty-student ratios, and graduation rates, to create composite scores. Interestingly, even commercial rankings have become more "scientized" over time, in the sense that their publication has been accompanied by increasingly more elaborate descriptions of methodologies, vetted by scientific advisory boards of some sort, and engaged in efforts to be—or at least appear to be—transparent and open for a genuinely scientific dialogue about the quantification practices behind rankings.

Scarcifying Status through Zero-Sum Tabulation

Comparison and quantification alone, even when understood as status related, do not necessarily lead to status competition among a group of colleges and universities. For status competition to be possible, the status of each institution in a hierarchy must be presented as relative to all others. This is where the zero-sum table comes in (Werron and Ringel 2017). In

1. For a more detailed account of the 1966 and 1970 ACE rankings, see Wilbers and Brankovic (2023).

plain terms, in a zero-sum table, universities or colleges are listed above each other, whereby the one with the highest score would be listed at the top, followed by the second highest, and so on. The positions in the status order are thus rendered *scarce*.

Although the zero-sum table we see in today's major rankings does not seem very different from those used by Cattell, Hughes, and Cartter, one element sets them apart: today's rankings are typically *open ended*. This allows for those not included in the ranking, and therefore not considered sufficiently "excellent," to become so in the future, provided they improve their *performance* (Wilbers and Brankovic 2023). In the early 1960s, improving performance, or "climbing," as the program officer at the Ford Foundation put it, meant "getting into the big league of graduate, and especially doctoral, study" (Berelson 1960, 135). It is thus not surprising that the ACE rankings from that period included only graduate departments. The tight coupling of the notion of excellence with university research is today visible in most so-called global rankings. Today, for many universities around the world, "climbing into the big league" means being included in the "Top 500" of a major global ranking. The open-ended table is especially critical here, as it makes these rankings potentially consequential also for the universities not ranked at all (Brankovic, Ringel, and Werron 2018).

With the popular press's growing interest in rankings, visual aspects would become even more pronounced. Today, rankings are visually adapted in myriad ways by the media producing or reporting on them, usually by spotlighting the "top performers" or those of most interest to their readers (Barats 2020). Finally, technological development, particularly the internet, would expand the horizon of possibilities for visually presenting comparisons based on quantification, which now may include colored maps, interactive charts, images, and even ways for individual users to customize rankings to their own preferences (Decuypere and Landri 2021). Quite certainly, pushing the zero-sum table more into the background may mean that the competition effect is being somewhat "softened" in the process. Yet, the pressure on colleges and universities to embrace competition does not come exclusively from the perceived scarcity of status.

Regular Publication and the Production of Dynamic Status Orders

One could argue that universities compete independently of rankings, for example, in the student market. These forms of competition are not *public*, however, in the sense that audiences cannot "see" winners, losers, or simply the game of competition itself, which is why they affect universities in different ways than rankings do. At the same time, the only goods the competitors can directly "win" in a ranking are essentially symbolic, which is what makes rankings "artificial zero-sum games" (Werron 2014, 63). The competition in a ranking can, of course, have consequences for the distribution of material resources: more directly, for example, if state funding is tied to performance in a ranking; or more indirectly, for instance, when a student chooses a university with the help of a ranking. In practice, however, the relationship between performance in a ranking and the distribution of material resources is much less straightforward than illustrated by these examples.

Competition, in the modern sense, is an *ongoing* state: There is never a definitive winner or loser, because another tournament, season, or rankings edition is always coming. In view of this, the only way rankings can produce the competition effect is for them to be published repeatedly and ideally *regularly* (Ringel and Werron 2021). Although the idea that changes in the relative quality of institutions (however one would define it) could be recorded over time had been entertained by Cattell, Hughes, and Keniston, they saw these changes as more gradual, taking years, decades maybe. Keniston's decision to compare his rankings in 1959 to the ones made by Hughes in 1925, or Cartter's decision to compare his results in 1966 to those obtained by Keniston and Hughes, speaks of their understanding of the pace of change. Even though the ACE would produce follow-up rankings of graduate departments five years later (Roose and Andersen 1970), it was not until the 1980s that a ranking would become regularly repeated.

U.S. News and World Report published its first college rankings in 1983, although they would not make their rankings an annual publication until 1989. And when the first global rankings emerged in the early 2000s, they would adopt the annual cycle from the outset. This is, however, not a trivial matter; in fact, the regularity of publication has significant implications for the effect rankings produce on higher education fields. Stabilizing the rankings interval at one year—instead of two (as it was for the first several cycles) or five (as Cartter had thought would be appropriate)—enables a temporal alignment between the ranking cycle and the academic year. For commercial producers, updating rankings each year makes rankings seem more relevant in the eyes of the public, particularly prospective students. Today, for the universities that simultaneously observe or participate in multiple rankings, the calendar is easily packed with new ranking releases, deadlines for submitting data, and informational events organized by rankings producers. It is thus unsurprising that rankings are experienced by many administrators as "engines of anxiety" (Espeland and Sauder 2016), which place administrators, faculty, and policymakers under great and constant pressure, urging them to ultimately *behave as competitors*.[2]

Conclusion

The recent withdrawal of top-ranked American law (and medical) schools from submitting their data to *U.S. News* and subsequent developments has been rather telling of how important rankings are to certain higher education institutions and their administrators (see Brankovic 2022 for elaboration). This effect, however, has hardly been the responsibility of ranking organizations alone. Higher education institutions and their administrators, but also policymakers and other actors in higher education, have contributed to the impact rankings have had on the higher education system, often believing that they have very little choice but to accept rankings as an irremovable facet of modern higher education.[3] Thus, when grappling with the puzzle of how rankings have come to wield so much influence, we must also factor in the ever more complex interrelationships between those who make rankings and other participants in higher education who—directly or indirectly, knowingly or unknowingly—make their effect possible.

In this chapter, we argue that the genesis of rankings in higher education is characterized by a much higher degree of continuity than is often assumed. Quantification of performances, comparison, visualization in the open-ended zero-sum table, and repeated publication morph together into a complex ranking operation, which effectively produces the competition effect on higher education fields. To understand rankings' grip on contemporary higher education, however, it is important to bear in mind that none of these suboperations is recent, nor are they exclusive to rankings. Performances of universities can be compared in other ways, such as by referring to qualitative criteria. Quantification, be it by counting, calculating ratios,

2. The pressure can sometimes lead to adverse behavior, including the manipulation and even fabrication of data submitted to a ranking organization.

3. This belief is well captured in the phrase "rankings are here to stay," which has been repeatedly used as a way of suggesting that rankings have no real alternative (see Brankovic, Ringel, and Werron 2022).

or producing composites, has also been a part of higher education evaluation for a very long time. Tables, listing, and hierarchical ordering of universities by some criteria had also been in circulation for many decades, as had their repeated compilation, data updating, and publication. What makes rankings unique, however, is that all these elements come together in a ranking to produce a particular suggestion of competition, whereby higher education institutions are urged to imagine themselves and each other as competitors—and act accordingly. And this had been long in the making.

References

Babcock, Kendric Charles. 1911. *A Classification of Universities and Colleges with Reference to Bachelor's Degrees*. Washington, DC: Bureau of Education.

Barats, Christine. 2020. "Dissemination of International Rankings: Characteristics of the Media Coverage of the Shanghai Ranking in the French Press." *Palgrave Communications* 6 (1): 1–11.

Berelson, Bernard. 1960. *Graduate Education in the United States*. New York: McGraw-Hill.

Brankovic, Jelena. 2018. "The Status Games They Play: Unpacking the Dynamics of Organisational Status Competition in Higher Education." *Higher Education* 75 (4): 695–709.

Brankovic, Jelena. 2022. "A Rankings Revolution? Hardly." *Chronicle of Higher Education*, December 8, sec. The Review. https://www.chronicle.com/article/a-rankings-revolution-hardly.

Brankovic, Jelena, Julian Hamann, and Leopold Ringel. 2023. "The Institutionalization of Rankings in Higher Education: Continuities, Interdependencies, Engagement." *Higher Education* 86 (4): 719–31.

Brankovic, Jelena, Leopold Ringel, and Tobias Werron. 2018. "How Rankings Produce Competition: The Case of Global University Rankings." *Zeitschrift für Soziologie* 47 (4): 270–88.

Brankovic, Jelena, Leopold Ringel, and Tobias Werron. 2022. "Spreading the Gospel: Legitimating University Rankings as Boundary Work." *Research Evaluation* 31 (4): 463–74.

Cartter, Allan Murray. 1966. *An Assessment of Quality in Graduate Education*. Washington, DC: American Council on Education.

Cattell, J. McKeen. 1910. "A Further Statistical Study of American Men of Science II." *Science* 32 (828): 672–88.

Decuypere, Mathias, and Paolo Landri. 2021. "Governing by Visual Shapes: University Rankings, Digital Education Platforms and Cosmologies of Higher Education." *Critical Studies in Education* 62 (1): 17–33.

Espeland, Wendy Nelson, and Michael Sauder. 2016. *Engines of Anxiety: Academic Rankings, Reputation, and Accountability*. New York: Russell Sage Foundation.

Flexner, Abraham. 1910. *Medical Education in the United States and Canada: A Report to the Carnegie Foundation for the Advancement of Teaching*. New York: Merrymount.

Geiger, Roger L. 2005. "The Ten Generations of American Higher Education." In *American Higher Education in the Twenty-First Century: Social, Political, and Economic Challenges*, edited by Philip G. Altbach, Robert O. Berdahl, and Patricia J. Gumport, 38–70. 2nd ed. Baltimore: Johns Hopkins University Press.

Godin, Benoît. 2007. "From Eugenics to Scientometrics: Galton, Cattell, and Men of Science." *Social Studies of Science* 37 (5): 691–728. https://doi.org/10.1177/0306312706075338.

Hammarfelt, Björn, Sarah de Rijcke, and Paul Wouters. 2017. "From Eminent Men to Excellent Universities: University Rankings as Calculative Devices." *Minerva* 55 (4): 391–411.

Hughes, Raymond Mollyneaux. 1925. *A Study of the Graduate Schools of America*. Oxford, OH: Miami University.

Hughes, Raymond Mollyneaux. 1934. "Report of the Committee on Graduate Instruction." *Educational Record* 15 (2): 192–234.

Keniston, Hayward. 1959. *Graduate Study and Research in the Arts and Sciences at the University of Pennsylvania*. Philadelphia: University of Pennsylvania Press.

Kunkel, B. W. 1924. "The Colleges and Scientific Leadership." *School and Society* 19 (484): 411–22.

Kunkel, B. W., and D. B. Prentice. 1939. "The Colleges and Scientific Leadership." *School and Society* 50 (1297): 600–608.

Morphew, Christopher C. 2002. "'A Rose by Any Other Name': Which Colleges Became Universities." *Review of Higher Education* 25 (2): 207–23.

Ringel, Leopold, and Tobias Werron. 2021. "Serielle Vergleiche: Zum Unterschied, den Wiederholung macht." *KZfSS Kölner Zeitschrift für Soziologie und Sozialpsychologie* 73 (1): 301–31.

Roose, Kenneth D., and Charles J. Andersen. 1970. *A Rating of Graduate Programs*. Washington, DC: American Council on Education.

Slosson, Edwin E. 1910. *Great American Universities*. New York: Macmillan.

Solorzano, Lucia, and Barbara E. Quick. 1983. "Rating the Colleges: Exclusive National Survey." *U.S. News and World Report*, November 28.

Thelin, John R. 2011. *A History of American Higher Education*. Baltimore: Johns Hopkins University Press.

Webster, David S. 1984. "The Bureau of Education's Suppressed Rating of Colleges, 1911–1912." *History of Education Quarterly* 24 (4): 499–511. https://doi.org/10.2307/367733.

Werron, Tobias. 2014. "On Public Forms of Competition." *Cultural Studies ↔ Critical Methodologies* 14 (1): 62–76.

Werron, Tobias, and Leopold Ringel. 2017. "Rankings in a Comparative Perspective: Conceptual Remarks." In *Geschlossene Gesellschaften. Verhandlungen Des 38. Kongresses Der Deutschen Gesellschaft Für Soziologie in Bamberg 2016*, edited by Stephen Lessenich, 1–10. Essen: DGS. http://publikationen.soziologie.de/index.php/kongressband_2016.

Wilbers, Stefan, and Jelena Brankovic. 2023. "The Emergence of University Rankings: A Historical-Sociological Account." *Higher Education* 86 (4): 733–50. https://doi.org/10.1007/s10734-021-00776-7.

Wilbers, Stefan, Leopold Ringel, and Tobias Werron. 2021. "Homöopathen, 'Quacksalber' Und Wissenschaftliche Mediziner: Zu Den Anfängen Der Hochschulrankings in Der Medizinischen Ausbildung Der USA, 1850–1930." In *Organisation und Bewertung*, edited by Frank Meier and Thorsten Peetz, 393–424. Wiesbaden: Springer VS.

R

Revenue

Dan Nemser and Brian Whitener

Since the 1990s and especially in the wake of the 2008 financial crisis, the US university system has been integrated into the reproductive circuits of capitalism in a new way.[1] A generalized crisis of capital overaccumulation—that is, a surplus of capital with little outlet for profitable investment—helped to transform universities into privileged sites for accumulation. Due to market conditions and credit availability, universities were able to increase tuition seemingly without limit, which in turn drove up their credit ratings and made borrowing cheap for them. As a result, banks, hedge funds, and institutional investors began channeling capital into and through universities at locations that operate as sinks, or pools, such as construction, endowments, and student loans. Through these mechanisms, the university came to serve as a key site for capital accumulation and the investment of overaccumulated capital.

The capacity to raise tuition was a major driver of these changes, and tuition has become the most important revenue stream for colleges and universities. At both public and private institutions, tuition has been rising for decades at a much higher rate than inflation. Skyrocketing tuition helps account for student debt in the United States, currently valued at $1.7 trillion, overtaking all other sources of consumer debt besides mortgages (Federal Reserve Bank of St. Louis 2024). Rising tuition has also generated a backlash, not only from students and families, who are increasingly reluctant to pay, but also from politicians, who have implemented policies like tuition freezes or ceilings in response. Additionally, tuition growth during and after the first Trump presidency has contributed to the return of the culture wars, which have their own long histories in white supremacy and patriarchy, by reinforcing the narrative of academia as "elitist" and universities as sites of "woke" indoctrination.

1. This chapter draws from and builds on Whitener and Nemser (2012, 2018).

A conventional narrative about why tuition has increased so much in recent years goes something like this: As state governments have cut funding for higher education, public colleges and universities have raised tuition to make up the difference. This story is often framed in partisan terms, such that Republicans (following a trail blazed by Reagan) are primarily responsible for this transformation. University administrators like this story because it lets them off the hook, blaming politicians for leaving them no choice but to take such action. There is some truth to this story, but it also gets important things wrong. For example, it cannot explain why private universities—which are not subject to the same funding pressures from states—have raised their tuition at similar rates over the same period. Most importantly, however, the conventional narrative gets the history backward. While budget cuts have done "enormous damage to public university finances," explains Chris Newfield (2016, 42), "tuition hikes preceded and were independent of the most serious cuts. Public colleges and universities raised tuition about 50 percent during the 1980s in constant dollars and another 38 percent in the 1990s, when real state funding actually increased slightly." How, then, do we explain rising tuition and its role as the principal revenue stream of the contemporary university?

We argue that a wider analysis that accounts for multiple revenue streams, along with the restrictions they carry, provides a better explanation than the conventional story. Colleges and universities have four main revenue streams: state appropriations, research funding, endowments and gifts, and student tuition and housing. The first three come with significant restrictions regarding their use. Generally speaking, state appropriations are supposed to be used for educational expenses, research funding is largely spent on specific research projects, and endowments and gifts go toward the pet projects of wealthy donors. Only tuition and housing are unrestricted and can be used for anything university administrators want, from higher administrative salaries, new deanships, and elite football coaches to new construction projects and real estate investments. In recent decades, university administrators have sought to maximize their revenues, but they have sought above all to maximize their *unrestricted* revenues—and have even been willing to sacrifice restricted state funding to do so. This is an important step in what Newfield (2016, 42–43) calls the "devolutionary cycle": As administrators at public schools have made tuition increasingly central in their budgets, states have been more willing to cut public funding.

By looking beyond state funding and student tuition, what we call the *four flows model* brings greater clarity to the critical analysis of university finances and the crisis of higher education more generally.[2] It helps us move beyond generalizations like privatization, corporatization, and neoliberalization, which are commonly used to describe the transformation of higher education over the last four decades, but which tend to center declining state funding as the key driver of this process. In this way, the model offers a fuller picture of how university finances have changed over time. Additionally, it lets us account for the specific conditions facing different kinds of institutions, according to the revenue streams on which they depend. For example, community colleges depend primarily on state funding, with a small stream of tuition and little to no research or endowment funds; small liberal arts colleges depend even more heavily on tuition and in some cases endowments, while going without significant research and state funding; and so on. These differences shape how specific institutions may respond to changing circumstances. In the same vein, finally, this model also helps us situate universities as sites of political struggle. It gives us a tool to critically evaluate the strategies administrators may look to, more or less successfully, in order to boost revenue in a context of crisis. It may also help organizers involved in political struggles against administrative restructuring and for alternative educational models to identify effective targets.[3]

What do we see when we look at the four flows? Consider the operating budget of the University of Michigan, which is often treated as a model for public research universities (figure 1). (We are using the university's 2019 financial statements, to avoid normalizing some of the exceptional impacts of the COVID-19 pandemic.)

---

2. Abigail Boggs and Nick Mitchell (2018) have advanced an important critique of what they call the "crisis consensus" in critical university studies. We agree with their critique of progressive or liberal nostalgia for the welfare state university, but we also want to hold on to the idea of crisis in its lineage with the Greek *krisis*, or a moment of decision, and as an operative concept in contemporary Marxism.

3. Consider, for example, the case of campus-based Palestine solidarity protests in 2023–24. Following the lead of the Boycott, Divestment, and Sanctions (BDS) movement, many organizers have centered divestment as a key demand, turning university endowments into an important site of struggle and challenging the managerial insistence on separating profitability from political and ethical considerations. At the same time, the four flows model could help to open a broader conversation about what divestment might entail. For one thing, not every institution has a substantial endowment, but even this sort of institution may still be implicated via other flows, such as research funded by the military-industrial complex and tuition from joint campuses and study-abroad programs.

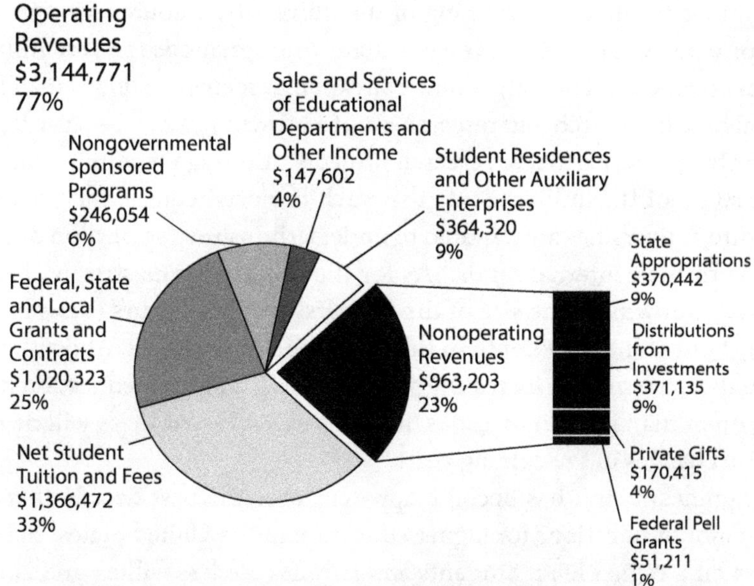

Figure 1. 2019 Revenues for operating activities excluding revenues from the health system and other clinical activities (University of Michigan 2019, 38).

Breaking down the numbers shown in figure 1, we find that net tuition and fees—net as in after taking out financial aid—bring in about $1.4 billion, one-third of the university's operating budget.[4] Research funding from governmental and nongovernmental sources combined contribute another $1.3 billion. The other two main revenue flows generate nowhere near this amount: Distributions from investments, or what the massive endowment

4. As the recent University of California COLA strikes have underscored, real estate plays an increasingly important role in university finances. We understand real estate as registering in two of the four flows. On the one hand, real estate is increasingly a site of investment for university endowments, best illustrated by UC's recent $4.5 billion investment in Blackstone's real estate income trust (Appel 2023; Schmidt, Feldblum, and Cohen 2024). In this circuit, real estate contributes to campus operations through distributions from the endowment. On the other hand, universities also operate as landlords, extracting rent directly from students living on campus. These students pay for room and board with the same loans they use to pay tuition and fees. In this sense, housing generates revenue for the university in the same way as tuition and is similarly unrestricted. That is, revenue would primarily cover operating expenses for dorms, for example, but profits could be used for any purpose. In university budget documents and financial statements, housing forms part of what are often labeled "auxiliary enterprises," a broad category that can also include things like cafeterias, parking, student unions, and athletics. Depending on how a given institution defines this category or breaks it down into its component parts, it can be hard to calculate what portion of the revenue from

contributes to the actual running of the university, accounts for $371 million, or 9 percent of the budget; and state appropriations for $370 million, another 9 percent. The only revenue stream that seems capable of matching tuition here is research, but research is not a growth strategy because it goes primarily toward particular research projects. Although research grants do cover some of the indirect costs that such projects require, such as infrastructure, universities are required to underwrite a growing portion of these costs with their internal funds.[5] As for the other revenue streams, even a massive endowment the size of the University of Michigan's ($12.5 billion in 2019) only funds one-tenth of the institution's operations. And although the political horizon for increasing public funding for higher education looks more open than it has in decades, it seems unlikely that there will be substantive changes in the coming years.[6]

A significant shift has become apparent over the past decade that will have major implications for higher education in the United States: the sector has hit a *tuition limit*. Students and families are less willing and able to pay ever-increasing tuition bills, despite the so-called wage premium that a college degree continues to confer. The tuition limit refers not to an absolute number beyond which tuition cannot be raised but to a trend by which, after growing rapidly over the past few decades, the rate of increase in tuition has begun to decline. As early as 2013, the credit rater Moody's revised its outlook for the higher education sector to negative, noting in particular, "Price sensitivity continues to suppress net tuition revenue growth" (Moody's Investors Service 2013, 3).[7] This forecast was prescient. At public four-year institutions, tuition and fees rose by 37 percent from 1992 to 2002, and again by 65 percent from 2002 to 2012, but declined by 1 percent from 2012 to 2022

"auxiliary enterprises" corresponds to housing. For the University of Michigan, this figure appears in the audited "Consolidated Statement of Revenues, Expenses, and Changes in Net Position" at the end of its financial reports: in 2019, of the $364 million in revenue from "auxiliary enterprises," $120 million, or about one-third, comes from student residences (University of Michigan 2019, 48). For institutions that do not record this specific figure, a rough estimation could come from multiplying the number of campus beds by the price of room and board.

5. In fact, according to Newfield (2016, 96), sponsored research "lose[s] an average of twenty cents on the dollar." On research funding and indirect costs more generally, see Newfield (2016, 85–115).

6. We are thinking here of the work of Scholars for a New Deal for Higher Education and legislative efforts like the College for All bill (Gavigan and Mittelstadt 2021).

7. The report adds, "All non-tuition revenue sources are also strained" (Moody's Investors Service 2013, 7).

(Ma and Pender 2022, 13). This trend is also visible in enrollment numbers, which have declined consistently since 2011 (Ma and Pender 2022, 25); in the politicization of tuition hikes, which has led many state governments to freeze or cap tuition since the mid-2010s (Kelchen and Pingel 2018; Newfield 2016, 157); and in eye-catching headlines about the growing number of schools slashing tuition to compete for price-averse students (Hartocollis 2022).

By bringing an end to a period of seemingly limitless tuition growth, the tuition limit marks the beginning of a phase of sustained crisis and recomposition. It will sharpen the ongoing crisis of higher education and intensify competition throughout the sector. Colleges and universities will attempt to turn to other sources of revenue to replace what has until recently promised unending growth in unrestricted dollars. The problem is that no other revenue stream runs as deep or offers as much flexibility as tuition did during the "golden age" of tuition hikes. We want to sketch out six possible trends that may unfold in response in the coming years.

First, the tuition limit will increasingly constrain the capacity of colleges and universities to continue to grow revenues straightforwardly through tuition hikes. Most administrators will be able to grow tuition revenue only to the extent that they can increase or restructure their enrollments. For example, they may try to max out the capacity of their campuses by increasing enrollment without expanding campus infrastructure. If they can no longer expect to squeeze more tuition out of every student, maybe they can squeeze more students into every classroom or dorm room. This strategy, however, will put increasing pressure on campus infrastructures and threaten educational quality. In the UC system, it has contributed to a profound housing crisis at campuses like Santa Cruz, where the COLA demand was first advanced during a militant wildcat strike in 2019 (Gilich and Boardman 2022; Hicks and Gross 2022; Nemser and Whitener 2020). Alternatively, administrators may double down on the amenities "arms race," using new capital projects like luxury dorms and other facilities to compete for out-of-state students capable of paying higher tuition. They will be limited in pursuing this strategy, however, because competition for such students will intensify and grow more expensive. Moreover, the tuition limit along with rising interest rates will put growing pressure on institutions' credit ratings, making borrowing more and more expensive.

Second, the end of ever-increasing tuition will limit the ability of colleges and universities to access cheap money in order to debt-finance operations and construction.[8] One area where this trend is already apparent is construction, as institutions increasingly turn to public-private partnerships (P3s) to build student housing. In these agreements, the university leases land to a private developer, which finances the construction project and pockets student rent in exchange. In recent years, for example, UC Berkeley, which, like Santa Cruz, is facing a serious housing crisis, has made deals with corporations like American Campus Communities, a publicly traded real estate corporation with 141,000 student beds in its portfolio, to build a new 775-bed dorm, which opened in 2018 (Dinkelspiel 2022). Eastern Michigan University recently approved a similar deal with a developer called Gilbane to demolish several old residence halls and build two new dorms to replace them. Strikingly, and in contrast to the UC Berkeley deal, this arrangement aims not to expand but to shrink student housing—the campus will end up with 1,000 fewer beds than before (Knox 2022). These deals provide relatively small sums of money to campuses in the form of land rent, but their primary contribution is to enable cost cutting and tuition growth. Whereas the UC Berkeley deal aims to increase tuition revenue by expanding housing and consequently enrollment, EMU aims to do so by drawing wealthier students and cutting costs, even as enrollment declines overall.

Third, pushed by growing competition, universities may begin to compete on price, something the industry has resisted as long as student debt has been able to circumvent, for a time and to some extent, the effects of skyrocketing tuition. As noted above, this is already beginning to happen at both private and public institutions (in the latter case for out-of-state students). Price competition is also visible in the area of tuition discounting. The latest Moody's Investors Service (2022, 4) report estimates that between 2010 and 2023, the discount rate will have risen from 32 percent for all colleges to 43 percent for private colleges and 38 percent for public.[9] But competing on price runs the risk of exacerbating rather than solving the revenue problem. What this suggests is that the era of price competition, which is well under way, will be complicated and potentially bloody. Smaller schools and institutions with high debt loads will be forced to cut first, while

8. One possible implication of this trend is that Bob Meister's (2009) important analysis of the UC system's pledging of tuition as collateral for its construction bonds will become less explanatory.

9. Notably, discount rates have grown more slowly at more selective institutions (NACUBO 2023).

larger institutions may try to wait out the price war until enough competitors go under. While it is unclear how these tendencies will play out, one result will certainly be the intensification of already existing racial, gender, age, and economic disparities, since the students served by community colleges and especially for-profit institutions are, as Tressie McMillan Cottom (2017, 59; see also 109) explains, "browner, poorer, older, and more likely to be female."

Fourth, universities will also attempt to look beyond tuition to restructure their revenue streams. These attempts will for the most part be unsuccessful. This was clear in the case of the University of California as early as 2017. During a presentation that year on how to close a $150 million revenue hole, UC Berkeley's chancellor outlined "six revenue streams" that would be emphasized under a new, highly touted plan: "non-degree enrollment (such as UC Berkeley extension or summer sessions), self-supporting degree programs, increased contract and grant activity, increased entrepreneurial activity, monetization of real estate and philanthropy" (Thatte 2017). Marginal tuition growth, more research, more philanthropy, more auxiliaries—the possibilities for growth in these areas are extremely limited, and this plan, like many others that have followed, are the institutional equivalent of squeezing a stone. Moody's (2022, 2) projects that sectorwide operating revenue growth will be limited to 1–3 percent, lagging far behind inflation, due to "muted" growth across every revenue stream. As a result, even more difficult choices or radical restructurings loom for some and have become a reality for others: dramatic cuts in health care and labor, degree program elimination, wholesale recomposition of colleges, certification-ization and ed-techification, and so on. There will also be greater jockeying for position, as institutions seek to outcompete regional and other rivals in the industry for student enrollment, state aid, and research dollars.

Fifth, as a consequence of these processes, the sector will be subject to a wave of school failures, closings, and mergers. After peaking in 2012–13, the number of aid-eligible institutions in the United States—one way of measuring the total number of college and university closures—has declined by 19 percent (NCES 2023). According to one tracking project, over a hundred colleges and universities have closed since 2016 (Higher Ed Dive 2023). This trend seems poised to continue, especially in the wake of three years of a global pandemic. On a political and discursive level, an important part of this process will be a debate over the extent to which these closures are the result of excess capacity, measured either in terms of the number of institutions nationally or compared with the available student body. Both the centrist/liberal press and rightwing think tanks have begun to advance arguments that there are simply "too many colleges," and that there has been a "massive public overinvestment" in higher education (Thompson 2017; Vedder 2016). These arguments have gained ground in sync with the increasingly popular narrative of a looming "demographic cliff" (Whitener and Nemser 2021).

What these kinds of arguments miss is that the crisis of university enrollments was created not by overinvestment but by price increases at many times the rate of inflation and the requirement to take on massive debt loads to access these institutions. It is not difficult to imagine that if college were free, classrooms would be overflowing, as the problem for many students is not a desire to attend but the means. Arguments about the need to reduce the number and size of universities will play a role in naturalizing the coming "new normal" of higher education as an elite or upper-middle-class activity. Furthermore, debates over excess capacity will be particularly important for the way they dovetail with the educational agendas of hardline conservative, far-right, or techno-libertarians to push students into technical, manufacturing, or health care training programs or to "disrupt" or "unbundle" the university by replacing it with professional or technical certificates. The "fact" of excess capacity will have many potential uses.

Sixth, we expect to see new kinds of crisis-based experimentation, potentially remaking the university in ways that today we can barely begin to imagine. The crisis will give a toehold to the most extreme, fringe ideas about how best to "disrupt" higher education—the disastrous 2012 wave of MOOCs and online education could seem tame in comparison to the "solutions" that will be rolled out as more and more parts of the system are called into question (Bady 2013). Whatever form they take, these "disruptions" will most likely find traction in a part of the system fighting for survival and spread outward from there. They will "succeed" as long as the administrators who created this crisis and the unsustainable model of debt-financed education into which it has congealed remain in power and no alternative social force emerges.

To those wishing to resist such transformations, the battle will clearly be an uphill one. Still, there are certain opportunities to be found, for example, in the fact that as profit margins narrow, so too will managers' room for error, maneuver, and cooptation. This means that campus-based struggles by students and workers—whether through recognized unions or voluntary associations—could be able to exercise greater leverage on administrations and perhaps put additional elements of the system into play. Recent unionization and protest activities across the country, including the massive and at times very militant UC strike in 2022 and the Palestine solidarity encampments in 2024, have shown how struggles like these can force an expanded conversation about what a truly autonomous university might look like. As the very idea of the university as a social institution of mass democracy comes under attack, those on the Left will have to name for themselves a future university or infrastructure of education and knowledge production worth fighting for.

References

Appel, Hannah. 2023. "Tenant, Debtor, Worker, Student." *New York Review of Books*, February 8. https://www.nybooks.com/online/2023/02/08/tenant-debtor-worker-student.

Bady, Aaron. 2013. "The MOOC Moment and the End of Reform." *New Inquiry*, May 15. https://thenewinquiry.com/blog/the-mooc-moment-and-the-end-of-reform/.

Boggs, Abigail, and Nick Mitchell. 2018. "Critical University Studies and the Crisis Consensus." *Feminist Studies* 44 (2): 432–63.

Cottom, Tressie McMillan. 2017. *Lower Ed: The Troubling Rise of For-Profit Colleges in the New Economy*. New York: New Press.

Dinkelspiel, Frances. 2022. "Why Hasn't UC Berkeley Built More Student Housing?" *Berkeleyside*, May 8. https://www.berkeleyside.org/2022/05/08/uc-berkeley-student-housing-building.

Federal Reserve Bank of St. Louis. 2024. "Student Loans Owed and Securitized (SLOAS)." FRED Economic Data, July 1. https://fred.stlouisfed.org/series/SLOAS.

Gavigan, Ian, and Jennifer Mittelstadt. 2021. "A New Deal for Eds and Meds." *Dissent* 68 (4): 30–37. https://www.dissentmagazine.org/article/a-new-deal-for-eds-and-meds.

Gilich, Yulia, and Tony Boardman. 2022. "Wildcat Imaginaries: From Abolition University to University Abolition." *Critical Times* 5 (1): 109–120.

Hartocollis, Anemona. 2022. "A Sign that Tuition Is Too High: Some Colleges Are Slashing It in Half." *New York Times*, December 14. https://www.nytimes.com/2022/12/14/us/college-universities-college-tuition-reset.html.

Hicks, Zach, and Rebecca Gross. 2022. "No COLA, No Contract: On the Ground at the UC Strike." *Brooklyn Rail*, December. https://brooklynrail.org/2022/12/field-notes/No-COLA.

Higher Ed Dive Team. 2023. "A Look at Trends in College Consolidation since 2016." *Higher Ed Dive*, December 1. https://www.highereddive.com/news/how-many-colleges-and-universities-have-closed-since-2016/539379/.

Kelchen, Robert, and Sarah Pingel. 2018. "Policy Snapshot: Postsecondary Tuition Capping and Freezing." *Education Commission of the States Legislative Tracking*, November 2018. https://www.ecs.org/wp-content/uploads/Postsecondary-Tuition-Capping-and-Freezing.pdf.

Knox, Liam. 2022. "A Cash-Strapped Public University Turns to the Private Sector." *Inside Higher Ed*, August 1. https://www.insidehighered.com/news/2022/08/02/emu-moves-forward-private-student-housing-partnership.

Ma, Jennifer, and Matea Pender. 2022. *Trends in College Pricing and Student Aid 2022*. New York: College Board. https://research.collegeboard.org/media/pdf/trends-in-college-pricing-student-aid-2022.pdf.

Meister, Bob. 2009. "They Pledged Your Tuition: An Open Letter to UC Students." *Council of UC Faculty Associations (CUCFA) News*, October 11. http://keepcaliforniaspromise.org/wp-content/uploads/2009/10/They_Pledged_Your_Tuition.pdf.

Moody's Investors Service. 2013. "US Higher Education Outlook Negative in 2013." Moody's Investors Service, January 16.

Moody's Investors Service. 2022. "2023 Outlook Negative as Revenue Rebound Stalls and Expenses Surge." Moody's Investors Service, December 8.

NACUBO. 2023. "Tuition Discount Rates at Private Colleges and Universities Top 50 Percent." NACUBO, press release, April 24. https://www.nacubo.org/Press-Releases/2023/Tuition-Discount-Rates-at-Private-Colleges-and-Universities-Top-50-Percent.

NCES (National Center for Education Statistics). n.d. "Number of Postsecondary Institutions in the United States that Award Federal Student Aid, 2002–03 to 2022–23." Integrated Postsecondary Education Data System (IPEDS). Accessed August 17, 2023. https://nces.ed.gov/ipeds/TrendGenerator/app/answer/1/1.

Nemser, Dan, and Brian Whitener. 2020. "From Occupy Everything to COLA for All." *Commune*, March 13. https://communemag.com/from-occupy-everything-to-cola-for-all/.

Newfield, Christopher. 2016. *The Great Mistake: How We Wrecked Public Universities and How We Can Fix Them*. Baltimore: Johns Hopkins University Press.

Schmidt, John, Samuel Feldblum, and Abbie Cohen. 2024. *Selling Sunset: Land and Financialization at the University of California*. UCLA Luskin Center for History and Policy, April. https://luskincenter.history.ucla.edu/2024/05/29/lchp-releases-report-on-land-endowments-and-ethics/.

Thatte, Revati. 2017. "UC Berkeley Has Cut Deficit in Half over 1 Year, Chancellor Announces." *Daily Californian*, November 3. https://www.dailycal.org/2017/11/02/uc-berkeley-cut-deficit-half-fiscal-years-2016-17-chancellor-announces.

Thompson, Derek. 2017. "This Is the Way the College 'Bubble' Ends." *Atlantic*, July 26. https://www.theatlantic.com/business/archive/2017/07/college-bubble-ends/534915/.

University of Michigan. 2019. *2019 Annual Report*. Ann Arbor: University of Michigan. https://2019.annualreport.umich.edu/uploads/fy19-financial-report.pdf.

Vedder, Richard. 2016. "The Death of a University? The Sad Story of Chicago State." *Forbes*, October 6. https://www.forbes.com/sites/ccap/2016/10/06/the-death-of-a-university-the-sad-story-of-chicago-state/.

Whitener, Brian, and Dan Nemser. 2012. "Circulation and the New University." *TOPIA* 28:165–70.

Whitener, Brian, and Dan Nemser. 2018. "The Tuition Limit and the Coming Crisis of Higher Education." *New Inquiry*, March 26. https://thenewinquiry.com/the-tuition-limit-and-the-coming-crisis-of-higher-education.

Whitener, Brian, and Dan Nemser. 2021. "Demographic Realism and the Crisis of Higher Education." *Los Angeles Review of Books*, May 11. https://lareviewofbooks.org/article/demographic-realism-and-the-crisis-of-higher-education/.

R

Risk Management

Mattie Armstrong-Price

In spring 2024, Palestine solidarity organizing shook US university campuses. Almost to a person, campus executives responded by authorizing violent police intervention, revealing how anxious they were to avoid being cast by conservative politicians, media outlets, and donors as insufficiently hostile to student demonstrators. Administrators were acting to ward off reputational damage. While their response to Palestine solidarity organizing was shaped by a singular set of circumstances, their notable preoccupation with reputational damage can be partially explained historically.

Around 2013, the notion of *reputational risk* entered the standard lexicon of university governance. That year, Janice M. Abraham, president of the Association of Governing Boards, published *Risk Management: An Accountability Guide for University and College Boards*. In contrast to earlier guides, Abraham's work is characterized by a persistent attention to questions of reputation. While legal liability and economic exposure receive their due attention, reputational risk functions as a sort of universal equivalent, allowing seemingly unrelated crises, from the drying up of endowments to the injury of students, to appear as commensurate: The fallout from each potentially includes damage to the brand. In this chapter, I explain how administrators and their advisers found in the notion of *reputational risk* an interpretive key with which to grasp the vagaries of university governance. Reputational risk emerged as a keyword of university governance at the precise moment when administrators were confronted with the tuition limit and compelled to compete on a wider geographic scale for potential tuition revenue—revenue that had recently become more challenging to access and yet more vital to university financial solvency. The turn to reputational risk management between 2011 and 2013 was woven together with new forms of policing on and around campuses. The story to follow thus helps explain historically the convergence of administrators' concern with reputational damage and their turn to aggressive techniques of policing, as seen in spring 2024.

The pertinence of reputational risk to emergent conditions of university governance was perhaps first made apparent to the administrative class when, in November 2011, Moody's decided to review for possible downgrade Penn State University's bond rating. In announcing their decision, Moody's (2011) noted that they would be studying the effect of the Jerry Sandusky sexual abuse case, determining "the potential scope of reputational and financial risk arising from these events . . . We will monitor possible emerging risks emanating from potential lawsuits/settlements, weaker student demand, declines in philanthropic support, changes in state relationship and significant management or governance changes." This appears to have been the first time that a ratings agency had decided to review for downgrade a university's bond rating based in part on reputation—that is, this was the first time that reputational damage was taken to directly threaten a university's financial solvency. A January 2012 article in *Business Insurance* featured a risk manager from the University of Denver conceding that, with Moody's review of PSU, "the awareness of reputational risk is certainly heightened" (Tsikoudakis 2012).

In 2016, I conducted a series of interviews with university risk managers. I wanted to know how they thought about reputational risk and how they imagined managing such risk. Reliably, these risk managers gave me reading recommendations. Janice Abraham's 2013 *Risk Management*, for example, was recommended by Gary Langsdale, risk manager at Penn State University. Langsdale insisted to me that Abraham had borrowed from the 2012 Freeh Report in composing her guide. In November 2011, PSU trustees commissioned former FBI director Louis Freeh to conduct an inquiry into the systemic governance failures that had shielded Jerry Sandusky from accountability over the decades when he was doing harm. Two recommendations from the Freeh Report stand out in light of risk and reputation management: first, a recommendation to "require regular Risk Management, Compliance and Internal Audit reports to the Board on assessment of risks . . . as well as on measures in place to mitigate those risks"; and second, a recommendation to "continue to provide all Board members with regular reports of local, national and academic media coverage of the University" (Freeh 2012, 135–36). Reports of media coverage might help board members anticipate "weaker student demand, [and] declines in philanthropic support," areas of concern noted by Moody's.

While bad press was coming into focus at this time as a potential drag on enrollments, the precise relationship between media coverage and matriculations remained for some time a matter of uncertainty to risk managers and to bond rating agents. In our conversation, Gary Langsdale noted that the "black eye" inflicted on the campus by the Sandusky scandal (a disconcerting metaphor given the context) had nevertheless not translated into reduced admissions, among either Pennsylvania residents or nonresidents. In recounting the nonevent of enrollment declines, Langsdale was reiterating the sort of argument he had been compelled to articulate in the winter of 2011–12 during regular conversations with Moody's representatives. Both he and they were involved in the detailed accounting of the financial costs of reputational damage. And while the results of this accounting suggested the relative imperviousness of PSU's enrollment and, to a lesser extent, fundraising efforts to reputation-induced declines, the case of the University of Missouri in the aftermath of the fall 2015 mass strikes against racism offered to risk managers a stark counterexample. In spring 2016, UC Berkeley risk managers shared an article with me that detailed Missouri's precipitous decline in out-of-state enrollments—a decline that the article attributed in part to "the fall protests and the resulting negative news-media coverage . . . For nonresidents, the barrage of media coverage created the image of a campus 'literally falling apart'" (Kelderman 2016). Here we can note an ideological inversion: an inspiring movement that brought together a campus community in opposition to anti-Black racism is recoded, through the imagined perspective of a nonresident student, into a scene of crisis and breakdown.

University risk managers' recent preoccupation with nonresident enrollments, and their concomitant preoccupation with national media coverage affecting their campus brand, can be seen to have certain structural causes—causes that can be traced to the 2008 financial crisis. For public universities in the United States, the 2008 financial crisis struck at least thrice. First, in fall 2008, the meltdown in the financial system brought significant losses for university endowments, pension funds, real estate holdings, and other investments (Brown and Tiu 2013; Wolinsky 2009). Then, in summer 2009, state budget allocations to public universities were cut—a result of recession-induced declines in state revenues—and would continue to fall through at least the 2011–12 academic year (Katsinas et al. 2016; Mitchell, Palacios, and Leachman 2014). The loss of state funds, however, was buffered by federal stimulus spending on academic research and student aid, which began in 2009 (Dinerstein et al. 2014). By 2011, much of this federal stimulus was discontinued, which created a third shock to university finances, especially given that state funding had not yet begun to recover toward prerecession levels.

In periodizing the history of the postcrisis US university, we can supplement this story of the three financial shocks by looking at university administrators' evolving responses to such shocks, as well as the ebbs and flows of university-based protest that at once reacted to and set limits on administrative and state actions. Up through 2011 at least, public university administrators dealt with financial losses and declining state support above all by raising tuition and admitting more out-of-state and international students, who generally pay higher tuition rates than in-state students. Caroline Hoxby, an economist who studies higher education, has argued that university administrators' turn toward tuition revenue in this moment was not wholly reactive to declining state funds but can be better understood as part of a bargain administrators forged with state governments, whereby universities accepted lower state funding in exchange for greater "autonomy" from state mandates around tuition and enrollment. According to this argument, the backstop provided by federal stimulus support for academic research enabled at least some public universities to weather the transition from state funding to tuition revenue (Dinerstein et al. 2014; Parker 2015).

This backstop fell away in 2011, though, a moment when state support for higher education was continuing to decline, creating another episode of crisis and uncertainty in university finance—a crisis period that many public university administrators attempted to resolve by pushing forward with further tuition hikes and other privatizing reforms.[1] Students at several public universities, particularly those in California, had already responded to the initial postcrisis privatizing sequence with militant protest, including a wave of building takeovers and walkouts in fall 2009. Such protest reemerged on a wider scale in fall 2011, as students concerned with tuition hikes, student debt, and police violence staged strikes and encampments at

1. A Moody's study of tuition increases since 2005 indicates that 2011 was the year of most intensive tuition hikes at public universities. Interestingly, tuition hikes at private universities began to slow in 2010, indicating that privates tended to use stimulus funding to limit tuition; see Douglas-Gabriel (2015).

many universities as part of the broader Occupy movement. In California, where Occupy protests on campuses reached a scale not seen since the 1970s, the protests of 2011–12 won a multiyear tuition freeze, linked to an increase in state support that was funded by a progressive tax measure. In other states as well, including states with relatively little student protest, the 2012–13 academic year was defined by a partial return of state funding and a decrease in the rate of tuition hikes, if not an outright freeze.

While 2012–13 was characterized by the slowing of certain privatizing trends and by the relative political stabilization of public universities, the conditions of university finances had still not returned to prerecession levels of solvency, as evidenced by a continuing trend of university bond rating downgrades. Ratings agencies such as Moody's and Standard and Poor (S&P) saw universities as overleveraged and burdened by structural deficits. To explain the dramatic slowing of tuition hikes despite universities' continuing relative insolvency, Dan Nemser and Brian Whitener (2018) have deployed the notion of the "tuition limit," which is a way of marking the political and economic constraints that prevented university administrators from keeping open the tuition spigot. An article by David Miles (2012) in *Trusteeship* magazine argued that, in the wake of the Occupy movement, regular tuition hikes could not be sustained, and that, as far as university finances were concerned, the "storm [had] not passed": "Nearly two and a half years after the formal end of the 'Great Recession,' federal stimulus funds have been exhausted, state budgets have not fully recovered, stock-market losses and low bond yields have reduced endowment returns, and most important, it is becoming ever more difficult for our students to afford tuition increases that have only partially offset declines in other income." As anticipated here by Miles, beginning in 2012–13, tuition hikes slowed dramatically at public universities, and administrators were compelled more actively to compete against each other in attracting nonresident student enrollments, as this was the only means they had to increase overall tuition income. When not doing so by attempting to scrub damaging stories from internet search engine results (as UC Davis Chancellor Linda Katehi infamously attempted to do with the pepper spray cop meme), they did so in part by pursuing public-private partnerships, as well as ground-lease agreements with private developers for the construction and management of new, high-end student housing—relatively affordable methods for attracting wealthier, out-of-state students. The consolidation of a reputation-oriented form of risk management occurred between 2011 and 2013, a period defined by the crisis and partial reconstruction of university financial models, and by a wave of mass campus protest. Reputational risk emerged as a keyword of university governance at the precise moment when structural factors drew administrators to compete on a wider geographic scale for students, whose tuition dollars they hoped would shore up tottering finances.

The notion of reputational risk, and the wider framework of enterprise risk management with which it tended to be associated, came ready-made from private sector managerial discourse. In the early 2000s, S&P had "significantly increased" its focus on reputational risk, and by 2011, *reputation* had become a keyword of corporate financial management. The private sector's increasing attention to reputational risk was a product of managers and ratings agents' recognition that quantitative measures of a firm's financial standing could not explain fluctuations in stock price, return on investment, and other conditions. Some intangible yet socially real quality must also determine a firm's standing. The notion of reputation came to name and give conceptual content to this intangible quality. Perhaps the most fully elaborated account of reputation's financial significance appears in Nir Kossovsky's *Mission: Intangible—Managing Risk and Reputation to Create Enterprise Value* (2010), a work that multiple university risk managers recommended I read.

While at times Kossovsky implies that business reputation is a concept that can be deployed transhistorically, he also seeks to explain how reputation and its management have become uniquely important to contemporary business practice. His argument turns on the increasing centrality of subcontracting and of geographically dispersed supply chains to production and distribution, as "'business-by-network'... creates a lack of visibility, awareness and control, which in turn creates financial and reputation risk" (17). Subcontractors' labor practices, as well as ever-present risks of supply chain disruption, make for greater operational and, more importantly, reputational exposure: "The 835 public companies that announced a supply chain disruption between 1989 and 2000 experienced ROI (Return on Investment) that was 33–40% lower than that of their industry peers" (19). Kossovsky takes such statistics as evidence that supply chain disruption is more consequential in its secondary effects, the damage it does to a firm's reputation over time, than in its primary effects, lost revenues from unrealized sales. In Michael Power's (2004, 32) study of risk management discourse, he identifies the prioritization of "secondary" over "primary" risks as a defining feature of post-2000 forms of corporate—and increasingly also public sector—risk management: "Reputation has turned the concept of materiality upside down; financially immaterial events may have huge potential significance for the organisation."

The delineation of inside and outside is a central aim of corporate risk management practices, particularly those entailed in *supply chain security*—a securitizing project echoed in recent practices of university risk management. Under the framework of supply chain security, inside and outside are delineated through the construction of physical barriers that seal supply chains off from the general population, through the policing of supply chains and the subjection of transit workers to background checks, electronic key access systems, or other security measures. While universities generally aren't in the business of physically sealing themselves off from the world beyond campus—my current workplace notwithstanding—the logic of inside and outside, often articulated in racialized terms, has long organized the policing of campuses and their surrounding neighborhoods, as evidenced by persistent conflicts over gentrification around major urban universities such as Columbia and the University of Chicago; by statistics indicating Black people's disproportionate arrests by campus police officers for trespassing; and by the anxious attention that even the earliest university "enterprise risk management" documents direct toward "nonaffiliates." With the mutation of educational risk and reputation management practices since 2011, however, the boundaries of inside and outside are being remapped at many campuses.

For one, campus police departments are being assigned wider jurisdictions and are increasingly patrolling student residential neighborhoods. With this expansion of police jurisdictions, student residential neighborhoods—and by extension the private lives of students—are being brought more clearly into the view of campus administrators. This making visible of students' private lives is also occurring through seemingly benign efforts to promote student safety, as, for example, in the adoption of policies that provide amnesty from conduct prosecutions to students who contact the police about potential alcohol overdoses. While these policies will hopefully reduce alcohol-related injuries, they also promise to offer administrators a clearer picture of student drinking patterns. Such harm reduction policies are being promoted within the trade publications of university risk managers in language that suggests the need to secure against reputational damage. Here, for example, is an excerpt from an essay published by Andrew Goldblatt and Hans Gude (2015), UC Berkeley's enterprise and traditional risk managers: "The traditional risk manager now heads Berkeley's Compliance and Enterprise Risk Subcommittee on Student Risk. He is working alongside students in the effort to reduce alcohol-related medical transports, injuries, and deaths—a role he would not have imagined for himself three years ago. And when he asks senior management for resources to support the committee's efforts . . . he makes an enterprise risk argument: that to continue attracting the highest-caliber students, the campus needs to address public perceptions that it condones a wanton, potentially lethal social environment." Since the publication of this essay, student members of the subcommittee, including student government representatives and residents of sororities and fraternities, have identified criminal acts in south Berkeley, including muggings, as a "student risk" they would like the subcommittee to address. In this way, efforts to manage the risks associated with students' off-campus lives, including by "enlisting students as risk managers," as this same essay puts it, have the potential to facilitate the more intensive policing of student residential neighborhoods in the name of keeping students safe from "nonaffiliates."

The remapping of inside and outside, and the securitization of the line dividing the two, is also increasingly taking place within the bounds of campuses. At UC Berkeley, for example, the majority of recently constructed buildings, especially those housing valuable equipment or funded through public-private partnerships, require key access and are surveilled more intensively than are long-standing academic buildings. In other words, certain buildings are less public than others, just as certain members of campus have less access or are less likely to be seen as "affiliates" than others. In 2015, students pushing for the redesignation of campus bathrooms as *all genders* encountered these discrepancies when they covered over the gendered bathroom signs with stickers in various buildings. While most of their guerrilla redesignations went off without a hitch, in the recently constructed Li Ka Shing Center for Biomedical Research, two students—one a white trans woman, the other a Black cis man—were immediately confronted by a building manager, who followed them for two blocks off campus while calling the campus police, who in turn stopped a city bus to detain the students. While the police almost immediately recognized the white trans student as an affiliate, they refused to similarly recognize the Black cis student, even after he had given them identifying documents and information. Evidently such protest tactics had an effect, as shortly after the students' detention, Berkeley adopted a policy to redesignate as all genders the campus's single user bathrooms. But in announcing this policy, administrators made clear that campus police officers would be patrolling single user bathrooms more intensively, purportedly to prevent "nonaffiliates" from occupying these rooms. In conceding to student demands, administrators and police representatives had ironically bolstered the same securitizing logics of inside/outside, and of affiliate/nonaffiliate, that had underwritten the harassment and differential detention of those very students who had taken action to win such reforms.

The persistence of bathroom policing at UC Berkeley illustrates a recurring irony of campus politics in an era of risk and reputation management. On the one hand, risk management frameworks present openings for campus organizers interested in counteracting forms of violence or exploitation condoned by university administrators. Such harms, if publicized, have the potential to damage a university's reputation, meaning that administrators informed by risk management frameworks may be more inclined to see these harms as matters of concern. Recent campus-based movements against, for example, sexual violence, anti-Black harassment, outsourcing, trans exclusion, or private prison investments have won victories that can be partially attributed to administrators' interest in avoiding reputational damage. In many cases, though, as with the bathroom redesignations at Berkeley, such reforms, insofar as they were filtered through the securitizing imperatives of risk management frameworks, bolstered administrative and police powers at the partial expense of students, workers, and community members' freedom dreams. And indeed, administrators' hostile response to the spring 2024 wave of Palestine solidarity organizing starkly demonstrates how a concern with reputational damage can be articulated with a turn to more aggressive forms of policing on and beyond the bounds of campus.

References

Abraham, Janice M. 2013. *Risk Management: An Accountability Guide for University and College Boards*. Washington, DC: Association of Governing Boards of Universities and Colleges.

Brown, Keith C., and Cristian Ioan Tiu. 2013. "The Interaction of Spending Policies, Asset Allocation Strategies, and Investment Performance at University Endowment Funds." In *How the Financial Crisis and Great Recession Affected Higher Education*, edited by Jeffrey R. Brown and Caroline M. Hoxby, 43–98. Chicago: University of Chicago Press.

Dinerstein, Michael F., Caroline M. Hoxby, Jonathan Meer, and Pablo Villanueva. 2014. "Did the Fiscal Stimulus Work for Universities?" In *How the Financial Crisis and Great Recession Affected Higher Education*, edited by Jeffrey R. Brown and Caroline M. Hoxby, 263–320. Chicago: University of Chicago Press.

Douglas-Gabriel, Danielle. 2015. "Moody's: Colleges Have Entered the New Normal of Flat Tuition Revenue." *Washington Post*, November 19. https://www.washingtonpost.com/news/grade-point/wp/2015/11/19/moodys-colleges-have-entered-the-new-normal-of-flat-tuition-revenue/.

Freeh, Louis. 2012. *Report of the Special Investigative Counsel Regarding the Actions of the Pennsylvania State University Related to the Child Sexual Abuse Committed by Gerald A. Sandusky*. Wilmington, DE: Freeh Sporkin and Sullivan, LLP. https://archive.nytimes.com/www.nytimes.com/interactive/2012/07/12/sports/ncaafootball/13pennstate-document.html?.

Goldblatt, Andrew, and Hans Gude. 2015. "The Two-Headed Monster of Risk: What Higher Ed Traditional Risk Managers and Enterprise Risk Managers Can Learn from Each Other." *URMIA Journal Reprint*. https://www.ucop.edu/risk-services/_files/Goldblatt_Two_Headed_Monster_20150728.pdf.

Katsinas, Stephen G., Mark M. D'Amico, Janice N. Friedel, J. Lucas Adair, Jake L. Warner, and Michael S. Malley. 2016. "After the Great Recession—Higher Education's New Normal: An Analysis of National Surveys of Access and Finance Issues, 2011 to 2015." Education Policy Center, January. http://ir.ua.edu/handle/123456789/3304.

Kelderman, Eric. 2016. "There's More than Protests to Blame for Mizzou's Enrollment Woes." *Chronicle of Higher Education*, March 18.

Kossovsky, Nir. 2010. *Mission: Intangible—Managing Risk and Reputation to Create Enterprise Value*. Indianapolis, IN: Trafford.

Miles, David. 2012. "Against the Wind: Governing Your University in an Era of Limited Financial Resources." *Trusteeship*, January/February.

Mitchell, Michael, Vincent Palacios, and Michael Leachman. 2014. "States Are Still Funding Higher Education below Pre-recession Levels." Center on Budget and Policy Priorities, May 1. https://www.cbpp.org/research/states-are-still-funding-higher-education-below-pre-recession-levels.

Moody's. 2011. "Moody's Places Pennsylvania State University's Aa1 Rating on Review for Possible Downgrade." Moody's, November 11.

Nemser, Dan, and Brian Whitener. 2018. "The Tuition Limit and the Coming Crisis of Higher Education." *New Inquiry*, March 26. https://thenewinquiry.com/the-tuition-limit-and-the-coming-crisis-of-higher-education/.

Parker, Clifton B. 2015. "Great Recession Spurred Student Interest in Higher Education, Stanford Expert Says." *Stanford Report*, March 6. https://news.stanford.edu/2015/03/06/higher-ed-hoxby-030615/.

Power, Michael. 2004. *The Risk Management of Everything: Rethinking the Politics of Uncertainty*. London: Demos.

Tsikoudakis, Mike. 2012. "Penn State Scandal Sharpens Focus on Reputational Risk." *Business Insurance*, January 1.

Wolinsky, Howard. 2009. "The Crash Reaches the Universities: The Global Financial Crisis Threatens Private and Public University Funding in the USA and Europe." *EMBO Reports* 10 (3): 209–11.

S

Sustainability

Kai Bosworth, Jesse Goldstein, Andy Hines, and Eli Meyerhoff

The twenty-first-century US higher education system has been significantly shaped by a turn to *sustainability*. As a code word for environmental concern, sustainability has risen in prominence alongside the increasingly unavoidable reality of global climate change. Through formal institutional structures such as offices of sustainability, as well as sustainability audits, pledges, and action plans, universities carefully acknowledge that serving the public's interest includes addressing climate change and environmental degradation. Some universities signal the need to create a fossil-fuel-free future, largely in response to global environmental movements, which are making demands for radical transformation of social, economic, and environmental systems.

We argue, however, that university sustainability mostly filters environmental goals through a reformist lens that seeks to insulate universities from radical and antisystemic demands, thus maintaining, as Sharon Stein puts it, "business as usual" as the "horizon of hope . . . for institutions (of higher education and otherwise) to become sustainable" (2019, 198). University sustainability draws a restrictive domain around what is socially, economically and technologically negotiable, selectively depoliticizing structural aspects of ecopolitics—such as a university's complicities with environmental racism, colonization, militarism, and the development of energy-intensive economies—either by asserting that things are as they must be, or by turning matters over to management by technical experts (Swyngedouw 2007). University administrators mostly promote individual action, technological innovation, and teaching and research as the terrains on which experts manage environmental impact. Sustainability pits a unified field of those who "trust the science" against both real and imagined foes, whether a rightwing steeped in climate change denial or a left invested in "politicizing" science to serve social and political aims.

Sustainability is broadly defined in the United Nations' 1987 Brundtland

Report as a program that meets "the needs of the present without compromising the needs of future generations to meet their own needs." These "needs" have been selectively interpreted by policymakers, government managers, and business leaders, who put forth three interlinked categories of social, environmental, and economic considerations, a "triple bottom line" meant to ensure that environmental efforts do not undermine economic growth. These "green growth" strategies rest on the dubious presumption that economic growth can be decoupled from the climate-changing impacts of growing material and energy throughputs (Buller 2022, 239–41). As early as 1990, university presidents sought to formalize a technocratic relationship to sustainability in the Talloires Declaration, which emphasized higher education's history of producing and managing expertise: "Universities educate most of the people who develop and manage society's institutions. For this reason, universities bear profound responsibilities to increase the awareness, knowledge, technologies, and tools to create an environmentally sustainable future" (ULSF 1990). The declaration highlights that universities focus on managing the environment as a support for economic growth, as opposed to confronting the capitalist systems causing environmental problems in the first place.

With this managerial focus, university sustainability disavows the settler-colonial and racial-capitalist histories of professional expertise and environmental improvement, while obscuring the histories of social movements that have linked environmental concerns with struggles for radical systemic transformation. In fact, the reformist, green growth narratives that largely define university sustainability are mutually reinforced by the professional training and credentialing of technocratic sustainability managers, engineers, and entrepreneurs at these same institutions. This managerial approach to sustainability persists, even as the UN's definition of "sustainable development goals" has evolved. Their newer definitions juxtapose environmental goals (e.g., "climate action" and "clean water and sanitation") with explicitly social, political, and economic aspirations ("zero hunger," "gender equality," and "decent work and economic growth"). These future-oriented definitions, however, offer institutions of higher education the language to avoid their historical and present role in extending coloniality in and through the climate crisis (Stein 2019). Universities have thus largely focused on the forward-looking environmental aspects of this push for sustainability in their development of campus-based policies, always looking toward what

Collard and Dempsey (2022) call the "future eco-perfect": a magical time-to-come when problems will be solved without the status quo ever having been upset.

The tendency toward reformist measures by university administrations has created challenges for campus-based environmental movements. Student environmental organizations face a complicated terrain in which enacting practical change within the norms of established university sustainability campaigns appears as one option, while many young people also feel a pull for radical action and connection with social and environmental justice movements *against and beyond* higher education institutions and their corporate partners. When young people frame their work as a response to the climate crisis or as a response to specific matters of environmental racism and injustice, they have pushed university sustainability in important ways. For organizers who grapple with these questions of environmental activism with varying relationships to universities and institutional power brokers, we offer further questions about how to approach university sustainability in a way that is not captured by the university's sustainability framing.

Sustainability and the Contemporary University

University sustainability today takes its language and strategy from corporate social responsibility initiatives. These programs allow any organization to act *as if* they are addressing environmental concerns while leaving core business operations intact, a strategy often criticized as *greenwashing*. More than simply a green veneer, however, universities' focus on metrics, pledges, and other related managerial tools allows them to function as if they were actively engaged in sustainability efforts while disavowing their role in creating the conditions for climate crisis and refusing responsibility to enact more transformative environmental action.

The driving force of university sustainability has become the *sustainability plan*, a blueprint for action that analyzes the current environmental impact of the university and maps potential tweaks to its operation. Sustainability plans usually focus on the material throughput of the university: energy use, procurement strategies, food and food waste, recycling and solid waste, and water efficiency. Sustainability plans also often focus on the university's physical environment, which can include an analysis of alternative transportation (such as ridesharing and bicycles for faculty and staff), the energy efficiency of built infrastructure, or landscape biodiversity (including gardening and composting). In addition, sustainability plans promote social means to support a campus culture of environmental stewardship and concern, such as promoting the inclusion of sustainability throughout the curriculum, messaging and awareness campaigns, and targeted research support. A minority of the most ambitious plans also discuss divestment of university holdings from fossil fuels and into environmental, social, and governance (ESG) index funds.

Sustainability plans often emerge from, or even help create, an Office of Sustainability, which supports and organizes these environmental stewardship efforts. Organizationally, these offices are usually situated within the management of the university's physical operations, as opposed to being situated within academic affairs. This limits the plans' ability to delve too deeply into questions of curriculum and research, which are often addressed through adjacent efforts that must abide faculty governance and academic freedom. Funding (or often the lack thereof) for things such as research centers, targeted hires, and curricular development activities demonstrate the prerogative of provosts, deans, and research leaders, who can influence what directions sustainability research and curricular redesign will take. For instance, West Virginia University touts its "silver" sustainability rating, while offering undergraduate and graduate programs in mining engineering, where students and faculty actively support the fossil fuel economy.[1] A public university in a coal-producing state is unlikely to highlight decarbonizing their energy system, for instance, and may instead elect to focus on energy conservation or zero waste targets (e.g., WVU Energy Sustainability).

Support for superficial standardized sustainability plans has been bolstered through the rising popularity of certification regimes and voluntary pledges. Some offer a seal of approval that a campus is bee or bike friendly, while others rate universities against their peer institutions, offering a means for institutions to publicize their purported superiority. In addition, some pledges "commit" (remember these are all voluntary and nonbinding) the university to changes in capital spending, operations management, and curricular/campus programming in various areas. The blend of investment

1. The program in mining engineering was not immune to cuts as part of WVU's so-called academic transformation, highlighting that wider programs of administrative austerity could generate surprising alliances between labor struggles and environmental movements.

and existing resource management, as well as the prioritization of these areas, depends on several factors, including regional setting, student body, historical mission, political and economic context (including composition of the university's governing board), and size of an institution's endowment.

Sustainability offices and their pledges nevertheless shape the quotidian landscape of campuses. Energy and water plans seek reduced consumption, climate-friendly systems, and decreased reliance on carbon-intensive sources for power generation. Transportation plans increase shuttle service from nearby bus and train stations, install electric vehicle chargers on campus, or provide increased opportunities for remote work. Managing the physical plant may yield new trees on campus, expanded park projects, or new energy-efficient buildings. Frameworks for harnessing "natural capital" and making it actionable and profitable include voluntary efficiency standards, triple bottom line accounting, and carbon permit and offset markets—though to date, these have had limited direct economic benefit. In short, once you start to look for sustainability on campus, it is possible to see it just about anywhere. Yet in the process, these tweaks reveal that any underlying reckoning with the history and present of unsustainable or climate-changing operations of the university, both within and beyond campus, is nowhere to be found.

The management and development of sustainability plans for higher education has become so prevalent that there is a professional organization, the Association for the Advancement of Sustainability in Higher Education (AASHE), devoted to "sustainability innovation." Founded in 2005, AASHE understands sustainability to reference "human and ecological health, social justice, secure livelihoods, and a better world for all generations" (Walton and Matson 2012, 53). Soon after its formation, the organization developed the immensely popular Sustainability Tracking, Assessment, and Rating System (STARS), "a voluntary, self-reporting system that provides recognition to participating institutions and enables them to benchmark their progress over time as well as compare to other institutions" (Walton and Matson 2012, 49–50). STARS and other pledge systems allow universities to self-report within a point-based system where dozens of individual or partial efforts translate into points (and fractions thereof), which accumulate into a single score that qualifies them for platinum, gold, or silver status. This *metric orientation* of sustainability has exploded into a variety of other rating systems acknowledged to be gestural signals of "sustainability leadership to alumni, local communities, and prospective students" (Walton and Matson 2012, 57).

Such metric-oriented rating systems introduce a somewhat perverse set of cost-benefit incentives to "find points" that will lead to the highest rating with the easiest or most cost-effective actions, as opposed to orienting work around the most strategic or impactful transformations. Of particular importance for universities, and an exemplar of sustainability's perverse incentives, are LEED building standards. Developed through a partnership between the US Green Building Council and leaders at the Natural Resources Defense Council (NRDC), LEED promotes voluntary standards for different levels of green building. These include options such as low-flow toilets, local material sourcing, renewable energy, and much more. As a nonpolitical review of sustainability history puts it, "From the standpoint of administrators, green buildings make financial sense because they pay for themselves over time. They have green marketing appeal and help [higher education institutions] differentiate themselves from other campuses" (Washington-Ottombre, Washington, and Newman 2018, 569). LEED construction ultimately fits perfectly within the modern university's mandate to mobilize bonds and other debt instruments for accelerating the wider regional economy via campus expansion. At the same time, university real estate investment supplies a means of growing endowments through asset price inflation and rentierism (see Adkins, Konings, and Cooper 2020; Baldwin 2021; Buller 2022). The triple-bottom-line approach ensures that sustainability does not impinge on economic growth; if the university is going to continue building its endowment and gentrifying its neighborhood, it might as well make sure these efforts are LEED certified.

University sustainability efforts tend to focus on seemingly more universal, abstract, easily measurable, and monetizable efforts such as energy efficiency and waste reduction, despite perfunctory gestures toward "social justice" in the definition of sustainability within higher education. These gestures rarely engage university-led or regional histories of environmental racism, colonization, or the university's direct participation in militarization and the development of increasingly materially and energetically intense economies. It is not difficult to see why. Social justice goals tend to be less measurable, require more careful community-engaging work, and have less assured outcomes. Critiques of specific lines of curricular engagement or research innovation might run afoul of both the academic freedom of individual faculty members and powerful political bases within and beyond the university. The few attempts at social equity usually involve universities nominally rewriting their histories of exploitation through apologies for their colonial injustice or historical involvement in slavery, again emphasizing gestural rather than structural reparations (Stein 2022). Nonetheless, despite an avowed focus on entwining social and environmental goals, university sustainability plans primarily address incremental shifts in future material resource flows.

This avoidance of history further demonstrates how the managerial approach remains resolutely future oriented in aligning university strategy with the preservation of capital accumulation through the deployment of land, labor, and financial capacities (Gilmore 2007). Sustainability plans and pledges have become ubiquitous at the same time as universities proclaim to be undergoing crises of accumulation and legitimacy (whether real or symbolic), which demand reorganization or even austerity. Though aspects of the "crisis in higher education" can be more performative than real at some institutions, universities have taken the declaration of crisis as an opportunity to subsume social and ecological action within the university's overall economic strategy (Nelson 2015, 468–70). Nature becomes a way to manage accumulation amid crisis.

For instance, the management of waste streams in more sustainable ways can be used to justify new labor strategies, be they outsourcing, reduction in low-wage jobs because of new pressures on individual responsibility, or speed-up and intensification of existing jobs. Net-zero and other decarbonization mandates can justify the mobilization of idle endowment capital toward energy "efficiency" that can be, at times, another code word for austerity cuts. Local biodiversity efforts and the creation, improvement, and expansion of green spaces help manage "safe" investments in real estate development close to campus, often going hand-in-hand with expansion of campus policing. Even calls for fossil fuel divestment and a turn toward ESG investment funds are predicated on stabilizing endowments by "minimi[zing] exposure to financial risks" (Buller 2022, 166). The presence of massive endowments is taken for granted and even justified with language eerily resonant with the UN's definition of sustainability: "[The university trustees'] task is to preserve equity among generations . . . Consuming endowment income so defined means in principle that the existing endowment can continue to support the same set of activities that it is now supporting" (Tobin 1974, 427). The minimum definition of sustainability is consistent with the preservation and growth of university endowments.

With this focus on sustainability as an accumulation strategy, institutions of higher education have tried to incorporate, redirect, or otherwise neutralize the political activity of student groups and wider social movements who are opposed to green growth strategies. Student environmental groups are often invited to participate in the activities of sustainability offices and plans, whether through curriculum (sustainability courses or certificate programs), campaign promotion (Bike to work! Compost! Reusable straws!), or changes to student life (free shower timers). Work-study programs in sustainability offices train students in these approaches and prepare them for work in business sustainability offices or consulting. In the process, latent transformational demands that might emerge out of student organizing are attenuated. For instance, demands by student groups for university leadership to "declare a climate emergency" or to "divest from fossil fuels" can now serve to accelerate or legitimize the managerial approach to sustainability.

The university is not alone among institutions that have contributed to what Patrick Bresnihan and Naomi Millner (2023) have termed "modern environmentalism," an approach to ecological preservation that brackets the activities of liberationist movements. Anticolonial movements, struggles over labor, and experiments in living otherwise—as embodied in movements such as the migrant farmworkers' unions, Third Worldism, the International Wages for Housework Campaign, and myriad struggles for Indigenous self-determination—have actively challenged the normative models of human dominance and control of nature foregrounded by capitalist political economy. These movements exist on the edges of calls for sustainability in part because their wider projects do not exclusively focus on the question of ecological conservation, but also because their figurations of, for instance, "agroecology, food sovereignty, territorial rights, Indigenous sovereignty, earth politics" do not fit within a framework that is friendly to capitalist strategies of sustainability (Bresnihan and Millner 2023, 2). While these ideas often find a welcome home in more critical corners of the university, they are excluded from conversations regarding university sustainability.

These elisions haunt university sustainability plans, which present themselves as innocuously and pragmatically depoliticized. While we understand the institutional and political pressures requiring this position, the effect insulates university sustainability from more critical movement demands, only to eventually—if forced—torque these demands to fit within institutional logics, which separate out safely technocratic questions from a more capacious or reparative vision. This strategy is not new to contemporary higher education but instead is built on a historical pattern of university administrations seeking to upend movements of social and environmental justice.

The History of the Sustainable University

The advent of university sustainability programs extends a long arc of institutional efforts to diffuse attempts to transform universities by radical movements. Importantly, these movements have rarely described themselves as "sustainability" driven, and not usually even as "environmentalist" or "ecological." Radical student and social movements have historically criticized university support for ecologically damaging materials such as military weapons, industrial chemicals, and fertilizers. They have demonstrated the links between ownership and policing of urban spaces like nearby parks, buildings, and land assets. And they have highlighted how "pilot programs" in sustainability frequently ignore the concerns of Indigenous peoples. What these examples demonstrate is that despite changes in form and orientation, universities have reactively neutralized these otherwise transformative and capacious demands and separated them from broader social justice movements "premised on the denial of our entanglement and the ceaseless racialised exploitation and expropriation of labor, land and 'natural resources'" (Stein 2019, 198). "Sustainability" is just the latest mantra for this counterinsurgent form of politics.

The origins of this firewall against politics, particularly as it consolidated around the sciences, can be found in the changing nature of university funding within settler colonialism. During the Civil War, the 1862 Morrill Land Grant Act systematized the financing of state universities through the dispossession of Indigenous people's land (Lee et al. 2020). In the postemancipation era, with capital facing an accumulation crisis from both the loss of profit from slavery and movements for alternatives to racial capitalism—what W. E. B. Du Bois called the "abolition democracy" of Reconstruction—universities offered new means of accumulation by taking and selling Indigenous land and by developing new sciences—of mining, agriculture, statistics, race, sex, and eugenics—that increased the efficiency and legitimacy of capitalist processes of accumulation, extraction, and division (Boggs et al. 2019; Du Bois 1935; Harris 2023; Marcus 1985; Wilder 2013). Capitalists used university-sanctioned racial science, for example, to develop discourses that depoliticized class conflict by seducing workers with the psychological and material privileges of whiteness, thereby frustrating potential working-class solidarity across races (Du Bois 1935; Roediger 1991).

The postemancipation university has continued to develop new means of accumulation and legitimation for capital in response to new crises. In the post–World War II era, universities prevented crises of unemployment by accumulating the surplus populations of returning veterans. University campuses increasingly became sites of struggle for these collected masses of people, who were not only connected across lines of difference but also given time and resources for studying the social and ecological contradictions they experienced under capitalism (Boggs et al. 2019). Much like university approaches to other 1960s social movements, emerging environmental movements were initially treated with skepticism to outright hostility. An efflorescence of political action threatened the political order sought by the state and capital, and many of these struggles contained environmental aspects (even if not named as such), such as the Black Panther Party's free breakfast, lead abatement, and pest control programs (Bloom and Martin 2016).

By the early 1970s, the university approach to environmentalism had begun to refine tactics of separation and neutralization, a counterinsurgent approach that would later be used against other radical movements. Consider the first Earth Day of 1970, proposed by US Senator Gaylord Nelson along with student activists and consolidated around the idea of a series of educational teach-ins, held on college campuses but usually open to the public. Teach-ins rested implicitly, if not explicitly, on university sanction for events that would not challenge its own status as a site of expertise. Though the movement surrounding Earth Day teach-ins was initially well connected to opposition to the Vietnam War, the broader peace movement, and organized labor, even at antiwar teach-ins, many faculty participants insisted on the norms of "academic discourse" and presenting "all sides of the issue" (Schrecker 2021, 143). Earth Day teach-ins were premised on assurances to universities, as one Iowa State faculty member put it, "that we weren't going to embarrass the university, that we weren't going to do anything radical, that we would be responsible" (quoted in Rome 2013, 104). Universities could act as purportedly neutral public squares through which civil debate and education would address environmental problems, marginalizing partisan tactics such as student occupations and their potential for systemic critique and disruption (Schwartz-Weinstein 2013). As historian Jason W. Moore notes (2024), "Earth Day's modest but influential infrastructure . . . sat on its hands" when the US invaded Cambodia the week after its teach-ins—while "four million students—half the American university student population—poured onto the streets."

What worked for Earth Day expanded to a general transition of ecological concern into the professional realm by the 1990s. The National Environmental Protection Act (NEPA) and the Environmental Protection Agency (EPA) in the early 1970s were somewhat explicitly understood by lawmakers as a chance to shift "environmental issues" such that they would be "debated and defined as technical issues" (Gottlieb 2005, 175). These policies also made litigation and lobbying the primary methods of improving environmental conditions, leading green organizations toward professionalization, supported by solicitation of money or signatures from a passive base rather than an active membership (Dowie 1995). Universities, of course, play an important role in professionalization (Harney and Moten 2013, 30–34); the student movements that followed in the wake of this moment demonstrate this shift. For instance, the Student Environmental Action Coalition (SEAC) organized Earth Day 1990 events on over 200 campuses. The group effectively pioneered and popularized the "campus environmental audit," through which energy, waste, and water flows through the institution are analyzed for potential inefficiencies (Gottlieb 2005, 396). Whatever their political aspirations (and undoubtedly some groups saw audits as a radical approach to the university's environmental responsibilities), the push for environmental audits was quickly absorbed into the professionalized campus sustainability culture, while SEAC eventually flamed out.

Sustainability and *sustainable development* thus arose as keywords to capture this particular technical and managerial approach to environmental issues, which seeks to neutralize and separate environmental concerns from political movements. Though sustainable development ostensibly seeks to "balance" the social, economic, and environmental aspects of sustainability, these terms are rarely used by radical social or political movements. If the

UN's international negotiations on climate change and its Sustainable Development Goals popularize particular approaches to environmental problem solving, US colleges and universities largely followed the oppositional path that the US government had taken to these policies. It was the US who emphasized voluntary and nonbinding commitments, such as standards, pledges, and goals, rather than enforceable agreements—often without even ratifying the nonbinding documents. In this regard, universities are laggards rather than the pathbreakers they believe themselves to be. As Ashley Dawson (2024, 3–4) explains, "The liquidation of the Kyoto Protocol's legally mandated emissions cuts and the principle of 'common but differentiated responsibilities' [among Global North and Global South countries] . . . was a severe blow to the aspirations of Global South nations and frontline communities to contain dangerous global warming."

Despite these selectively depoliticizing tendencies, universities have occasionally served as nodal points around and through which refuge and dissent can be organized. Youth and student movements, as well as radical movements across campus boundaries, have pushed these neutralizing institutions beyond what they are comfortable with. As part of such movements, university-related struggles will need to transform beyond the parochially climate related. Outside the university, movements can fight back against the separation and neutralization that would take the environment and the university as concerns unrelated to other political tendencies and contexts.

Conclusion

This chapter offers a generic portrait of university sustainability plans and offices. We have sought to unwrap some of the premises behind these approaches, as well as the historical underpinnings that universities otherwise seek to disavow. Along the way, we have argued that the sustainability efforts of higher education institutions have sought to neutralize environmental concerns by marking them as separate from broader transformative or radical movement visions and demands. By challenging technological solutions and recommitting to environmentalism anchored by anticolonial struggles, we could create alternative sociotechnical imaginaries that have justice and liberation, instead of profit, baked into their core. This project would not seek to "redeem" the university's future by forgetting the past, but would instead provide openings for *redress* for the coloniality of the university (Palmer 2023; Stein 2019), broadening our imaginative horizons beyond "settler modes of sustainability" and toward possible futures based on sustaining and amplifying practices of Indigenous land rematriation, sovereignty, and self-determination (Underhill, Sabati, and Beckett 2022).

Many questions remain to be explored by further movement-informed inquiry, whether by student organizations, researchers, or movements within or beyond higher education. For instance: how can environment-related student and faculty movements be stitched back together with contemporary struggles for abolition, decolonization, improving work conditions, communization, and land reclamation? How could movements critically interrogate what current sustainability regimes render as controversial and what they render as fact on different campuses? What relation do university endowments have to global and structural debt loads borne largely by Global South countries, and what obligations might they have to reversing or repairing these historical imbalances (Buller 2022, 183–226)? How do we prevent calls for disinvestment—whether from dirty industry or university-supported prison labor—from simply turning into new accumulation strategies for ESG? What tools and resources within universities can be reappropriated or "stolen back" by radical movements (Harney and Moten 2013)? How are land-grant, tribal, liberal arts, Ivy League, and community and technical colleges positioned differently within the higher ed sustainability landscape? How can youth go beyond the limits of the campus, such as student transience, that impede links with environmental justice and land-based struggles?

These are just some pathways for inquiry that we hope this chapter can open.

References

Adkins, Lisa, Martijn Konings, and Melinda Cooper. 2020. *The Asset Economy: Property Ownership and the New Logic of Inequality*. Cambridge: Polity Press.

Baldwin, Davarian L. 2021. *In the Shadow of the Ivory Tower: How Universities Are Plundering Our Cities*. New York: Bold Type.

Bloom, Joshua, and Waldo E. Martin Jr. 2016. *Black against Empire: The History and Politics of the Black Panther Party*. Berkeley: University of California Press.

Boggs, Abigail, Eli Meyerhoff, Nick Mitchell, and Zach Schwartz-Weinstein. 2019. "Abolitionist University Studies: An Invitation." *Abolition: A Journal of Insurgent Politics*. https://abolitionjournal.org/abolitionist-university-studies-an-invitation/.

Bresnihan, Patrick, and Naomi Millner. 2023. *All We Want Is the Earth: Land, Labour and Movements beyond Environmentalism*. Bristol: Bristol University Press.

Buller, Adrienne. 2022. *The Value of a Whale: On the Illusions of Green Capitalism*. Manchester: Manchester University Press.

Collard, Rosemary-Claire, and Jess Dempsey. 2022. "Future Eco-Perfect: Temporal Fixes of Liberal Environmentalism." *Antipode* 54 (5): 1545–65.
Dawson, Ashley. 2024. *Environmentalism from Below: How Global People's Movements Are Leading the Fight for Our Planet*. Chicago: Haymarket.
Dowie, Mark. 1995. *Losing Ground: American Environmentalism at the Close of the Twentieth Century*. Cambridge, MA: MIT Press.
Du Bois, W. E. B. 1935. *Black Reconstruction in America*. New York: Free Press.
Gilmore, Ruth Wilson. 2007. *Golden Gulag: Prisons, Surplus, Crisis, and Opposition in Globalizing California*. Berkeley: University of California Press.
Gottlieb, Robert. 2005. *Forcing the Spring: The Transformation of the American Environmental Movement*. Rev. and updated ed. Washington, DC: Island.
Harney, Stefano, and Fred Moten. 2013. *The Undercommons: Fugitive Planning and Black Study*. Wivenhoe, UK: Minor Compositions.
Harris, Malcolm. 2023. *Palo Alto: A History of California, Capitalism, and the World*. New York: Little, Brown.
Lee, Robert, Tristan Ahtone, Margaret Pearce, Kalen Goodluck, Geoff McGhee, Cody Leff, Katherine Lanpher, and Taryn Salinas. 2020. "Land-Grab Universities: A *High Country News* Investigation." *High Country News*, March. https://landgrabu.org.
Marcus, Alan. 1985. *Agricultural Science and the Quest for Legitimacy: Farmers, Agricultural Colleges, and Experiment Stations, 1870–1890*. Ames: Iowa State University Press.
Moore, Jason W. 2024. "The Fear and the Fix." *Baffler*, May 15. https://thebaffler.com/latest/the-fear-and-the-fix-moore.
Nelson, Sara Holiday. 2015. "Beyond *The Limits to Growth*: Ecology and the Neoliberal Counterrevolution." *Antipode* 47 (2): 461–80.
Palmer, Meredith Alberta. 2023. "Good Intentions Are Not Good Relations: Grounding the Terms of Debt and Redress at Land Grab Universities." *ACME: An International Journal for Critical Geographies* 22 (4): 1239–57.
Roediger, David R. 1991. *The Wages of Whiteness: Race and the Making of the American Working Class*. Brooklyn: Verso.
Rome, Adam. 2013. *The Genius of Earth Day: How a 1970 Teach-In Unexpectedly Made the First Green Generation*. New York: Hill and Wang.
Schwartz-Weinstein, Zach. 2013. "Not Your Academy: Occupation and the Futures of Student Struggles." In *Is This What Democracy Looks Like?*, edited by A. J. Bauer, Cristina Beltrán, Rana Jaleel, and Andrew Ross. New York: Social Text Collective. https://what-democracy-looks-like.org/not-your-academy-occupation-and-the-futures-of-student-struggles/.
Schrecker, Ellen. 2021. *The Lost Promise: American Universities in the 1960s*. Chicago: University of Chicago Press.
Stein, Sharon. 2019. "The Ethical and Ecological Limits of Sustainability: A Decolonial Approach to Climate Change in Higher Education." *Australian Journal of Environmental Education* 35 (3): 198–212.
Stein, Sharon. 2022. *Unsettling the University: Confronting the Colonial Foundations of US Higher Education*. Baltimore: Johns Hopkins University Press.
Swyngedouw, Erik. 2007. "Impossible 'Sustainability' and the Postpolitical Condition." In *The Sustainable Development Paradox: Urban Political Economy in the United States and Europe*, edited by Rob Krueger and David Gibbs, 13–40. New York: Guilford.

Tobin, James. 1974. "What Is Permanent Endowment Income?" *American Economic Review* 64 (2): 427–32.

ULSF (University Leaders for a Sustainable Future). 1990. *Report and Declaration of the Presidents Conference.* Talloires Declaration, ULSF.

Underhill, Vivian, Sheeva Sabati, and Linnea Beckett. 2022. "Against Settler Sustainability: California's Groundwater as a Vertical Frontier." *Environment and Planning E: Nature and Space*, July 7.

Walton, Judy, and Laura Matson. 2012. "Measuring Campus Sustainability Performance: Implementing the First Sustainability Tracking, Assessment, and Rating System (STARS)." In *The Sustainable University: Green Goals and New Challenges for Higher Education Leaders*, edited by James Martin and James E. Samels, 49–62. Baltimore: Johns Hopkins University Press.

Washington-Ottombre, Camille, Garrett L. Washington, and Julie Newman. 2018. "Campus Sustainability in the US: Environmental Management and Social Change since 1970." *Journal of Cleaner Production* 196:564–75.

Wilder, Craig Steven. 2013. *Ebony and Ivy: Race, Slavery, and the Troubled History of America's Universities.* New York: Bloomsbury.

T

Title IX

Rana M. Jaleel

Title IX of the Education Amendments Act of 1972 prohibits discrimination based on sex in education programs or activities that receive federal assistance, from K–12 to institutions of higher education. This keyword focuses exclusively on the latter site. Title IX states: "No person in the United States shall, on the basis of sex, be excluded from participation in, be denied the benefits of, or be subjected to discrimination under any education program or activity receiving Federal financial assistance."[1] The law exempts from coverage religious institutions, military academies, and single-sex private colleges. The US Department of Education's Office for Civil Rights enforces Title IX. Under Title IX and Title VI of the Civil Rights Act of 1964, federal funding is contingent on the promise that the recipient will not discriminate on the basis of sex (Title IX) or race, color, or national origin (Title VI). Congressional spending power, as well as Congress's ability to withdraw funding for those recipients who discriminate, give the enforcement mechanism of Title IX and Title VI its teeth. In this way, as the American Association of University Professors explains, "[Title XI and Title VI] form a contract between the federal government and the recipient of federal funds" (Lieberwitz et al. 2016, 71).

By many lights, Title IX might be understood as a feminist victory in lawmaking. At the time of its enactment, women faced flagrant inequality within higher education. They were outright excluded from some colleges and universities and from programs and spaces within those schools. They were evaluated by higher admissions standards than men, endured more frequent tenure denials than men, and otherwise faced structural obstacles that put them at a disadvantage due to their sex. Title IX covers and has prompted action to address inequitable admissions policies, the unequal promotion of women in math and sciences, deficiencies in vocational edu-

1. Title IX, Education Amendments Act of 1972, 20 USC §§1681–1688 (2018).

cational opportunities, and discrimination against pregnant students and mothers, among other areas of concern. But ultimately, this triumph of feminist organizing has proved to offer inconsistent and uneven results. While the purpose of Title IX might seem straightforward and its textual meaning plain, the statute has been inconsistently applied, and the content and scope of what constitutes *discrimination* and *sex* has been a subject of intense sociocultural and legal controversy. During its 50-plus year history, Title IX has weathered repeated legislative attempts to weaken or entirely demolish its aims. Indeed, Title IX has gone back to Congress more times than most other laws—24 times by 2007 (Chan 2012).

There is an enormous amount of scholarship on Title IX, much of it legal or policy oriented. Because the meaning of *sex discrimination* is legal and cultural—and deeply politicized—the interpretative guidance issued by the Office for Civil Rights (OCR) can shift with each presidential administration, making a definitive survey of Title IX law and policy difficult. For example, President Biden's administration advanced new administrative rules that effectively undo key interpretative changes advanced by Betsy DeVos and the first Trump administration. The new rules clarified that Title IX's prohibition of sex discrimination does in fact apply to bias on the basis of sexual orientation and gender identity, although the issue of transgender athletics has not been definitively addressed (US Department of Education 2024).

In light of such political fluctuations in the interpretation and application of Title IX, in what follows, I do not offer a comprehensive legal or social history of Title IX and sex discrimination, but instead foreground how interpretations of Title IX have as often as not put the contradictions in the social and legal meanings of *sex* and *discrimination* on public display. Today, Title IX has become practically synonymous with two particular issues: (1) gender equity in sports, including controversies surrounding transgender athletes; and (2) sexual harassment and assault. In the case of college athletics, for example, contestations over the application and scope of Title IX foreground the contested relationships between gender and biology, testing concepts of sex and strategies of sex segregation as a vision of social equity.

We can also witness feminist tensions in recent popular conceptions of Title IX that (1) reduce sexual discrimination to sexual harassment and assault at the expense of other forms of sex discrimination on campus and

(2) expand the meaning of sexual harassment by conflating speech and conduct. These new understandings of sexual harassment have been criticized as running afoul of free speech, academic freedom, shared governance, and due process, while also ignoring and exacerbating racial and other forms of bias that have long accompanied accusations of sexual danger and harm. The emphasis on sexual harassment as sexual violence has also provided a rationale and cover for enhanced surveillance and policing on campus (Doyle 2015), contributing to what Elizabeth Bernstein (2007) has termed "carceral feminism," or the idea that social problems can be best met by punitive responses that in turn enhance the coercive power of the state. This is due in part to another unintended consequence of Title IX: the growth of bureaucratic and administrative structures, practices, and logics necessary to comply with federal guidance concerning campus allegations of sex discrimination (Doyle 2015; Gersen and Suk 2016; Gersen and Suk Gersen 2016).

History

As a case study, Title IX's origins and subsequent interpretations and applications attest to both the power and limits of appeals to state-based protection. The passage of Title IX is the fruit of dedicated campaigning by feminists and others who were disturbed by discrimination in educational employment.[2] Before the passage of the Education Amendments Act of 1972, which included Title IX, educational employment had been deliberately excluded from antidiscrimination legislation on the grounds that educational institutions should not be subjected to governmental control or interference.[3] But the 1960s had seen an increase in the number of colleges and universities across the nation, and as more women joined the faculty,

2. The gender composition of Congress during these organizing years is worth noting. From 1965 to 1975, the number of female representatives increased from 11 to 19, including 4 Black representatives, but women nonetheless composed less than 5 percent of the House. Meanwhile, the number of female senators plummeted from an already meager two to zero (Congressional Research Service 2019, quoted in Wu and Mink 2022, 130).

3. The Higher Education Act of 1965, Pub. L. No. 89–329, provided in Section 804(a): "Nothing contained in this Act shall be construed to authorize any department, agency, officer, or employee of the United States to exercise any direction, supervision, or control over the curriculum, program of instruction, administration, or personnel of any educational institution, or over the selection of library resources by any educational institution."

the problem of sex discrimination on campus became a heated public issue at a moment when the ultimately unsuccessful attempts to ratify the Equal Rights Amendment were in full swing.

Bernice Sandler, a lecturer at the University of Maryland, College Park, who later directed the Project on the Status and Education of Women for the Association of American Colleges, became a central figure in the ensuing debates. Sandler demanded Congress take up the issue of sex discrimination in higher education employment, and to evidence the need, she conducted a systematic analysis of the gender composition of university faculty. She subsequently used these data as the basis of a class action lawsuit against hundreds of colleges and universities for sex discrimination (Lieberwitz et al. 2016, 70; Wu and Mink 2022, 150). Studies by the Ford and Carnegie Foundations, as well as the US Department of Labor, the US Civil Rights Commission, and the commissioner of education provided further proof of sex discrimination in higher education.

In 1972 Patsy Takemoto Mink, the first Japanese American female lawyer in Hawai'i and the first woman of color US congressional representative, became a key sponsor of Title IX. An antimilitarist and environmentally conscious feminist, Mink worked closely with Rep. Edith Green (D-OR), who drafted the legislation, and several feminist organizers working broadly on social justice issues to ensure its adoption. In 1972, President Richard Nixon signed Title IX into law. Shortly after her death in 2002, Title IX was renamed the Patsy T. Mink Equal Opportunity in Education Act (Pub. L. No. 92318, 86 Stat. 235).

Title IX undoubtedly had a sizable impact on women's access to higher education by decidedly refuting the notion that women were by nature, as Edgar F. Herman, a member of the 1970 Democratic Policy Council's Committee on National Priorities (CNP), declared, subject to "certain biological conditions that may be lunar, may be puberty, during pregnancy, and menopause" that rendered them unfit to navigate the vicissitudes of public life. As Herman remarked before the CNP in 1970, "Suppose we had a President in the White House, a menopausal woman President, who had to make the decision of the Bay of Pigs . . . Anything can happen, knowing women, psychologically during this period, or during their lunar problem. Anything can happen from going up and eating the paint off the chairs" (quoted in Wu and Mink 2022, 137). Despite this sort of public sentiment, the passage of Title IX opened the door to educational access for many, although certainly not all, women.[4]

On Athletics and (Trans)gender Panics

While many people might agree that sex discrimination has no place in higher education, what constitutes *sex* and *sex discrimination* has been subject to charged debate, particularly in the realm of women's athletics. Shortly after its passage and for several subsequent decades, Title IX was popularly associated with promoting women's participation in sports. This was due in part to the short sightedness of Congress: they had not, prior to its passage, fully considered the impact of Title IX on college athletics. Initially, the National Collegiate Athletics Association opposed Title IX. Soon after the law's passage, some members of Congress attempted to "exclude athletics from Title IX's scope due to concerns regarding the law's impact on men's athletics programs, especially revenue-producing programs" (Shizue McKenna 2023, 406). Notably, in 1974, Senator John Tower (Texas) proposed an amendment to Title IX to exempt collegiate athletics from its auspices; when that did not pass, he introduced an amendment to exclude "revenue-generating" sports from Title IX's mandate. While the Tower amendments failed, subsequent years saw a spate of court cases that tested the limits of Title IX remedies for sex- and gender-based inequities in athletics (Shizue McKenna 2023). Yet Title IX nonetheless transformed the terrain of women's collegiate athletics. As Katie Barnes (2023) explains, "According to a 1971 survey by the National Federation of State High School Associations (NFHS), the number of girls participating in sports that year totaled 250,776, which was less than the number of boys participating just in wrestling that year (265,039). By the 1975–76 school year, girls' participation in basketball alone had jumped to almost 405,000 students."

As Title IX was interpreted to include women's athletics, the question became whether a sex-segregated or gender-integrated model would achieve the best results. Because women had little opportunity to train or participate in athletics as children and young adults, many worried that a cold intro-

4. To give one example: "In 1972, 15.4% of men and 9% of women in the United States had completed a four-year degree or more. As of 2021, women in the United States are outpacing men in higher education attainment: 39% of adult women ages 25 and older have a bachelor's degree versus 37% of adult men ages 25 and older" (NOW 2022).

duction into integrated collegiate athletics would perversely have a chilling effect on their participation in sports, even if an integrated athletics system was understood to be the ultimate goal. As the National Organization for Women (NOW) wrote in a 1974 memo, "NOW is opposed to any regulation which precludes eventual integration. Regulations that 'protect' girls and/or women are against NOW goals and are contradictory to our stand on the [Equal Rights Amendment]" (quoted in Sharrow 2017, 55). Nonetheless, in 1975 the OCR and the Department of Health, Education, and Welfare (what preceded the Department of Education) issued guidelines for implementing Title IX and ended sex discrimination that explicitly allowed, and in some cases recommended, sex segregation in athletics.

The suppression of this history has helped naturalize a scientifically contested idea of gendered (and racialized) sex difference that has in turn shaped subsequent policy governing women's participation in college athletics.[5] While scholarship in feminist science studies, transgender studies, and critical ethnic studies has criticized the separation of sex from gender—the rendering of sex as fixed and gender as fluid (Butler 2024; Gill-Peterson 2018)—as a recent historical invention, the issue of women in sports has, as Barnes (2023) observes, helped stabilize a notion of sex segregation as a form of social equity. The political utility of gender has fueled an "'anti-gender ideology movement,' which treats gender as a monolith, frightening in its power and reach" (Butler 2024, 4). As Judith Butler suggests, gender has become "no longer a mundane box to be checked on official forms, and surely not one of those obscure academic disciplines with no effect in the broader world. On the contrary: it has become a phantasm with destructive powers, one way of collecting and escalating multitudes of modern panics" (Butler 2024, 5).

This fear of gender has in turn influenced national debates on the meaning of Title IX at a moment when a spate of antitrans bills in Republican-led states have occupied much of the US political discourse (Currah, Levi, and Minter 2024). Within this context, on April 19, 2024, the Department of Education released the Biden administration's Title IX Final Rule. Notably, this guidance explicitly extended sex discrimination under Title IX to the

5. For more information about the science of gender, see Bailey (2016); Fausto-Sterling (2008); Gill-Peterson (2018); Nyong'o (2010); Samuels (2014).

protection of sexual orientation and gender identity. Applying the reasoning of the Supreme Court's 2020 ruling in *Bostock v. Clayton County*—discrimination on the basis of sexual orientation or gender identity is prohibited under Title VII of the Civil Rights Act—the new Title IX regulations fully prohibit discrimination and harassment based on sexual orientation, gender identity, and sex characteristics in federally funded education programs (US Department of Education 2024). A history of sex-segregated statutory and regulatory carve-outs, however—particularly ones that allow federally funded educational institutions to provide gender-segregated bathrooms and living facilities—have left some commentators concerned about the rule's ultimate effect on transgender athletes, especially since a former June 2022 proposal from the Biden administration had floated the possibility of forbidding schools from outright banning transgender athletes from participation (Binkley 2024).[6]

Sexual Harassment Bloat

If sports had previously occupied the popular understanding of Title IX, the 2010s brought new debates and transformations in the reach and application of Title IX. Beginning in the 1980s, student and feminist organizing helped usher some forms of sexual harassment and conduct on campus into the ambit of actionable sex discrimination for the purposes of Title IX. Sexual harassment is not mentioned in either Title IX or Title VII legislation. In 1977, sexual harassment was juridically recognized as a form of sex discrimination for the first time, when the DC Circuit Court of Appeals held Title VII to be applicable to a claim alleging that a supervisor conditioned a job promotion on sexual favors (Sherer 1993, 2123).[7] In 1980, the National Advisory Council on Women's Educational Programs reviewed Title IX

6. But note, in 2023, the Department of Education's OCR issued a Notice of Proposed Rulemaking that sought to amend its Title IX regulations. If adopted, categorical bans on transgender students participating in sports consistent with their gender identity would be prohibited even as the proposal would allow some restrictions for each grade level, sport, and level of competition. Such restrictions would be tolerated if they "are substantially related to an important educational objective and are aimed to minimize harm" (Cole 2023). Yet even if the department issues a Title IX athletics rule, the June 2024 US Supreme Court ruling overturning the long-standing Chevron doctrine leaves the impact of the rule in question. The Court's decision in *Loper Bright Enterprises v. Raimondo* (603 US _ 2024) undermines federal agencies' powers to interpret and apply statutes, often carried out through rules and regulations.

7. See *Barnes v. Costle*, 561 F.2d 983, 990 (DC Cir. 1977).

and recommended the explicit addition of sexual harassment to Title IX prohibitions due to a particular concern for students (Mango 1990–91, 381), defining academic sexual harassment as "the use of authority to emphasize the sexuality or sexual identity of a student in a manner which prevents or impairs that student's full enjoyment of educational benefits" (Till 1980, 7).

The prohibited conduct here concerned individual actions; hostile environment, or the creation of a workplace climate that could interfere with student education, had yet to be explicitly taken up (Lieberwitz et al. 2016, 74). Courts rejected claims of "environmental harassment" until 1991, when sex scandals—from Clarence Thomas's confirmation hearings to Tailhook—dominated the news cycle. After a series of lawsuits, in *Davis v. Monroe County Board of Education* (526 US 629, 650 (1999)), the Supreme Court concluded that schools may be found liable in private damage suits for student-to-student sexual harassment when the behavior is "so severe, pervasive, and objectively offensive that it can be said to deprive the victims of access to the educational opportunities or benefits provided by the school." In 2001, the OCR stated that "despite some differences in wording, the Court's definition of a hostile environment is consistent with the definition used by the OCR in administrative enforcement of Title IX" (Lieberwitz et al. 2016, 75). The OCR then defined hostile environment sexual harassment as "conduct of a sexual nature [that] is sufficiently severe, persistent, or pervasive to limit a student's ability to participate in or benefit from the education program, or to create a hostile or abusive educational environment" (US Department of Education OCR 2001, v–vi).

The 2001 and 2003 OCR guidelines that govern the interpretation and application of Title IX were very cognizant of the tension between First Amendment principles and workplace speech and conduct restrictions in the context of higher education (US Department of Education OCR 2001, 2003). But the Obama administration's 2011 "Dear Colleague" letter put the issue of hostile environment sexual harassment under Title IX front and center in a new way. As the AAUP noted, the 2011 OCR "Dear Colleague" letter, in its efforts to take survivors of sexual harassment seriously, risked conflating conduct and speech cases in ways that limited permissible speech (Lieberwitz et al. 2016, 77). For example, in an April 22, 2016, letter regarding allegations of sex discrimination at the University of New Mexico, the US Department of Justice asserted that compliance with Title IX required defining sexual harassment as "unwelcome conduct of a sexual nature," including "verbal conduct" and "regardless of whether it causes a hostile environment."[8]

Scholars like Janet Halley (2016), Aya Gruber (2015, 688), and Joseph Fischel (2019) have further challenged the definitions of unwanted sexual conduct by asking whether government regulation of sex on campus should occur through rubrics of affirmative consent. As Gruber (2015, 686) argues, "there are various meanings of 'consent' and 'affirmative consent' to sex" that are neither unambiguous nor easy to legally evaluate. Is consent, for example, "an internal state of agreeing or being willing to do something, an external act of expressing agreement to something regardless of internal feelings, or both internal agreement and external communication"? Debates over the meaning of sexual harassment, the scope of First Amendment speech and expression guarantees, and academic freedom continue to be taken up by feminists and other campus stakeholders, particularly as administrative and bureaucratic structures on campus continue to expand to address a broadened Title IX mandate (Gersen and Suk 2016; Gersen and Suk Gersen 2016). Logics of punishment and surveillance come to define campus "safety" in ways that put racialized and minoritized sexual and gender identities, Indigenous people, and working-class people at risk (Doyle 2016; Halley 2014, 2016; Jaleel 2021; Kennedy and McCann 2020; Nash 2019). The pitfalls of Title IX's treatment of sexual harassment has led many to question its efficacy and look for new models premised on abolitionist feminist principles, DIY strategies, and mutual aid (Coker 2017; Jaleel 2021; Walsh 2021).

While Title IX has undoubtedly transformed the meaning of sex discrimination in the 50-plus years since its inception, these changes have been as charged as the meaning of *sex* itself.

References

Bailey, Moya. 2016. "Misogynoir in Medical Media: On Caster Semenya and R. Kelly." *Catalyst: Feminism, Theory, Technoscience* 2 (2): 1–31.

Barnes, Katie. 2023. *Fair Play: How Sports Shape the Gender Debates*. New York: St. Martin's.

Bernstein, Elizabeth. 2007. "The Sexual Politics of the 'New Abolitionism.'" *differences* 18 (3): 128–51.

8. US Department of Justice Civil Rights Division to President Robert G. Frank of the University of New Mexico, April 22, 2016, https://www.justice.gov/opa/file/843901/download, quoted in Lieberwitz et al. (2016, 78).

Binkley, Colin. 2024. "Biden's New Title IX Rules Protect LGBTQ Students and Sexual Assault Victims: Transgender Athletes Aren't Mentioned." PBS News, April 19. https://www.pbs.org/newshour/politics/bidens-new-title-ix-rules-protect-lgbtq-students-and-sexual-assault-victims-transgender-athletes-arent-mentioned.

Butler, Judith. 2024. *Who's Afraid of Gender?*. New York: Knopf.

Chan, Kristina. 2012. "The Mother of Title IX: Patsy Mink." The She Network (sponsored by the Women's Sports Foundation), April 24.

Coker, D. 2017. "Crime Logic, Campus Sexual Assault, and Restorative Justice." *Texas Tech Law Review* 49 (147). https://papers.ssrn.com/sol3/papers.cfm?abstract_id=2932481.

Cole, Jared P. 2023. "Transgender Athletes: Education Department Proposes Amendment to Title IX Regulations." US Congressional Research Service, June 23.

Congressional Research Service. 2019. "Women in Congress: Statistics and Brief Overview." Congressional Research Service. https://fas.org/sgp/crs/misc/R43244.pdf.

Currah, Paisley, Jennifer L. Levi, and Shannon Price Minter. 2024. "Inside the Legal Fight for Trans Rights." *Boston Review*, March 6. https://www.bostonreview.net/articles/inside-the-legal-fight-for-trans-rights/.

Doyle, Jennifer. 2015. *Campus Sex, Campus Security*. South Pasadena, CA: Semiotext(e).

Fausto-Sterling, Anne. 2008. *Myths of Gender: Biological Theories about Women and Men*. New York: Basic Books.

Fischel, Joseph J. 2019. *Screw Consent: A Better Politics of Sexual Justice*. Oakland: University of California Press.

Gersen, Jacob, and Jeannie Suk. 2016. "The Sex Bureaucracy." *California Law Review* 104:881.

Gersen, Jacob, and Jeannie Suk Gersen. 2016. "Administering Sex." *Administrative and Regulatory Law News* 42 (1): 18.

Gill-Peterson, Jules. 2018. *Histories of the Transgender Child*. Minneapolis: University of Minnesota Press.

Gruber, Aya. 2015. "Not Affirmative Consent." *University of the Pacific Law Review* 47:683–707.

Halley, Janet. 2014. "Trading the Megaphone for the Gavel in Title IX Enforcement." *Harvard Law Review* 128:103.

Halley, Janet. 2016. "The Move to Affirmative Consent." *Signs: Journal of Women in Culture and Society* 42 (1): 257–79.

Jaleel, Rana M. 2021. *The Work of Rape*. Durham, NC: Duke University Press.

Kennedy, Rosanne, and Hannah McCann. 2020. "Splitting from Halley: Doing Justice to Race, Unwantedness, and Testimony in Campus Sexual Assault." *Signs: Journal of Women in Culture and Society* 46 (1): 79–102.

Lieberwitz, Risa L., Rana Jaleel, Tina Kelleher, Joan Wallach Scott, Donna Young, Henry Reichman, and Anne Sisson Runyan. 2016. "The History, Uses, and Abuses of Title IX." *Academe* 102:69–99.

Mango, Kimberly. 1990–91. "Students versus Professors: Combatting Sexual Harassment under Title IX of the Education Amendments of 1972." *Connecticut Law Review* 23:381.

Nash, Jennifer C. 2019. "Pedagogies of Desire." *differences* 30 (1): 197–227.

NOW (National Organization of Women). 2022. "Title IX: The Civil Rights Law that Opens Doors—50th Anniversary." NOW, June 15. https://now.org/title-ix-the-civil-rights-law-that-opens-doors-50th-anniversary/.

Nyong'o, Tavia. 2010. "The Unforgivable Transgression of Being Caster Semenya." *Women and Performance: A Journal of Feminist Theory* 20 (1): 95–100.

Samuels, Ellen. 2014. *Fantasies of Identification: Disability, Gender, Race*. New York: New York University Press.
Sharrow, Elizabeth A. 2017. "'Female Athlete' Politic: Title IX and the Naturalization of Sex Difference in Public Policy." *Politics, Groups, and Identities* 5 (1): 46–66.
Sherer, Monica L. 1993. "No Longer Just Child's Play: School Liability under Title IX for Peer Sexual Harassment." *University of Pennsylvania Law Review* 141 (5): 2119–68.
Shizue McKenna, Sabrina. 2023. "Transgender Women in College Athletics: The Next Era of Title IX." *University of Hawai'i Law Review* 45 2): 403–15.
Till, Frank J. 1980. *Sexual Harassment: A Report on the Sexual Harassment of Students*. Washington, DC: US Department of Education.
US Department of Education. 2024. "U.S. Department of Education Releases Final Title IX Regulations, Providing Vital Protections against Sex Discrimination." April 19.
US Department of Education Office for Civil Rights. 2001. *Revised Sexual Harassment Guidance: Harassment of Students by School Employees, Other Students, or Third Parties*. Washington, DC: US Department of Education.
US Department of Education Office for Civil Rights. 2003. "First Amendment: Dear Colleague." July 28. http://www2.ed.gov/about/offices/list/ocr/firstamend.html.
Walsh Fuchs, Lyra. 2021. "When Title IX Is Not Enough." *Dissent* 68 (4): 48–56.
Wu, Judy Tzu-Chun, and Gwendolyn Mink. 2022. *Fierce and Fearless: Patsy Takemoto Mink, First Woman of Color in Congress*. New York: New York University Press.

U

Union

Zach Schwartz-Weinstein

Workers in US universities have organized collectively since before the 1935 Wagner Act established the Fordist collective bargaining regime, which is still in effect for the dwindling percentage of the workforce represented by it. The union, the collective entity organized and authorized by workers as their collective bargaining representative, has frequently, but not exclusively, been the form that organization has taken. Not only have faculty of various ranks and statuses organized, but so have graduate student instructors and researchers, clerical workers, glassware cleaners, janitors and cafeteria workers, security guards and cops, library workers, hospital workers, medical residents and interns, undergraduate resident assistants, and plumbers and pipefitters. They have unionized at community colleges and state schools, at small liberal arts colleges (SLACs) and HBCUs, as well as at exclusive private research universities (Kelley 1996). More than once, universities have proved the site of critical challenges to, and expansions or rollbacks of, what counts as a union and who is legally entitled to form one. Unions have played important roles in organizing and supporting the struggles of university workers, and universities have been important spaces for incubating, expanding, and containing and constricting the organization of work and workers across the entire landscape of industrial and postindustrial labor in the United States (Lafer 2003).

If the history of American higher education unions has distinct waves, it is not always useful or possible to define each by a particular category of work or worker: Janitorial and custodial staff at many institutions began organizing earlier than clerical, technical, and instructional staff did, but university librarians had organizing drives at the tail end of the explosion of white-collar organizing that accompanied the "age of the CIO" in the 1930s and 1940s, and there was at least one graduate employee union (at the University of California, Berkeley) during this era.[1] Organization of graduate employees and contingent faculty began in earnest in the 1960s, the same decade that saw a significant wave of clerical worker organizing, in universities and in nonacademic workplaces, and of autonomous worker organizations as well as more traditional labor unions.

Frequently, the unions that university workers have organized rejected the conservatism of traditional *business unionism* and the so-called postwar compact between capital and labor in favor of more capacious visions of social transformation and the role of labor movements in broader struggles for social justice. The role of campus unions in supporting boycotts of and divestment from the South African apartheid regime is an important example here, but so are more recent initiatives, such as the 2006 campaign launched by the Yale Graduate Employees and Students Organization (GESO, now Local 33 of Unite Here) against Yale's investments in the private prison corporation CCA via Tom Steyer's hedge fund, Farallon Capital Management, and the groundbreaking resolution passed in 2015 by UAW Local 2865, the graduate employee union for the entire University of California system, calling on the AFL-CIO to expel police unions from its membership (GESO 2006). The disparate backgrounds of the different workforces universities employ, and the high degree of racial and gender segregation, both between labor grades in individual unions and between larger categories of work and workers (e.g., between janitors and tenured faculty), have at times presented an obstacle to solidarity. As during the 1971 strike by Yale janitors, dining hall workers, groundskeepers, and maintenance workers, university administrators and antiunion faculty have at times attempted to use forms of segregation in the labor force produced and reproduced by their own hiring practices to attack unions as racist and retrograde (Schwartz-Weinstein 2015, chap. 5). In such moments, the university administration and allied faculty have deployed critiques of structural racism as a weapon against the university's own workers, a pattern that has repeated many times in many different contexts. Elsewhere, and in other instances, university unions have under-

1. Edward Logue to Walter Brock, December 11, 1946, Folder 11, Box 1, RU 488, Yale University Manuscripts and Archives; UOPWA-CIO, "The Professional Angle," New Haven, December 1946, Folder 11, Box 1, RU 488, Yale University Manuscripts and Archives; Robert Cohen to Natasha Raheja, June 7, 2015. In the mid-1940s, for instance, competing CIOs attempted to organize Yale's libraries: United Construction Workers, a UMWA affiliate that then represented maintenance and custodial workers, and United Office and Professional Workers of America.

taken forms of solidarity and industrial organization, which have been offered as models for the broader labor movement to follow (Gilpin et al. 1995).

Sometimes, university unions have been sites of struggle. Here, the conflict early in the second decade of this century between Academic Workers for a Democratic Union (AWDU) and the United Auto Workers' Admin Caucus is paradigmatic. Emerging from the wave of antiausterity occupations across the UC system following the 2008 financial crisis, AWDU spread eastward from California and expanded from a struggle for union democracy on one campus to a struggle for union democracy at the highest levels of the International Union leadership, feeding into the Unite All Workers for Democracy (UAWD) slate's victory in the International's first one member/one vote general election for its presidency and regional directors. Among those elected to the latter position was Brandon Mancilla, a leader of the fight to organize the Harvard Graduate Students Union—UAW Local 5118 (and that local's former president), as the regional director of UAW Region 9A, which includes eastern New York, Puerto Rico, and New England (Press 2023; also see Wertzberger and Woo 2020).

Early waves of unionization on university campuses accompanied waves of unionization in the larger landscape of early twentieth-century capitalism, prompted by the founding of the American Federation of Teachers in 1916 and the formation of the Building Services Employees International Union in 1921. Here, too, there was considerable solidarity and cross-pollination. Consider, for instance, the career of Jerome Davis, a firebrand communist sociologist at Dartmouth and then Yale's Divinity School, and a strong supporter of the early organizing by janitors and maintenance workers on the latter campus. After his tenure denial, Davis served as the international president of the American Federation of Teachers from 1936 until 1939 (Elkin 1995). Others who began their careers organizing at universities would similarly go on to prominent positions of leadership in the broader labor movement. University employees unionized in response to the Great Depression, when university administrators sought to take advantage of the slack labor market to undertake significant capital projects. They unionized in response to the Second World War, during which many universities became "war production plants," housing and training military soldiers and turning their research objectives toward military use (Elkin 1995, 172–73). They sought to unionize when the GI Bill infused higher education with federal funds, and again during the Kennedy years, when the federal government again increased education expenditures to accelerate growth and control unemployment (Caffentzis 1975, 130). The most significant waves of both faculty and clerical worker unionization coincided with the twenty-year highwater mark of public sector and white-collar unionization in the 1960s, 1970s, and into the 1980s, before the Supreme Court's *Yeshiva University* (444 US 672 (1980)) ruling stripped ladder faculty at private institutions of the right to organize on the grounds that they were, in essence, management. Even after *Yeshiva,* faculty at state institutions have continued to join unions and engage in collective action. The spring 2024 semester began with a statewide strike by the 29,000 faculty members of the California State University system (Smith 2024).

Graduate employee unionization in its contemporary incarnation began with the Teaching Assistants Association at University of Wisconsin–Madison in 1969, the Graduate Employees' Organization at the University of Michigan in 1970, and the incorporation of graduate students into what is now the Professional Staff Congress at the City University of New York in 1972. First in public universities and then spreading into private institutions, the 1980s and 1990s saw a slowly building wave of organizing—UAW 2865 began at Berkeley and then spread, first to UCLA and then across the entire UC system between 1988 and 1999. Graduate employees in the University of Massachusetts system won recognition at Amherst in 1990, at UMass Lowell in 1993, and at UMass Boston in 2000. Grad workers in the State University of New York system organized with the Communication Workers of America and won recognition in 1992. At the University of Iowa in 1995, graduate employees affiliated with UE, the leftwing union that had been expelled from the CIO in an anticommunist purge 46 years earlier. Graduate students at the University of Wisconsin–Milwaukee, the University of Kansas, Wayne State, and Oregon State all joined the AFT in the 1990s, as did grad workers at Temple, Michigan State, and the University of Illinois Urbana-Champaign in the early 2000s.

The National Labor Relations Board (NLRB) extended its jurisdiction to private universities in 1970 (Cornell University, 183 NLRB 329 (NLRB–BD 1970)) but ruled in 1972 that graduate assistants at Adelphi University were "working toward their own advanced academic degrees, and their employment depends entirely on their continued status as such. They do not have faculty rank, are not listed in the University's catalogues as faculty members, have no vote at faculty meetings, are not eligible for promotion or tenure, are not covered by the University personnel plan, have no standing before the University's grievance committee, and, except for health insurance, do not participate in any of the fringe benefits available to faculty members." The board thus found that graduate teaching and research assistants "although performing some faculty-related functions, are primarily students and do not share a sufficient community of interest with the regular faculty to warrant their inclusion in the unit" (Adelphi University, 195 NLRB 639 (NLRB–BD 1972)).[2] Two years later, in a decision at Stanford, the NLRB clarified that graduate employees "were not employees" (Leland Stanford Junior University, 214 NLRB 621, 623 (1974)). By 1989, however, graduate employees at Yale were unionizing, and by the mid-1990s, graduate employees at NYU had joined them. Organizing campaigns at Columbia, Brown, Penn, and Cornell would soon follow. In 2000, the NLRB reversed the *Adelphi* precedent and ruled that private university graduate employees were workers and entitled to National Labor Relations Act (NLRA) protections. Four years later, the board reversed that reversal, restating *Adelphi's* "primarily students" definition as grounds for exclusion from the NLRA (Brown University, 342 NLRB 483 (2004)). The organizing campaigns at Brown, Columbia, and Penn stalled, and the NYU grad employees struck for six months of the 2005–6 term to try to force NYU to negotiate a second contract. The strike ended shortly after the spring semester, but the members of NYU's Graduate Student Organizing Committee remained in legal limbo for another eight years, until NYU agreed to voluntary recognition of the union, sensing another NLRB reversal on the horizon. That regulatory reversal finally came in 2016 at Columbia, amid and at the forefront of a new wave of organizing. Rather than being tempered by the arrival of the COVID pandemic in 2020, the wave of organizing and militancy instead intensified at both public and private institutions, with lopsided organizing victories at the University of Chicago, Northwestern University, Johns Hopkins, Brown, and the University of Minnesota; as well as inter alia and strikes at Columbia, NYU, Indiana, Michigan, Rutgers, and the entire University of California system. There were even organizing victories at Stanford, once the site of the NLRB's blanket exclusion of graduate employees from employee status,

2. Interestingly, it was the administration who wished to include graduate assistants in the Adelphi unit, not the faculty.

and, in 2023, at Yale (Kim 2023), where graduate employees had been organizing since 1989 against a particularly intransigent administration.[3] In starkly underscoring the literal disposability and structural indisposability of contingent labor to university administrators, the pandemic made clear the stakes of an expanded struggle, which continues today.

Administrators and some faculty, graduate employees, and professionalized workers have often objected to unionization on the grounds that it forces a brute materiality onto the idyllic self-representation of the university as a space of pure cognition, that it challenges, in the words of the late historian and labor lawyer Staughton Lynd (1969), the assumption that "universities are assumed to be institutions governed by reason, not by power." Unionization, that is, challenges what Lynd called the "non-coercive mystique" that held that it was "Socratic dialogue" rather than a hierarchy dominated by corporate executives on university boards of trustees and reproduced in the power of senior over junior faculty and of faculty over students that ruled universities. Indeed, an entire genre of administrative communiqué and student newspaper opinion column is devoted to restating the very logic that is here the object of Lynd's critique. Certainly the sentiment that industrial unions like the UAW and SEIU have no place representing university faculty and graduate students stems nearly as much from this idealized, platonic misconception of the political economy of higher education as from nose wrinkling at the prospect of having to face the unwashed masses at the bargaining table. It is this logic that lends to such sentences as "Duke's relationship with its graduate students is quite different from that of employer to employee, and we do not believe that representation of students by a non-academic third party, focused on just one piece of a student's experience, is in the best interest of students or the university" ("Duke's Position," n.d.) whatever credence faculty or other employees may place in such claims. The same is true of the frequent assertion, repeated in the Duke antiunion messaging, that the creativity and flexibility that characterizes the faculty-student mentoring relationship "could be lost when these matters are ruled by binding collective agreements." Yet to attribute too much to the anxiety

3. Stanford GW-UE (@StanfordGWU), "We Won," Twitter, July 6, 2023, https://twitter.com/stanfordgwu/status/1677048098080845824?s=61&t=fcL81poVtbcFNSiKdxwMmw.

over the loss of the bucolic myth of the university is, in a sense, to reproduce its studied negligence and exceptionalist erasures.

Not only were the "third party" and the "lost creativity and flexibility" tropes frequently deployed in antiunion campaigns against university clerical and technical workers decades ago, but they are also in fact commonly deployed against union organizing campaigns with little direct relationship to higher education (beyond the broadly "infrastructural" role that universities play in sorting and preparing the labor force, and in capturing surplus population; Boggs et al. 2019, 2023). In a "New Associate Orientation" video produced by Walmart and leaked to YouTube, an actor portraying a Walmart worker informs the viewer, "the truth is, unions are businesses, multimillion-dollar businesses that make their money by convincing people like you and me to give them a part of our paychecks." Another actor explains, "I'm in control of my own career. With a union, you put that control into someone else's hands." The video's main host adds, "Here, all associates are free to talk openly with their leaders . . . I'm encouraged to speak on my own behalf. I speak for myself. And, frankly, I don't think Walmart associates should *have* to have someone speak for them" ("Walmart's Sickening 'New Associate Orientation' Video" 2015). What the university administration frames as a case against unionization premised on the exceptional nature of the academic workplace, then, in its similarities with the language of antiunion offensives in retail and other industries, undermines the argument for the academic workplace as exceptional.

Furthermore, the language of antiunion campaigns against organizing by graduate employees, undergraduate workers, and contingent faculty often strongly echoes the language administrators used against clerical and technical worker organizing drives in the 1960s, 1970s, and 1980s.[4] That is no mere coincidence, but rather suggests a continuity in the logics of exception that characterize the class relations of the university as workplace and its relation to the broader service industry whose rise corresponds with its own ascent to a hegemonic position in the political economy of postindustrial urban space (Baldwin 2021). One reason the union has become the most important form for the struggles of contingent academics is that unions

4. Kimble Williams to Yale Employees, Re: Information about Local 104 NCDWA, November 2, 1971, Folder 1, Box 1, RU 488, Yale University Manuscripts and Archives.

have been the most important and successful venue for the labor struggles of other university workers. Although rarely given the attention afforded to academic organizing, at least in scholarly writing on the university, unionization of nonacademic university workers continues to not only inspire graduate employees, adjuncts, and researchers to wage their own struggles, but has in its own right continuously reshaped the landscape of work on campuses and in the cities and towns that surround them.

References

Baldwin, Davarian L. 2021. *In the Shadow of the Ivory Tower: How Universities Are Plundering Our Cities*. New York: Bold Type.

Boggs, Abigail, Eli Meyerhoff, Nick Mitchell, and Zach Schwartz-Weinstein. 2019. "Abolitionist University Studies: An Invitation." *Abolition Journal*, August. https://abolitionjournal.org/abolitionist-university-studies-an-invitation/.

Boggs, Abigail, Eli Meyerhoff, Nick Mitchell, and Zach Schwartz-Weinstein. 2023. "Marx, Critique, and Abolition: Higher Education as Infrastructure." In *The Palgrave International Handbook of Marxism and Education*, edited by Richard Hall, Inny Accioly, and Krystian Szadkowski, 509–35. Cham: Springer International.

Caffentzis, George. 1975. "Throwing Away the Ladder: The Universities in the Crisis." *Zerowork* 1:128–42.

"Duke's Position on Unionization of Graduate Students." n.d. Duke Graduate Student Unionization. Accessed February 10, 2024. https://sites.duke.edu/union/dukes-position-on-unionization-of-graduate-students/.

Elkin, Deborah Sue. 1995. "Labor and the Left: The Limits of Acceptable Dissent at Yale University, 1920s to 1950s." PhD diss., Yale University.

GESO (Graduate Employees and Students Organization at Yale). 2006. *Endowing Injustice: Yale University's Investment in Corrections Corporation of America*. GESO. https://www.prisonlegalnews.org/media/publications/yale_geso_yale_univ_investment_in_cca_exec_summary_.pdf.

Gilpin, Toni, Gary Isaac, Dan Letwin, and Jack McKivigan. 1995. *On Strike for Respect: The Clerical and Technical Workers' Strike at Yale University, 1984–1985*. Urbana: University of Illinois Press.

Kelley, Robin D. G. 1996. "The Proletariat Goes to College." *Social Text*, no. 49, 37–42.

Kim, E. Tammy. 2023. "How the Yale Unions Took Over New Haven." *The New Yorker*, October 23. https://www.newyorker.com/news/dispatch/how-the-yale-unions-took-over-new-haven.

Lafer, Gordon. 2023. "Land and Labor in the Postindustrial University Town: Remaking Social Geography." *Political Geography*, no. 22, 89–117.

Lynd, Staughton. 1969. "Campus Activism." *New York Times*, April 9, sec. Letter to the Editor.

Press, Alex. 2023. "A Night at the Movies with Brandon Mancilla." *Nation*, December 14. https://www.thenation.com/article/politics/brandon-mancilla-united-auto-workers/.

Schwartz-Weinstein, Zach. 2015. "Beneath the University: Service Workers and the University-Hospital City, 1964–1980." PhD diss., New York University.

Smith, Ashley A. 2024. "Cal State Faculty Staging Historic Systemwide, Weeklong Strike."

EdSource, January 22. https://edsource.org/2024/cal-state-faculty-stage-historic-system-wide-week-long-strike/704294.

"Walmart's Sickening 'New Associate Orientation' Video Demonizing Labor Unions." 2015. Posted by May 21 by Christian G2, YouTube. https://www.youtube.com/watch?v=sdHSFWZZAkU.

Wertzberger, Jillian, and Frances Woo. 2020. "Graduate Student Organizing Timeline: 1984–2020." Associated Students Living History Project, July 30. https://livinghistory.as.ucsb.edu/tag/awdu/.

Appendix

Questions to Consider for Composing a Keywords Entry

1. Define your term in relation to institutions of higher education. What parts of the institution does your term affect and which among those feel its impact most intensely? Who are the people in and outside the university for which this term is a preoccupation or special interest and why? The answer to this question may have changed over time. If so, attend to the different phases and movements of a term's development.
2. How is your term experienced daily? Think about how it affects different groups of people based on their position with respect to the university and race, gender, class, sexuality, and ability.
3. How does your term affect different types of postsecondary institutions?
4. Why is your term essential for understanding the current state of the US university and the wider system of which it is a part?
5. Outline significant political or economic developments that have made this term central to postsecondary institutions of higher education. Political developments may include federal and state legislation, nonbinding committee reports, or political campaign promises (realized or not). Economic developments may engage the history of capital, monetary and financial policy, budgeting commonsense, or broad trends in the philosophy of management of land and labor, among other phenomena.
6. What social and political movements have directly engaged the development of this term? What was/has been/is their approach and position about this term's function within the university? What have they demanded in response and how have those demands been adopted, reconfigured, or met with reactionary refusal?

7. What are the common misconceptions about your term? What do the form and nature of those misconceptions highlight about the history of your term?

8. To what degree has the history of your term's development within postsecondary institutions been something internal to higher education? Alternatively, is the adoption of the logics, materials, and practices related to your term reflective of wider political, economic, social, and historical shifts? With respect to your term, did the university system shape the US and global political economy on this issue or vice versa?

Contributors

Mattie Armstrong-Price is an assistant professor of history at Fordham University. They are currently working on a book about early railway labor in Britain and colonial India. They were active in recent antiprivatization struggles at the University of California.

Davarian L. Baldwin is the Raether Distinguished Professor of American Studies and founding director of the Smart Cities Research Lab at Trinity College in Hartford, Connecticut. He is the award-winning author of several books, most recently *In the Shadow of the Ivory Tower: How Universities Are Plundering Our Cities* (2021).

Wayne L. Black is an assistant professor of sports administration at the University of Cincinnati, where he examines college athletics using sociopolitical theories. He has published articles on issues in college athletics, such as athlete activism, housing insecurity, and commercialization. His work has been featured in *Sociology of Sport Journal, Journal of Sport Management, Journal of College Student Development*, and *Journal of Issues in Intercollegiate Athletics*.

Abigail Boggs teaches in the Sociology Department, College of Education Studies, and Feminist, Gender, and Sexuality Studies Program at Wesleyan University. She is currently revising her first book, *American Futures: A Genealogy of the Noncitizen Student and the US University*. Her scholarly work can be found in *Feminist Studies, Abolition Journal, American Quarterly, S&F Online*, the *Journal of Academic Freedom, History of the Present*, and the edited collection *Mobile Desires: The Politics and Erotics of Mobility Justice*.

Kai Bosworth is a geographer and assistant professor of international studies in the School of World Studies at Virginia Commonwealth University.

He is the author of *Pipeline Populism: Grassroots Environmentalism in the 21st Century* (2022).

Jelena Brankovic is a sociologist with an interdisciplinary background and an interest in theoretical, qualitative, and historical research. Her research focuses on the practices of comparison and quantification, global governance, and dynamics of institutionalization, with particular attention to the university sector. Currently, she is a research fellow at the Robert K. Merton Center for Science Studies at the Humboldt University of Berlin.

Scott Gelber is a professor of education at Wheaton College (Massachusetts). His research focuses on the development of American higher education during the nineteenth and twentieth centuries. He is the author of *Grading the College: A History of Evaluating Teaching and Learning* (2020), *Courtrooms and Classrooms: A Legal History of American College Access, 1860–1960* (2015), and *The University and the People: Envisioning American Higher Education in an Era of Populist Protest* (2011).

Jesse Goldstein is an associate professor of sociology at Virginia Commonwealth University, where he directs the Environmental Humanities Lab at VCU's Humanities Research Center. He is also founder and co-director of the Billion Worlds Lab at VCU, which is a space for experimentation with liberatory study. He is author of *Planetary Improvement: Cleantech Entrepreneurship and the Contradictions of Green Capitalism* (2018) and is currently collaborating on a new manuscript about student entrepreneurship in higher education.

Andy Hines is author of *Outside Literary Studies: Black Criticism and the University* (2022). He is senior associate director of the Aydelotte Foundation at Swarthmore College.

Dennis M. Hogan is a scholar, writer, and organizer based in Providence, Rhode Island. He writes widely for academic and popular publications on literature, culture, labor, politics, and the US university. He holds a PhD in comparative literature and teaches at Harvard University.

Rana M. Jaleel is an associate professor of gender, sexuality, and women's studies and Asian American studies at the University of California, Davis.

She is the author of *The Work of Rape* (2021), which received a 2021 Duke University Press Scholars of Color First Book Award and was co-winner of the 2022 Gloria E. Anzaldúa Prize from the National Women's Studies Association. A longtime member of the American Association of University Professors, she presently chairs Committee A, the Committee on Academic Freedom and Tenure.

Isaac Kamola is an associate professor of political science at Trinity College, Hartford, Connecticut. He is author of *Free Speech and Koch Money: Manufacturing a Campus Culture War* (with Ralph Wilson, 2021) and *Making the World Global: US Universities and the Production of the Global Imaginary* (2019).

p. s. kehal investigates how racism, cisheterosexism, and colonialism are experienced in cultural organizations, asking what constitutes antiracist and anticolonial strategies of equitable cultural inclusion. In ongoing research efforts, they founded and currently lead the Sikh LGBTQIA+ Oral History Project to understand how queerness, transness, and Sikhi manifest in mundane life experiences. They received their PhD in sociology from Brown University.

Annie McClanahan is an associate professor of English at University of California, Irvine, where she is also educational co-director of UCI-LIFTED, an in-prison BA degree program at Richard J. Donovan Correctional Facility. She is the author of *Dead Pledges: Debt, Crisis, and 21st Century Culture* (2016) and the forthcoming *Beneath the Wage: Tips, Tasks, and Gigs in the Age of Service Work*.

Louise McCune is a PhD candidate in English and associate instructor at University of California, Irvine. Her research focuses on modernist fiction and criticism, as well as the political culture of the American left.

Eli Meyerhoff is author of *Beyond Education: Radical Studying for Another World* (2019) and the co-author of "Abolitionist University Studies: An Invitation" (with Abigail Boggs, Nick Mitchell, and Zach Schwartz-Weinstein).

Dan Nemser is an associate professor of Spanish at the University of Michigan and the author of *Infrastructures of Race: Concentration and Biopolitics in Colonial Mexico* (2017).

Christopher Newfield was distinguished professor of English at the University of California, Santa Barbara, and is now director of research at the Independent Social Research Foundation in London. He is past president of the Modern Language Association. He has written a trilogy of books on the university as an intellectual and social institution, is co-author or co-editor of two books on the limits of quantification in social and cultural knowledge, and is currently writing one book about budget injustice in universities and another about the social effects of literary knowledge.

Juan Pablo Pardo-Guerra is an associate professor in sociology at the University of California, San Diego. He is the author of *The Quantified Scholar: How Research Evaluations Transformed the British Social Sciences* (2022) and *Automating Finance: Infrastructures, Engineers, and the Making of Electronic Markets* (2019).

Jennifer Ruth is an associate dean in the College of the Arts and a professor in the School of Film at Portland State University. She is a contributing editor for *Academe Blog* and the author, with Michael Bérubé, of *It's Not Free Speech: Race, Democracy, and the Future of Academic Freedom* (2022). She has written about academic freedom and higher education in such publications as the *New Republic,* the *Chronicle of Higher Education,* and *Ms.* and is a co-editor, with Ellen Schrecker and Valerie C. Johnson, of *The Right to Learn: Resisting the Right-Wing Attack on Academic Freedom* (2024).

Eleni Schirmer is a writer, educator, and organizer. Her writings have appeared in the *New Yorker,* the *New York Times,* the *Nation, Boston Review,* and elsewhere. She works as a postdoc at Concordia University's Social Justice Centre and as a research associate with the Future of Finance Initiative at UCLA's Luskin Institute on Inequality and Democracy. She also organizes with the Debt Collective.

Ellen Schrecker is well known for her scholarship on McCarthyism, academic freedom, and higher education. A retired professor of history at Yeshiva University, her latest book is *The Lost Promise: American Universities in the 1960s* (2021). Along with Valerie C. Johnson and Jennifer Ruth, she is a co-editor of *The Right to Learn: Resisting the Right-Wing Attack on Academic Freedom* (2024). The former editor of AAUP's magazine, *Academe,* she currently serves on that organization's Committee A on Academic Freedom.

Zach Schwartz-Weinstein teaches courses in American studies, labor history, and race and capitalism for Bard Prison Initiative, where he is site director for Woodbourne. His current book project is a history of food service and custodial workers at Yale in the 1960s and 1970s.

Elizabeth Tandy Shermer is a professor of history at Loyola University, Chicago, where she teaches courses on labor, capitalism, and politics. She has written about those topics in op-eds, academic articles, and scholarly books, including her history of student loans, *Indentured Students* (2021), *Sunbelt Capitalism* (2013), and edited collections, such as *Barry Goldwater and the Transformation of American Politics* (2013) and *The Right and Labor* (2012, with Nelson Lichtenstein). She is currently finishing a book on the public/private character of American higher education, tentatively titled *The Business of Education.*

Asheesh Kapur Siddique is assistant professor of history at the University of Massachusetts Amherst. He has written about the politics of higher education for publications such as *Inside Higher Ed, Teen Vogue,* and *Truthout.*

Richard Simpson is associate professor of English at the University of Maine, Presque Isle. His research examines the pedagogical qualities of urbanization and environment in contemporary American culture. His development of collaborative modes of knowledge making through civically engaged participatory pedagogies and digital mapping has been awarded a National Endowment for the Humanities Digital Humanities Advancement Grant. His recent essays have been published in *Lateral: The Journal of the Cultural Studies Association* and *Claims on the City: Situated Narratives of the Urban.*

Vineeta Singh joined the Interdisciplinary Studies Program and the VCU community in fall 2021. She has previously taught at the University of Maryland, College Park, the College of William and Mary, and the University of California in Santa Barbara and San Diego. She completed her PhD in ethnic studies at the University of California, San Diego, in 2018, with a dissertation historicizing contemporary conversations around diversity, equity, and inclusion in higher ed by placing today's controversies and confrontations in the context of 400 years of US racial democracy.

Heather Steffen is an adjunct professor and core faculty member in the MA Program in Engaged and Public Humanities at Georgetown University, where she also teaches in the writing program. Her research focuses on the history and present of academic labor in US universities; critical, decolonial, and abolitionist approaches to university studies; and the applied humanities. Steffen also serves as assistant director of Faculty First Responders, a small mutual aid organization dedicated to direct action in defense of academic freedom.

Yalile Suriel is an assistant professor of universities and power at the University of Minnesota. Her research explores the intersections between the histories of higher education and carcerality to better understand how institutions of higher learning have shaped power relations within and beyond the institution.

Grace Watkins is a student at Yale Law School and a DPhil (PhD) candidate in history at the University of Oxford. She is a co-editor of the volume *Cops on Campus: Rethinking Safety and Confronting Police Violence* (2024).

Brian Whitener is an associate professor of Spanish at the University at Buffalo. He is the author of *Crisis Cultures: The Rise of Finance in Mexico and Brazil* (2019) and editor of *Border Abolition Now* (2024) and *Raquel Gutiérrez: In Defense of Common Life* (2024).

Stefan Wilbers studied social sciences and history (BA) and sociology (MA) at Bielefeld University. His interests include sociological theory, historical sociology, and sociology of science and higher education. Currently, he is a researcher at the Leibniz Center for Science and Society in Hannover.

Jeffrey J. Williams started working on critical university studies in the 1990s, particularly on academic labor and student debt, through editing *Minnesota Review* as well as his own writing. He also writes on contemporary American fiction and the history of modern criticism and theory, publishing in both academic and more general journals. He has published seven books, notably *How to Be an Intellectual: Essays on Criticism, Culture* (2014), and he is an editor of the *Norton Anthology of Theory and Criticism*. He is professor of English and of literary and cultural studies at Carnegie Mellon University.

Jason Thomas Wozniak is an associate professor in the Educational Foundations and Policy Studies Department, coordinator of the Transformative Education and Social Change Program, and co-director of the Latin American Philosophy of Education Society at West Chester University. He is also a long-term organizer with the Debt Collective.

Acknowledgments

This book would not exist if not for the work of its many contributors. I am incredibly grateful for their time, effort, and analysis, as well as for all those who support them and make their work possible.

Conversations with friends and collaborators also helped me develop this book, from deciding on terms, discussing exciting recent work, and following insights found through organizing to figuring out what would make this book useful to its readers. These people include Davarian Baldwin, Abigail Boggs, Timothy Burke, Rachel Buurma, Sam Cohen, Sarah D'Adamo, Shannan Hayes, Dennis Hogan, Jodi Melamed, Eli Meyerhoff, Nick Mitchell, Lindsey Muniak, Chandan Reddy, Stuart Schrader, Zach Schwartz-Weinstein, Vineeta Singh, Heather Steffen, and Jason Wozniak, as well as the Bryn Mawr, Haverford, and Swarthmore College students in the "University City" course in spring 2024 and the participants and attendees of the "Universities and Democracy" symposium held at Haverford College in February 2024. This project is difficult to separate from the work I do at the Aydelotte Foundation at Swarthmore College; Marianne Dages, Kati Gegenheimer, and Patricia White have thus also made key contributions.

Greg Britton at Johns Hopkins University Press has provided support and encouragement for this project since our first conversation. I am also grateful to the feedback from several anonymous reviewers who made this book better at various stages.

I am fortunate to have a partner and spouse in Keegan Cook Finberg; she is a constant inspiration, interlocutor, and advocate for me. Our dog, Olive, has provided necessary perambulatory distraction, essential for problem solving. Finally, our children, Zev and Muriel—the latter of whom was born as I finished editing the manuscript for this project—are beautiful, personal reminders of why we must fight for a university that serves the imagination and the potential of many people, young and old. This book is for them.

Index